GENERAL
PSYCHOLOGY

David C. Edwards
IOWA STATE UNIVERSITY

GENERAL
PSYCHOLOGY

The Macmillan Company
Collier-Macmillan Limited, London

Library of Congress catalog card number: 68–12716

THE MACMILLAN COMPANY
COLLIER-MACMILLAN CANADA, LTD., TORONTO, ONTARIO

Printed in the United States of America

Preface

General Psychology is intended as a short introductory text, suitable for a one-quarter or semester traditional and comprehensive course. Its topic coverage, though, is comparable to most longer texts. The reduced length is achieved principally by an attempt to avoid unnecessarily elaborate exposition and discussion of the obvious. The traditional content includes also a sprinkling of old yet still somewhat useful material and new, though speculative, topics.

The brevity of the text has several intentions. Primarily, the text will be useful for short courses for which the instructor cannot justify a lengthy text or is unwilling to make an arbitrary selection of parts of a longer text. Second, the text may be profitably used in a longer course for which some other learning experience is desired. The short text will permit use of one of the excellent collections of readings in psychology, a substantial laboratory program, or perhaps a program of participation in research projects. Third, the short exposition presents terms, concepts, and principles in a fashion which many readers find easier to study. Lengthy exposition of each point often becomes burdensome during a second reading when the student's intention is to learn the material.

The primary purpose of this text is to aid the instructor by presenting the basic concepts and principles of the established science of psychology. This breadth allows the instructor to focus upon certain topics and issues or present entirely new material of his own choosing in lectures, and yet expose the students to the field as customarily defined.

The presentation is flexible in that chapters (and even parts of most chapters) may be presented in any order to suit the instructor. There is a logic to the text order, but almost any order of topics can be defended. The general psychology course is a picture of behavior and its determinants from a variety of directions, and it is not necessary to present those views in any particular order.

The names and dates associated with research on each topic have been only occasionally presented, and then in an indirect fashion with superscript numbers which refer to references at the end of the text. The beginning student usually has no use for extensive documentation, and the more advanced student will consult textbooks on individual topics. Many such texts are listed in the annotated Suggested Readings at the end of each chapter.

The author sincerely appreciates the encouragement, help, and criticism which several colleagues and friends have given. Wayne Bartz, James Bruning, Melvin Marx, David Mills, Ronald Peters, John Schuck, and Charles Uhl each gave a greater or lesser measure of criticism which improved the book, though the complete final version is not to be held against them. Thanks are due also to the several associations, publishers, and individuals who permitted parts of their works to be reproduced herein, a department head (Wilbur Layton) who pretended to not notice that research activity was postponed, several typists, including Jannella Kamin and Sherryl Trampel, and to my wife, Jeanne, who did her best to keep Jennifer away during the serious hours of writing.

D. C. E.

Contents

Contents

GENERAL
PSYCHOLOGY

Chapter *1*

INTRODUCTION

Among the most fascinating topics in science are those concerning the mind of man and the ways in which he behaves. What are the motives and goals which guide man's actions? Why are certain objects valued over others? What is the nature of feelings of emotion, and what produces emotional experience? What determines the accomplishments of an individual? How can they be improved? What behavior can be changed through punishment, and how should it be done? These are some of the broad problems which are typically presented to psychologists. Psychologists have developed a philosophy of solving these problems which has shaped the science of psychology.

What is the nature of psychology? What are the methods and techniques which give information to psychology? How does psychology differ from other disciplines of knowledge? What are the historical roots of psychology? This introductory chapter will describe the characteristics, methods, and background of the present science of psychology.

The Definition of Psychology

Psychology is the *science of behavior*. Using the approach, methods, and values of science, psychologists formulate questions and uncover principles about behaving individuals. The subject matter for scientific psychology is the observable behavior of individuals. The primary aim

1

of psychology is to find the laws which relate behavior to situations, conditions, and other behaviors.

Psychology seeks to *understand, predict,* and *control,* as do all disciplines which use scientific methods. The goals of all disciplines using scientific methods are dictated by the desires of the scientist. There is first a desire for knowledge and *understanding* of the phenomena under investigation. What are the factual relationships, and how does the information fit into a larger organization of what is already known? The related notion of explanation will be discussed later. Scientists also wish to *predict* phenomena; they wish to be able to predict that phenomenon X will usually occur under conditions Y and Z, but almost never in the presence of Q. A further desire of the scientist is *control* over phenomena, which complements understanding and prediction. Control may take the form of harnessing a phenomenon for practical purposes, or it may involve the careful staging and exclusion of relevant events to produce the phenomenon upon demand. Some phenomena, for example the movements of celestial bodies, cannot be controlled in this sense with our present knowledge, but the attainment of such control represents a certain goal of scientific investigation.

The major *difference* between scientific psychology and other scientific disciplines is the choice of subject matter. Psychologists are primarily interested in observing and understanding behavior.

BEHAVIOR

The psychologist defines *behavior* as being all of those activities of an individual which can be noted by another person, with or without the aid of instruments. This subject matter of psychology includes a variety of familiar things. A movement of an eye, the choice of a particular group of words, the redness of skin areas, the content of a story told about a picture—all are important behaviors which may be observed and studied in a situation. Psychologists divide and classify behaviors into topic areas for discussion, with the belief that similar principles describe the behaviors so grouped. The division of psychology into different areas also yields some convenience of description and study. Thus, behaviors classified under the labels motivation, emotion, physiological psychology, perception, maturation, learning, thinking, personality, social psychology, adjustment, mental health, and applied psychology will be considered as separate topics. Each of these groups and others are discussed as an independent aspect of behavior, but always keeping in mind that the other processes are concurrently affecting the individual's behavior. While studying perception, the psychologist must consider the effects of motives, learning, and physiological states upon the observed behaviors. The perceiving individual is also a motivated and learning individual, having a particular personality and experiencing physiological conditions as well as social constraints, and so on. Behavior is determined by all of these concurrent conditions.

SCIENCE

Science in psychology is a way of going about the study of behavior. The procedures and methods of scientific psychology are basically the same as those which are used to obtain knowledge in other fields of inquiry. These methods have been quite successful in psychology, as they have been in other fields. *Science* is a collection of operating principles that have been shown in the past to produce useful information.

The usefulness of information obtained by scientific methods may be assessed in more than one way. Information may be useful if it yields accurate predictions of behavior. For example, tests of the mental age or brightness of grade-school children were found to predict accurately the relative success of those children in school studies. Knowledge of the previous experiences of an individual with such incentives as money or job-satisfaction may allow a prediction as to which is the best motivating device for extracting a greater amount of work from that person. The utility of the information produced by scientific methods may also be judged by the extent to which it fits into a larger organization of information. Does the information fill gaps in our knowledge? Does it bolster and reaffirm what has already been learned?

Some of the characteristics which informally describe the scientific methods of gathering knowledge may be labeled *measurability, repeatability,* and *control.* By the term *measurability* is meant the degree to which the terms and concepts under consideration can be precisely specified. This measurement does not require the application of numbers, though the use of numbers is desirable and is a higher level of refinement of measurement. Measurement does require unequivocal identification of the situations and behaviors named, in such a fashion that the same identification may also be made by others. Consider the statement "Pigs can think better than horses." To put this statement to a meaningful test, the words must be objectively defined. Pigs and horses are usually not difficult to identify. A definition of "thinking," though, must be established. This may perhaps be done by equating performance on each of a series of complex tasks (such as responding to commands) with thinking ability. Precise application of these tasks allows others to know exactly what was meant by "thinking" in the test, forestalling argument based upon misunderstandings and confusions over the term. The usefulness of the definition is another problem; only the measurability of the term has been guaranteed.

Repeatability refers to the generality of the observations that have been made. Is the relationship stable and one that will occur again under the same conditions, or is it a chance happening, a fluke? Some estimate of the stability of observations may be made by repeating those observations on an independent occasion. Whether pigs think better than horses must be determined by testing more than one pig and one horse. A suitably large number of pigs and horses must be tested to give credence to the conclusion. The possibility that the selected pig made a "lucky" response or was an unusually "bright" pig must be made unlikely by observations of a greater number of pigs.

Control is the methodology which reduces the number of factors which may have contributed to an observed behavior. Factors X may be said to produce behavior Y only if Q factors, which are also known to produce Y, have been controlled. Control may be accomplished by removing the Q factors, or simply by knowing their probable effects. For example, an emotion-arousing situation may be said to have produced an increase in the size of the pupillary opening of the eye only if the intensity of light striking that eye, which also effects the same change, has been controlled. Light stimulation in this case may be controlled by holding it constant, or by assessing the magnitude of the pupillary reflex to such light changes as did occur. The experimenter must see if *all* of the important conditions and factors which may affect that behavior have been identified and described. The degree of control in a situation is difficult to assess, and most assuredly varies in practice somewhere between "no control" and "complete control." Control improves with knowledge of relevant factors and refinements in methods. The pigs and horses must be tested under similar conditions, insofar as the relevant factors are known. Control of the factor of hunger motivation would be poor if pigs were tested before feeding and horses after feeding. Similarly, both animals must not be tested in the natural surroundings of but one, such as the hog feed-lot. Generally, differences between the testing situation of the pigs and that of the horses must be minimized or systematically studied, so that their effects do not contribute to the behavior differences that are used to measure thinking.

Science is also used as a name to describe the collection of information which is obtained by these methods. The term "science," then, is used to refer both to the methods of obtaining useful information and to the collection of ordered information which has already been found.

This definition of the content and requirements of scientific psychology does not appear to provide a place for a certain content which many people feel to be a natural part of what we call psychology. What of personal experiences, conscious processes which are not observable to others, unconscious processes described so vividly in both popular and scientific discussions of psychology, and similar subject matter? These mental contents cannot be observed in others by an impartial observer, nor are they measurable and repeatable. It would appear that they do not have a respectable status in psychology as a science. This conclusion is both correct and incorrect. To the extent that such things are and remain discussed in terms which do not allow observation by others, they have no place in scientific psychology. However, many happenings of a personal nature *can* be measured and observed indirectly using a technique called *inference*. *Inference* allows prediction of likely mental content from observations of the situation and ongoing behavior. We may infer that a group of students oriented towards a lecturing professor are having personal experiences and conscious processes that are directly related to the content of the professor's speech. We might similarly infer with a fair degree of accuracy the mental content of a group of college men who are visually oriented towards a coed ascending a stairway. We might miss our guess, that is, infer incorrectly, about some of the individuals, but on the average our inference will be valid. In a carefully structured situation, where it is known what has happened recently and what is presently occurring, the mental contents of the participants may be inferred and thus admitted to an acceptable status in scientific psychology.

It is true that there is no clean dividing line between study of the clearly experiential or personal mental contents and many kinds of observable behavior or states of the mind of an individual, such as motivational conditions, learning abilities, or the limits of the sense of vision. All scientific psychology must use some amount of inference. Any "psychological" process involves inferring some kind of internal process. The process is studied by controlling and measuring behavior, which is either deliberately evoked or naturally occurs and is merely observed.

Methods of Psychology

The many methods that are actually used to gather information about behavior for scientific psychology can be described as consisting of some combination of the four basic methods described below. These methods are termed *naturalistic observation, testing, the experimental method,* and *the clinical method.* Systematic differences exist between these methods in the kind of information which they may produce and in the relative value and purpose of the behavioral laws derived from their use. Such differences between the methods will be discussed, along with their separate descriptions.

NATURALISTIC OBSERVATION

The hallmark of gathering data by *naturalistic observation* is that the investigator only observes and does not interfere with the ongoing behavior. Observation-without-interference is often difficult to achieve, but is perhaps the only way to assure that the behavior being studied is not directly or indirectly affected by the presence of the observer. The existence of a psychologist with a notebook, for example, will affect the course of discussion of any group of people, except more psychologists. The naturalistic observation of behavior is said to produce behavior assessments of a high degree of *generalizability.* That is, the results may be generalized easily to similar situations. The behavior is "true" and not "artificial."

This generalizability, however, is not attained without cost. Naturalistic observation requires a great deal of time to complete. Often hours of observations (for example, of children at play) must be completed before the one bit of behavior under study (for example, aggression) occurs in the group or individual. Many additional hours of waiting may be required before that sort of behavior will be repeated under similar conditions which can be used as a check. When using this method, the observer takes the risk that the desired behavior may *never* occur in the individual under observation. It is thus apparent that certain kinds of problems and questions may never be studied efficiently using this method. The generalizability of naturalistic observations is also obtained at the cost of knowing the determinants of the behavior. That is, a very low degree of control is exerted over the behavior studied, and almost no statements may be made about the probable causes of the behavior. Generally, control and interference in scientific observations go together.

Naturalistic observation can make possible an accurate description of behaviors which are too elaborate for any of the other techniques. For example, certain social behaviors in established groups have been observed and described. The complex dominance or pecking-order relationships among the members of natural monkey colonies may be discovered. The social relationships or the actual channels of function in a group working in a business office may be discreetly studied by a suitably positioned observer. An "inside observer" often anonymously joins the group he wishes to study. Assessments of many kinds of behavior can only be accurately obtained by the naturalistic observation method applied without interference.

TESTING

The *testing* method requires that a standard stimulus situation be presented to each individual. Primary interest is in the types of and differences among responses to this standard situation. Comparisons of the frequency of occurrence of different responses, rather than an analysis of a particular type of response, are the usual goals of this procedure.

A well-known use of the testing method is the typical course examination, whether it is in multiple-choice, true-false, fill-in-the-blanks, or essay format. Test scores define categories of behavior of individuals for classification or further study. Another familiar variation of the test method of gathering information is the survey or questionnaire. All persons surveyed are asked the same question, such as "do you feel that dogs shoud be permitted inside food stores and why?" Answers to these open-ended questions provide a richness of behavior to be categorized and analyzed.

The testing method is most frequently employed where relatively quick assessments of behavior are necessary. Psychological testing of intelligence and other aptitudes, personality characteristics, and achievement or proficiency in a variety of subjects has been built upon the premise that certain kinds of responses to test questions indicate a more general pattern of behavior. Tests are efficient predictors of such more general behavior patterns, which by their nature are quite complex or require considerable periods of time to be completed.

In psychological study of social relationships, the testing method is used to sample opinions and attitudes of individuals. The testing technique evokes relevant social behavior for study which could otherwise be effectively hidden from observation.

The testing method does interfere with the behavior to be assessed. It interferes to the extent that it presents stimuli and situations of the investigator's choosing. This limits the range of behavior which is likely to be given by the subject, but such structuring saves time by producing behaviors of greater interest to the psychologist. The interference and degree of control introduced by use of the standard stimulus situation (including the investigator's presence) results in some amount of artificiality of behavior, and thus limits the generalizability of the results. The way a question is asked or the status of the questioner may shape the responses in an unnatural manner. An extreme example of bias in responses would be obtained by a clergyman surveying people in a public setting and using the "loaded" question, "You *do* go to church often, do you not?"

THE EXPERIMENTAL METHOD

The distinctive feature of the *experimental* method is the relatively high degree of control which may be exerted in this situation. The important factors of this method can be given by a simple experiment in which two groups of subjects, selected so as to be equal at the start of the investigation, are treated alike except for one manipulated difference. One of these groups is called the *control group* and does not receive that treatment, but in all other respects is treated exactly like the *experimental group*. Any difference in resulting behavior can then be attributed to the differences in treatment. The condition of difference in treatment between the groups, the manipulation being studied, is called the *independent variable*. The measured behavior changes which may reflect that variable are called the *dependent variable*. The function of the control group is to insure that the changes in the dependent behavior are a result of the operation of the independent variable. The use of a control group allows the experimenter to assess the effects of other factors which may be present by chance, and it provides a standard of comparison in the units of the behavior-measurement procedures.

The experimental method is generally the preferred technique for studying problems in such topics as motivation, learning, and perception. Factors such as the kind of materials most easily memorized, the pairs of colors which are not readily differentiated, and the effectiveness of electric shock punishment for wrong responses in a maze, are most efficiently and convincingly demonstrated by the experimental method. In order to answer the question "does factor X affect behavior Y?" One must exert control over other factors such that only X was likely to

Figure 1-1. A medical polygraph used in experimental research of physiological responses to psychologically different stimuli. (Photo by author)

have been the cause of the behavior Y. The inherent control in the experimental method is largely lacking in the other information-gathering techniques.

The experimental method, which obviously rates high in the control which may be exerted, at the same time rates very low in generalizability. The requirements of control operate in such a way that they usually restrict the natural range of behavior, and the resulting observation may then be described as somewhat artificial or unnatural. Such artificiality is not automatically present, however, and many experiments isolate and allow study of behaviors which are quite natural in all respects.

THE CLINICAL METHOD

The *clinical* method, or as it is sometimes called, the *case-history* method, combines some of the techniques of testing and naturalistic observation to produce a body of information about an individual. Information may come from interrogation of the individual, from written records and diaries, or from accounts related by other individuals, as well as the personal observations of the investigator. The end-product, the case-history, may be of varying degrees of reliability, depending upon the sources used in the compilation.

This neat-appearing, friendly but extremely nervous individual, who continually bit her fingernails and twisted the rings on her fingers, was articulate and clinically displayed much impulsive behavior. For example, she would quickly answer questions before thinking about them, move the cards of the Picture Arrangement sub-test of the WAIS in an impulsive manner, etc. She recognized all her errors readily and was able to correct most of them. Eye contact was fair; she was oriented in all spheres and cooperated well with all instructions given.

When seen later for projective evaluation, the patient appeared initially to be extremely bland, but ill at ease/tense. She appeared unable to give specific information about her feelings regarding her asking to be seen at this installation, and when pressured, she began to block, to become extremely tense and to smile nervously. At one point in the interview, tears streamed down her face without any other indications of crying. She described an interest in "mystics" and felt that her reading of Jung, St. Thomas Acquinas, etc., might have some relationship to her feelings toward the "other man," which she states are prompting her ideas of divorce. She described vaguely marked mood swings from "extreme depression to feeling so good that it is out of proportion." In marked contrast to her construction/tenseness/blocking clinically, she displayed some appropriate affect, warmth, and some coyness while engaged in the Rorschach.

Bender designs were drawn in a methodical order on both phases (one sheet of paper being used to draw each design on the Tachistoscopic Phase). Modification of the curvature, sketching, and fragmentation were noted in both phases, suggesting qualitatively an aggressive labile individual who over-compensates and has marked sexual disturbance. Human figure drawings suggest an impulsive, self-centered, dependent individual with some guilt feelings regarding sex.

The MMPI is a valid protocol suggesting an immature, anxious, depressed individual with paranoid tendencies, hostility, and some looseness of reality contact; these results could portend an incipient schizophrenic condition with its accompanying anxiety. The extremely low Masculine-Feminine score suggests an attempt to make herself appear more feminine than she actually is. Ten critical items were listed and an inquiry of them yields suggested aggression, acting-out potential, sexual concerns, guilt, feelings of unreality ("from day to day things seem to change"), a feeling that things are "on two different levels" and much philosophical rumination.

The patient's Rorschach displays the exceedingly poor form quality which is associated with lack of adequate reality ties. Her percepts lack the morbidity of the deteriorating schizophrenic, but are idiosyncratic and display marked tendencies to distort and view her environment in terms of her own very regressive, infantile needs. Much of the protocol is very suggestive of an extremely hysterical, denying, regressive individual who functions in a borderline psychotic manner. She is "clingingly" dependent, extremely anxious in all spheres, and quite labile. She displays a child-like fear of heterosexual contact and a marked sensitivity to environmental cues.

OVERALL IMPRESSION

Ambulatory schizophrenic with marked anxiety/regression. It is not felt that the patient would benefit from hospitalization, though possible medication and out-patient therapy might bring her defenses up enough to continue her marginal adjustment. It is difficult to decide what the therapeutic goal should realistically be with this patient because the exact etiology and precipitating stresses of her present discomfort are not clear.

Figure 1-2. One form of a case-history. This summary was based on several clinical contacts including counseling and testing. (Courtesy of D. H. Mills)

Some psychologists say that this method of gathering information is not really scientific because of both the fairly high degree of subjectivity and the unreliability of much of the material in such compilations, and because of the emphasis upon the non-repeatable behavior of the unique individual rather than upon generalizations which may hold for all individuals or for the typical individual's behavior. These critics perhaps hold an unnecessarily severe and restrictive definition of both science and of the scientific methods which they claim to be acceptable. A more liberal and pragmatic criterion for scientific methods, by which those that produce information useful for prediction and explanation are accepted, has been met by those investigators who have contributed case-history or clinical evidence to the body of our knowledge of behavior. Many of the useful generalizations described in Chapter 12, *Behavior Disorders,* were obtained by use of the clinical method.

Theory in Psychology

Psychology, like other sciences, has found it useful and stimulating to construct theories about its subject matter. By formulating a symbolic representation or organization of observed behavior, psychologists may talk and think about complex behaviors more easily, discover possible underlying similarities of different behaviors, or rationally bridge larger gaps in the available knowledge in some areas of behavior. These kinds of uses of theory may be described in terms of two basic functions. Theories may act as *tools* and as *goals.* As a *tool,* theory in psychology may give order to observed relationships, permitting deductions and predictions of other, new relations, and thus guiding further research. As

a *goal*, a theory may conform to the end state of science, which is ordered knowledge. The working theory or conceptual organization is an
approximation of the ordered knowledge of behavior which is sought.

Based upon a mixture of empirical evidence, common sense, rational
thought, hopes, and dreams, a variety of complex and simple theories of
behavior have been erected and found useful. Some of these theories have
been concerned with a particular type of behavior. These theories have
attempted to account for learning, personality disorders, or depth perception, for example. Other theories have tried to describe essentially
the factors underlying all human and animal behavior.

Two theories which have been extremely influential in psychology are
those of Sigmund Freud and Clark Hull. A brief sketch of each of these
theories is given below as an example of the function such speculative
organizations of behavior have served in psychology.

FREUD'S THEORY *

Sigmund Freud (1856–1939) developed a theory of personality structure and development. Freud's theory was designed to understand and
guide the cure of those patients exhibiting abnormal behavior patterns.
Freud based this theory upon a background of evidence obtained in his
clinical relationships with patients and experimentation with the *free
association* or talking-out methods of therapy. The theory consisted of a
plan of development of personality (outlined in some detail in Chapter
10, *Personality*), in which sexual impulses are transformed through various stages during childhood, and aspects of later personality depend
upon the success of those changes or transformations. Notions and
terms which were a part of Freud's theory, such as *repression, superego,
ego,* and *id,* have become common and accepted labels in other aspects
of the study of behavior, as well as a part of the layman's language.

One of the most important parts of Freud's theory concerns the effect
of *unconscious* processes determining the course of behavior. Experiences of the individual determine the form and structure of the
unconscious and this dynamic unconscious directs behavior of the individual. Freud considered dreams to be repressed unconscious forces
circumventing or trying to get around the conscious *resistances* of the
patient. The content of *dreams,* therefore, present to the therapist in
symbolic form the sorts of problems and experiences at the root of the
patient's troubles. One way in which the unconscious slips by the conscious resistances is through the use of symbols.

Objects and factors in the repressed experience are given expression in the parts which symbols play in dreams and other experiencs. Another process by which the unconscious manages to slip by the conscious resistances is by means of slips-of-the-tongue, slips-of-the-pen, and other small accidents of action and communication which change or expose some hidden meanings. The poor fellow trying to explain something to a voluptuous female acquaintance and being obviously distracted when he says "There are two important points, Miss Sweater, ..." illustrates two Freudian slips of differing subtlety. Freud's notion is that all of these things are determined. They are determined by the processes of the unconscious, and are consistent with the needs and wishes of the individual.

In the clash between the unconscious forces and active conscious control, the rational processes of man are largely ignored by Freud. Freud felt that logical thinking is influenced by personal desire, and that the most rational kinds of thought are really just expressions of instinctual cravings and primitive desires.

The talking-out method, or free-association, was developed by Freud as a means to achieve *catharsis*. *Catharsis* is a release of emotions which functions by bringing repressed experiences into memory and out of the unconscious. Basically, the talking method involved requiring the patient to say anything that occurs or comes to mind. Two phenomena were noted by Freud in his early studies using free-association. These were called *transference* and *resistance*. *Transference* was an especially obvious love or hate of the therapist by the patient. Freud considered this to be additional evidence for the sexual nature of the problems being treated. *Resistance* was an unwillingness or inability to continue talking. Freud considered this to be a sign of being close to the forgotten experience; the inability to continue implying an increase in tension brought about by the closeness of the repressed troubled experience.

The details of Freud's theory concerning the formation and transformation of the personality from infancy through adulthood are available elsewhere in numerous books and articles. The notion of sexuality and sexual urges as the primary determinants of the unconscious and thus as the primary motives of the individual should be clarified somewhat. Note especially that Freud's view of the term "sex" included not only specific sex interests and activities, but what he would call the whole "pleasure life" of human beings. The term might be more closely linked to the way we presently use the word "love," implying things as diverse as artistic endeavors, religious experiences, serious avocations, as well as sexual activity in the specific sense of heterosexual intercourse and related activities.

HULL'S THEORY

Clark L. Hull's (1884–1952) theory of learning and motivation was also a theoretical system of large scope and lasting influence. Hull constructed a detailed and rational theory of behavior upon a base of a small amount of empirical evidence of the principles of learning and motivation. Hull guessed at the laws where there was poor evidence, and gave further specific testable suggestions about physiological mechanisms which might underlie certain aspects of behavior. Hull's published theory in 1943 and 1951 was stated in such a positive and testable way that it incited a great deal of research upon problems of learning. It is not true that all of the research which Hull's theory provoked has been useful, but it is probably true that many psychologists have become active in seeking new knowledge of learning because of the research motivation generated by Hull's theory of learned behavior.

Hull chose to design this theory using the *intervening variable technique*. Certain constructs of the theory intervene between the stimulus situation and the behavior that is observed. Hull gave names and letters to these constructs such as "habit" (H) for the learning factor of behavior, "drive" (D) for a motivational factor, incentive motivation (K), delay in reinforcement (J), and stimulus intensity (V). These factors were explicitly defined and were assumed to combine in a specific way to form reaction potential (E). Reaction potential was in turn linked in an explicit fashion to such observed behaviors as running speed of animals in a maze and percentage of correct choices in a discrimination task.

The major focal characteristic of Hull's theory concerned the nature of the formation of the learned response. What sort of events are necessary and sufficient for learning to take place? Hull espoused what is called a *reinforcement theory*. His reinforcement theory held that any response which is followed by a reinforcing state of affairs would be learned. Reinforcement, in turn, was defined as a state of affairs which leads to a reduction in needs or other primary motivations (hunger, thirst, escape from pain, etc.). Food given to a hungry animal reinforces associated behavior because that food reduces the need for food. Hull's reinforcement position, which stated that increments or increases in habit strength occur only as a result of the reduction in drive or need state, was especially provocative. This particular assumption of the theory was perhaps the irritant which incited the greatest amount of research energy toward disproving the theory. But this hypothesis also made Hull's theory an efficient and elegant theory of the evidence of learning then available.

A second important and lasting contribution of Hull's theory was his conception of motivation using the concept *drive*. The construct *drive* was meant to summarize all of the sources of motivation acting upon an individual at a given moment. The motivation comprising drive is supplied by states of hunger and thirst, the presence of aversive stimulation and fear, and other sources regardless of their relevance to the particular learned behavior. The quantity of drive directly determined performance in the theory by multiplying the amount of habit strength for the ongoing responses (Performance = Drive × Habit).

Since it first appeared in detail in 1943, Hull's system has had an influence upon a wide variety of problems. It has been widely applied beyond the original experimentation on which it was based into such diverse areas as motor skills learning, behavior disorders and therapy, and even the assumptions underlying the investigations by many physiological psychologists.

RECENT TRENDS IN THEORY

Large systems or theories of behavior like those of Freud and Hull have not been constructed anew in psychology in recent years. Aside from some continuation and reworking of the older theories, the trend in conceptual organization or theorizing has been toward smaller, less ambitious formulations. Even the name "theory" has gone somewhat out of style in favor of the term "model." Where there were once a few large-scale theories of learning, there are now several smaller treatments of limited aspects of learning. The smaller theory or model has generally included more empirical evidence in its premises and less of the rational guessing of past years. This reflects, in part, the increase in knowledge about behavior, but it also reflects a lessened willingness of theorists to concern themselves with models which are not likely to be very accurate.

Explanation of Behavior

One of the pervasive and troublesome problems of the field of psychology for many students is the source of explanations for behavior. Explanation, of course, is troublesome and controversial even for those who study it as a part of the philosophy of science. The basic problem of explanation in psychology is simply this: A particular behavior pattern has been regularly observed. How is that behavior pattern to be explained? We will attempt an answer later in this section.

First some words about an approach that is not likely to be fruitful in accounting for behavior at present. Some students, especially those who have had extensive studies in the biological sciences, believe that the obvious way to understand behavior is to break it into physiological units for study. The suggestion is to use physiological knowledge and principles to explain the more gross behavior. To explain the behavior pattern of running from a snake, for example, a physiological analysis would consider the principles of nervous system activity in response to fear-producing stimuli. Indeed there are available some of the principles of nervous system activity during emotional states. A complete analysis, however, cannot be made with the present degree of physiological knowledge. Some understanding can be contributed, but an explanation would require more complete information of the physiological bases and principles governing processes like the reception of stimuli, how these stimuli are coordinated with physiological memory traces of past experiences, and how this information is transmitted into the action of running, which is the observed behavior. The main point is that quite detailed physiological information is required before we can appeal to that level to explain the behavior phenomena. One might also ask why or how the reduction is stopped at the physiological level. Physiological function may be broken into biochemical function, which in turn may be reduced to physics, and so on. This sort of reduction leads to no firm level of particles or pieces which may not in turn be reduced, at least with our present knowledge in the various fields of scientific investigation. Some writers hold that one of the eventual goals of science is such a reduction from one discipline to another, and this point will not be disputed here. The question of interest here is the selection and use of methods to explain behavior satisfactorily at the present time.

If reduction to physiology is not a useful approach, what then *is* a source of explanation of behavior? A very simple way of looking at explanation which answers much of the question is to consider what it is that one does when asked to explain something. The first step is to assess how much the person already knows and then to slowly present a chain of information until the fact or concept to be explained is included. That is, the fact or concept is presented in terms with which the person is already familiar. Explanation may be defined as describing a new thing in terms of what is already known—relating the new to the old and established.

Two patterns of explanation which are often used in psychology can be identified in terms of the organization of information that is used in the explanation. These two patterns of information are called *developmental* explanation and *interactive* explanation.

Developmental explanation relates a new behavior to an established sequence of known behaviors. It is historical explanation, in the sense of requiring some knowledge of the historical sequence of this and similar behaviors. For example, the appearance of some behaviors in children may be "explained" in this way by comparing that behavior to known knowledge of the timing or sequential development of the behavior in similar situations.

Interactive explanation accounts for behavior by describing its position in the organization of the present situation and using the known laws relating to that present situation. The behavior to be explained is fitted into the present interaction of events. We might explain the perception of an illusion by considering the organization of the various stimuli which have been selected to make that figure appear different from what it really is. The present situation is all that is needed: no knowledge of what has just happened is required.

Psychology's Past

Compared to many other disciplines, psychology is very young. Writers who identified themselves as psychologists did not appear until about the beginning of the present century. Definite influences upon psychological thought, though, can be seen in the work of certain earlier philosophers and in the general trend of theory and knowledge in biological disciplines. Three such influences are *associationism, faculty psychology,* and *Darwinism.*

PHILOSOPHICAL INFLUENCES

Associationism was a philosophical view of the makeup of the mind. This view held that the content of mind was formed of the association of ideas. Ideas are patterns of images originally obtained from the senses. The ideas were associated according to the operation of principles named contiguity, similarity, and contrast. Ideas which were present at nearly the same time were more likely to be associated than those occurring at disparate times. Similar ideas were easily associated. Contrasting ideas were more readily associated than were unrelated ideas.

The associationistic view held further that there were no substantial inborn differences in the mind. Experience was the factor which produced differences among the minds of individuals. Definite influence of the associationistic position can be seen in many thories of learning which also emphasize experience as the primary factor effecting changes in behavior.

Faculty psychology presents a philosophical position which is opposed to the associationist view in many respects. Faculty psychology describes an individual as composed of a number of inborn faculties which determine the mind of that individual. While associationism held that differences were produced by experience in structurally identical individuals, the faculty psychology view assumed that differences in mental structure from birth were the most important determining factors for mental behavior. Some later developments of this view held that these faculties were directly related to the size of certain parts of the head. By measurement and cataloging the bumps upon a person's head, the faculties and hence the mind of the individual would be known. This extreme view, called *phrenology*, is no longer seriously maintained in psychology, but the influence of the notion of inborn differences *is* present in the modern study of individual differences and of personality.

Darwinism includes the notions of *species evolution* and *natural selection* which have had an influence upon the course of investigation of all of the life sciences. These notions hold man to be the end product of a long, slow change from more primitive and less complex forms of life. This assumed gradual development of the structure of man has specific implications for behavior and provides a rationale for the study of animal behavior.

Survival-of-the-fittest can be applied not only to the study of changes in the form of a species, but also to the long-term development of specific behaviors of the species. Behaviors which impair or facilitate the survival of the individual will affect the likelihood of changes of the behavior patterns of the species. Behaviors which are useful remain, and those which are not useful for survival tend to be eliminated through the partial removal of those individuals from the breeding population.

Darwinism has had other, less specific influences upon psychology and related fields. Darwinism forced a consideration of man as a more complex animal on a continuum with other forms of life rather than as a unique type of being with mystical capabilities which by definition cannot be directly studied and understood. As a continuation of other life forms, man is viewed as being subject to the same influences and factors as are animals. Though man is more complex, his behavior is of the same kind.

VIEWPOINTS OF THE RECENT PAST

Some of the more recent general viewpoints in psychology can be seen to be influenced directly by these older, historical philosophies, by present influences from other fields, and from views developed around specific problems, some of a practical nature. The successive eras of *structuralism, functionalism,* and *behaviorism* have had a major influence upon present scientific psychology. In this period also, the concurrently developing views of *psychoanalysis* and *gestalt psychology* have given direction to aspects of present psychology. These views are located approximately on the time scale of Figure 1-3.

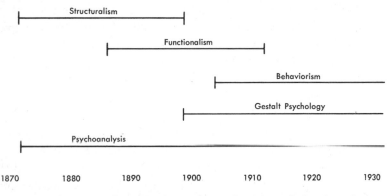

Figure 1-3. **The approximate dates of origin and duration of major influence of several important viewpoints in psychology.**

Structuralism was perhaps the first psychology which did not identify itself with philosophy. The subject matter of this new psychology was held to be experience. Trained subjects analyzed their own experiences by *introspecting*, describing personal mental contents according to certain rules. The goal of introspection was to break up experience into elements which were called *sensations*.

German structuralists, especially Wilhelm Wundt, brought the new psychology into the laboratory and performed experiments to analyze experience further. An example of these experiments is that of the com-

parison of the speed of reaction of the hand to a lever at the appearance
of a light signal (simple reaction time) with the speed of a similar
reaction when the subject must note which of several light signals has
been given and also make an appropriate discrimination response
(choice reaction time). The greater length of time to perform the latter,
more complex reaction was given as evidence for the greater structure
of mind which was required for that task. Furthermore, it gave a
precise time measurement of the relative amount of such mental activity.

Though structuralism was reasonably rigorous for its time, it was
also judged to be sterile, unreliable, and unproductive for the purposes
of the American psychologists at about the turn of the century. Structuralism tried to study what it called the "facts" of the mind as they
existed, while the new and developing American view was more interested in the "functions" of the mind.

Functionalism included the *goal* of the mental activity in its description of the mind. The functionalists also used an introspective analysis
of experience as the basic data-collection method for psychology, but
the functionalists were more interested in the adaptive function of the
mental processes than their structure. The influence of the biology of
the times and of Darwinism in general was evident, along with the
American temper of practicality. The pragmatic view presented by
functionalism accounted for the development of many practical questions (for example, concerning education) which some functionalists
posed.

A modern viewpoint which also is called functionalism and can be
traced to the earlier functionalists is so named because of its interest
in "functional relationships." Modern functionalism seeks laws relating
behavior to situations and variables, with an emphasis on the usefulness
of the relationships rather than upon theoretical considerations. The
similarity of interest in function, though, must be tempered by the
difference in methods of the old and new functionalists. While the
older functionalist view applied the prior introspective techniques,
modern functionalists have adopted the methods and procedures usually
associated with the succeeding behaviorism.

Behaviorism displaced introspective functionalism as the dominant
viewpoint in American psychology. Behaviorism's leading vocal expo-
nent, John B. Watson, decried the use of the introspective technique
and the analysis of experience as the content of psychology. Watson
claimed that the only proper subject matter for psychology was behavior
that could be observed. Such *objective* behavior study soon was the

most popular technique for gathering information in psychology. The early behaviorists developed some rather extreme and reactive viewpoints which left no place for introspection, the mind, or any other concept having "experiential" overtones. Watson, on one occasion, proclaimed an extreme associationistic view in which behavior was said to result entirely from experience, suggesting that control of experience in the proper manner could result in *any* child becoming *any* kind of person. Behaviorism is still the label applied to most of scientific psychology today, though the tolerance to other positions and the use of other kinds of concepts than those based solely upon directly observable behavior indicates that a considerable softening of Watson's extreme stand has taken place.

Displacing structuralists, more recent German psychologists have described a theory of behavior called *gestalt psychology,* which has had some influence upon psychology, especially the study of perception. The word "gestalt" translates from German to something like "form" or "organization" in English, and these words describe the basic notion of the view. Gestalt psychology is concerned with organization as the dominant mechanism in mental processes. The method of gathering of information is that of *phenomenology,* which is a kind of introspection made by untrained or naive subjects. Instead of observable behavior, verbally reported experiences of subjects are the basic subject matter of gestalt psychology.

The interest of gestalt psychologists has been primarily in perception. The simple experiential reports of what was seen by naive observers provide the basic information. The gestalters were interested in patterns rather than elements. They conceived of learning in perceptual terms of changes in patterns or organization of the related stimuli. Some contemporary "field" theories in psychology can be seen to come very close to the gestalt position, but the major contribution of gestalt psychology has perhaps been the rich collection of perceptual phenomena and principles it has yielded rather than its procedural philosophy.

One final viewpoint which has very strongly determined the form of present psychology is that of *psychoanalysis.* Sigmund Freud and his theory, of course, are the major sources for this view which combines a theory of personality, a theory of development, and a tool for the treatment of mental disorders. This view stemmed from a practitioner's observations and biases. The general views and tenets of psychoanalysis which have been influential in all of psychology include the notion of an unconscious motivational structure, and that there are some dynamic, causative processes which determine behavior, but which themselves are not observable.

Summary

Psychology is the science of behavior. It deals with observable behaviors which are measurable, repeatable, and under some degree of control. Mental events are inferred from observations of behavior in carefully planned situations.

Four methods of gathering information comprise the typical approaches of psychology. Naturalistic observation requires observation of behavior without interference with that behavior. Testing presents a standard stimulus and notes the variations in behavior which result. The experimental method holds constant all known influences upon the observed behavior except one, the independent variable. The clinical method combines personal data from a variety of sources into a case-history of one person. These methods differ on two factors called control and generalizability.

Theory in psychology may function as a tool for organizing information or as a goal, a description of ordered knowledge. An era of elaborate theories of behavior, illustrated by those of Freud and of Hull, has given way to a period of limited theories or models of smaller segments of behavior.

Explanation of behavior cannot be usefully accomplished by breaking it into physiological units, at least with our present knowledge. Instead, a behavior is explained by its position in an organization of other information. The new is explained by its relation to the already known. Organizations of information explaining behavior may use historical knowledge of the development of behavior or knowledge of present factors as they interact to include the behavior.

The philosophical background of psychology includes the associationism view of mind as developing from associations of ideas, the opposite faculty psychology view of mind as resulting from inborn mental differences or faculties, and the Darwinism notion of man and animals developing physically and mentally through natural selection from less adaptive forms of life.

Recent philosophies of psychology have influenced the choice of methods of present psychology. Structuralism analyzed mental events or facts of mind by introspection, a description of personal mental content. Functionalism also used introspection but included the function or goal of the mental activity in the description. Behaviorism refuted introspection and allowed only the study of observable behavior. Gestalt psychology studied the organization of materials as they determined the phenomena of experience. Finally, psychoanalysis contributed the view of behavior as being influenced by unconscious motivation processes, causes for behavior which can be noted only indirectly through their effects.

SUGGESTED READINGS

Marx, M. H. (Ed.) *Theories in contemporary psychology.* New York: Macmillan, 1963.
A collection of papers on the nature and status of theory in psychology. Special emphasis upon the role of theory in scientific psychology and the controversy which different viewpoints have generated.

Marx, M. H., and Hillix, W. A. *Systems and theories in psychology.* New York: McGraw-Hill, 1963.
A presentation of a philosophy of the science of psychology, the philosophical and other historical backgrounds to present psychological thoughts, and the contemporary developments of the older systems of psychology.

Scott, W. A., and Wertheimer, M. *Introduction to psychological research.* New York: Wiley, 1962.
A basic introduction to the theory and the practicalities of psychological research. The problems and refinements of the methods of psychology are elaborated.

Sidowski, J. B. (Ed.) *Experimental methods and instrumentation in psychology.* New York: McGraw-Hill, 1966.
A sophisticated presentation of the experimental method and the accumulated lore of research in topic areas of experimental psychology. This work serves as a handbook of techniques in several specialized areas.

Underwood, B. J. *Experimental psychology* (2nd edition). New York: Appleton-Century-Crofts, 1966.
A standard approach to the application of experimental methods in a variety of topic areas.

Chapter 2

PHYSIOLOGICAL PSYCHOLOGY

If psychology studies and answers questions about the behaviors of individuals, why is an introduction to psychology concerned in part with matters of the structure and physiology of the body? What kind of contribution does study of physiology make to knowledge of behavior? What is the physiological "apparatus" underlying behavior? What are the principles of operation of the nervous system which structure behavior events? How is the brain studied? What do we know of "systems" in the brain which organize patterns of behavior? These questions are among those answered in this chapter.

Purposes of Physiological Psychology

Study of the structure and of the physiological functioning of the body *is* important in psychology. As discussed in Chapter 1, biology is not able at this time to describe, predict, and explain behavior completely, but it can help immensely in the study of behavior. This help may be given in several ways.

Physiological principles contribute to the understanding of behavioral phenomena. Knowledge of physiological function adds to the organization of facts surrounding those phenomena. As an example, if a person is forced to perform a rather simple but boring task over a long period of time, measures of that skill may show a decrease in performance after a lengthy period of practice. Accompanying these performance measures will be statements by the workers that they feel "tired." These facts lead to the conclusion that the long-term work has produced some sort of physiological fatigue, a physical slowing-down in the motor systems involved. Physiological experimentation, though, is likely to demonstrate that there is little or no such impairment of the motor systems. Direct stimulation of the motor neurons will immediately evoke the original high level of performance. A change in the task conditions and incentives (like a brief electric shock for poor performance) may also restore the "fatigued" motor performance. The source of the performance decrement and of the tired feelings must be found elsewhere. Coordinate information about sleep and arousal control in certain nervous system structures of the brain may also help in this attempt to understand the observed behavior decrement. Physiological information has clarified the problem by changing it from one of muscle fatigue to some process of nervous system control in other parts of the body. In this case the physiological analysis has eliminated one rational explanation for the observed phenomenon and suggested a new direction for research. In other cases analyses may direct the psychologist in a more positive fashion to sharpen a particular explanation.

In many cases the simple knowledge of what is and is not possible physiologically will guide the behavioral scientist. An example of this function is given by the story of the fellow who had a fly which he had trained to jump over a pencil upon command. He was an experimenting sort of fellow and he decided to pull off two legs from the fly. He then commanded the fly to jump, and the fly jumped easily over the pencil. He removed two more legs from the fly and commanded it to jump. The fly tried, but the best it could do was crawl across the pencil using his remaining legs. After this performance the fellow pulled off the remaining legs from the fly and commanded "jump!" The fly did not move. The fellow wrote of this research to a scholarly journal of animal behavior and concluded "when all of the legs of the fly were removed, the fly became deaf." Knowledge of where we believe the fly's auditory receptors are located makes this example humorous. But this is not the entire story. Study has shown that the primary auditory receptors, those sensitive to sound and other vibrations, are located on the fore-legs of the fly. The removal of the final pair of legs may well have produced "deafness." Knowing more about physiological processes which directly affect a behavior may change the whole picture. The use here is not so much of the explanatory function of biological knowledge as of the related guidance it provides to behavioral research and interpretation.

Study of physiological structure underlying and related to behavior is also the goal for some psychologists. The aspects of behavior of greatest interest to these psychologists are the many physiological functions and changes which make up behavior. Often, what are clearly "physiological" mechanisms are also the most important behaviors in a situation. It is very difficult to define a difference between physiological processes and other sorts of behavior. Is a "blush" a physiological change or a bit of behavior? Blushing and a long list of other observable behaviors can be noted in an individual undergoing an emotional experience. Moist palms, a dry mouth, and pounding heart are indeed physiological changes, but they are also the major observable behaviors during an intense emotional reaction. In these situations the contribution to knowledge of behavior of researchers with an interest in physiological processes is quite large. Other topics of research by physiological psychologists and psychophysiologists will be discussed later.

These examples of gifts of physiological analysis to behavior research have been relatively direct and simple. Physiological experimentation may also be valuable for the psychologist in an indirect fashion. For example, about a half century ago the developing theories of learning assumed as a source and model the accepted physiological knowledge of the times. The notion of a simple "neural arc" (See Figure 2-3) and related neural "circuitry" of the body was assumed to be the means by which information was received, stored, and converted into behavior. It was rationally assumed that there existed a memory center in the brain responsible for the storage of information—a place where memories are located. An implication of this notion was that if this center could be located, further analysis of the learning process would be greatly facilitated. Later physiological investigations have shown that it is unlikely that there is such a unitary center and that the notion of basic circuits is too simple to be an adequate description of the workings of the brain. Most recent physiological analysis of this same kind of question, the action of learning in the brain, has centered upon lower brain areas and the relationships between affective or motivational conditions and learning. But the influence of the earlier reflex view was strong and still may be seen in the ways in which psychologists view the hidden processes underlying behavior. The psychologist's view of physiology, whether it is right or wrong, new or old, plays a strong role in his thoughts about behaviors.

Structure and Function

Some parts of the structures of organisms have been shown to affect behavior more directly than do other parts. The action of a muscle has been more useful and interesting to students of behavior than has been the process of formation of skin. Similarly with functions of the body, some are more directly connected to psychological problems as we presently know them than are others. Knowledge of the mechanism of action of a neural cell has given much more useful information to the psychologist than that of the actions of leukocytes in the blood. Thus this chapter does not pretend to overview all that is important in physiology and biology. Rather, an overview of structure and a few detailed topics of general utility to behavior study will be presented.

THE RECEPTORS AND EFFECTORS

The *receptors* and the *effectors* are means of receiving information and making responses. The *receptors* include the senses, with which everyone is familiar, plus a few other channels of information input which are not consciously experienced. The *effectors* are the muscles and glands which directly or indirectly produce observable behavior.

The familiar receptors include those which convert energy for sight (vision), hearing (audition), the sense of smell (olfaction), the taste sense (gustation), the skin senses (warmth, cold, and pressure), and the sense of pain. Less well-known are the very important senses which give information about movements of the parts of the body with respect to one another (kinesthesis) and which inform other parts of the body about movements of the head in space (equilibratory senses). All of these receptors will be discussed more fully in Chapter 4, with an emphasis upon the ways in which they affect perception.

A *muscle* is a bundle of fibrous cells which contract upon neural stimulation. There are three basic types of muscles. Those which are easily visible in the arms and the legs are the *striped* (or striate) muscles. Striped muscles produce movements of the parts of the skeleton, both the voluntary and the involuntary movements required in walking, talking, writing, and so on. A second type of muscle is the *smooth* muscle. The smooth muscles control the automatic functions necessary for the maintenance of the body, such as digestion, with the exception of the heart muscles. Smooth muscles are relatively slow in operation but are also slow to fatigue as compared with the striped muscle. Muscles of the heart are the third major type, the *cardiac* muscle. These muscles produce the pumping action of the blood in the heart.

The *gland* affects behavior in an indirect way by action on the internal environment of the body. Internal glands called *endocrine glands* secrete chemical substances directly into the bloodstream to perform various regulatory functions. At least one of these endocrine glands is known to have a direct and immediate relationship to observable behavior. The adrenal glands, as one of their functions, secrete a substance, commonly called "adrenaline," into the bloodstream during states of emotional excitement. Adrenaline has been found to be directly responsible for many of the lasting physiological effects observed in emotional states, such as cessation of digestion, muscle tremor, and "pounding" heart.

The *duct glands* secrete substances through ducts onto the surface of the body rather than into the bloodstream. The secretions of the tear, salivary, and sweat glands are often useful observable behaviors, as indicants of emotional states or as a part of other behavior mechanisms.

THE NERVOUS SYSTEMS

The channels which pass information from the receptors and eventually to the effectors are called the *nervous systems*. Nervous systems are made up of *nerves* which are, in turn, composed of various sizes and shapes of specialized cells called *neurons*. Some neurons are fast conductors of information, some slow; some are automatic, and some are subject to a high degree of voluntary control. These connectors, to and from the many parts of the body, have by no means been all located and categorized as to function. Only rough ideas of the neurons in many body areas are known. Some particular divisions of the total nervous system, however, may be identified and their function in behavior specified.

There are two ways in which the nervous system may be divided. First, the nerves may be identified as members of the *central nervous system* and those of the *peripheral nervous system*. The central nervous system is composed primarily of the spinal cord and the brain. The peripheral nervous system includes most of what is left, those connectors which lead from the receptors to the spinal cord and brain, and those connectors which go to the muscles and the glands from the spinal cord and brain. A second division of the entire nervous system can be made between the nerves of the *somatic nervous system* and the *autonomic (visceral) nervous system.* The somatic nervous system effects skeletal control, primarily the voluntary processes of the body. The autonomic nervous system controls the glands and smooth muscle processes which are not generally subject to voluntary control.

Four nervous systems may be identified by these two divisions of the nerves of the body: the central somatic system, the peripheral somatic system, the central autonomic system, and the peripheral autonomic system (See Figure 2-1). This last named subdivision holds

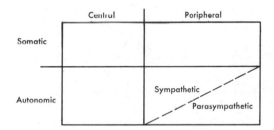

Figure 2-1. Two divisions of the nervous system establishing four subdivisions having somewhat unique general properties. The peripheral autonomic subdivision is further divided usefully into two parts.

special interest for the student of emotional behavior. The *peripheral autonomic system* consists of the nerves leading to and controlling the glands and smooth muscles. This system has been further divided into two parts labeled the *sympathetic nervous system* and the *parasympathetic nervous system.*

The two branches of the peripheral autonomic system can be identified by their somewhat different spatial locations and also by the method and function of their activity. The *sympathetic nervous system* is active during states of emotional excitement, tends to act as a unit, and functions to expend the resources of the body into action. The *parasympathetic nervous system,* conversely, is most active during resting states, acts in a piecemeal fashion as needed, and serves to conserve the resources of the body. Some of the organs which are partly controlled by one of the two parts of the autonomic nervous system are shown in Figure 2-2. Note that some organs are activated

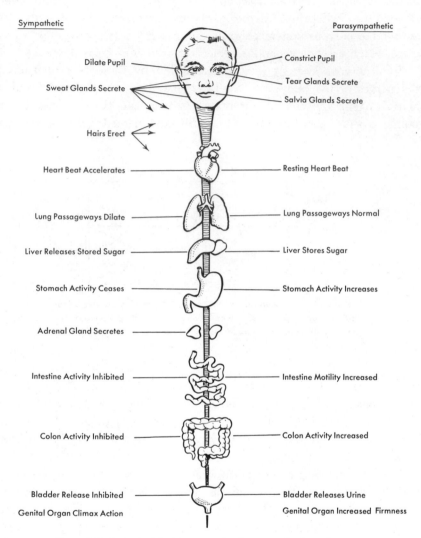

Figure 2-2. Control of body organs by the sympathetic and parasympathetic branches of the peripheral autonomic nervous system.

by only one of these two branches, while others are controlled by both.
These facts help in understanding the nature of responses to emotion
discussed in Chapter 3.

LEVELS OF NERVE FUNCTION

Three levels of nervous system functioning can be usefully identified: *reflex action, old brain action,* and *new brain action.* These levels are primarily conceptual views, but they have some basis in structural and functional differences.

Reflex action is of a very low level of complexity. It is analogous to a simple electrical circuit activating a doorbell by means of a button. A stimulus activates a receptor cell which, in turn, stimulates an incoming or *afferent* neuron. At the spinal cord or brain stem the pulse of the afferent neuron stimulates an *efferent* or outgoing neuron which stimulates an effector cell structure. Sense information is transmitted almost directly into action. This simple kind of function is called a *reflex arc* and is illustrated in Figure 2-3. As indicated in the figure, more than just two neurons are probably involved, and even such a simple circuit as this probably also receives controlling stimulation from

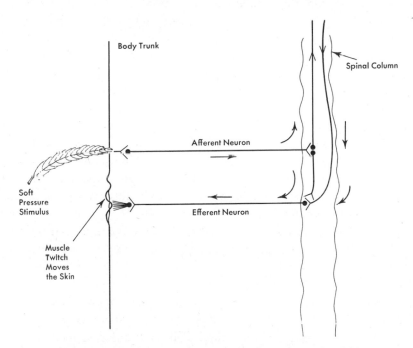

Figure 2-3. A reflex arc conception of nervous system functioning at the spinal cord level. The stimulus activates a circuit of neural cells which evokes a response. Information of this neural activity is probably carried to higher nerve centers as indicated.

centers in the brain. Some writers describe the reflex arc as the smallest *functional* unit of the nervous system. The smallest structural unit is considered to be the neuron. The reflex arc concept has been borrowed and used heavily in behavior theories, especially in theories and interpretations of learning.

Old brain action is a more complex level of functioning in the nervous system. Old brain or lower brain areas refer to the major brain areas found in phylogenetically "older" and, hence, simpler species. These brain structures control the automatic and life-preserving processes of the body, including breathing and regulation of food and water intake. Other old brain actions include the automatic (and, loosely, unconscious) aspects of motor acts like riding a bicycle or typing. In early attempts at riding a bicycle one is very much aware of each movement that is made. As the skill develops, less and less attention is paid to these component movements until they are definitely out of awareness. At this level the skills may be thought of as being controlled by old brain action. All old brain functions may be characterized as unconscious, complex behaviors which are controlled by areas of the old or lower brain.

The third level of function, termed *new brain* action, is the most complex. Functions such as sensation, thinking, problem solving, and other voluntary or conscious acts fit into this category. These functions are presumed to be controlled in the phylogentically "new" or recently-evolved brain areas, especially the cerebrum. In most cases, new brain actions involve conscious experiences of incoming stimulation and the actions to them. This higher level of function is often considered objectively unmeasurable because it underlies a private experience of the individual. Hence it has largely been set aside in favor of study of more observable and less variable processes. But it is also recognized that these new brain functions are necessarily more complex and difficult to study in view of the greater structural complexity of the new brain.

NEURAL FUNCTION

Each *nerve* is composed of bundles of neurons. A *neuron* is a specialized cell. Like other cells, it has a *cell body* and a *nucleus*. (See Figure 2-4.) Part of the body of the neural cell is tubular shaped and of substantial length, which serves to transmit information through a distance within the body. This tubular portion, called the *axon*, generally receives impulses of activity from the *dendrites* at one end. The axon transmits impulses of activity towards the other end of the cell where

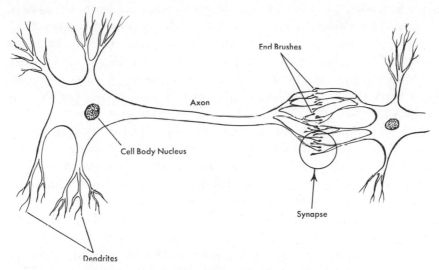

Figure 2-4. A simplified picture of a single neuron. An impulse is normally received by the dendrites at the left, passes along the axon, and produces action at the end brushes which potentially stimulate firing of other neurons.

there are parts called *end brushes*. These end brushes, through processes to be described later, either activate other neurons or other types of cells, including muscles and glands.

A typical neuron from man has an axon of about 1/100 of a millimeter in diameter and transmits impulses at about 100 meters per second. The speed of the impulse and the length and diameter of neurons vary. The larger the diameter of the axon, the faster is the neural transmission. Some of man's neurons are covered with a white, fatty material which serves to insulate the neuron from the surrounding tissue. Neurons so covered are said to be *myelinated*. Myelinated neurons are found to develop more slowly in a growing individual, but when fully developed, transmit impulses at a much faster rate than unmyelinated neurons.

Neurons are sometimes compared and likened to electric wires, but some important differences should be noted. The speed of neural conduction is far slower than the speed of electrical transmission. Electrical activity in a copper wire approaches the speed of light. The interior of an axon is about 100 million times more resistant to electrical transmission than is the copper wire.

The evidence [21] strongly suggests that the movement of an impulse along a neural axon is primarily a chemical and not an electrical process, though we measure that neural impulse indirectly by devices sensitive to electrical activity. The measurable electrical properties of neural transmission are merely a side effect or property of the chemical changes. This relationship between electrical and neural activity has interesting implications for many uses of electrical activity measurements. Does every neural impulse have an electrical counterpart? Do all such measured electrical changes result from neural activity?

At least two principles of neural conduction, which have been known for some time, follow directly from a description of the chemical process of neural conduction. One is that the impulse transmission along a neuron generates itself and either happens or it does not. The impulse is of a constant strength if it exists at all. That is, the strength of the impulse along the axon is determined solely by the chemical action along the axon membrane and not by any characteristic of the situation which initiated the activity of the neuron. The strength, duration, or quality of the stimulus at the dendrites has no effect on the impulse as long as that stimulus was sufficient to elicit a neural impulse. Once begun, each impulse along a neuron is exactly like all other impulses along that particular neuron in the past or future. The second principle of importance is that the time taken for the chain of chemical events at one point along the axon is of a substantial, finite length. Therefore, the *number* of such impulses which may travel along a neuron in a given period of time is limited. A typical neuron may transmit no more than a few hundred impulses in a second under ideal conditions.

Again in comparison with electrical transmission along a wire, both the size and number of electrical impulses which may travel along a wire are almost without limit, but the neural impulse is always of a constant size and is limited in frequency of occurrence by the impulse time and chemical rebalance time.

The transmission of impulses along the length of a single neuron is only part of the picture of nervous system activity. The junction of the end brushes of one neuron and the dendrites of the next is called a *synapse*. Neurons do not touch one another at this junction but are separated slightly at the ends. (See Figure 2-4.) How then does the impulse which reaches the end of one neuron travel to the next neuron?

The mechanism of transmission of the impulse across the synapse is called *synaptic transmission*. This process, like the transmission of the neural impulse, is chemical in nature. The end brushes of each neuron emit a chemical substance which stimulates the dendrites of the next neuron. This process takes a slightly longer period of time than that required for an impulse to pass along an equal distance of axon, thus it would take longer for an impulse to travel along a simple neural "circuit" of many synapses than it would to travel a comparable distance crossing fewer synaptic junctions.

There is further evidence that the type of chemical emitted at the synapse differs for neural fibers in the different branches of the peripheral autonomic system. The synapses of neurons of the sympathetic system are believed to use acetylcholine secretions (cholinergic stimulation), while the synapses of the parasympathetic nervous system require norepinephrine secretions (adrenergic stimulation). This difference in chemical transmission may provide some interesting though crude explanations about the effects of drugs taken into the body. Chemicals may be administered which counteract or neutralize the action of one or the other of these two substances. For example, the sympathetic nervous system and consequent emotional behavior may be enhanced by the administration of cholinergic or acetylcholine-like drugs.

Though we have been describing single neuron functions, the interconnections between neurons are immensely complex and should not be viewed as a simple system. Some neurons require the simultaneous stimulation of a large number of other neurons for activation. This many-to-one principle is called *spatial summation*. A neuron which requires a mass of stimulation before it is activated could perhaps also be fired by the repeated stimulation from one or more nearby neurons in a short period of time. This is termed *temporal summation* of neural activity. Similarly, some neurons have sufficient potency to activate a number of other neurons with a single impulse. The variety of complex connections between neurons indicates the variety and richness of neural circuitry that is possible.

The Brain

BRAIN STUDY TECHNIQUES

The brain is the common name given to a collection of organs located at the top of the spinal column. Each part of the brain generally has a different function. These functions may be collectively described as the organization and control of stimulation and behaviors of the body. A collection of mechanisms as complex and as extensive as the brain has allowed a variety of approaches by those who study it. Five different approaches are called here *anatomical, developmental, removal, stimu-*

lation, and *electrical recording.* One can see in these five basic brain-study techniques described below some of the characteristics of the methods of general behavior study which were described in Chapter 1.

The *anatomical* techniques provide basic knowledge of the structural units of the brain and describe connections between various organs. By using techniques of nerve degeneration and selective tissue stains, the neural map of the brain may be determined in a fairly precise way. Such anatomical analysis, though, generally locates only the larger groups of nerves of the estimated 10 billion neurons present in the human brain. The precise detail of individual neurons and their inter-connections has not been cataloged simply because of the enormity of the task and the lack of any helpful way to record the information for ready reference. But another factor hinders anatomical description of single neuron location. One brain is not exactly like all other brains. There are significant individual differences in structure which complicate the more detailed anatomical description.

The *developmental* technique compares brain structure and behavior to estimate the functions of the parts of the brain. This may be accomplished in two different ways. One may study the development of structure of an individual over time during periods of change through growth, comparing the structural changes with corresponding changes in behavior. One may also compare the brain structure and behaviors of the various species of animals. In conjunction with the anatomical technique, one might infer that the well-developed olfactory bulb of the dog controls its correspondingly strong relative ability to distinguish and locate sources of odors. Similarly, the enlarged temporal lobes of the bottle-nose dolphin correspond to the presence of its remarkable acoustic abilities. Man's well-developed occipital lobes correlate with his acute visual sensitivity. The presence of a given unusual behavior and a uniquely developed structure in one species as compared with another species or with development of similar areas in that species suggests the function of that organ.

Removal of selected brain tissues is also an effective method of determining the function of those organs. The relationship between a specific damage to the tissue, called a *lesion,* and behavior may again be described in two different ways. A change in behavior may be noted between observations before and after the lesion, or the lesion may be produced in what is assumed to be a normal animal followed by attempts to modify that individual's behavior. This last technique is most often used in studies of the locus in the brain of processes like learning.

Thus, by use of the removal technique, it can be determined whether that area is used for the performance of an already learned response or whether it is necessary for the acquisition of that learned behavior. The removal technique is generally used as an experimental technique upon animals, but similar kinds of observations can be made of existing brain damage in man which has resulted from injury or disease.

Figure 2-5. A sheep having electrodes implanted into brain areas. The packs on its back allow information to be transmitted to remote receivers without the nuisance of wires. (Courtesy of D. Sussman and T. Pepper)

Stimulation of the brain tissue has produced valuable information of brain function. Mild electrical stimulation of the exposed surface of the cerebral cortex of patients undergoing brain surgery has provided a sort of mapping of the functions of these cortical areas. This mapping will be presented, in part, later. Experimental stimulation of interior parts of the brains of animals has produced some remarkable findings. There are brain areas which apparently produce pleasurable sensations for the stimulated subjects. Animals will learn and work for further stimulation in these areas. This phenomenon will also be discussed later in the chapter. Electrical and chemical stimulation of other interior or lower brain areas has begun to describe the rather precise and delicate mechanisms which control eating, drinking, temperature regulation, emotional sensitivity, and wakefulness.

The fifth technique of brain study is that of *electrical recording*. The very small electric currents produced with each neural firing (on the order of a billionth of a watt of power) are measured with sensitive electronic amplification devices. All of the electrical activity reaching the pick-up device is amplified and presented as a complex pattern. Thus any single neural firing is hopelessly buried in the record of several thousand nearby firings. The surface recording of these electrical changes is known as electroencephalography, or simply, the *EEG*. The EEG record is usually described in terms of the amplitude, frequency, and synchrony of the tracings. Figure 2-6 shows a characteristic high-

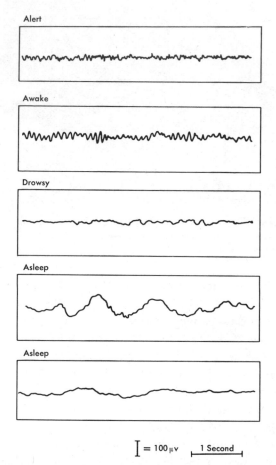

Figure 2-6. Some frequently occurring EEG tracings during psychological events as noted. (From Brazier, M. B. *The electrical activity of the nervous system.* Macmillan, 1960.)

amplitude (large vertical movement), well-synchronized (consistent and regular pattern of the tracing), and low-frequency (few patterns per unit of horizontal distance) EEG record from the back of the brain of a relaxed subject with eyes closed. This particular brain wave of about 10–12 cycles per second is called an *alpha wave*. Opening of the eyes or almost any other stimulus which arouses or attracts the attention of the subject results in the disappearance or "blocking" of the alpha wave. In the place of the alpha wave there appears a desynchronized, low-amplitude, high-frequency brain wave.

EEG records have been used to identify different stages or phenomena of sleep. Desynchronized waves of lower amplitude and frequency mark the onset of drowsiness. Light sleep brain waves are of low frequency with occasional "sleep spindles" of faster wave pattern. Deep sleep is marked by very high amplitude and low frequency brain waves with occasional periods of low amplitude and high frequency waves. These occasional desynchronized patterns are called "paradoxical sleep."

Microelectrode recording is a promising new attempt to record electrical changes in a single cell or fiber. Very small electrodes may be placed into or next to a single neural unit to monitor its activity apart from surrounding activity.

CEREBRAL CORTEX

The most modern or phylogenetically most recent development of the human brain is the cerebral cortex. The cerebral cortex is the outermost layer of the cerebral hemispheres next to the skull. It is composed of thin hemispherical layers of convoluted (folded) grayish neuron tissue. As might be expected from the reasoning of the developmental approach, the cortex controls and coordinates those activities which are most nearly unique to the human and higher mammalian species.

Probing by electrical stimulation has determined that there are specific areas on the surface of the cortex which are involved with sensory and motor function. These areas are called the *projection areas* and are located upon the hemispheres as indicated in Figure 2-7. The visual projection area is located at the back of the cortex in the occipital lobe. Neural activity from stimulation received in the right side of the retina of each eye is transmitted, eventually, to the right hemisphere visual area, while stimulation to the left half of each retina is transmitted to the corresponding area in the left hemisphere of the cortex.

The auditory projection areas are located in the temporal lobes at the side of the cortex. Unlike the visual area, both temporal areas

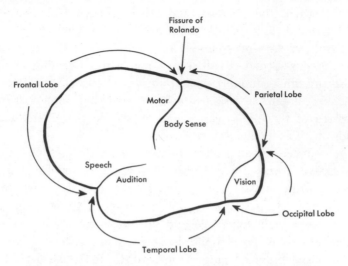

Figure 2-7. **Cortical projection areas and terms describing features of the cerebral cortex.**

receive information of auditory stimulation from both of the ears. A major speech control area is located in the frontal lobe near the auditory area. The control of speech is more complex than those aspects of control which are located in just this area, but it has long been maintained that the speech area is localized in only one hemisphere and that this localization is related to handedness. Left-handed persons have a speech area localized in the right hemisphere and right-handed persons have a speech area localized in the left hemisphere. The motor and body-sense projections areas are located upon opposite sides of the deep vertical fold in the cortex called the *fissure of Rolando*. The extent of the area which controls or receives sense stimulation from each part of the body corresponds to the degree of complexity of the control or the sensitivity of that area, as indicated in Figure 2-8.

The remaining areas of the cortex have been given vague names such as "association areas," indicating the belief that these areas, not having a known specific function, must have a general associating function for the neural information arriving from the many sensory channels. There is evidence, for example, that the frontal lobes are involved in the ordering of sequential phenomena and that damage to the frontal lobes removes the capacity to perform simple discrimination problems which involve a time delay between cue and response.

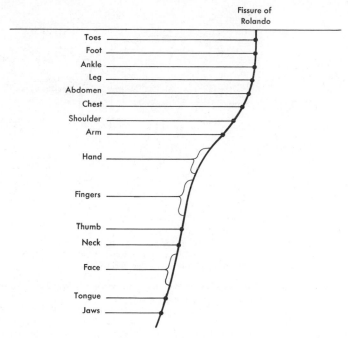

Figure 2-8. Cortical representation of body sense and motor control.

Recently the lower areas of the cerebral cortex have been experimentally probed and the beginnings of meaningfully ordered knowledge have emerged. Most research attention to the cerebral cortex has been concerned with the exploration of the surface layer of neural cells with the likely assumption that what is directly below these areas does not differ in function. Six layers of nerves and neurons exist in the cortex, which is roughly one tenth of an inch thick. The basic evidence comes from work in the visual cortex. Single neurons in the cortex have been shown to respond to a particular stimulus such as a vertical line. All neuronal cells in a vertical column respond to similar stimulus patterns and researchers have theorized that the process leading to identification of shapes, for example, may take place at the different levels of the vertical column.[34]

LOWER AND INTERNAL BRAIN STRUCTURES

The older brain stem areas which are located between the spinal cord and the cerebral cortex have many and varied functions of importance

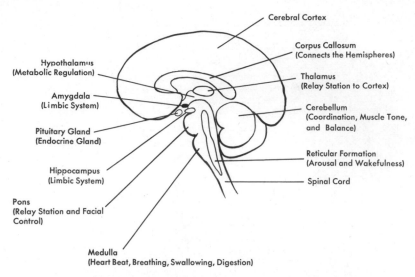

Figure 2-9. **A drawing of the brain as viewed toward one side from a slice down the middle.**

to behavior. Some indication of the kinds of behaviors controlled by these areas and their locations are given in Figure 2-9.

The *thalamus* is located at the top end of the brain stem deep between the cerebral hemispheres of the brain. The thalamic structures receive neural information from many of the receptors in the body and relay this information to areas of the brain. The thalamus sifts and controls this information in a fashion that is not precisely understood.

The *hypothalamus* is named for its position below the thalamus but has little to do with the thalamus. The hypothalamus is a primary control center for autonomic function, for the regulation of metabolism. It senses the level of water and food stored in the organism. It regulates the temperature of the body. Such metabolic regulation is known as *homeostasis*. Homeostasis names an hypothesized mechanism of control and maintenance of the level of some states of affairs like temperature. According to the principle of homeostasis, for example, deviations in body temperature from some optimum level are corrected in a fashion much like the relationship between the common thermostat and furnace in a heated building. Changes in the temperature state are sensed by the thermostat mechanism, and processes of the furnace are initiated to reestablish the preferred temperature level. This kind of control effected by the hypothalamus tends towards maintaining a constancy of internal processes of the individual. The mechanisms of control of each of these metabolic functions in the structures of the hypothalamus are not yet completely known, but extensive direct stimulation research has been aimed at these questions. The hypothalamic mechanisms are further discussed in Chapter 3 as they relate to survival motivation.

The *reticular formation* in the brain stem samples a wide variety of incoming information channels and partly controls the state of arousal and wakefulness of the organism. This structure shuts off certain incoming stimulation when the lowered arousal condition of sleep is present.

The *cerebellum* coordinates and controls the fine muscle movements of the body. Balance and muscle tone throughout the body are maintained by this quite necessary but phylogenetically old center. The coordination of the movements of different parts of the body in physical activities is controlled in this center.

Finally, the *medulla* provides the autonomic control necessary for such vital processes as swallowing, digestion, heartbeat, and breathing.

Some Functioning Systems

One characteristic of physiological research in psychology in recent years has been the study of certain functioning systems. These systems include groups of structures which are interrelated in the performance of emotional behavior, wakefulness, and other bodily functions. The parts of these systems do not necessarily have structural similarities nor are they necessarily located close together, yet the separate parts function as an identifiable system. Study of these systems is an obvious first step in the understanding of the functioning of the human brain.

THE LIMBIC SYSTEM

One functional system is that which has been called the *limbic system.* The basic function of this system is control over states of emotion and emotional behaviors. It is composed of the hippocampus, amygdala, septum, hypothalamus, parts of the thalamus, and others. The limbic system was first thought to be a part of the olfactory system or sense of smell, and it has been only in recent research that the emotional functioning of this system has been demonstrated.

As an example of some of the experimental analyses of this system, fear and rage behaviors have been found to result from stimulation of certain areas of the amygdala. Lesions in the amygdala produce docility or an absence of emotions even in typically vicious species as the lynx and the agouti.[72] Similar analyses in other areas of the limbic system have lead to the conclusion that these areas are important in the development and expression of emotional behavior.

Other studies of the role of the limbic system in emotional behavior concern its interaction with the cerebral cortex. Certain structures included in the limbic system are also a part of the cerebral cortex. It has been found that animals which have had all of the cortex removed except these limbic structures display a markedly placid behavior. They appear to be so peaceful that any kind of anger response or intense emotion is quite effectively suppressed or absent. It seems impossible to get them emotionally upset. Animals which have had the entire cerebral cortex removed, including the limbic structures, exhibit a very intense emotional reaction characterized by a very sensitive and undirected, but short-lived, emotional state. It would appear then that those limbic structures in the cortex exert a suppression or inhibiting force upon the emotion-exciting action of the limbic system.

THE RETICULAR SYSTEM

Certain areas of the brain stem and thalamus called the *reticular system* are believed to regulate the level of neural activity and wakefulness of the organism. Two parts of this reticular system are the *brain stem reticular formation* and the *thalamic reticular system.*

The *brain stem reticular formation* is a neural network extending from the medulla upward through various bodies and eventually reaching to the cortex. Sensory stimulation excites the reticular formation, but all sense channels are not equally effective. Evidence has shown that, of the sensory inputs to the brain stem reticular formation, visual stimulation seems to be least effective in producing alertness in a sleeping animal, while somatic stimulation including pain seems to be most effective in waking a sleeping animal. Stimulation from the cortex above may also excite the reticular formation. Sensory information is sorted out and interpreted by the cortex so that certain physically weak but meaningful and important stimuli excite the subject to wakefulness. Common examples include the sleeping mother who responds to the weak cry of her baby, yet is not awakened by the loud rattling of the windows during a thunderstorm. Similarly, sleeping animals may be awakened by the very mild scent of an approaching enemy, yet are quite unaffected by much stronger odors from nonthreatening sources.

Cortical areas sift the stimuli and excite the reticular system to arouse the individual.

The *thalamic reticular system* is a neural network which does not have direct projections to the cortex but does receive stimulation from sensory channels like the brain stem reticular formation. Direct electrical stimulation of some parts of the thalamic reticular system produces sleep that appears to have a slow natural behavior pattern in its onset and exhibits the typical EEG record of a sleeping subject. Stimulation in other parts of the thalamic reticular system may produce an immediate alerting response in a subject which was sleeping.

THE REWARD SYSTEM

Electrical stimulation to certain brain areas has been suggested to be rewarding, perhaps even pleasureable. Electrodes intended for portions of the reticular activating system were instead placed in a nearby area of the brain. Stimulation of that particular area seemed to reward or reinforce whatever response the animal was making. That is, the rat repeated responses made just prior to the stimulation. Rats learned responses which were followed by direct electrical brain stimulation. This kind of stimulation and its effects have since been called *Intracranial Stimulation (ICS)* and *Intracranial Reward.*

Rats allowed to control the onset of a short period of such stimulation by pressing a lever to receive the stimulation do so for continuous periods of 15–20 hours or until responses stop because of the subject's exhaustion. Rats also endure aversive motivations such as degrees of hunger, thirst, and pain in order to receive intracranial stimulation. Given a choice between ICS and food when 48 hours hungry, rats choose ICS.[62]

Later studies have mapped the intracranial stimulation effect and have shown that there are many areas which have rewarding functions, though not all areas produce effects as strong as that of the original observations. There are also close areas which produce aversive or unpleasant states in the organism. Additional experiments have indicated the complexity of the effect by showing that intracranial stimulation may, on different occasions, produce both positive reward functions and aversive states with the same electrode placement.[9] There does not seem to be any systematic relation between the various locations which have been shown to be rewarding, though it appears that most of the rewarding areas are located in or near the limbic system and appear to be separate from those areas of the brain which have sensory or motor functions. The areas of stimulation which yield punishing or aversive states appears to be located in the area between the thalamus and the hypothalamus.

Summary

Physiological psychology is a study area dealing with the states and processes of the body which underly behavior. This study may guide behavior studies in a direct or an indirect fashion. It may also be the primary subject matter for the behavioral scientist.

Physiological processes may be classified as involving the receptors, the effectors, or the nervous system. The effectors include three muscle types and two kinds of glands. The receptors are the familiar senses and a few channels of information about movements and positions of the body.

The total nervous system may be divided in several ways. Two structural divisions of the nerves of the body define four nervous systems of differing locus and function. One of these, the peripheral autonomic nervous system, is especially valuable for understanding emotional reactivity.

Three conceptual levels of nervous system functioning are named for reflex action, old brain action, and new brain action. These levels basically separate nervous system action of differing complexity and structural locus.

Nerves are composed of neurons. Neurons are elongated cells which transmit impulses through a distance in the body. The mechanism of transmission is primarily a chemical process having measureable electrical effects. It is not like electric current in a wire. The passage of the impulse from one neuron to another is also a chemical process and is called synaptic transmission. The actual complexity of neurons at any point in the body is such that a simple model of interconnecting wires or neural plumbing is grossly inaccurate.

The brain stem and brain have been studied using five different approaches. Anatomical techniques attempt a mapping of neural connections. Developmental techniques compare the presence of certain structural developments with behavior patterns to infer the function of those structures. Removal studies answer the same questions by noting the effects of elimination of the structure. Stimulation studies artificially activate structures to note their effects upon behavior. Finally, electrical recording attempts to correlate the electrical properties of neural activity with ongoing behaviors.

The marked difference between human and other animal brains is the human cerebral cortex, implying cerebral involvement in the behaviors and processes which are uniquely human. Stimulation of the cerebrum surface has revealed specific (projection) areas of involvement with vision, hearing, body sensitivity, and motor control. The remaining cerebrum surface has less specific known functioning and is called "association area." The depth of the cortex is only about 1/10 of an inch and the lower levels are thought to interpret aspects of the stimulation received at the surface.

Lower brain structures play various parts in effecting behavior. The thalamus is largely involved in relaying neural information to the brain, regulating the flow to some extent. The hypothalamus appears to be a primary control center for autonomic functions, regulation of aspects of metabolism. The reticular formation controls arousal and wakefulness. The cerebellum coordinates muscle activity of the body and the medulla regulates the autonomic parts of breathing, heartbeat, digestion, and so on.

The limbic system controls emotional states and behaviors. A collection of lower brain structures have been shown by stimulation and removal studies to be necessary for certain emotional behavior and sufficient to produce others. Parts of the cerebral cortex are also in the limbic system and serve to suppress the emotional states excited by other parts of the limbic system.

The reticular system has two parts located in the thalamus and in the brain stem. The brain stem reticular formation filters stimulation from receptors and reacts to stimulation which has been filtered from the cortex. The function is one of alerting or allowing sleep in response to such stimulation. Artificial stimulation of the thalamic reticular system has been shown to evoke immediate sleeping and alertness.

The reward system is a collection of areas which react to electrical stimulation with behavior effects resembling those following administration of a reward. Presumably pleasurable and aversive states result from this intracranial stimulation.

SUGGESTED READINGS

Altman, J. *Organic foundations of animal behavior*. New York: Holt, Rinehart and Winston, 1966.
A textbook of physiological psychology which presents a biological point of view of behavior. Requires a greater depth of physiological terminology and concepts than other secondary sources.

Deutsch, J. A., and Deutsch, D. *Physiological psychology*. Homewood, Illinois: Dorsey Press, 1966.
An advanced textbook of physiological psychology providing a well-documented introduction to topics of hunger, reproduction, learning, arousal, emotion, the senses, and others. Excellent for the student with some sophistication in physiology.

Grossman, S. P. *A textbook of physiological psychology*. New York: Wiley, 1967.
A very detailed and comprehensive summary of the topics of physiological psychology. Suitable for advanced students or when considerable experimental evidence is desired.

Morgan, C. T. *Physiological psychology* (3rd edition). New York: McGraw-Hill, 1965.
A beginning text in physiological psychology.

Sidowski, J. B. (Ed.) *Experimental methods and instrumentation in psychology*. New York: McGraw-Hill, 1966.
Several chapters of this handbook of experimental psychology research methodology are directly concerned with physiological analyses.

Thompson, R. F. *Foundations of physiological psychology*. New York: Harper and Row, 1967.
A textbook which emphasizes an understanding of basic brain organization and functions.

Chapter *3*

MOTIVATION
AND EMOTION

*What gives behavior its push? What causes a group of drowsy
students to become alert when "sex" is mentioned by the lecturer?
How does money come to have such a strong influence over the
behavior of man? What is your motive for reading this book?*

Defining Motives

Motivation is not a particular behavior or a thing or event which can
be observed directly. Motivation is an invented construct which describes certain aspects of behavior. Two aspects of behavior which are
described by motivation concepts are the *goal-direction* of the behavior
and the *relative energy* put into the behavior. Behavior is usually identified as motivated either (1) when it is aimed at some goal or (2) when
its intensity or apparent energy level is fairly strong or different than
would be expected from the stimuli apparently evoking the behavior.
The energy is the source which seems to compel the behavior in a
determined manner. What we mean by motivation then is the energy
and directional aspects of observed behavior.

In practice a motive may be defined or described in at least two
ways. It may be defined by the internal states of an individual which
have apparently caused or brought about some behavior; it may also be
defined from its effects upon behavior which is directed toward some

goal or end condition. These two different approaches to the identification of a motive may alone or together describe motivated behavior. A
thirsty man approaching a water source and hence drinking may be
said to be motivated both by an internal condition brought about by
a lack of water and by the attraction of the goal condition of consuming
water. In many instances, though, the motivation for a behavior is
identified in just one of these ways. Children may be strongly motivated
to the goal of eating sweet candy though there is no reasonable evidence of hunger, or animals may become very active and behave in
an energetic but apparently undirected fashion when they are deprived
of food.

Either of these defining procedures, whether identifying states and
conditions of the individual or the goal-direction of the behavior, must
be used with restraint. If not, a separate motive could be defined for
every observed behavior. Though such a situation would be in accord
with the defining procedures for motives given above, there would be
little that is useful in such a scheme. To say that we drive fast because
of a motive to travel rapidly, look at the mountains because of a
motive for viewing nature, or eat candy because of a motive for consuming sweets, adds nothing to the basic facts that we drive fast, look
at the mountains, or eat candy.

The use of motives adds something to a description of behavior.
Motivation concepts add a simplicity to behavior description by reducing a group of behaviors to a few principles. This may be done
in several ways, as listed below.

A given behavior may be related to similarly motivated behaviors. By
using the concept of a motive to describe a collection of behaviors, such
as seeking and consuming needed materials for the maintenance of the
body, behaviors in response to a new similar motive may be described
by the same or similar principles. To say that a certain motive is in
operation, such as a need to be with others of the same species, directly
implies that the behavior of that individual is directed towards satisfaction of this need state rather than others. Thus, if a person seeks out
other individuals, we say that he is satisfying the conditions of this
particular state of affairs which we call the motive for affiliation, as
opposed to describing the behavior in terms of other possible factors.

By using a particular motivational concept, the behaviors in a given
situation may be linked to certain sets of facts as opposed to others.
Thus, negatively, theorizing the operation of a particular motive may
direct attention away from learning, maturation, and certain other fac-

tors which under other conditions might be said to determine the observed behavior. When a factor, for example novelty of stimuli, is identified as a motivator, that factor is now predicted to affect behavior like other motivators. It is considered to have the properties of a motive rather than an instinct, a facet of personality, or a state of development.

The use of a motivational concept also implies a degree of regularity of function rather than form of the behavior in similar future situations. The use of the term motive implies that behavior is directed towards a goal. There is a particular regularity of the purposes of this behavior as opposed to the specific form that behavior may take on each occasion. The individual in need of company will direct his behavior towards seeking others and being in their company, rather than make a particular relatively unchanging response on each occasion. On one occasion he may join a bridge club, on another occasion he might take up bowling, and on a third occasion he might engage in social activities at a local pub. Each time we say that his behavior is directed towards increasing affiliation or company of others. The form of the behavior has changed in each particular occurrence of the motive state.

It is quite reasonable to assume that there will be several motives operating at any one time. Thus, the behavior observed may be the result of not one, but several simultaneous motives. The same behavior, such as running, may also reflect the action of different motives on different occasions. Furthermore, a given motive may be expressed in several different kinds of behavior. It has been well established that learning may modify the form of expression of behaviors influenced by motives. Thus the varied learning experiences of individuals could easily produce the complex relations between motives and behaviors suggested above. For these reasons, also, it would appear to be unlikely that a good account of motivation of behavior may be derived from defining motives by labeling each behavior.

REFLEX, TROPISM, AND INSTINCT

Three kinds of behavior which are related to the problem of identifying motives are *reflexes*, *tropisms*, and *instincts*. These three behaviors represent different levels of complexity of processes which intervene between relatively simple stimulus situations and particular behaviors.

A *reflex* is a simple stimulus-response reaction, such as the closure of the eyelid to a tap on the cheek, the closure of the pupil of the eye to a bright light, or the crouching position adopted in reaction to an intense, startling stimulus.

A *tropism* adds a bit more latitude in the range of behaviors in response to the stimulus, though the end result can still be simply described. The attraction of a moth to a light, the tendency of young rats to climb upwards, the orientation of fish to the current of water, and the response of the sunflower to the position of the sun are all tropistic responses. They differ from reflexes primarily in their involvement of the whole body, rather than just a part of the body as in the reflex.

Finally, an *instinct* is a complex, unlearned behavior of a species set off by relatively simple stimuli. The seasonal migration of birds and fishes, the mating behaviors of many species, and the reactions of some species to the characteristic visual forms of predators are all examples of instincts which have been studied.

To what extent should these kinds of behaviors be described as motivated and is there any use for so classifying them? This is essentially an unanswerable question, though it must be noted that there is no clear line between some instinctive behaviors which have a learned component and many other motivated behaviors which fit the general definitions given above.

HOMEOSTASIS

One way of viewing the operation of many motives is that described by the term *homeostasis*. The principle of homeostasis has been developed in physiology to describe the operation of mechanisms which maintain a state of the organism. The regulation of body temperature, the maintenance of food stores, and the means of maintaining a certain amount of moisture in the body tissues are all examples of the principle of homeostasis. It describes a compensating function which takes account of deviations from some value of the condition and sets in motion processes which will restore the proper conditions.

Homeostasis can be seen to describe nicely the operation of hunger, thirst and several of the other physiologically based motives of man. Homeostasis has been used also as a hypothetical mechanism to describe the operation of more complex, learned motives. Assume, for example, a motive involving social contact. A particular amount of social contact is the preferred amount. Lesser or greater experiences of social contact than this preferred amount would be said to set in operation a motive which will energize and direct behavior towards restoring the base amount of contact.

The homeostatic mechanism often describes the operation of a motive usefully, but care must be taken that all motives are not pounded into this hypothetical homeostatic mold. Account must be taken of factors which might change the base level towards which the homeostatic principle operates. Experience, for example, may dictate a particular base level toward which a principle of affiliation might operate. As we become more and more accustomed to certain kinds of people we may wish to have less such contact or more contact as the case may be. Sometimes a change from the base level of a motive appears to be the goal for behavior. Experiencing higher than usual levels of fear or danger is a goal motivating behavior in many sports activities, while similar risks in our day to day activities would not be undertaken. The same individual who would avoid exertion by taking the elevator on every occasion might on the weekends decide that climbing mountains is an enjoyable activity. Thus, to the extent that there is a unitary motive behind each of these dual situations and examples, we might say that the homeostatic principle is not the primary principle describing the operation of that motive.

MOTIVATION AND OTHER BEHAVIORS

Motivation is not an old topic in psychology, appearing as an acknowledged separate study area not more than 30 years ago. Motivation as a concept, however, has been around as long as psychology and is at the root of some of the greatest unknowns of behavior. It usually answers the questions of how and why. There is no clear conceptual dividing line between motivation and learning, perception, emotion, personality traits, and other factors which also describe changes in behavior. Each factor has topics and principles which are somewhat unique, but there are many behaviors which bridge two traditional areas of study and for which a satisfactory discussion of causes requires principles from both.

As an example of such mixing of principles, many of the goals of human behavior, such as money, have acquired a power to motivate behavior through the action of experience or learning. Through experience, having money has become a goal and hence is an effective motivator of behavior. The effects of the two factors, motivation and learning, are here quite inseparable. A more complex example of the mixing of motivation and other constructs in a particular behavior is given by the judgments of subjects in an unpublished demonstration asking how many dollar bills equal in weight one silver dollar. Their guesses, based presumably upon past perceptual learning and memory, averaged to about 1600 paper dollars for each silver dollar. Other subjects made independent judgments of how many 10 dollar bills equalled in weight the silver dollar and their guesses averaged to about 600.[73] Apparently, the learned value of these incentives or goals which is presumably directly related to their motivating power, has influenced the perceptual-memory-judgment process of relative weight, and the relationships between the motivational, learning, and perceptual aspects of this behavior are quite completely mixed.

One important factor serving to structure the area of motivation has been its close ties with particular theoretical viewpoints. For example, Hull's theory of learning [35] identified one of the conditions for learning as the reduction in motivation which attends the learned response. Further, the energy for behavior in this theory was determined by the many need states or conditions of deprivation from materials needed for survival suffered by the individual. This energy, called *drive*, influences broadly any and all behaviors which are present. This is sometimes called a *general drive* view rather than a *specific drive* view. Any source of drive is assumed to contribute to the pool of general drive which motivates any ongoing behavior. The specific drive position holds a more restrictive notion of each source of drive effecting only specific behavior related to that source of drive. Hunger, in the specific drive view, would affect only food-seeking behaviors. The general drive view holds that hunger contributes to the pool of drive which energizes any responses in progress.

The details of Hull's view of the importance and effects of motivation were instrumental in shaping the topics studied towards those motives which are closely connected with the survival of the animal. Those motives which were not defined by deprivation from some obvious and measurable biologically needed material were basically ignored at first by those working with this theoretical formulation. One result of this special interest has been a large amount of research and information concerning those particular motives and relatively little investigation (and some amount of hostility) towards study of the more complex learned and social varieties of motivation.

CLASSIFYING MOTIVES

One method of identifying and organizing motives which may prove to be useful is to group them according to similarities among their causes and conditions. A classification which has been proposed in a similar form by several writers [29] separates motives into three groups,

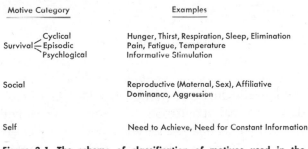

Motive Category	Examples
Survival⟨ Cyclical / Episodic / Psychlogical	Hunger, Thirst, Respiration, Sleep, Elimination / Pain, Fatigue, Temperature / Informative Stimulation
Social	Reproductive (Maternal, Sex), Affiliative / Dominance, Aggression
Self	Need to Achieve, Need for Constant Information

Figure 3-1. **The scheme of classification of motives used in the text.**

here labeled *survival, social,* and *self* motives. An outline of this scheme is presented in Figure 3-1.

Survival motives are those which are based upon a physiological necessity or other condition of an individual which may directly affect the survival of that individual. Included are the motives which follow the deprivation-satiation cycle in time (hunger, thirst, and the needs for air, elimination, and so on), motives which depend upon some episodic stimulation (pain and fatigue), and motives which orient the individual to stimuli in his immediate environment (curiosity and the needs for manipulation and exploration).

The *social* motives are those which require the presence or participation of another individual for their expression or instigation. Included in this social category are motives which are labelled aggressive, reproductive, affiliative, and dominance. There are, of course, physiological causative and regulating factors in social motives, but the primary direction of the behavior energized by these motives can be described as towards other individuals rather than towards external stimuli or to rectify internal needs.

The *self* motives are those which contribute towards the maintenance of the concept of self or ego which each individual has personally developed. These motives have also been called ego-integrative motives, implying the structure and the organization which attends the concept of the ego or self. Self motives include the need to achieve, the need for consistency in belief and action, and similar motives which defend and enhance the picture which each individual holds of himself.

These three categories do not have perfectly sharp boundaries, but they serve as a useful organizational framework in which to discuss similar motives. It will be seen that some similar principles of operation exist in several instances from the motives which are grouped together.

Survival Motives

The survival motives require for their development a change in the condition of the individual as a result of either time or of some particular kinds of external stimulation. The change in condition is such that, if it is not corrected and is allowed to develop to an extreme level, the individual will not survive. It is not necessary, however, for death to be hovering nearby before the individual can be said to have a survival motive. The motive is present long before the extreme state is reached and may be thought of as serving the purpose of altering conditions so that they do not reach that fatal level.

It is useful to separate further the survival motives into three categories named *cyclical, episodic,* and *psychological* survival motives. The *cyclical* survival motives include the needs for food, water, air, elimination, and other things or processes which occur on a regular basis purely as a function of the normal operation of the organism over a period of time. When these processes are interrupted, a motive is said to exist which energizes behavior directed towards resuming the normal processes. The *episodic* survival motives are those which are produced by the application of certain stimulation conditions. Painful stimuli and situations which produce fatigue are the major motives which fall into this category. The *psychological* survival motives are those which are linked with the reception and interpretation of information necessary for immediate response and survival in the environment. Included are the motives labeled manipulation, exploration, curiosity, and the nonspecific need for at least a certain amount of informative stimulation. Examples of these motives will be considered separately in the following sections.

CYCLICAL SURVIVAL MOTIVES

Hunger is a condition of an individual in need of food. The degree of hunger may be measured and defined by the extent of known deprivation from food, by the strength of approach to a goal state of consuming food, and by the amount of eating that an individual will do when given free access to food. The existence of a hunger motive underlying an observed behavior may be inferred from the direction of that behavior towards food as a goal or from a change in the intensity of the behavior in the presence of a known deprivation from food. Hunger is also a conscious experience known to most people in some degree. This conscious experience contributes part of the total picture of hunger and its effects upon the regulation of the food resources of the body. The hunger experience is a feeling of mild pain in the stomach sometimes joined by a general feeling of loss of strength. This usually is sufficient to cue or stimulate the experienced individual to seek food. But how does this hunger feeling come about? What is the means by which a state of insufficient food is detected in the body, where is the detector located, and how does it work? A complete answer to these questions is not yet available, but some good approximations can be given.

Early notions about hunger and food intake regulation centered around the intestines, holding that contractions and distension of these organs with the presence and absence of food may be the adequate detection devices. Evidence does link such contractions with experienced hunger pangs, but other evidence is hard to assimilate to this simple notion. For example, individuals without stomachs report that they feel hungry, even though they do not report hunger pangs as such. This notion of stomach-controlled hunger has been called a "local" theory of hunger.

Local theories have been generally displaced by recent "central" theories of hunger control which specify that mechanisms controlling food-intake are located in the hypothalamus and other brain areas. The exact mechanisms are not yet known, but theories based upon evidence from direct stimulation and removal studies hold that the hypothalamus samples the bloodstream for some substance such as a type of "blood sugar." The glucostatic theory of J. Mayer,[49] for example, holds that the ratio of glucose in the bloodstreams entering and leaving the brain varies directly and quickly with feeding. A low ratio, which indicates lowering amounts of body stores of food and glucose, serves as a cue for hunger mechanisms. Other evidence suggests that this notion is not complete, but to date it accounts reasonably well for the regulation of eating behavior. Included in Mayer's glucostatic theory are further suggestions that this mechanism is not the total picture of hunger, but that the learned value of foods and experience with stomach distensions and contractions also contribute cue functions to the determination of eating behavior.

Hunger is a name which we apply to a collection of many needs and appetites. A person in need of salt, sugar, certain vitamins, and many similar substances may engage in behaviors which will lead to satisfaction of those specific needs and hungers. Thus, hunger is not a unitary concept. It is instead composed of a collection of individual need states and appetites each of which may be assumed to have a physiological basis.

Demonstration experiments have shown that rats, when deprived of a particular substance, will select from a cafeteria-like arrangement of foodstuffs those materials which will rectify that need. Some caution though must be applied in the interpretation of this kind of specific hunger demonstration. Not all specific needs will result in behaviors rectifying those needs. If an evolutionary basis for the origin of such specific hungers or needs is hypothesized, it is apparent that each individual species including the rat or man will have developed a particular set of tastes corresponding to his needs for certain food materials. Thus, only specific substances which have been available and usefully distinguished in the history of that species are likely to be selected by an individual when so deprived.

Experiments have also demonstrated that learning plays an important role in specific hungers of an individual. In a similar cafeteria arrangement, one might demonstrate the learned selection of foodstuffs containing a substance like Vitamin B, which has been carefully removed from the subject's diet for a period of time prior to the experiment. The learning takes place because of the results of that selection. Thus, individual rats may experience pleasant effects and improvements in their physiological condition after having selected the materials which have been experimentally removed from their diets. Experiments have borne out the prediction based upon the notion of learned dietary selections such that if the vitamin or deprived substance is now removed from the compound which the animal had learned to select, the animal will continue to choose and consume that particular compound.

Thirst is a condition of an individual in need of water. Thirst is very similar to hunger in many respects. The cue to produce water intake is partly the unpleasant dryness of the mouth and throat regions, though the regulation of moisture stores in the body is more complex and seems to be centered also in the hypothalamus. Certain hypothalamic structures seem to be triggered by a decrease in the concentration of water reaching those cells. An additional mechanism of thirst detection may be sensitive to the presence of hormone substances in the bloodstream.

The need for *sleep* fits the definition of a cyclical survival drive though it also is similar in some respects to fatigue, which will be considered later. The goal state for the sleep need in man consists of various degrees of lowered responsiveness and alertness occurring in a regular cycle for an average of one-third of each 24 hour period.

Measurement of the presence and extent of sleep in an individual has proved to be a difficult task. Sleep can be identified by the subject's EEG brain wave pattern, loss of consciousness, or generally lowered activity level separately or in combination with observations of lowered states of alertness and responsiveness. None of these criteria is entirely adequate in all sleep measurement situations. For example, loss of consciousness, though usually correlated with the sleep state, is in many cases present when the individual is not sleeping. Human infants, individuals who have had certain brain injuries, and subjects who have been given certain drugs, exhibit other behavior characteristics which indicate that they are not sleeping, yet there is a definite loss of consciousness. In the typical sleep measurement situation, however, the use of the EEG brain wave from normal, undrugged adults has given meaningful indications of depth or degrees of sleep, as described in Chapter 2.

The motive state produced by deprivation of sleep has obvious sensations and feelings of sleepiness and leads generally to a lessened responsiveness to stimulation and a more rapid onset of sleeping when sleep is possible. After about 48 hours of sleep deprivation, there is no further increase in sleepiness feelings but the individual will fall asleep more rapidly and requires a greater amount of activity to keep from falling asleep.

There is a general decrement in motor skills performance with increasing sleep deprivation, but the pattern is not a regular one. Decrements in performance occur in daily periods of onset of light sleep which are correlated with slight decreases in body temperature over the period of measurement. Other study has shown a general deterioration of cortically controlled functions with increasing sleep deprivation. Speech, handwriting, and simple conceptual tasks are more prone to errors of various kinds.

Recovery from extended sleep losses does not require that the total lost time be spent in sleep. Even after many days of sleep deprivation, individuals require only about 11 or 12 hours of sleep to regain the normal state of wakefulness. There has been no demonstration of systematic after effects of such long term sleep deprivation.

Other cyclical survival needs include those for *respiration* and for *elimination*. The cue to the motive to breathe does not depend directly upon the deprivation of oxygen from the individual as might be supposed. The mechanism which produces the sensation of "suffocation" responds to carbon dioxide in the blood. Thus, no feeling of suffocation (and hence no motive for breathing) is produced if the individual is deprived of both oxygen and carbon dioxide as would happen, for example, upon reaching high altitudes by airplane. On the other hand, an intense feeling of suffocation occurs when an unusually large concentration of carbon dioxide is present in air which may or may not contain adequate amounts of oxygen. The control of breathing and suffocation feelings is effected in the medulla of the lower brain.

The need for elimination has not been extensively studied, though frequency and amount of urination and defecation are widely used as indications of "emotionality" in animals. Also, one not so surprising study demonstrated that human males adopt numerous postural changes in the presence of such a need when, for example, an attempt is made to inhibit urination.[19]

EPISODIC SURVIVAL MOTIVES

Painful stimulation produces a strong motive to avoid such stimulation. Through learning, stimuli which have been associated with pain acquire a negative goal status in that they also are avoided. The presence of these learned cues for pain is one of the primary sources for the motive which we call fear. The response to painful stimulation is immediate. The intensity of the response indicates that it is highly motivated though that same response intensity frequently prevents behaviors which are effective in removing the pain stimulus. The high degree of control over time and intensity values of electric shock has led to extensive use of this method of evoking a pain motive in studies of learning.

Direct response to a pain stimulus, though intense and important at the time, is not the most frequent contribution of the pain motive towards determining behavior. The anticipation and avoidance of pain of various kinds is far more important in shaping a large proportion of day to day behavior. Having experienced various kinds of pains, we are motivated to avoid any further such pain. We need not even experience directly each particular variety of pain before we are able to take such action as is necessary to avoid that kind of pain. The wide use of commercial analgesics or pain suppressors, even in anticipation of pain symptoms, provides good anecdotal evidence for pain avoidance behavior.

Fatigue is another episodic survival motive, though the precipitating stimuli are not so obvious and do not produce a motive state as rapidly as do those of pain. The conditions of intense or constant activity produce a decrement in performance of that activity along with subjective reports of being tired. A rest period or reduction of that activity restores both the original performance and removes the tired feeling. The fatigue may be a local effect involving just the muscles of one finger, or it may be a more complex effect involving larger functional units of the body.

The physiological changes which occur in a state of fatigue are many. At the point of the muscle action, there may be either an accumulation of substances in the blood caused by the activity, or there may be a reduction in certain energy reserves. Experiments have shown that with increasing fatigue there is an accumulation of substances such as lactic acid in the blood. Other studies have shown that an insufficient supply of oxygen, blood sugar, or glycogen is sufficient to yield an early fatigue. The source of fatigue effects may also be located in the neural systems which control the muscles involved in the activity. A reduced synaptic transmission and a failure of neural conduction have been shown to occur with fatigue states.

The effects upon performance of a state of fatigue are not just a decrement in performance itself, but may be much more complex. During the onset of fatigue, individuals are likely to change the pattern of the task performance itself. The subject may use an increased amount of effort, use different and more extensive muscle systems than those which are adequate, or require excessively long rest periods after a given amount of work. Any or all of these factors are a distortion of the performance under a state of fatigue.

Subjective fatigue, which may be described as local or general feelings of tiredness or exhaustion, is often found to exist before any substantial amount of fatigue of physiological processes leading to inactivity accumulates at the level or the effector muscle. A hand movement, for example, which has been stopped because of reported subjective fatigue may be reinstated to some degree by supplying a change in the motivational situation. Electrical shock for inactivity or a promise of great financial reward for better performance may be made. Sudden increases in performance after applying these changes indicate that the source of fatigue was not in the effector muscles. A central inhibiting factor is believed to be important in producing fatigue in addition to the changes and physiological reactions which occur in the muscles and local nervous systems.

The maintenance of a moderate *temperature* of the body is the goal state of an additional episodic survival motive. The regulation of internal body temperature seems to be controlled in the hypothalamus, as studies show that damage to various regions of that structure lead to losses in temperature regulation. Extreme temperature changes, not quite strong enough to produce pain, motivate an individual in a manner not unlike pain. The avoidance of and the reaction to such situations motivates a good deal of man's behavior in most climates. Many aspects of seeking housing and clothing are guided by the attraction of maintaining a moderate and comfortable body temperature in the face of anticipated temperature changes. As will be discussed in Chapter 4, though, the temperature sensors adapt to small changes in temperature. Those small differences in temperature to which the individual readily adapts would not be expected to motivate behavior significantly.

PSYCHOLOGICAL SURVIVAL MOTIVES

The psychological survival motives labelled *curiosity, exploration,* and *manipulation* can be considered to be different behavior names for a motive to receive *informative stimulation.* The term "information" is used in a sense of being a quality of stimulation, the quality of being neither highly repetitive nor monotonous. The informative value of stimulation has proved to be difficult to specify absolutely, since it may depend on subjective factors such as past experience with similar stimulation, the present activities and goals of the individual, and/or the momentary set and attention behaviors of that individual. Most experimenters have relied upon comparisons of responses to stimuli which are obviously different along some information dimension. For example, subjects are allowed to choose between observing other members of the same species at play as opposed to observing only a blank cage box. There have been some attempts, however, to apply information theory concepts to the specification of stimuli in this type of investigation. Information theory attempts to describe stimuli in units called "bits" of information, somewhat like the descriptions of things as they are presented to computers and other data-processing devices. Stimuli which can be so measured may be selected for the amount of information which they possess. The primary problems of this approach, however, are that many stimuli are not subject to analyses into units of information, and that such analyses do not, in practice, describe all dimensions and features of complex stimuli. For example, artificial forms have been generated which have specifiable amounts of information considering numbers of points, lengths of lines, etc. But the phenomenally familiar form of a house or a star has an information content which is not revealed by the theoretical measurement techniques. These forms obviously affect behavior differently than informationally similar forms which do not correspond to familiar objects.

The active behavior of seeking informative stimulation is apparent in most individuals as soon as orientation and locomotion behaviors are possible. The curiosity and explorations of the members of some species are legendary. Those who live with a cat are aware of the powerful attraction of new, dark, and small hideouts, whether they are big enough for the cat to enter or not. The first behaviors of a dog brought into a new place are usually directed towards carefully exploring the scents of that place. A monkey or a baby given a toy will carefully explore and manipulate that toy with fingers, lips, and teeth, if any.

There is no question of the presence of this kind of behavior to these stimuli, though there is an important question as to the motivation status or attributes which these behaviors may represent. What is the defining state of affairs for a motive called curiosity? Some use has been made of terms like "novelty" of stimuli or of the relative "complexity" of the situation. This quality of stimuli has been defined by Berlyne [6] as the measured amount of time which individuals would look at stimuli. He required subjects to press a lever for a very brief peek. The greater the number of presses that an individual would make for a visual stimulus, the greater, presumably, was the curiosity evoked by that stimulus. Berlyne identified and manipulated three dimensions of stimuli, all of which affected the strength of curiosity behaviors. These dimensions were called incongruity, complexity, and surprisingness and are illustrated in Figure 3-2. This approach emphasizes the power of the informative stimulus in a certain situation to evoke and arouse the behavior.

Another way of studying the psychological survival motive of need for informative stimulation is to increase that need. Instead of assessing the effects of new stimuli presented in a normal stimulus environment, an individual may be deprived of informative sensory stimulation to some degree. The motive produced by this "sensory isolation" is directed towards the goal of receiving a moderate amount of informative stimulation. A typical sensory isolation experiment has required the subject to lie quietly on a soft bed wearing translucent goggles and heavy gloves in a sound-deadened room for as long as three days, breaking this pattern only to satisfy the cyclical survival needs of the body.[91] Though there are individual differences, a strong motive to receive some stimulation can be measured by, for example, the willingness of

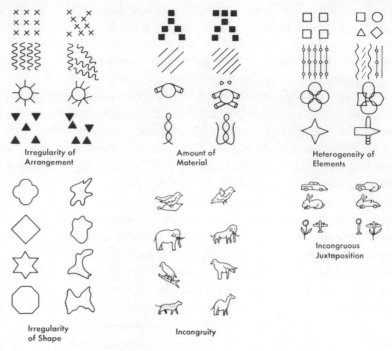

Figure 3-2. Samples of the stimuli used in Berlyne's studies of stimulus complexity and the factors of incongruity and surprisingness.

the subjects to listen to an outdated stock market report or a children's lecture. The isolation situation is reported as "unbearable" by many subjects who voluntarily stopped the experiment early. From further studies it has been established that the greater the deprivation of sensory input, the stronger is the motive for informative stimulation. A similar isolation situation was presented to monkeys by R. A. Butler.[10] Rhesus monkeys learned a discrimination problem for the sole apparent reward of being allowed to peek outside of a box in which they were placed.

Social Motives

Socially motivated behaviors involve other individuals in their goal attainment. If achieving the goal state requires interaction with other individuals, behavior is said to be socially motivated. The identification of each social motive depends upon the definitional rules described earlier. A classification as a social motive is primarily one of convenience for discussion.

The social motive may be controlled by specific known physical stimuli and physiological mechanisms, or it may have an unknown and more complex origin in individual past experience and socialization. There is good evidence of hormone control of some behaviors reflecting social motives in animals, for example, but in the more complex species such as the primates and man, direct physiological control appears to be masked by extensive socialization or learning. The absence of an identification of physiological factors in a particular social motive in man, however, is no assurance that there is no primary physiological control which is hidden by learned behaviors. But it should not be considered a requirement that each motive have a known physiological basis before that motive can be used in an effective manner describing the course of social behaviors.

REPRODUCTIVE MOTIVES

Certain social motives may perhaps be viewed as directed towards the goal of reproducing the species. The maternal behaviors of many animals seem to be highly motivated toward the goal of caring for the young and sex behaviors may be seen to be aimed at the goal of initiating the reproduction of the species. But more immediate goals and factors have been shown to be important in describing these motivated behaviors.

Maternal behaviors in animals include such activities as nest building, retrieving young, and providing for the feeding of the young. The typical maternal behaviors of each species will involve specific patterns of each of these particular activities. Systematic studies of the controlling factors or maternal behaviors have generally used the rat. The nest building activity of the female rat has been found to be dependent primarily on external room temperature. That is, under higher temperatures the rat ceases or limits nest building activity, while under lower temperatures, the rat mother builds more elaborate and complex nests. Research has indicated that the nest building activity is essentially a heat regulating process for the mother rat. The building of the nest is not an altruistic motive to protect the young but may be viewed as a hedonistic need to keep the mother's bodily temperature at some optimum level. Certain gland secretions before, during, and after the delivering of the young have been found to affect directly the temperature control of the mother rat.

Retrieving of the young usually is linked with the nursing behaviors. The retrieving behaviors exist as long as there is a need for continued nursing of the offspring. Retrieving has also been found to be a function of temperature regulation elicited by certain characteristics of the young, such as size. Learning does seem to play some role in the retrieving behaviors of higher species. It has been found that the young chimpanzee will not be missed if it is removed immediately after birth. But if the young chimpanzee is removed after it has been with the mother chimpanzee for a fairly long period of time, the mother becomes quite distressed over its loss.

The nursing behaviors of many small animals seem to consist primarily in the female maintaining a motionless position over the young. The actual nursing activity depends upon an automatic behavior pattern (instinct?) which is present from birth. If for some reason the infant is unable to engage in sucking, it will perish. The mother will make no other attempts to help the young.

Social traditions of maternal behavior are much more important in shaping these behaviors in human mothers, though presumably there are physiological changes and hormones which regulate particular aspects of the behavior. Primarily the dictates of fashion determine the form of maternal behavior which the individual administers, whether it be breast-feeding vs. bottle-feeding, carried vs. left-alone, and so forth. Because of Freud's emphasis upon the basic and fundamental nature of sucking experiences in early childhood and their effect on the development and formation of later character, interest in nipple feeding and time of weaning to a cup has received a great deal of experimental attention. Basically, the question is whether there exists an independent sucking need or drive which will persist even in a well fed infant. Experimentation with dogs has indicated that there is such a basic sucking need and that it is independent of the amount of food taken. However, with human infants, the situation of being well-fed from a cup or any other non-sucking device has not led to an unusual frequency of other kinds of sucking behaviors. Speculation is that perhaps the sucking experiences during feeding in children result in a learned behavior which continues beyond its need in normal children. Sucking has perhaps become a comforting behavior because of its past association with the pleasant aspects of receiving food.

Some interesting studies that vary the rearing conditions of macaque monkeys were made by H. F. Harlow.[27] Artificial, substitute mothers were used to provide the food, warmth, and comfort normally given by live monkey mothers. Basically, two mothers, one wire and one cloth-covered were presented to each monkey, but each monkey was fed by only one. Thus, one group of monkeys was "wire" fed and the other was "cloth" fed. Later testing indicated that the cloth mother was a more preferred security figure or stimulus regardless of which mother fed that monkey. It was found that the monkeys spent a greater amount of time on the cloth mother independent of feeding activities. A further important result of these studies with artificial monkey mothers is that the social development of the young monkeys was not normal.[26] Some critical factors of early experience were missing for these monkeys over and above the factor of maternal contact. A general conclusion is that certain experiences with other monkeys, whether they be mothers, peers, or other colony members, are necessary for the monkey to develop certain social skills and techniques necessary for sexual activity, aggressive behavior, and other normal monkey business.

Sex as a motive is extremely influential in producing and directing a variety of behaviors. Like maternal motives, sexual behaviors are found to be subject to close hormonal control in lower animals and the form of these behaviors is relatively fixed and rigid. Sexual behavior in higher animals and man, though, is not unequivocally responsive to hormone conditions and does not follow a fixed behavior pattern. There are definitely physiological functions and processes which contribute to and make possible sexual behaviors, including heterosexual intercourse, but it is also true that there has not been identified a uniform cyclical need state for this behavior like that for the cyclical survival drives. The apparent strength of sex motivation in determining behavior often is such that an analogy to hunger and thirst seems appropriate, but the known physiology and other evidence indicates otherwise.

Why, then, is sex such a powerful motivator? There are two questions here: What are its characteristics as a motive, and why is sex powerful? One theoretical answer to these questions [24] holds that sexual appetite has been slowly learned from the early years of life. Exploratory stimulation of genital organs is generally treated in a fashion which leads the young child to expect something exciting and pleasant. Attention is strongly directed to behaviors which are so vigorously suppressed for no obvious (to the child) reason. Suppression of these behaviors connected with sexual experience enhances and directs interest in them. Later in life definite social training from many sources establishes the cultural norms of sex-arousing stimuli. The preferred forms of partners, movements, words, and phrases are associated with the excitement arising from the suppressed behaviors and the pleasurable sensations of exploratory genital stimulation. Inhibition of the overt behaviors connected with sex may be firmly established, but the excitement of the whole topic is not suppressed. From this point, experiences of various kinds with the learned symbols and with many forms of sexual stimulation lead to a consistent pattern of learned motives and responses to previously neutral stimuli.

Sex is a *powerful* motive in shaping behavior only when there are few other competing motives and behaviors, and then only in a culture where it is treated as exciting and different. Sex is not an important motive affecting individuals in cultures where sex is treated in a matter-of-fact and nonsuppressed way. The strength of the sex motive is also weak when pitted against other motives. Individuals who are subjected to the effects of a reasonably strong hunger motive or who are engaged in attaining other social or self-motivated goals are not affected by sex-arousing symbols.

Control of sexual appetite could be gained according to this viewpoint by a controlled contact with sex-arousing cues and by regulation of other attention-consuming activities. The disturbances caused by sex-motivating stimuli should not be expected to diminish as long as those stimuli are frequently experienced. Frequent voyeurism and contact with sexual symbolism will strengthen, not satiate, the desire for further sexual experience.

AFFILIATION

The tendency to be with other similar individuals may be termed an affiliative motive. Not all species engage in such grouping, but man considers the individual who lives alone, the hermit, to be unusual. When affiliation or grouping is not present, behavior is usually energized towards such a state.

Experiments have shown that threatened, female students preferred to wait for an additional part of an experiment with other students rather than alone.[71] The threat in this case was the anticipation of an electric shock in an experiment for which she was waiting. Other studies have shown that individuals who were not accepted for membership in a fraternity to which they desired to belong had more frequent themes of separation-belonging in stories which they invented about pictures than did students who were accepted. This suggests an increased interest in affiliation because of the fraternity rejection experience. The initial equality of the groups must be certainly questioned in this comparison though, since the fraternity acceptance was probably based upon many personal characteristics related to social motivation.

The motive for some sort of social affiliation has proved to be a useful concept to account for many behaviors. On a crude level one may speculate that college fraternity and sorority groups as well as other fraternal organizations satisfy the need for some amount of belonging or affiliation. The basis for this motive is most probably a learned dependence upon the support and comfort given by others during socialization training, though specific analysis of such past experiences has not yet been made.

DOMINANCE

The social motive of *dominance* is well known to students of animal behavior. The familiar "pecking order" of barnyard chickens is a clear example of the relative dominance of the individuals in a group. Higher chickens in the order have the right to and do peck other lower chickens. Though the motive for such behavior undoubtedly has a substantial learned component in more complex species, it has been demonstrated that a simple physiological change by hormone injections may temporarily alter the pecking order of individual chickens. The baboon also sets up dominance rankings. The dominance among baboons is expressed in grooming behavior such that higher baboons are groomed by those lower in rank. The grooming is done with two hands if the individuals are close in rank. However, if a great difference in ranking separates the individuals, the lower baboon grooms the higher with but one hand. Presumably the lowest ranked baboon is rather unkempt.

The effects of dominance-like motives are quite apparent in the prestige-seeking societies of man. Seating at formal dinners and the unnecessary trappings associated with military and corporate ranking are some socialized expressions of dominance. The size and quality of offices often does not correspond to needs for space. We continually search for and develop ways in which we may appear of higher rank than our fellows. Each of these behaviors may be viewed as the result of the operation of a motive for dominance. The dominance motive, perhaps second only to sex, has been exploited in many ways by commercial promotions and advertising. At this writing there are frequent themes in advertising suggesting the attainment of dominance by the consumer. The letters and names on automobiles allude to great speed, performance potential, and importance of the owner. Extra long cigarettes are promoted as the mark of excellence and distinction. The strength of the motive in this setting can be measured by the extent of sales. Each of these observations appears to support the usefulness of a motive called dominance, but because they are not controlled observations they cannot be considered as more than speculative observations. The origin of each pattern of behavior suggested may be quite different from the effects of dominance motivation, yet the concept may be usefully maintained.

AGGRESSION

Aggression as a social motive illustrates many of the problems of such motives. Aggression is a type of behavior characterized as hostility and destructiveness directed towards other individuals, but the motive behind that behavior may be quite difficult to identify. Aggressive acts occur in partial response to motives of hunger, sex, and dominance, but is there also an independent motive for aggression?

Aggression is prominent as an instinctive motive in Freud's theory of personality, linked with the death instinct. Other theorists such as Miller and Dollard [58] connected aggression with the state of frustration, holding that aggression is learned to certain cues in which the emotion of anger is normally elicited. The aggressive motive has a logical basis in theory, but the isolation of examples of aggression as a "pure" motive, uncontaminated by other motives has been difficult. It is known what kinds of situations will evoke aggressive behaviors (frustrations, constant irritations, and so on), but the identification of a separate aggression motive has been quite elusive and has not been proved to be useful.

Self Motives

The self-motives are even more complex than most of those motives which were classified as survival and social, in that the personality structure upon which the motive is based is also acquired in the process of socialization. Motives which defend the ego or self from incongruent actions and information provide examples for study of this kind of motive. Two self-motives have been reasonably well-specified by theorists and experimentation. They are the *need to achieve* and the *need for consonant information*.

NEED TO ACHIEVE

The *need to achieve* is one of several motives included in an attempt to measure and study human motivation by McClelland and his associates.[50] An objective scoring of a projective test was devised. The test consisted, basically, of counting the number of "achievement" themes present in stories invented by subjects about test pictures. The theoretical reasoning was modified from the "projective techniques" of personality measurement and holds that the stories which are invented by individuals will consist of information about the past experiences, present motives, and the plans of the individual without his being aware of the disclosure. This has been called "motive assessment by fantasy."

Research in which achievement motivation is studied has used individuals classified by the fantasy assessment technique as having a high or a low need to achieve. Note that this experimental procedure does not guarantee that the groups of individuals selected are equal in all other relevant factors before the behavior assessment, but only that they are different in achievement test performance. Nevertheless, achievement motivation experimentation has shown that individuals with a high need to achieve are seen to take fewer great risks on simple game-like tasks than those with a low need to achieve. High need achievers prefer a moderate risk, presumably in the hope of scoring consistently. Those with a high need to achieve have also been found to dislike games of chance or any situation in which the skill of the operator has little bearing on the outcome. High need achievers prefer a difficulty level for which a success is valuable, yet not so difficult that successes are few.

Using more complex behavior tests, the status of arousal of the achievement motive becomes more obscure. Whenever an individual's achievement goals are not known, it is difficult to determine if substantial achievement has already been made, or whether the individual is presently deprived of and is seeking achievement.

NEED FOR CONSONANT INFORMATION

The need for consonant beliefs and information and its opposite, the presence of dissonance between these things, arose as a motivational concept from a theory by L. Festinger [17] in which it was claimed that the presence of dissonance leads to a need-state like hunger. The notion of dissonance holds that in the presence of a belief, information to the contrary arouses a motive which will be directed towards reducing that conflict. Thus, believing that you are a good student and getting a high B on a test is consonant information and leads to no particular motive state. Information that you had flunked a test, however, would be dissonant information and would produce a tension or motivational state.

The direction of the behavior motivated by this dissonance is towards establishing consonance. This may be done, according to the theory of dissonance in one or two general ways: by denying or discounting the dissonant information, or by changing the original belief. If the F on the exam was information received through a friend, consonance could be temporarily achieved by rejecting the information, claiming an error in the friend's perception or memory. If, on the other hand, the exam performance was verified by your own observation and no other dissonance reducing recourse was open which would remove the information (like discounting the value of the exam or finding a good excuse for a momentary lapse in performance such as illness) the consonance might be achieved by changing the original belief. You might now believe that you are not that good as a student, at least not consistently.

The dissonance reduction motive has enjoyed a good deal of attention among psychologists and has been influential in stimulating a collection of experimental studies of various consonant and dissonant cognitive sets. It has also sharpened interest and attention towards rigorous experimental control and definition upon problems of strategies and choices which have, in the past, been complex and vague.

Emotional States

There is no clear distinction between the terms "motivation" and "emotion." Indeed it is difficult to separate a condition of strong motivation from one of strong emotion by simply observing an individual's behaviors. It is clear that there is a great communality between these differently named things. But there are many useful differences as well.

While motivation has only recently become a separate area in psychology, the topic of emotion is very old. An early theory of emotion called *hedonism* emphasized the pleasantness and unpleasantness of emotional experiences or feelings. While this viewpoint is still held by some present psychologists, there have also appeared other theories of emotion and motivation which emphasize instead the arousal and activation factors of emotional states and motivations. Concepts from both of these approaches have provided useful information in the study of emotion.

A working definition of an *emotional state* is that it is an affectively toned experience, psychological in origin, and revealed in behavior and physiological functions. The pleasantness aspects of emotional states are contained in the word "affective." The words "psychological in origin" restrict the term to conditions which are not primarily physiological states (for example, it excludes hunger), though this distinction, to avoid complexity, will be vague. Both behavior patterns and changes in physiological indicators reveal strong emotional states. A listing of these physiological changes is given in the following section.

Physiological Functions in Emotion

PHYSIOLOGICAL INDICATORS OF EMOTION

Changes in measureable events at the surface of the skin during emotional states have received a good deal of investigation. The factors behind many of these changes are not precisely known, but some indications and general principles will be given later. The basic listing follows Lindsley's [42] survey of the literature.

1. Electrical conductance of the skin increases with the degree of emotional arousal of the individual. The resistance to the flow of a very weak and unnoticeable electrical current from one point to another on the skin decreases with increases in arousal. This measurement is commonly called the *galvanic skin response,* or simply *GSR.* Those who are aware that moisture, especially salty fluids, increase such conductivity of electricity might hasten to ascribe the GSR effects to sweating during emotion states, but though the GSR is very much involved with the physiology of the sweat gland, evidence shows that the moisture secreted during emotion contributes only part of the GSR effect.

2. Changes in the pressure, volume, and composition of the blood and the rate of heart beat may be used as indicators of changes in emotional state. Increases in blood pressure and increases in rate of heart beat (measured by the electrocardiogram or EKG) usually occur with increases in excitement of emotional experience. Blood volume in an area is regulated by the constriction or dilation of blood vessels and is responsible for the changes in "color," usually redness, of the skin with emotion. The blush of anger and the blanch of fear reflect the relative concentration of the blood. The composition of the blood may be analyzed before and after emotional excitement to determine a change in the presence of blood-sugar, adrenalin, red blood cells, and the acid-base balance.

3. Respiration or breathing cycle changes are apparent without special instruments in persons undergoing an intense emotional experience. Quicker and more shallow breathing, for example, is characteristic of

an intense emotional experience of anger. Close measurements of respiration also show small and brief changes to very weak emotion-evoking stimuli. A sudden interruption in breathing in response to an emotion-provoking stimulus may not be noticed except with the aid of sensitive instruments.

4. The temperature and sweating of the skin are linked to some extent in emotional states. Literature describes the frightened person as having cold, clammy hands and the angry person as being hot under the collar. Some confirming research attention has shown that continued emotional stress is related to a lowered skin temperature. Sweating is detected in part by the GSR, but some patterns of moisture produced over the surfaces of the body are believed to be related to emotional states in which both the sympathetic and parasympathetic nervous systems are involved.

5. The change in size of the pupil of the eye has long been known to vary with emotional state as well as light level. Some recent speculation is that this emotion-indicating mechanism distinguishes between unpleasant states (a constriction of the opening) and pleasant states (a dilation of the pupillary opening).[28] Firm evidence has long indicated that the pupil opens wide during strong sympathetic nervous system activity.

6. Salivary gland secretion is controlled by both sympathetic and parasympathetic nervous systems, but there is evidence that these glands stop secreting, producing a dry mouth, during emotional (sympathetic) reactions such as fear.

7. Muscle tension and tremor are also easily observed in emotional states without instruments. The familiar shaking and tightness of the muscles can be ascribed to these factors.

8. A group of other changes may be measured during emotional states. The pilomotor response produces "gooseflesh" and makes hairs "stand on end." Dermographia is the measurement of the length of time that redness of the skin persists after a sharp, momentary pressure has been applied. Gastrointestinal motility is the relative activity of the digestive processes. The metabolic rate may be monitored by bodily heat given off. Eyeblinks and movements may be recorded. Analyses may be made of changes in the content of urine and saliva.

These many known indicators of emotional states suggest that emotions may be easily identified and monitored by the proper selection of instruments and responses. This has not been shown to be true. Relatively poor success has been achieved in identification of type of emotion and only slightly better techniques are available to monitor changes in emotional arousal. The process of monitoring bodily changes, however, has gained considerably with the development of sensitive and accurate recording devices. The modern medical recording polygraph can give a sensitive and continuous written record of the state of each of several responses selected for study. But the many named emotions appear to be complexly related to various bodily processes and no one pattern of the indicators appears to be identical with what we have called emotion.

The techniques and instruments of polygraph recording of emotional changes have been taken over for practical application into what has been called the "art of lie detection." This application depends upon the assumption that one who has committed some act and is lying will experience a change in emotional state when he tries to conceal his guilt. Thus, the situation is really one of detecting emotion change. The process of lie detection becomes more complex and is called an art based upon science because of the considerable polygraph-operating experience and questioning skills necessary to infer the existence of a lie from emotional state measurements.

The changes usually monitored for lie detection are those of the GSR, blood pressure and pulse rate, and respiration. Polygraph recordings of these changes are not easily interpreted. A thorough mastery of the machine based on experience with observing known changes requires more than a casual acquaintance with an instruction book. There are very few hard and fast rules which may be applied to the records and there are many problems of interpretation of individual differences.

The second aspect of lie detection is the specification and phrasing of the questions to the subject. A common procedure is to intersperse several "critical," emotion-evoking questions among a series of neutral, non-emotional and neutral, emotion-inducing questions. The levels of emotional response to the two kinds of neutral questions serve as bases for determining whether an emotional change has been made to the "critical" questions. Great care must be directed to the selection and sequence of presentation of the questions. The "critical" questions are ideally non-emotional to all but the guilty. The presence of questions which are both neutral and non-emotional provides a non-emotional "baseline" from which to infer an emotional reaction. Questions which are neutral yet emotion-inducing give an indication of the reactivity to be expected from the subject and they provide a sort of "cover" which attracts attention away from the critical questions. Sequencing, of course, would be calculated so that each kind of question is interspersed among the others.

Lie detection findings are seldom admitted as evidence for legal proceedings, but there is another use of the lie detection process which is frequently exploited. Lie detectors have served as an effective deterrent to illicit activities for those who believe that they will be given such a test on a regular basis. Industrial pilferage and petty theft has been reduced markedly where the threat of lie detection is made and periodically carried out. No endorsement is intended for the use of such a technique of involuntary self-incrimination except to note that as a social "motivator" the lie detector can be and is so used. This use is morally objectionable to many.

NERVOUS SYSTEM CONTROL

Nervous system activity during emotional states was mentioned in Chapter 2. Basically, emotional states are identified with sympathetic nervous system activity, while parasympathetic control dominates during quiet, energy-conserving states, though there are numerous specific exceptions to this general rule. Figure 2-2 indicates the rough location and function of these peripheral autonomic nervous system activities.

The sympathetic system is organized for general action. One of the responses produced by sympathetic system activity is stimulation of the adrenal gland, which in turn secretes into the blood stream a substance commonly called *adrenalin*. This hormone serves to continue the action of the parts of the sympathetic nervous system. That is, it serves to *maintain* activity in many of the organs which were *originally* excited by the sympathetic activity which was in response to an emotion-producing stimulus. This chemical action is partly responsible for the lingering emotional sensations which are present after the fear or anger stimulus, for example, has disappeared.

PSYCHOSOMATIC ILLNESS

One of the consequences of an enduring emotional state is the possibility that it might disrupt the normal (non-emotional) physiology of the body. The physiological changes which accompany an emotion state of fear and anxiety, may, if present for an extended period of time, lead to or facilitate physical damage. The presence of such symptoms as peptic ulcers, bronchial asthma, high blood pressure, ulcerations of the colon, rheumatoid arthritis, and some diseases of the coronary arteries have been found in many cases to have an origin in a prolonged emotional experience. These emotion-produced symptoms are termed *psychosomatic*.

Search is just beginning for the factors which lead to a psychosomatic disorder in one individual and no such illness in another person who has had similar experiences. The suggestion has been made that the afflicted organ may have been weakened before the emotion-produced stress. Another viewpoint concerning psychosomatic disorders is that they are the direct result of a certain kind of personality structure of the sufferer undergoing a particular kind of stress. That is, each kind of disorder is considered to be typical of a particular personality problem, according to this view.

Experimental production of psychosomatic disorders has suggested some conditions which are sufficient to produce such illness. A classic example of these experiments is that of Brady. Two monkeys were paired in an apparatus as shown in Figure 3-3. In front of each monkey

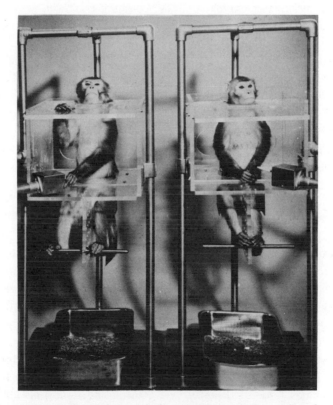

Figure 3-3. The monkeys and physical situation used in studies of long-term psychological stress. The executive monkey on the left pressed the lever periodically to prevent shocks reaching both monkeys. (Courtesy of J. V. Brady; U.S. Army Photograph)

was placed a lever switch. Electrodes capable of delivering shocks were attached to the feet. A learning task was arranged so that if the monkey pressed the lever at the appropriate time, shocks which were otherwise delivered every 20 seconds would not occur. Only one monkey was allowed to prevent the shocks in this fashion and he was designated the "executive" monkey. The other monkey was a "yoked control," in that he simultaneously received the same shocks and general treatment as did the executive, but his behavior had no effect on the shocks he received. The monkeys were given this experimental treatment for periods of 6 hours alternated with 6 hours of rest. After about 23 days the executive monkey died of gastric ulcers. The control monkey was found to be in good physical health. Further replications under the same conditions established the repeatability of the finding. Other studies have indicated that the stress of the task combined with the rhythmical pattern of stomach acid production (which was in turn a function of the work-rest-feeding timing) were sufficient conditions for producing a psychosomatic disorder in these subjects.

The complexity of emotion physiology and the variety of different ways in which physical disorders have arisen from prolonged emotional states makes generalization difficult. But the evidence suggests that perhaps a good deal of the physical illness that we suffer results from the emotional states and conditions which we daily endure. A prognosis of good physical health depends upon avoiding some conditions of long-term emotional experience.

Behavioral Expression of Emotion

The attempts by psychologists to differentiate among the emotions such as anger, fear, surprise, disgust, love, and so on by using physiological changes have not been successful. On the whole there are far too many responses in common and too few physiological changes which reliably differentiate these named emotional states. Two reasons may be suggested for this lack of success.

First, the existence of "different" emotions may come from word usage rather than clear differences in phenomena and, further, these emotion names tend to describe the stimulating situations rather than the emotional response. A second reason for the lack of clear physiological differentiators of emotions may be that many of these changes, like other behaviors, are learned or acquired through experience. If this is true, as some learning theorists have suggested, then the individual variability of learned expression may mask whatever innate or natural physiological reactions to emotion are also present.

FACIAL EXPRESSION

A different approach to the identification of the emotions has been to consider the overt behaviors corresponding to these states. The most obvious behaviors of man which attend a change in emotion are those of facial expression. The pattern of relative changes in position of parts of the face could be easily measured. But first it must be established that there exist distinct, recognizable facial expressions for the emotions. It has been shown that observers can identify the emotions portrayed in unposed candid photographs with a fair degree of accuracy when the background has been removed, leaving only the face. An even better job of identification is done when the pictures are taken of experienced actors assigned to show the emotions. The actual degree of accuracy depends upon how fine a distinction is requested between similar emotions. That is, into how many categories are the emotions to be classified? The increased accuracy of judging purposeful actor's expressions as opposed to the natural reactions of the unaware individual is clearly a function of the ability of the actor to exaggerate slightly the socially accepted characteristic of the emotion and conversely the tendency of the average individual to suppress much emotional expression in accordance with socialization training.

LEARNED REACTIONS

The simple observation of the actor's exaggeration of emotional expression provides some evidence that such expressions can be learned. The behavioral expression of an emotion can be modified through experience. For example, fear may be expressed in man by flight, by "turning the other cheek," by attacking, or by fainting. Which of these behaviors is the "natural" reaction to fear? Consider, respectively, the rabbit, the porcupine, the bobcat, and the opossum. The typical reactions of members of these species indicate that there are several kinds of "natural" responses among the species.

If a man was described as exhibiting the following behaviors, successively, what emotional states would you guess that the person was experiencing? His eyes were opened wide and round. His tongue was stretched out. He clapped his hands. He scratched his ears and cheeks. If the observer was Chinese, the emotions would have been identified as those of anger, surprise, disappointment, and happiness, respectively. An American observer would perhaps identify surprise, sassiness, approval, and embarrassment as the emotion names closest to the states that these respective behaviors indicate in our society. Cultural training results in certain conventions of emotional expression of its members. Further, the language of emotional expression is an important part of the established means of communicating in each society.

Acquiring Emotional Reactions

Some situations evoke the emotions of anger, others evoke fear, and still others evoke love. It is apparent that we learn to respond with certain emotions to particular meaningful situations. Anger is the appropriate emotion with which to respond when a member of our culture has been insulted. We experience joy when a particular goal has been attained. We are sorrowful at the death of someone close. All of these kinds of emotional reactions were acquired in the process of learning the established ways of behaving in our society. We will consider some methods by which these emotional responses may be acquired. But first a related question should be examined. To what extent are the different emotional responses a function of the normal structural development of the individual? Is the normal development of the individual a sufficient cause for the appearance of the different named emotions?

DEVELOPMENT AND MATURATION OF EMOTIONS

The pattern of emotional responsiveness with age in the early years has been well established by study. Soon after birth the emotional state can only be described as *excited*. It appears to be an unpleasant excitement judging by the kind of stimulation which is adequate for its arousal. At this early age there is no evidence of a "pleasantness" reaction other than inactivity or resting. At about the age of three months the response of general excitement remains and is called *distress*, contrasted with *delight* which appears as a reaction characterized by "cooing," and other positive behaviors. By the age of one year the emotions of *anger, disgust, fear, elation,* and *affection* have been distinguished.

It is, of course, certain that some learning has taken place during the first year of life, but the apparent regularity of the appearance of these emotions in a large number of differently-reared children indicates that there is likely a substantial component of structural development or maturation which effects some differentiation of emotional behavior. The extent of the contribution by development vs. learned factors, though, is not known and is probably not a useful question to ask.

LEARNING EMOTIONS

The wide variety of situations which evoke emotion in different individuals suggests a substantial effect of experience or learning. There are three ways in which we may view the learning of emotional reactions to certain stimulus situations. Emotions may be acquired by *imitation*, by *conditioning*, and by *understanding*. The occasions for each of these methods will be clear after discussion.

Imitation is perhaps most easily observed in little children (before the disapproval of "copying" has been learned). At about the age of two years, most children mimic and imitate the behaviors of those around them. In this way they seem to learn quickly to judge the emotional states of their mothers, and will respond to situations in the same way. After the mother angrily scolds the cat, the child also shakes her finger and "scolds" the cat. The mother later may become upset when the child strikes other persons (including the cat). Still later, the child displays a similar emotional reaction when a "fight" is seen on the television screen.

Emotional reactions change very quickly in children; they do not stay unhappy or angry for very long. Happiness and laughter are easily induced in a child, assuming other conditions are satisfactory, by simply allowing their observation of others acting happy and laughing. This imitation can, of course, be used to advantage by purposefully avoiding the display of emotion in the presence of things of which you do not wish the child to be afraid. Associate the darkness with laughing and games instead of promises of "monsters," and the child will probably never be afraid to enter a dark room.

A different picture of learning emotions is given by *conditioning*. This method requires the association of a neutral stimulus with another stimulus which already has the power to evoke that emotion. The neutral stimulus comes to evoke the emotional reaction after conditioning. A classic experiment describing the operation of this method was that of Watson and Rayner.[92] A small boy named Albert was placed upon a table, and in front of Albert was placed a white rat. Albert showed no fear of the animal and reached to touch it. At this time a very loud noise was made which was sufficient to frighten the child into crying. As a result of a few more presentations of the white rat followed by the loud emotion-producing noise, Albert was quite unwilling to approach the rat again. Other things similar to the fuzzy white rat were also avoided by the child. The fear was said to "generalize" to similar white, fuzzy stimuli.

This method of learning emotion has been given a good deal of theoretical support by the many experiments using fear conditioning in the study of the learning process. There is a danger, though, of trying to explain too much by this mechanism. There are many learned emotional responses which are not easily described by the conditioning notion, or by the imitation schema of learning emotions.

The third way in which emotions may be learned is called *understanding*. This term is intended to describe the complex factors of information reception and interpretation which are required to elicit the emotion. Certain fears may be described as rational fears, in that the knowledge of the consequences of a situation is sufficient to elicit a fear reaction. The fear of being in high, precarious positions is based upon the knowledge of the danger of falling. A fear of "zaps" of high voltage electricity may be aroused even though the pain of such electricity has never been experienced. Situations in which there are unknown, complex-looking machines produce a mild fear (which disappears when the operations of the machines are understood). The acquisition of many emotional reactions is most simply described in this way, by appeal to a rational understanding of the consequences. It is also possible, though, to hypothesize a chain of "conditioned" emotional reactions to account for many of these "understood" reactions, though the chain often becomes very long and conceptually unwieldy.

Theories of Emotion

Two distinct kinds of interpretations have been given to emotion and its role in determining behavior. *Hedonic* theory has a substantial background of philosophical concepts traceable to the writings of the ancient Greeks. Activation theory is of more recent origin, arising from the physiological studies of the arousal systems of the body. Some highlights and problems of these theories are briefly given below.

HEDONIC THEORY

Modern hedonic theorists have tried to account for the goal direction aspects of motivated behavior, by assuming that as certain states of affairs are pleasant and that others are unpleasant, these affective states are transferred to new behaviors. The affective aspects of emotion are linked to new situations, and they push and prod behavior. One problem for hedonic theory has been to describe and define the affective processes in a way that is independent of the behaviors that they are expected to explain. Thus, to theorize that candy is eaten *because* it is pleasant requires, further, a definition of pleasantness that does not include the eating behavior. A second major problem for hedonic theory has been to show how the pleasant consequences of a state of affairs act backward in time to draw an approach response from an individual. How does eating candy motivate the seeking of that candy? This problem has been partially solved by the addition of some theoretical mediation concepts. Certain covert responses are conditioned to the earlier stimuli which in turn provide motivation and stimulation for maintaining the response sequence which is completed by the affective consummatory reaction. The mediators may be thought of as a sort of picture of the affective goal state which becomes conditioned to the early stimuli and serves to keep the subject oriented toward that goal.

As a theory of emotion, hedonism has emphasized experiential feelings. The pleasantness and unpleasantness of various emotional states are alleged to be the essence of the emotion and these feelings are what distinguish the emotion from other kinds of states.

ACTIVATION THEORY

A different approach to the description of emotional behavior has come from an emphasis upon the relatively high energy output which emotional behaviors exhibit and from physiological evidence of what has been called an arousal system in the brain stem. Activation theory has presented the view that behavior can be aroused to different degrees, varying on a continuum from deep sleep to excited, emotional states. The different degrees of arousal have been shown to be measureable by the electroencephalograph (EEG). Figure 2-6 shows some of the typical patterns of brain activity which have been identified with certain levels of arousal. Activation theory has identified the maintenance of arousal level as the function of the reticular system of the brain (See Chapter 2). Direct electrical stimulation of particular areas in the reticular system has produced immediate changes in the degree of the arousal.

One of the concerns of the activation theory of emotion is predicting the relative efficiency of behavior as a function of level of emotional

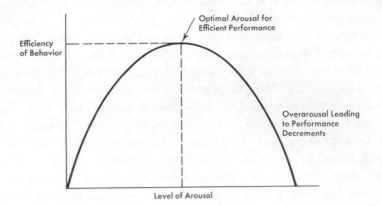

Figure 3-4. The efficiency of behavior as a function of level of arousal according to one view of arousal theory of emotion. An optimum efficiency is obtained at a moderate arousal. Greater or lesser degrees of arousal are less efficient.

arousal, as shown in Figure 3-4. Behavior efficiency is alleged to increase in arousal up to moderate amounts of arousal. With further increases in arousal, the measured behavior deteriorates. Some behavioral and also some physiological evidence has supported this inverted U-shaped function of the effects of arousal.

The primary interest of activation theory is the relative energy as opposed to the direction that emotional states give to behavior. It can be said to be an incomplete theory of emotion to the extent that it does not consider all aspects of emotional experience. But it has done a fairly good job of measuring and manipulating variations along the arousal dimension.

Summary

Motivation is a construct devised to describe the goal-direction and relative energy of behavior. Motivation concepts are useful to the extent that they contribute to the organization and understanding of behavior.

The reflex, tropism, and instinct describe three levels of increasing complexity of a fixed response pattern to simple stimuli. Homeostasis is a name for a hypothetical mechanism which achieves a relatively constant level of something by setting in action the processes necessary to compensate for deviations.

Motives may be classified into three groups labelled survival, social, and self motives. Survival motives have a basis in a condition of need which may likely affect the survival of the individual under unprotected conditions. Cyclical survival motives follow a recurring, natural pattern of need for food, water, air, elimination, and so on. Episodic survival motives are produced by a periodic situation of pain, fatigue, and others. Psychological survival motives include curiosity, manipulative, and explorative behavior patterns, which may be thought to be based upon a need for informative stimulation.

Social motives require the presence or participation of another individual for expression or instigation. Reproductive, affiliative, and dominance motives are among those presented as reflecting varying amounts of social learning and biological influence in their development.

The self motives depend upon an assimilated personality structure. The need to maintain a congruence between beliefs and information and the need to achieve certain goals are considered in detail.

An emotional state is an affectively toned experience, psychological in origin, and revealed in behavior and physiological function.

A listing of physiological changes during emotional states is presented followed by a discussion of the process of lie detection using those changes.

Psychosomatic illness is a physical disability induced by certain kinds of prolonged emotional experience.

The different emotion labels reflect the instigating situation rather than different states of the individual. Expression of the "emotions" is modified by learning to conform to the expectations of the culture.

The acquisition of emotional responses to new situations may be viewed as reflecting in part the effects of normal growth of the child called maturation. Learned emotional responses may be accomplished in the situations called imitation, conditioning, and understanding.

Hedonic theory of emotion stresses the affective pleasantness of the states. Actuation theory reflects the studies of behavioral arousal and the measurement of general arousal of the individual.

SUGGESTED READINGS

Cofer, C. N., and Appley, M. A. *Motivation: Theory and research.* New York: Wiley, 1964.
A comprehensive summary of research upon a wide range of motivational topics. Findings are summarized in considerable detail such that this book makes a good starting point for delving more deeply into a particular topic.

Haber, R. N. (Ed.) *Current research in motivation.* New York: Holt, Reinhart and Winston, 1966.
A collection of original research reports and other writings on the topic of motivation.

Hall, J. F. *Psychology of motivation.* New York: Lippincott, 1961.
A textbook of motivation stressing research studies.

Young, P. T. *Motivation and emotion: A survey of the determinants of human and animal activity.* New York: Wiley, 1961.
A survey of motivation and emotions organized by a noted hedonistic theorist of emotion. Sections describing emotional behaviors and affective processes are exceptionally rich in information.

Chapter *4*

PERCEPTION

How bright must an object be before it is seen on a moonless night?
Why don't things that are closer look bigger than things more dis-
tant? Can we more easily see things that we want to see? Why does
the moon appear to be larger when nearer the horizon than over-
head? Can one learn to find underground water with a forked
stick by careful practice?

One of the basic processes in the interaction of man and his environment is that governing the reception of information about the stimuli
and events around him. He must stop at the lighting of a red light,
slap at the biting mosquito, and answer the ringing telephone. He distinguishes the voice of a friend, the appearance of his automobile, and
the smell of a bakery. He judges the quality of a new drink, the texture
of a sweater, and the feel of a carnival ride. Innumerable of such behaviors depend in a basic way upon the mechanisms of receiving and
interpreting information.

The study of the reception and function of stimulation may be usefully broken into two parts. That part which considers the mechanisms
of receiving information may be called *sensation*. That part which considers the received information in combination with other information
and past experiences may be called *perception*. In another sense we
can describe these two topic areas as being the study of the senses
themselves and the study of the experiences received through the senses.

These definitions are not rigorous, nor are the boundaries between these
areas sharp, but the separation serves to group similar kinds of knowledge together for convenience in presentation.

Perception has historically been fractionated into many parts for
study. Scientists, who use different methods, emphasize different problems, and have different theoretical backgrounds of approach to the
area, have produced this fractionation. These different approaches have
made the field appear piecemeal in principles and concepts. There are
collections of facts describing certain kinds of phenomena, which do
not integrate well with other collections of principles in a slightly
different problem area. Where there has been overlap, such as the
explanations put forward for the "moon illusion" or for the perception
of depth, some substantial and apparently non-integrative arguments
have arisen. That is, the protagonists, by and large, have not attempted
to resolve the problem by incorporating all of the knowledge of the
problem, but instead have centered about the knowledge obtained from
their own separate approaches. This fractionation is not unique to perception, but appears more pronounced than in the study fields of
learning, motivation, social psychology, etc.

Because of this kind of research history in perception, there is a
corresponding lack of overall organization in surveys of the field such
as this chapter. Some rough divisions have been made, however, and
are represented by the major section headings. Within these divisions,
though, there may be a notable lack of continuity.

The Senses

The mechanisms which convert stimulus energy into neural energy
are called the *senses*. Discussed below are the senses of *vision, audition,
olfaction, gustation,* the *skin senses, kinesthesis,* and the *equilibratory
senses*. Some of the structure and functions of each of these energy
transducers will be considered. For example, knowledge of the kinds,
locations, and sensitivity of the visual receptors allows an understanding
of the kinds of light stimuli which may be seen in the dark.

The old question of how many senses man has is an interesting topic
for discussion, but is meaningless unless it is specified what sort of
distinctions are to be made. The senses may be classified in terms of
the kinds of physical energy which are transferred into neural energy.
They may also be divided in terms of types of energy conversion cells

or transducers that are located in the various parts of the body. The definition used becomes especially important in considering the skin senses. There is more than one kind of receptor for pain and more than one kind of receptor for pressure, and the two mechanisms which sense temperature changes operate in a complex interacting fashion. Considering the sense of vision, there are separate cells which receive certain colors and other cells which convert only black and white information to neural energy. The question of the number of man's senses does not have a definite and easy answer.

VISION

The main points of the structure of the eye are given in Figure 4-1. Light passes through the *pupillary opening* in the *iris,* is focused by the lens, and is projected through the *vitreous body* of the eye to the light-sensitive cells on the *retina.* Two structural features of importance shown in Figure 4-1 are the *foveal pit,* the depression in the retina at the point at which light is received from stimuli centered in front of the eye, and the *blind spot,* the point of exit of the fibers which connect the light receptive cells to the optic nerve. This exit point for neural fibers has no receptor cells. The blind spot is not usually noticed, but may be demonstrated by fixating the "X" at the bottom of Figure 4-1 and holding the page about 18 inches away. The airplane then disappears.

The approximate path followed by neural information from the points of light reception to the occipital lobes of the cerebrum is indicated in Figure 4-1. Note the separate routes of information received in roughly each half of each retina as it passes along the *optic nerve* toward the *optic chiasma* or crossover point, along the *optic tracts* to the *lateral geniculate nuclei,* and finely, in less well-defined bundles of fibers, to the occipital lobes of the cerebral cortex. Note also that information which is presented in the left visual field eventually is projected to the right cortical lobe and that of the right visual field reaches the left cortical lobe. The crossover at the chiasma effects a particular organization relating cortical lobes and the *side* of the eye from which the stimulation is projected, rather than from *which* eye the information was received.

The retina is composed of light sensitive neural cells called *rods* and *cones,* and collateral connector and bipolar neurons. Differences in location and in function between these two receptors lead to some predictions and explanations for various sensory phenomena. These two

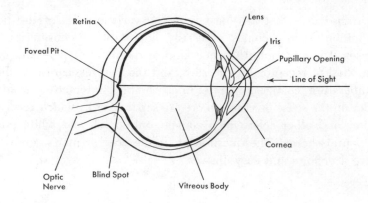

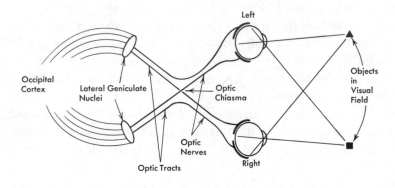

Figure 4-1. **Approximate structure of the eye, including those parts which function as described in some basic phenomena of perception, and the main pathways of neural information from the sides of each retina to the occipital lobes of the cerebral cortex.**

kinds of cells are distributed differently upon the retina. The 5 million cones in each eye fill the foveal pit and surrounding areas, but as the distance from the fovea becomes greater, the concentration of cones becomes less and less and the density of the greater than 125 million rods increases. The cones receive and transmit information of color, while the rods transmit only black, grays, and white. When adapted to

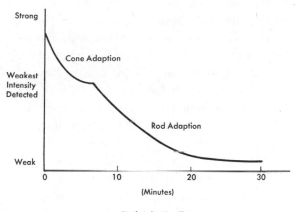

Figure 4-2. Increasing sensitivity of the eye to weak light as a function of adaptation to the dark. Cone cells adapt more quickly, but the rods are eventually able to detect a much weaker light stimulus.

darkened conditions, the rods detect a far weaker light stimulus than do the cones. This last difference is illustrated by the adaptation curve (Figure 4-2) which describes the weakest intensity of light which may be detected after the indicated length of time has passed in darkness since exposure to a bright light. The two curves describe the course of adaptation over time of the cones and the rods respectively. The cones adapt more quickly but the rods adapt to a much weaker light, that is, the rods become much more sensitive than cones after a long period of adaptation time. After 20 minutes, the rods may detect a stimulus which is 1/100,000 as bright as the light stimulus which was detectable immediately after exposure to the bright light.

The differences between the two kinds of light receiving cells in spatial location upon the retina and in extent of adaptation to a dark stimulus lead to some predictions about perception. For example, in a sufficiently darkened situation, and as the eye is dark adapted, objects which are projected upon the cone cells of the foveal areas of the eye will not be seen. Objects in such darkened conditions are best seen when the eye is aimed to one side, allowing the weak light to reach the more sensitive rods. To see a dimly lighted object at night, look around it and keep the eye moving, resisting the tendency to focus directly on the object.

The difference between the cells in adaptation rate plus the difference in transmission of color information accounts for the lack of color in stimuli observed in darkened areas. Once the level of illumination is less than that required for cone cell operation, only the rods give their black and white information. Thus, all cats look gray at night.

Another dimension of operation of the eye is that of *acuity,* the detection of small-sized stimuli. It has been established that the human eye can detect stimuli which cover a retinal area which is considerably smaller than the size of each retinal cell. A single line which covers 1 second of arc can be detected, while the average cone in the fovea covers about 24 seconds of visual angle. This discrepancy may be partially understood by noting the constant motion of the eye, both the sweeping and jerky movements which can be easily sensed and the very small and rapid "fixation" movements which are not usually noticed. The stimulus thus reaches a much wider area on the retina than the measurements of the physical stimulus would indicate. The acuity of the eye depends to a great extent upon the amount of light falling on the stimulus. The greater the illuminance, the smaller is the stimulus which may be seen.

The dimensions of subjective sensation of the visual stimulus are *hue, brightness,* and *saturation,* which correspond fairly close to the physical dimensions of the light stimulus called *wave length, amplitude,* and *complexity.* The correspondence between changes in the physical dimension of the stimulus and changes in sensations is not perfect, however. Figure 4-3, describing the contours of constant hue, indicates that

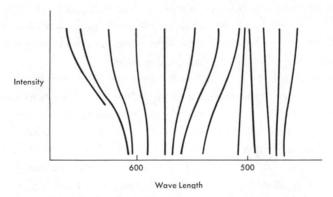

Figure 4-3. **Wave-lengths of constant hue with changes in intensity of the light stimulus. Only the three colors at 572 (yellow), 503 (green), and 478 (blue) do not change hue as the stimulus is changed in intensity.**

the perceived color of a certain wave length stimulus may shift with changes in amplitude (brightness) of that stimulus. With the exception of certain wave lengths close to yellow, blue, and green, the hue of a stimulus shifts towards either yellow or blue as its brightness is increased. The subjective hue at each wave length depends upon the intensity of that stimulus.

Some of the limits of operation of the sense of vision are given by measures called *thresholds*. (Some techniques of threshold measurement will be discussed later.) The *absolute threshold* is the least amount of energy required to produce a consistently reported sensation. One use of threshold measurements is that given in the curve of adaptation over time in Figure 4-2. A different absolute threshold function is described separately for the rods and cones at each color of light stimulus given in Figure 4-4. These curves show that the point of greatest sensitivity differs for the rods and for the cones. A stimulus of 510 millimicrons wavelength (bluish-green to cone receptors) marks the greatest sensi-

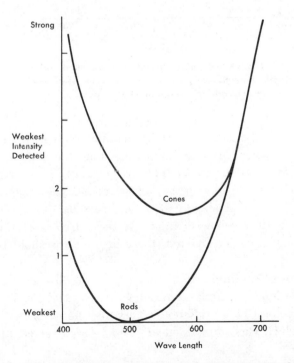

Figure 4-4. Weakest detectable stimulus intensity at each wavelength after dark adaptation. Cones are less sensitive to very weak light, but are more sensitive to differences in wave length than are rods.

tivity for the rods, while the cones can detect most easily a stimulus which is yellowish green (555 millimicrons).

A measure of the sensitivity of the eye to changes in wavelength or color is given by the difference threshold. The *difference threshold* is an answer to the question of how much can the stimulus be changed before a change in the sensation is consistently reported. Figure 4-5

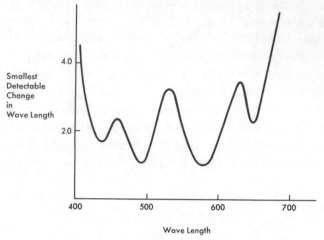

Figure 4-5. **Smallest detectable change in wave-length at each wave-length. Bottom points indicate a maximum sensitivity to change in wave-length at blue-green and at yellow.**

plots the amount of change that must be made at each wavelength for a detection of a change in hue, indicating that the amount to be changed differs with various colors. The eye appears to be most sensitive to minimal changes in blue-green and in yellow. The relative insensitivity to change in hue at about 540 millimicrons on this curve corresponds to green with a yellowish tinge. At the extremes of the range of visual wavelengths, violet and red, the difference threshold becomes quite large.

If the measures of sensitivity to change are made on each dimension of color (hue, brightness, and saturation) there are about 7½ million distinguishable colors. These different colors may be displayed upon a *color solid* in which each dimension of color is represented upon one axis.

A colored stimulus may be found to be composed of several wave lengths presented simultaneously. The mixture of two or more differently colored stimuli may produce a single apparent hue. There are two kinds of color mixture, *color addition* and *color subtraction*. The mixing of pigments as in painting is a color subtraction process in which a mixture of a little blue pigment in a yellow paint produces green. This effect is obtained because yellow pigment absorbs all colors except yellow and green, these it reflects. The blue pigment reflects blue and green, absorbing all others. The mixture of the blue and yellow pigment reflects only green; all of the other colors are subtracted by one of the pigments. The incident white light, which is usually a mixture of all wave lengths, is reflected as green.

Additive color mixture is produced by colors projected together upon the same white surfaces. White surfaces reflect all wave lengths. In color addition, red and green lights are reflected as yellow. When the spectrum of colors is bent into a circle and this spectrum is stretched and compressed in certain places as shown in Figure 4-6, the additive

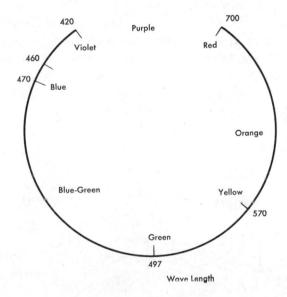

Figure 4-6. **Color-wheel for which opposite colors are complementary and mix additively to gray.**

mixture of colors at opposite positions on the color "wheel" produce shades of gray or white, depending upon the saturation of the colors. These opposites are said to be *complementary* colors. The complementary of a color is also perceived under certain conditions as a negative after-image, as discussed in a later section. A further principle of additive mix-

ture is that any three colors can be combined in a certain way to produce any other color, so long as one of the three is not formed by the
mixture of the other two. In this way, given three "primary" colors, the
entire range of perceived hues may be produced.

AUDITION

The stimuli for the sensations of hearing are normally the changes in
air pressure produced by vibrations or movements of the sound source.
The vibration of a taut string, the back and forth movements of a loud-
speaker cone, or the sharp movements of air as a firecracker explodes are
carried through the air much like the visible ripples of water spreading
out from where a fish has jumped.

Three dimensions describing the sound stimulus are its intensity, its
frequency, and its complexity. In a fairly close correspondence, these
dimensions of the sound stimulus give rise to the sensory dimensions of
loudness, pitch, and *timbre.*

The ear receives, amplifies, and transduces the vibration movements
of the air such that they yield information to the nervous system. The
structures of the ear (Figure 4-7) which perform these tasks may be
divided into three parts: the *outer, middle* and *inner* ears. The *outer ear*
is composed of the external ear tissue, an approximately one-inch-long
canal, and the *tympanic membrane,* commonly called the eardrum.

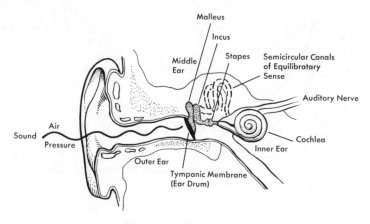

Figure 4-7. Approximate structure of the ear. Sounds enter the
outer ear as waves of changing air pressure which move the ear
drum. The middle ear bones connected to the ear drum transmit
the movements to the face of the fluid-filled cochlea. Cells sensitive to those fluid movements give neural information of the
sounds to the auditory nerve.

Changes in air pressure are funneled to this flexible membrane and cause it to move in response to the pressure changes. The *middle ear* structure is composed of three bones: the *malleus,* the *incus,* and the *stapes.* These act as a mechanical system of leverage to transmit the movements of the tympanic membrane to the inner ear. These mechanical movements of the middle ear are applied to another membrane which is attached to the *cochlea,* the superstructure of the inner ear. The cochlea is a fluid filled boney structure which looks much like a snail shell. Located inside the cochlea are the mechanisms which transduce the movements of the fluid into neural events or information. The cells which accomplish this task are called the *hair cells of the organ of Corti,* and are distributed along the length of the complex inner structure of the cochlea.

The details of the inner workings of the cochlea will not be described except to note that one of the most controversial aspects of the history of the study of hearing has concerned theories of how pitch or frequency of the sound stimulus is transmitted to the brain. A "place" theory holds that each frequency is detected at one place in the cochlea and separate neurons lead from each of those different receptors. "Frequency" theory has described ways by which frequency of the vibrating stimulus may be faithfully carried along neurons; one of these is the "volley principle" in which a collection of neurons fire in succession so that, taken as a whole, the actual vibration frequency is carried over a distance on neurons which singly could not fire that rapidly.

The range of frequencies which can be heard is generally agreed to be from 20 to 20,000 Hertz (cycles per second) for a normal young adult observer. The upper limit is not reached by everyone, however, and the highest frequency detectable typically declines with age in a regular fashion. The lower limit of 20 Hz. reflects not so much a limit of hearing but a limit of the quality of tonality of the stimulus. Below 20 Hz. the stimulus appears to be a series of rapid beats instead of a tone.

The intensity threshold for hearing has been found to be a function of the frequency of the stimulus, with the lowest intensity threshold for stimuli of about 2000 to 3000 Hz. The bottom curve of Figure 4-8 is an *absolute threshold curve,* indicating the lowest intensity of sound detectable at each frequency. The *equal-loudness curves* pictured above the absolute threshold curve represent tones which sound equally loud to a particular reference tone. Thus, the 20 db. contour connects the intensities of tones which sound equally loud to a standard 1000 Hz. tone which has been increased 20 db. above its measured absolute threshold value. Note that as the relative loudness of the tone increases, the rela-

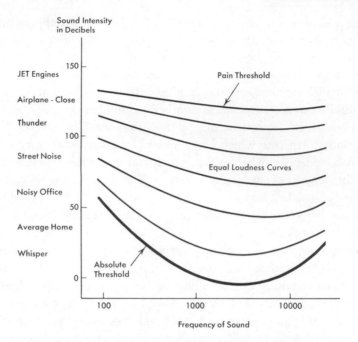

Figure 4-8. Absolute threshold of intensity for sounds of different frequency, tones which appear equally loud, and the intensity of sound for each frequency where pain is sensed. Some approximate sound intensities of common sounds are located on the scale at the left.

tionship with frequency becomes less curved. At equal-loudness values of about 110 db. there is little difference in intensity as a function of frequency. At about 130 db. tones of any frequency are judged to be painful. This upper limit or pain threshold can be easily exceeded by many sounds such as an unmuffled jet engine at close range. Sounds which approach or exceed these values can produce damage to the transmission structures of the ear and consequent *hearing losses* or deafness.

Normal experience is with complex as opposed to simple sounds and, except in rare circumstances, the pure tones of a single frequency used to obtain the curves and functions above are not experienced. A *complex sound* is simply one which is composed of many frequencies presented together.

If all of the audible frequencies are represented in an intensity proportional to the abilities of normal hearing—that is, at an equal loudness—the resulting complex sound is called *"white noise."* *Noise,* in general, is any non-orderly collection of tones, though the term is also applied to certain other collections of sounds which are judged to be unpleasant (a value judgment). The effect of noise added to a listening situation is to raise the threshold intensity required to hear specific sounds. Specific auditory stimuli are *masked* by the noise present. The masking function of complex sounds is usefully applied to some situations. A constant level of white noise in a laboratory will reduce the likely detection of unwanted sounds. Collections of sounds at the various frequencies of normal speech may be used to mask or render undetectable the sounds of speech.

Another kind of complex sound is that produced by the combination of a small number of pure tones. If two tones of different frequencies are presented at once the result may vary from the hearing of one tone which fluctuates in loudness to the clear sensation of three tones. The result is directly predictable from knowledge of the frequencies of the two tones and of the range of hearing. If two tones are selected such that the difference is *less* than 20 Hz., the two tones will be heard as one tone which fluctuates in loudness at a rate equal to the difference in frequency. This phenomenon is called *beats*. It is frequently experienced on a highway when two vehicles, which are close together as in passing, have nearly equal frequencies of engine sounds. If two pure tones are *greater* than 20 Hz. apart in frequency, each of the presented tones will be heard plus the *combination tone* which will be equal in frequency to the difference in frequency of the presented tones.

A third variety of complex sound is that of a single base tone plus components or *overtones*, which represent multiples of the base frequency. Musical instruments produce different proportions of the various overtones. This difference in complexity accounts for the easy distinguishability of several instruments playing the same basic note and is a good example of the dimension of sound experience called *timbre*.

Overtones are usually present in the stimulation finally received by the hair cells in the cochlea of the inner ear regardless of the purity of the sound presented to the outer ear. There are substantial distortions called *aural harmonics* that are produced as the sound passes through the outer ear cavity and is converted from changes in air pressure to mechanical movements to changes in fluid pressure by the various devices in the ear. These aural harmonics are enhanced as the intensity of the stumulus increases. There is considerable justification for saying that no one has ever heard a loud pure tone.

OLFACTION AND GUSTATION

The senses of olfaction (smell) and gustation (taste) have been often called the *chemical senses*. An obvious characteristic of the stimuli for these senses which separates them from the stimuli of other senses is that they are substances having chemical properties. The receptors of olfaction and gustation, along with some additional sensations that we usually associate with the outside of the skin, such as temperature, pain, and pressure differences arising from texture qualities, generally function together to give the sensations we report as "taste" of a food or drink. The taste of a food involves several of the senses, though it is probably true that the majority of the sensation comes through the olfactory sense.

The receptors for olfaction are called *olfactory rods*. These receptors are located very high in the nasal passage and out of the normal pathway of air inhalation. A substance can reach these receptors only by reaching the air of that area by diffusion or by mixing that substance into the air through sniffing or tongue movements.

Though several theories exist concerning how these receptors work, there is still considerable doubt. Similarly, little is known about the specific properties of substances which give rise to the olfactory sensations. There are no established chemical rules or other physical characteristics which allow for the description of similar odors. All attempts at establishing categories for smells have met with some degree of trouble; there always seems to be some group of substances which does not fit into the scheme. One such ordering which is used in practice by industrial chemists employs four categories named fragrant, acid, burnt, and caprylic (goaty). Each substance to be measured is experientially analyzed and rated as to how much it resembles the standard of each category. This yields a numerical description of the smell sensation of each substance in a standard framework.

The olfactory sense adapts to a constantly presented substance. The adaptation to a constant smell is quite complete after a few minutes and can be easily demonstrated by spending a considerable period of time in an enclosed area having a particular odor. Upon departing and reentering, the constantly present odor will be detected again. The olfactory sense also responds to a reduction of olfactory stimulation with an increased sensitivity to odors.

The receptors for gustation are called *taste buds*. They are located in many areas of the mouth cavity. Taste buds are present on the tip, sides, and base of the tongue (but not in the center of the top), as well as on the tonsils, palate, larynx, and epiglottis. Some individuals also report sensitivity on the floor of the mouth and the inside surfaces of the lips and cheeks. The taste buds appear in groups on *papillae* ("bumps") on the surface of the sensitive area. The stimuli for gustation have been considered to fall into the four classic subjective dimensions: sweet, sour, salt, and bitter. The strength of the sensation depends upon both the quality of the substance and the location to which it is applied.

Neurophysiological analyses of taste buds have shown that the classic four-receptor view is an oversimplification. There does not appear to be separate taste buds sensitive to each of these subjective qualities. Instead, recent theory and research describe an "afferent code" for taste.[65] Some receptors are sensitive to one kind of stimulus and others to several or a range of stimuli. The afferent neural discharge in one channel or set of fibers yields different taste sensations depending upon what activity was present in another channel. The afferent code is a composite of activity in a number of taste fibers.

There is some variation in sensitivity to gustatory stimulation depending upon the point of application and the temperature of the substance. Consider just the surfaces of the tongue: the tip is most sensitive to sweet substances, sour tastes are strongest when applied to the sides, and bitter substances are most strongly sensed when they are applied to the base of the tongue. Salt solutions do not seem to vary greatly in effectiveness with area of stimulation. The threshold or strength of sensation is also found to vary in a complex way with the temperature of the substance. Salt or bitter solutions must be stronger to be detected when warm. Sweet solutions must be stronger when their temperature changes in either direction from approximately body temperature. These relationships provide a basis for the observation that we prefer some foods to be warm and others cool and that we prefer certain methods of combining and eating foods.

There may be complete adaptation to fixed gustatory stimuli as well as olfactory stimuli. By constantly replenishing the stimulus solutions applied to the receptor areas in the mouth or in some other way preventing dilution of concentration by normal saliva flow, even very concentrated salty, sweet, sour, or bitter solutions will not be detectable after a few minutes of continuous exposure.

THE SKIN SENSES

Mechanical and thermal stimuli normally excite a variety of specialized nerve endings in the skin which result in reported sensations of pressure, pain, warmth, and cold.

The stimulus for the *pressure sense* is a mechanical deformation of the skin, a small bending or stretching of the surface. Sensitivity to pressure stimulation varies on the different surfaces of the body. The hands and face areas near the mouth are quite sensitive, whereas calloused areas of the feet and the expanse of the back are quite insensitive. Another kind of threshold which has described the sensitivity of the pressure sense is called the *two-point threshold*. This is the smallest distance by which two points of pressure may be separated and still yield a sensation of two separate points rather than one. Two stimuli must be separated a great deal (about 2½ in.) before they are distinguished from a single stimulus on the surface of the back as compared to the very small detectable distance between stimuli applied to the tip of the finger. The pressure sensations adapt with a reasonably constant pressure. Thus, sensations of a wrist watch, shoes, or a ring are not noticed after a short period of wearing. If the appropriate body areas are not moved for a few minutes, such stimuli are not only unnoticed but they are not detectable.

The sense of *pain* is not a simple one. It can arise from the extreme stimulation of many different kinds of stimuli in a wide variety of bodily areas. Sufficiently bright lights, loud noises, high or low temperatures, or great pressures all yield pain sensations. Some skin areas (for example, the back of the knee) appear to be far more sensitive to sharp mechanical stimulation than are other areas (the tip of the nose). It has been noted, in general, that the further toward the extremity of a limb that mechanical stimulation tests are made, the greater is the pressure sensitivity and the less is pain sensitivity. There are certain other areas of the body which give especially sharp pain sensations to simple mechanical stimulation. The cornea of the eye and the eardrum yield strikingly intense pain.

A long standing controversy concerns whether pain is a separate sense with its separate neural structure like vision or whether pain results from a pattern of intense stimulation from any of a variety of receptors. Part of the difficulty involves the psychological assumption of pain as an existing state rather than recognizing that pain is only a class of response from an instructed subject. The class of events evoking this response are sought in study of pain, and such investigations may be hindered by premature assumptions of the nature of the stimulus. A recent view of pain sensitivity has been formulated which recognizes this distinction and postulates a control system which regulates sensory input from the skin. This control is affected by other ongoing neural activity, recent similar stimulation, and more general central nervous system states.[55]

There are separate sense receptors for certain stimuli which alone and in certain combinations give the sensations of *hot, warm, cool,* and *cold.*

The measurement of sensations from moderate temperature changes, however, is hampered somewhat by the many processes of temperature regulation in the body, including the control of blood flow near the surface of the skin and of surface moisture production. It has been found that adaptation of temperature sensations is complete for any stimulus applied to the skin in a limited area when that stimulus is within the range of 16° to 42° C. (or about 60° to 108° F.). Beyond these values the stimulus remains cool or warm.

The sensation of very *cold* appears to be simply the stimulation of the cold receptors plus, in extreme situations, some pain sensations. The experience of *hot* is quite different. It has been found that a hot stimulus excites simultaneously the warm and cold receptors. The cold receptors, then, are responsive to temperatures which are cooler than the body and those which are much warmer than the body. The warm receptors respond only to stimuli that are warmer than the body. The sensation of hot can be demonstrated artificially by a special apparatus designed to excite both of these cells at the same time without using a hot stimulus. Two coils of tubing are wound in a parallel fashion such that a warm solution (42°-44° C.) may be passed through one coil and a cool solution (12°-15° C.) through the other to almost the same areas of the skin. This simultaneous excitation of the warm and cool sense receptors yields a sensation of hot called *paradoxical heat*.

KINESTHESIS

Kinesthesis receptors in the joints, muscles, and tendons yield neural information of the relative movements of the limbs of the body. Receptors in the joints give information about movement and relative position of the limbs. Comparisons of the sensitivities of the various joints have shown that small movements at the shoulder are the most easily detected and that movements of the ankle are relatively undetectable. Other kinesthetic sense organs are located in the muscles and in the joints to provide information of relative strain and tension. All of these kinesthetic senses provide what has been called *feedback* information about the success of movements which are in progress. For example, to regulate the amount and duration of force of arm muscles necessary to lift a box from the floor to a table while blindfolded requires continuous information as to the amount of muscle force applied, the speed of the movement, and the extent of the movement of the box at any given time. A quite sophisticated interaction of kinesthetic information may be seen to be necessary to perform this simple task efficiently.

Two kinds of receptors give information about movements of the head and permit a sense of balance of the body. These *equilibratory senses* are called the *semicircular canals* and the *vestibular sacs*. Both are located in the inner ear next to the cochlea (See Fgure 4-7).

The three *semicircular canals* in each ear are shaped like tubes bent into a donut, each located on a different geometric plane, such that rotations of the head in any direction will be detected. Each of these canals is filled with a fluid which resists movements by remaining stationary and causes hair cells attached to the moving walls to be stimulated.

Mild rotational movements yield sensations of moving, while more extreme activity may produce dizziness, rotating visual sensations, and perhaps motion sickness. Motion sickness ranging from moderate discomfort to nausea has been shown to be produced by slow (about once every 3 seconds) vertical movements through a distance of approximately 7 feet in a specially constructed elevator. This erratic elevator has produced motion sickness in a substantial proportion of experienced naval officer volunteers when the motion was presented in a continuous fashion.

The *vestibular sacs* lying between the semicircular canals and the cochlea operate on a similar principle. Resting upon hair cells are a group of crystals of calcium carbonate called *otoliths*. Vertical acceleration movements of the head change the pressure of the otoliths upon the hair cells, thereby stimulating them. The primary sensitivity of the vestibular sacs is therefore to the position of the head with respect to the pull of gravity. But accelerations or decelerations of movements in a forward direction of the head have been found to give rise to similar sensations attributable to changing otolith pressure. Accelerations forward are sensed as movements upward and a decelerations are sensed as movements downward.

Psychophysics

The precise measurement and description of the responses made to stimuli presented to the senses characterize the problem facing *psychophysics*. What are the psychological events which correspond to the presentation of physical stimuli of various intensities? Are there simple increases in the sensation for constant increases in the physical stimulus, or does some more complex rule better describe this relationship? These rules have been shown to have both a practical value and a usefulness for the study of the bases of sensory mechanisms and perception.

Some traditional methods which try to answer questions of the limits of sensory reception under controlled conditions will be described first. Certain practical applications of sensitivity and the influence of characteristics of the observer have been influential in developing new and important ideas about the measurement of stimulus-detection limits. These newer methods of *signal detection* are presented briefly in the following section. Finally, some of the ways in which psychologists can quantify stimuli which are not near threshold values or which have no apparent meaningful physical dimension will be considered.

TRADITIONAL THRESHOLD MEASUREMENTS

A *threshold* is a point along some measured dimension of stimuli at which greater values elicit one kind of response and lesser values produce a different kind of response. One important such point is the *absolute threshold,* the value on the stimulus dimension which is sufficient to separate the following responses of an instructed observer: "the stimulus is present" and "the stimulus is not present." The visual sensitivity curves of Figure 4-4 and the bottom loudness contour of Figure 4-8 illustrate measurements of absolute thresholds of intensity of stimuli differing in adaptation and frequency, respectively.

Another point on the continuum of stimuli defines the *difference threshold,* the point on either side of which the observer makes responses of "the stimulus has changed" and "the stimulus has not changed." Difference thresholds may be determined along any dimension of a stimulus. Successive difference thresholds along a dimension may be determined by using the stimulus, which was just detected as different, as the new reference for determining a successive difference threshold. The sensitivity to changes in hue pictured in Figure 4-5 may be obtained by successive difference threshold measurements.

An observation which has been noted with many kinds of stimuli is that the size of the difference threshold depends upon the size of the reference stimulus. An early approximation to this relationship stated that, for a range of moderate stimulus values, the size of the difference threshold is a constant proportion of the reference stumulus. This relationship is called *Weber's law.* Recent evidence dictates a *power law;* that changes in the stimulus which produce equal stimulus ratios result in equal ratios of the reported stimulus. The comparison of two car horns versus one is the same stimulus ratio as 20 car horns compared to 10. These comparisons would be judged to be equal. That is, 20 as compared to 10 is the same psychological ratio as 2 to 1.

Determination of threshold points requires (1) a procedure for the presentation of the stimuli which will average out any systematic biases and errors of measurement, (2) careful control of the presented and the background stimuli, (3) an observer trained in detecting the stimuli and in responding in the fashion of the experiment, and (4) a specific procedure for definition of the threshold value of stimulation. Two kinds of approach to determining thresholds are the *method of limits* and the *frequency methods*.

The *method of limits* presents a series of stimuli one at a time and in order of magnitude for the observer to judge. With this method several "runs" along the stimulus dimension from either direction serve to bracket the threshold point. Stimuli are changed toward the presumed threshold in small steps from points known to be unnoticeable on some trials and from points which are easily received and noticed on other trials. The observer reports, with each stimulus change, whether the stimulus is detected or not. The average stimulus value marking a change of the observer's responses defines the threshold, after an equal number of runs from above and below the presumed threshold.

The methods of limits are not without some constant errors of measurement. A resistance or inertia against changing a response, called an *error of habituation,* or conversely, a tendency to change the response too soon, called an *error of anticipation* may affect the judgments of the observer. The range of values of the stimuli which are presented to the observer may also bias the judgments, especially towards middle or average values of the range of presented stimuli. This has been called a *context effect.* Despite these biases on the measurements, when it is used in a consistent fashion, the method of limits reliably and usefully measures thresholds.

The *frequency methods* of threshold determination present, randomly, a narrow range of stimuli within which the threshold point is assumed to lie. As each stimulus is presented the observer judges the presence or absence of the specified stimulus difference. For example, each test stimulus may be presented in conjunction with a comparison standard, requesting the judgments of *"same"* or *"different."* Measurements of absolute threshold by frequency methods may require that the subject, at a given signal, judge whether the stimulus is detected, or is not detected.

Frequency or probability judgments of the occurrence of each class of response (Same or Different, Yes or No) to each stimulus may be combined into a curve of the sort given in Figure 4-9. A common convention is to fit a curve through the points, interpolating the threshold value as that corresponding to the stimulus yielding 50% "Yes" judgments.

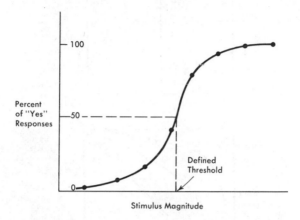

Figure 4-9. **Threshold stimulus value defined by use of a curve fitted to points marking percentage of "Yes" responses at each of several stimulus values. The point corresponding to 50 percent "Yes" judgments is conventionally used to describe the absolute threshold value.**

DETECTION THRESHOLDS

In the application of techniques of traditional threshold measurement to perceptual detection problems like the detection of a critical sound signal on a background of noise, it became apparent that the responses of the observer were not just a function of the intensity of the stimulus. Detection was found to be importantly and systematically influenced by (1) properties of the stimuli, (2) prior information about the stimulus and the method, (3) properties of the sense employed, and (4) motivation and other variables which affect the response made by the observer. A new set of sensitivity measurement procedures have been developed which take into account the effects of most of the additional factors. Representative of these methods is the *theory of signal detection* (TSD).[80]

Signal detection theory methods may be illustrated by a fundamental problem of detection. Suppose that only one stimulus value is either pre-

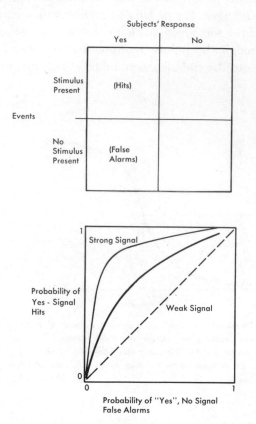

Figure 4-10. Event-response categories for a simple detection experiment allowing only "Yes" or "No" responses to the presence or absence of a weak stimulus event. The lower "iso-sensitivity" curve describes response probabilities for the same signal under differing conditions of testing. See text.

sented or not presented within a specified interval of time. Thus a stimulus of energy level X may be randomly presented on say, 50% of the detection trials. The subject's response of "Yes, I hear it" or "No, I don't hear it" may be distributed into the various cells of the table given in Figure 4-10. The subject may conceivably say "Yes" or "No" for both those trials on which there was no stimulus presented and on those trials on which the stimulus was presented.

The occurrence of "yes" responses when the stimulus was not presented (a false alarm) may be considered to be a measure of the extent of the situation pressures toward making that response. By replicating the detection experiment many times for each observer a useful relationship may be described. In each of these experiments the probability of the "Yes" response is changed by instructions. Instructions yielding a large number of "Yes" responses may liken the task to one of finding a valuable object. Any hint of the presence of the object will be reported, while errors are not punished. Similarly, "Yes" responses may be made quite infrequent by suggesting that the task is one of selecting and removing the harmless snakes from a mixture of similar appearing poisonous and non-poisonous reptiles. Experiments demonstrate that the ratio between the "hits" (correctly reporting "Yes" when the signal *was* present) and the "false alarms" (incorrectly reporting "Yes" when the signal was *not* present) varies with the likelihood of the "Yes" response being made at all. This function, presented in Figure 4-10, has been called a *iso-sensitivity curve*. The curve connects points determined in separate experiments in which the stimulus did not change, yet the instructions and other factors led to differing proportions of hits and false alarms.

The shape and level of the iso-sensitivity curve depends upon the strength of the stimulus presented to the subject. The curve above and to the left in Figure 4-10 illustrates the iso-sensitivity curve for a stronger stimulus, while a weaker stimulus would result in an iso-sensitivity curve approaching the position of the diagonal line. The empirical data, predicted by the theory of signal detection, have shown the importance and relative value of the strength of the stimulus, the expected frequency of that stimulus, and the values and costs of making certain responses in the detection situation.

PSYCHOLOGICAL SCALING

A set of stimuli may be "measured" by the responses of human observers, even though there are no corresponding physical dimensions of those stimuli. For example, one may estimate his own personality characteristics, such as "cheerfulness" or "hostility." Many of our common observations of the behavior of others concern the ordering and comparing of behaviors. The measurements and comparisons of things using man as a measuring device may be done according to two general procedures. The measurement may require comparisons among the stimuli to be measured, or it may specify the rules for judgments of the absolute value of each stimulus along the subjective dimension. Some highlights of the comparison and absolute judgment procedures for scaling stimuli are given below.

The *comparison judgment* scaling task may simply be to place all of the stimuli in order on the characteristic. One may rank seven friends in order of decreasing sense-of-humor. This method of rank ordering establishes the greater-than, less-than relationship for a moderate sized collection of stimuli, but it does not give information directly about the size of the differences among the items. In the similar paired-comparisons approach, judgments are made between pairs of the stimuli, requiring in each case only a statement of which is greater. Certain statistical treatments can then provide estimates of the size of the step between each stimulus in addition to the average rank order of the collection of stimuli.

Observers can also make *absolute judgments* of the magnitude of the characteristics possessed by each stimulus. The task may be to assign numbers ranging from 0 to 100 to the stimuli, or the task may be to sort the stimuli into categories of specified magnitude differences. Sit at a piano and strike one key high on the keyboard and assign the value 100

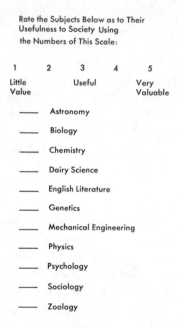

Figure 4-11. **A rating scale applied to a quality of stimuli for which there is no one objective definition. Consistent scale values may be obtained after a large number of students have judged each stimulus. The wording of the labels, the number of categories, and several response biases of the raters, however, make the rating scale useful only as a first approximation to the measuring stimuli.**

to it. Strike a lower note and call this tone 0. Now pick around with your eyes closed to avoid visual bias to select the note that you would judge to be 50, 75, 25, etc. Strike other keys at random and assign numbers according to the range already "tied down" by 0 to 100. The commonly used rating scale is a form of such absolute judgments of stimulus characteristics. By using the rating scale technique illustrated in Figure 4-11, each stimulus may be assigned to one of the ratings.

The value of these kinds of measurements of stimuli may be judged by the usefulness of the scales which are the end product. If reliably ordered numbers can be applied to the members, dimensions of objects and events which are physically unspecified may be measured and thus readily studied.

Perceptual Organization

Some of the basic and relatively undisputed facts of the organization of information received by the receptors may be divided into two groups: (1) those seemingly dependent upon the pattern of the simple stimuli presented, and (2) those involving the interpretation of the pattern of stimuli and other information reaching the senses.

STIMULUS FACTORS

The perception of certain stimulus patterns depends upon characteristics of that pattern. The perception of units as groups because of the *similarity* or *proximity*, the tendency to see things as *continuous* patterns rather than as separate parts, and the tendency toward achieving *closure* or to fill-in missing stimulus parts to perceive a meaningful whole, illustrate stimulus factors of perception. These kinds of factors are illustrated in Figure 4-12. Some theories of perception hold that these ways of viewing a stimulus are unlearned, built-in characteristics of the perceiving individual.[8] This question of the extent and complexity of innate determinants of perceptual behavior has proved to be difficult to resolve but is probably not immediately necessary for the understanding of the operation of the principles in simple applications.

In almost any stimulus presentation there is one part of the stimulus which stands out as the figure at any given moment against a background. This *figure-ground relationship* of different parts of the stimulus may change at different times in what has been called a *reversible*

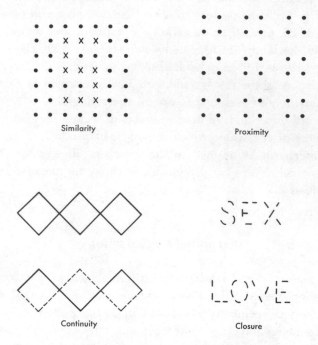

Figure 4-12. Similarity, proximity, continuity, and closure as factors determining the perception of a pattern.

figure. Reversible figures (Figure 4-13) have been used to show that past experiences with similar stimuli and the mental sets of the observer, can determine which of the parts of the complex stimuli will dominate as the initial figure. Experience, in this case, can be demonstrated to determine that aspect of a complex stimulus which stands out as the figure.[40]

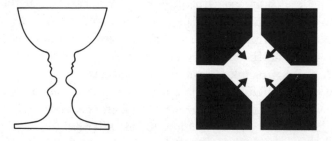

Figure 4-13. Reversible figure-ground relationships. First one then another part of the figure stands out as the figure.

OBJECT CONSTANCIES

The perception of an object and all of its properties as constant and unchanging in spite of the continuously changing sensations of those properties received by the sense organs outlines the scope of the object constancies. How is it that the light green door to a familiar room is recognized as having a variety of stable properties in the face of retinal information which is different? The door's brightness is correctly reported regardless of wide variations in physical intensity of light reaching the eye from sunlight to a lone weak night lamp. Its color appears the same in the blue daylight, the yellowish lamps of evening, or under the spot from a flashlight. The door does not appear to vary in size when one moves towards or away from it as does the size of the retinal image. The shape of the door is judged to be rectangular though the retinal image appears a rectangle only in a particular position. In spite of the movements of the head in space, the door appears at rest in an unchanged position. The recognition of the door as a stable and constant object is not the obvious process that its commonplace nature might suggest.

Typically the constancy of each of the properties of an object is considered and studied separately from the others. *Brightness, color, size, shape,* and *location* constancy will separately be considered for a given visually perceived object. This separation for study does not imply that they are unrelated processes. Some interactions will be demonstrated.

Brightness constancy allows the perception of objects as having an unchanging brightness regardless of the intensity of the incident illumination. A white rabbit in the shade appears brighter than his gray cousin in the sunshine even though the physical intensity of light reflected from the gray rabbit is greater than that from the white rabbit. This brightness constancy may be destroyed if each stimulus is viewed separately in the absence of the comparison cues given by the background. Thus, by using a *reduction screen,* a device such as a blackened tube held to the eye and aimed at the object to remove other stimulation than that from the object, the true physical brightness of the object is perceived. The gray rabbit appears to be the brighter of the two when viewed through a reduction screen.

In a similar fashion the *color constancy* of a stimulus may be shown to be determined by color information from the stimulus and its background. The apparent color of objects remains unchanged when background comparisons are available despite the use of deeply colored sunglasses or illumination by colored lights. The color constancy

Figure 4-14. Distorted room demonstration. (Courtesy of H. Cantril)

mechanism allows the correct identification of the color of objects as long as some cues to that true color are present.

The perception of object as having a *constant size* in spite of changes in the size of the image reaching the retina of the eye has been found to be closely linked with the perception of depth. As the distance of an object from an observer is increased, the retinal image size decreases, yet the object is seen as unchanged in size. Removal of the cues to depth is usually sufficient to make judgments of the size of unfamiliar objects impossible. Familiar objects, however, are seen as having a constant size. If a familiar appearing object such as a golf ball is presented to an observer in a darkened room which allows no cues of

Figure 4-14. Distorted room demonstration. (Cont.)

depth, distance to the lighted ball will be judged with the implicit assumption that the ball is of that familiar size. The observer may be tricked by the presentation of a mock-up 2-foot golf ball. This large ball will be judged to be much closer than it really is, consistent with the assumed size of golf balls. If an object such as a balloon is varied in size in a situation where no cues to depth are present, it will not be seen as changing in size, but as varying in distance. As the balloon is made larger, it will be seen as coming closer.

Shape constancy allows us to recognize the shape of familiar objects. A window is seen as being rectangular, even though the retinal image is almost never that shape. A dinner plate is judged to be circular even though the usual angle of viewing produces an image of an ellipse upon the retina. Less familiar stimuli achieve a certain constancy of shape when they are presented upon a background of known spatial orientation and depth cues. The object's shape is judged by knowledge of depth and size of its parts.

Shape and size constancy may both be seen to operate to produce an illusion of normality in a display called a *distorted room*. As shown in Figure 4-14, the distorted room is constructed to appear quite normal from one position only. Stimuli which are moved from one side to another in this distorted room are seen to change in size because of an unperceived change in distance from the observer. The size constancy of a test figure placed in the room is insufficient to overcome the perception of the room as a normally shaped stimulus background.

Location constancy refers to the apparent stability of objects in space despite the changing location of the retinal pattern reaching the eye. When the head position is changed, the world does not dance about with each movement. This constancy has been studied by changing the usual optical relationship between the direction of the stimulus light and the retina.[39] These experiments used prisms worn as glasses which reverse the up-down, left-right relationships of the stimuli and the retina from the normal. There was an initial expected disorientation for a time. But after repeated attempts to get about in this reversed world, subjects have successfully learned a variety of complex tasks requiring vision, including fencing and riding a bicycle. These experiments suggest that the stability of the position or location of objects is influenced by learning and may be a learned perceptual mechanism.

Perceptual Topics

The following sections are neither exhaustive of the field of perception in psychology nor complete in the treatment of any of the various problems selected. A sampling has been made which is believed to reflect the significance and the importance of knowledge of perceptual principles. Further study by the interested reader may begin with the suggested readings at the end of the chapter.

DEPTH PERCEPTION

Important to the perception of an object as having unchanging properties of shape and size is information about the nearness of that object.

If all cues to depth are removed, unknown objects become uninterpretable as to size and shape.

Some knowledge of the cues for depth perception come from a review of the simple principles of making a drawing convey depth, as illustrated in Figure 4-15. Near things often appear in front of and hence

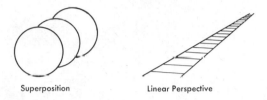

Superposition   Linear Perspective

Figure 4-15. Two-dimension cues conveying information of depth.

cover up parts of more distant objects. This is the depth factor of relative position or *superposition.* Objects appear smaller when further away than when near. This *linear perspective* accounts for the convergence of the image of parallel lines as they become more distant, and for the gradients in texture produced by a collection of items of the same size as they become more distant. The *lights* and *shadows* upon parts of an object also give depth cues. The usual direction of light sources is from above. This light direction produces some characteristic brightness differences upon solid objects whose variously shaped parts are exposed or not exposed to that light. This light and shadow assumption is illustrated in the picture of the surface of a grain storage bin in Figure 4-16. Lack of clarity or the presence of haze also conveys information of depth. In the atmospheric conditions of most parts of the world clarity of vision is obscured by substances in the air as distance is increased. Dramatic evidence is given by the underestimation of distances by observers when experiencing for the first time the exceptionally clear air of parts of the Rocky Mountains.

An additional stimulus-produced cue to depth is the *relative movement* of near and far objects when the observer is moving with respect to those objects. The common observation of rapid, almost-blurred movement of near objects as opposed to the slower movements of distant objects when traveling in a vehicle is one example of the relative motions cue to depth. Another, less obvious variation of this distance cue is given by the slight side-to-side head movements which observers make when asked to judge the relative distances of objects in the

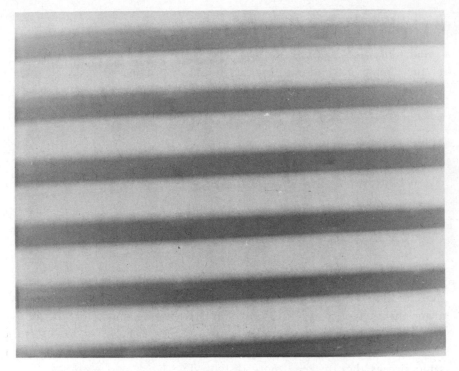

Figure 4-16. An illustration of light and shadow cues to depth. Turn the page upside down and the depressions become projections. (Photo by author)

visual field. These head movements are usually sufficient to yield small amounts of relative motion of objects at varying distances.

Other cues to depth come from the form and operation of the sensory receptors. The *convergence* of the two eyes upon the closer stimulus, the change in focus or *accommodation* of the lenses of each eye, and the slightly different picture received by each eye, called *retinal disparity*, which is a function of the spatial separation of the two eyes and their consequent different perspective. These physiological sources of depth information are illustrated in Figure 4-17.

A new stimulus-pattern analysis of depth perception and its determinants has come from Julesz [36] in which different patterns of dots are presented to each eye. Normal inspection of these patterns reveals no general differences, yet when presented one to each eye as with a stereoscope, properly constructed patterns yield three-dimensional pictures. The pattern of dots presented to one eye is a matrix of black and white squares randomly distributed. The other pattern is the same

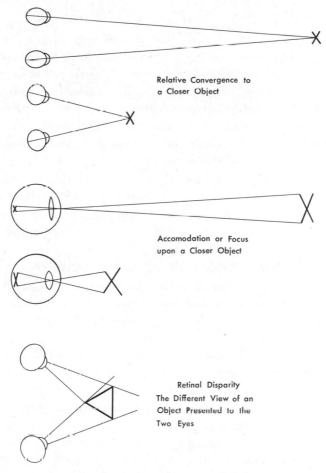

Relative Convergence to
a Closer Object

Accomodation or Focus
upon a Closer Object

Retinal Disparity
The Different View of an
Object Presented to the
Two Eyes

Figure 4-17. Convergence, accommodation, and retinal disparity
as cues to depth.

except that one block of these dots was displaced one column away, the displaced column filling the empty space. The area of the displaced block now appears in a different depth plane than the surrounding parts of the matrix, with no brightness gradient marking the border.

These demonstrations have shown that depth perception does not require the recognition of the form of the stimuli nor depend upon the convergence and accommodation of the eyes. The depth perception indicated is not a result of an analysis in each eye, but may take place at the cortical level. Further work with this disparity pattern technique of separation of the various cues to depth will undoubtedly be of great importance.

MOVEMENT PERCEPTION

The perception of a stimulus that is moving against a background may at first glance seem to be a trivially simple thing. But with some thought the notion becomes very complex. The detection of movement in one part of a retinal image which itself is constantly changing is not simple. This relationship between stimulus and retinal image may be partly learned, as indicated by the reversing-lens experiments mentioned above in relation to the perception of location constancy. The reversal by the lenses of the apparent location of stimuli reverses also the direction of relative motion of the image of that stimulus on the retina. It has been found that the confusion of both location and direction of movement behaviors while wearing the reversing lenses leads to new habits which are in accord with the actual rather than the apparent location of the stimulus.

Some information to guide understanding of the perception of movement concerns the minimal stimulus change which will produce movement. Apparent movement may be produced by the rapid, successive presentations of slightly different pictures. This artificially produced movement has been termed *stroboscopic movement* and has been found to depend upon the brightness of the stimulus, the duration of the presentation of the stimuli, the length of the interval between stimuli, and the amount of change of parts of the stimulus which are to be seen as "movements." The movement perceived in motion pictures is produced by such discrete picture presentations. A simple form of stroboscopic movement is given by the *phi phenomenon*. The successive lighting of two lamps in different positions in front of a subject in a darkened room gives the appearance that the light is moving. Again, the brightness, durations, and distances may be studied to determine the limits of such artificially produced movement perceptions.

ILLUSIONS

The study of illusions or misleading perceptions of the physical stimulus has been a rich source of evidence and information about the perceptual processes. The previous discussion of the principles of perceptual organization revealed that one method of studying these principles is to change the stimulus situation so that illusory depth, shape, form, or brightness perceptions are reported. Some classic illusions which have been studied are described and illustrated in Figure 4-18.

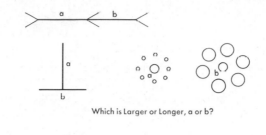

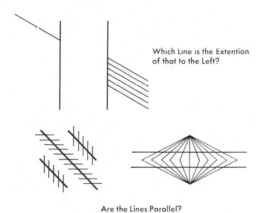

Figure 4-18. Illusions of size and directions are effected by organizing the elements to take advantage of perceptual habits.

One special problem of perception which has proved to be remarkably resistant to satisfactory explanation is that known as the "moon illusion," the appearance of the moon at the horizon as being much larger than when it is overhead. A variety of attempts to explain this phenomenon have called attention to upward movements of the eyes, the contrasting background at the horizon, and the presence of terrain between the observer and the moon. But none of these discussions has been entirely satisfactory, probably because the moon illusion is a function of a collection of principles operating at the same time. The relative reliance upon one factor as opposed to another may be a difference attributable to the individual observer.

One final class of illusions has been popularized recently though they have been known for many years. These illusions are the composite figures which represent what have been called *impossible figures*. Separate parts of these drawings, as illustrated in Figure 4-19, are meaningful and in accordance with expectations, but when the whole stimulus

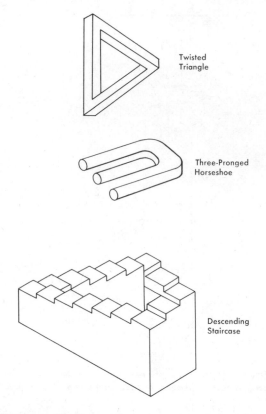

Twisted
Triangle

Three-Pronged
Horseshoe

Descending
Staircase

Figure 4-19. Impossible figures whose elements are in accordance with the way we perceive the outlines of objects but which, as wholes, become impossible to visualize.

is observed, the picture loses meaning. The staircase is drawn correctly at any one place, but the whole depicts a never ending ascending or decending unit which is unreal. The basic drawing or construction technique in making impossible figures is to link together two or more unrelated figures which happen to have similar or common connecting parts. The incongruous pictures used in the study of motivation (Figure 3-1), consisting of interchanged parts of animal bodies, illustrate the same basic principle. The perceptual illusion here is merely an illustration of the tendency of the observer to make meaningful complete wholes from the complex stimuli presented to him.

SOUND LOCALIZATION

The perception of the direction of a sound source depends upon the separation of the two ears as well as some properties of the sound source and the situation. The ability to distinguish accurately the direction of sound can be highly developed with practice as demonstrated by, for example, the remarkable performance of many blind individuals. Sound localization is also a reasonably accurate perceptual ability which is often used in an unnoticed but direct fashion in many activities. Responding to a call or the act of listening to music presented by sophisticated "stereo" sound reproduction systems require the perception of differences in the location of sound sources.

The separation of the receptors and the relatively slow speed of travel of sound waves allows for several possible differences in the sounds reaching one ear at a given moment as opposed to those reaching the other ear. The sound can be shown, as in Figure 4-20, to differ in intensity or loudness, time of arrival, and, less importantly, phase of

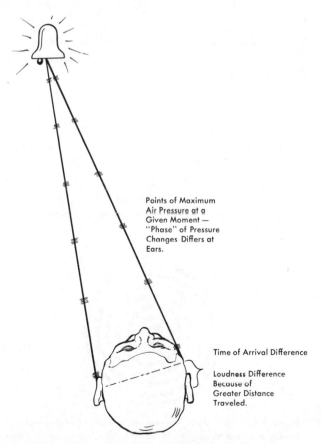

Points of Maximum
Air Pressure at a
Given Moment —
"Phase" of Pressure
Changes Differs at
Ears.

Time of Arrival Difference

Loudness Difference
Because of
Greater Distance
Traveled.

Figure 4-20. **Sounds arriving from one side of the head differ in time, intensity, and phase of pressure changes.**

the changes in pressure reaching the eardrum. Only sounds that arrive from one side of the head will be detected using these cues, however, as shown in Figure 4-20; sounds which arrive from points equally distant from the two ears will not differ in these characteristics.

Other properties also supply cues to sound localization. The learned direction from which many sounds arrive leads one to look upward for airplanes, and toward a familiar road for sounds of automobiles, trucks, and so on. These learned localizations may cause one to look in error for familiar sounds coming from strange places. A friend calling from a position in a tree above the observer may not be located immediately because the usual localizations of that familiar sound, the ground and surrounding area, will be searched first.

The various echoes and distortions which are present for every sound in a reasonably enclosed space may also contribute to its identification and location. Knowledge of the distinctive features of a given place such as a hallway will allow determination of the direction and distance down such a hall that the sound source was located. The quality and strength of echoes usually allows determination of which side of a room a sound is coming.

PERCEPTUAL AFTEREFFECTS

Certain kinds of stimulus situations produce not only immediate sensations and perceptions but also a further sensation after the stimulus has physically ceased. Commonly experienced aftereffects are the visual sensations which persist after a glance near the sun or other intense light source, and the lingering sensations after persistent viewing of a colored stimulus. This latter lingering sensation is of a reversal (negative

Figure 4-21. Spiral demonstration of movement aftereffects. Following a period of rotation in one direction, the stationary figure appears to rotate in the opposite direction with continued fixation.

afterimage) of the colors to their complementaries when the observer's gaze is shifted to a neutral background.

Aftereffects of the perception of motion can be demonstrated by a device like the "spiral," as shown in Figure 4-21. Another movement aftereffect is the sensation of moving backward in a vehicle after having come to a rest. When the surroundings begin to move forward, as often occurs in heavy vehicular traffic, railroad yards, or in a cluster of taxiing air transports, a strong sensation of moving backwards is usually induced.

ATTENTION AND VIGILANCE

Of the many possible stimuli which may be detected and perceived at any moment a certain proportion are attended to. This attention seems, experientially, to be under both conscious and external stimulus control. Attention can be directed voluntarily to certain sources of stimulation. The shadow caused by the incident light upon the center crease of this book or the pressures presently reaching your right thumb are now attended to. On occasion certain kinds of stimuli seem to be forced into attention by external factors. Stimuli which have the quality of greater intensity, size, or vividness than other stimuli or stimuli which are presented in an unusual manner like the repetitive ticking of a loud watch in a quiet room, are so forced into attention. Skillful use of the attention determining factors of stimuli can guide the perceptions of an audience away from the true mechanism of a magician's trick or toward selected information about the product being advertised.

The related concept of *vigilance* refers to the long-term attention of an individual toward a certain restricted set of stimuli. Practical problems of vigilance have been studied in military situations. Continuous watch-ing of radar screens and simple guard duty require vigilance. The closer the stimuli sought are to a detection threshold, the greater is the effort of detecting these stimuli, and, consequently, the greater is the decrement in the detection performance after a period of time on the task. Stimulus changes which would have been easily detected at the beginning of a watch session are missed entirely after surprisingly short periods of continuous vigilance.

SUBLIMINAL PERCEPTION

Responses and behavior changes to stimuli which are not reported to be consciously experienced are assumed to reflect what has been termed *subliminal perception*. That such responses and behaviors do exist is quite apparent. The phase, intensity, and time differences in sounds reaching the two ears which allow localization of the source are not consciously noticeable differences. Nor are the physiological changes in the muscles which move the lens of the eye and the position of the eyeball detectable experienced stimuli changes, though there are definitely responses and behaviors which depend upon the cues so provided. In this sense, then, there are definitely subliminal perceptions.

In another sense, though, this term has been applied to a possible sequence of events which has not been demonstrated satisfactorily. This usage refers to the presentation of information including printed words and statements at such a speed that they are not consciously noticed, with a view toward changing the behavior pattern of that person without his awareness. This notion assumes that the skills of reading and looking at complex stimuli can take place at a much faster pace than that of which we are consciously aware, and that further, the individual would respond to these unconscious messages.

Two questions must be answered and neither has had convincing affirmative answers. The first question is whether such complex stimuli can be detected at an unconscious level. The second question is whether an individual would respond to the demands (or suggestions) of such information if it were detected. The evidence suggests that there need be no fear at the present time of these techniques changing the behavior of individuals viewing a television screen.[52]

PERCEPTION AND MOTIVATION

The joint determination of behavior by factors of motivation and those of perception was discussed earlier in Chapter 3. There is little question that these factors are usually present in the determination of behavior. The question to be considered here is whether motivational factors influence the process of perception *in addition to* their effect on behavior. Does, for example, a state of intense hunger produce perceptions of more food-related objects in ambiguous visual stimuli, or does the food deprivation operation just affect the sorts of responses which are likely to be available and used by an individual? Experiments show that more food-related responses are made under these conditions of ambiguous or nonexistent stimuli presentations.[51]

Reference to Figure 4-22 will present these possibilities in another way. Responses may be observed to stimuli under a certain set of instructional and situational conditions. The process called perception is assumed to intervene. Question is directed toward the source of the difference in behavior. Are the stimuli actually perceived differently, or

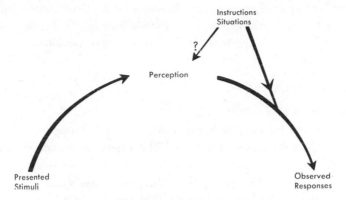

Figure 4-22. A schema of the perception process as it relates to presenting stimuli situations and instructions, and observed responses. Is the perception of stimuli affected by different instruction and stimuli or do these factors only affect the responses which the observer is likely to make in the situation?

does the subject simply respond in a different fashion to the same perceptions because of other factors? The known effects upon responses alone of motivational and similar variables tend to support the simple interpretation of the response differences as due not to different perceptions but rather to the action of motivation upon responses.

Another kind of experiment which belongs in this problem area is that called the study of *perceptual defense*.[54] The basic observation has been that stimuli which are threatening to the defenses of the individual are more poorly perceived. These threatening stimuli are assumed to be perceived at an unconscious level and suppressed. The information is detected at a subliminal level and is consciously suppressed through the mechanism of raising the threshold value for that stimulus. Thus, the stimulus must be stronger to be perceived. A response bias interpretation of these findings of different thresholds for the perception of neutral versus threatening stimuli is that both kinds of stimuli are equally detected, but that the information of a threatening nature is voluntarily withheld until a greater degree of certainty is obtained as to its identity and until the absolute necessity of making such responses is verified. Thus, in comparisons of "neutral" versus "taboo" words, the greater observed thresholds or exposure duration for the taboo words including "whore" and "penis" may be attributed to the greater need to be sure of the identity of the stimulus before it is spoken to the experimenter. Individuals act to be sure that the stimulus really is "whore" before they publicly emit that response. A response of that nature which was in fact incorrect would obviously allow "all sorts of Freudian interpretations about that individual's past history and personality." At least the subject is likely to think that it is.

EXTRASENSORY PERCEPTION—ESP

An intriguing and persistent irritation to the psychology of perception is the belief that information may be transmitted through other channels than the known sensory mechanisms. The phenomena include notions of thought transmission from one mind to another, called *telepathy*; knowledge of the happenings at another time or place, called *clairvoyance*; and predictions of future events, called *precognitions*. There are also beliefs in the ability of inanimate objects to be moved by mental power, called *psychokinesis,* and recent reports of the abilities of certain "sensitive" individuals to detect the color of a stimulus by touch without the aid of vision.

Serious studies of these kinds of phenomena, that is, those which use no trickery or intent to defraud, have persistently appeared from some researchers. The effects reported are never very large. They often depend upon the power of unusual statistical tools for the demonstration of their slight non-chance nature. The effects are often reported to be the special powers of a few "sensitive" individuals rather than a general phenomenon of all individuals. Further, the effects have often been shown to decrease in magnitude when increased experimental control and rigor are applied.

It is no secret that many psychologists dismiss these effects as unbelievable and prefer not to discuss the matter any further. There is a certain justification to this personal position which is based upon some knowledge of the ESP research. A psychologist can easily find sufficient significant and interesting projects of perception to study. Time need not be spent upon a will-o'-the-wisp quality of a very small percentage of the population of normal individuals, a quality which, furthermore, does not mesh with any information which we have about perception. As a very small, elusive, and hard-to-believe phenomenon, it is perhaps justifiably ignored. The past connections at times with exposed charlatans, frauds, and others whose interests are clearly at variance with scientific psychology is also a significant contribution to the personal decision which most scientific psychologists have made to avoid the whole topic. The door is always partly open, however, for future evidence which is compelling.

Summary

Perception is the process of receiving and interpreting information. Sensation is that part of perception dealing with the mechanisms of receiving information, including study of the senses.

Vision converts light to neural energy through the retinal cells at the back of the eye. Neural information travels hence to the occipital lobes of the cerebral cortex. The differences in location and operation of two kinds of retinal cells allow description of several visual phenomena. The sensitivity of the eye to small-sized stimuli, very weak stimuli, and small changes in dimensions of the light stimuli describe the limits of vision.

Audition changes air pressure differences into neural counterparts at the inner ear, after passing through the mechanisms of the outer and middle ears. The human ear is sensitive to tones ranging from 20 to 20,000 Hz. Tone detectability varies with intensity in a systematic fashion. Complex sounds, including noise, combinations of tones, and overtones comprise the sounds normally experienced.

Olfaction (smell) transducers are located in the nasal cavity, but the properties of the stimulus leading to neural transmission are largely unknown. Gustation (taste) receptors are located on the tongue and adjoining mouth surfaces. Four dimensions of gustation labeled sweet, sour, salt, and bitter vary in spatial location of the receptors and interact with the temperature of the stimulus.

Senses of pressure, pain, warmth, and cold are distributed over the skin. Kinesthesis gives information about movements and positions of parts of the body with respect to one another. Equilibratory senses give information about movements of the head and position of the head with respect to gravity forces.

Psychophysics includes measurement and description of observer responses to specified stimuli. Thresholds are average values on an ordered dimension of stimuli at which an instructed observer's response changes, reflecting a change in sense phenomena. Absolute thresholds indicate minimal sensitivity and difference thresholds indicate sensitivity to changes in the stimulus. Weber's law describes the finding that the size of the difference threshold is a proportion of the magnitude of the stimulus; the greater the stimulus, the greater must a change be to be noticed. Threshold measurements follow certain procedures, including the methods of limits and the frequency methods.

The theory of signal detection follows a newer viewpoint of psychophysics which includes techniques for measuring factors other than the stimuli themselves which influence observer responses. The nature of the instructions and the relative consequences of reporting accurately or missing some stimuli are two such factors. Stimuli may be psychologically scaled by asking subjects to compare or rate stimuli on dimensions which have no physically measureable counterpart.

Factors affecting the perception of patterns of stimuli include similarity, proximity, and continuity of the parts, and the closure and figure-ground aspects of the whole stimulus. Objects are perceived as having constant, unchanging properties of brightness, color, shape, size, and location.

Depth perception is influenced by factors of stimulation from near and far objects, and by properties of the receptors, such as the spatial separation of the two eyes and two ears. Sound localization is effected by different stimulus cues reaching the ears, and the distortion of the stimuli by echoes and reflections. The nature of the perception of movements of a stimulus is illustrated by the apparent motion produced by discrete presentations of changing pictures in proper sequence called stroboscopic movement. Illusions provide useful tests of knowledge of perception and demonstrate the nature of the assumptions we make about stimuli. Similarly, perceptual aftereffects provide cues of the perceptual functioning. Attention to stimuli is determined both by certain properties of the stimulus and the expectations of the observer, including motivational states. Subliminal perception describes information received which is not consciously noticed. Extrasensory perception includes the reception of information through other than the known sensory mechanisms, and, for various reasons, is not seriously entertained as a plausible notion by scientific psychology.

SUGGESTED READINGS

Geldard, F. A. *The human senses*. New York: Wiley, 1953.
   An older but still outstanding source for what is known about all of the sensory mechanisms and capacities.
Graham, C. H. (Ed.) *Vision and visual perception*. New York: Wiley, 1965.
   An excellent source of knowledge of vision and some types of perception.
Hochberg, J. *Perception*. Englewood Cliffs, N.J.: Prentice-Hall, 1964.
   An advanced treatment of stimulus aspects of perception. Detailed figures illustrate and contribute to the text material.

Leibowitz, H. W. *Visual perception.* New York: Macmillan, 1965.
   A consideration of eight topics in perception, with a background introduction and a significant reading for each.
Mueller, C. G. *Sensory psychology.* Englewood Cliffs, N.J.: Prentice-Hall, 1965.
   A more recent treatment of sensation than that of Geldard, but it is also written for those not familiar with the area.

Chapter 5

SIMPLE LEARNING

How can behavior be modified to meet the demands of new situations? What are the components of a demonstration of learning? What sorts of factors affect the learning of simple changes in behavior? What sorts of situations have been used by psychologists in the study of learning?

Learning refers to the plasticity of behavior which results from experience. Learning may be quite apparent and deliberate, as in assigned academic studies, or it may be quite subtle and unnoticed, as in the gradual dependence of a beginning smoker upon the movements required for smoking in particular social situations. This sort of experience with new situations producing changes in behavior is often held to be the basic and perhaps the most important determiner of the variety of man's behavior. Learning has been extensively studied and has provided the basic topic of interest for many behavior theories in psychology.

A precise and all-encompassing definition of a term so broadly used as learning is not possible, but some attention to the general bounds of what is called learning will be useful. Common to most definitions of learning are (1) some mention of practice or past experience with events, (2) the notion that the performance changes must be relatively permanent changes in behavior, and (3) some use of the concept of reinforcement. These three factors can be put together into a working definition. Learning is "the relatively permanent change in behavior which results from (reinforced) practice."

There are three conceptual phases in any demonstration of learning: (1) the practice or learning itself, (2) a time delay, and (3) a performance test of what was learned. Certain of these phases may be emphasized in some situations of learning. For example, in studies of the retention of a learned behavior the time delay is the primary experimental variable and its effects are assessed by noting changes in performance after various different delays. In other studies of learning the time delay consists only of some slight pause between successive practice periods (the intertrial interval). The third phase, the performance test, may be a subsequent, special test, or simply the measured strength of the learned response during the next period of practice or trial. Each of these phases are part of a demonstration of learning.

Learning can never be observed directly. Changes in the performance of some bit of behavior are the indications that learning has taken place. But changes in behavior result from other factors as well as learning, including motivation, adaptation, and fatigue. In the usual demonstration of learning the organism is motivated, and the behavior is directed towards a goal. To insure that the observed performance changes are the result of associative or learning factors rather than of changes in motivational states or similar conditions, these latter factors must be held reasonably constant or controlled over the course of the practice trials. When this control has been accomplished, the inference may be made that the remaining performance changes reflect the effects of learning.

The treatment of the topic of learning in this chapter follows a general pattern of moving from simple to more complex forms of learning situations. Section division is made on the further basis of concentration of kinds of experimental investigations which have developed in the course of the study of learning by psychologists. The study of what are believed to be simple, less complex forms of learning are discussed in this chapter.

The majority of experimental research upon simple learning has been with animal subjects, and many of the theoretical formulations have been built upon animal research. The use of animal subjects has been based upon a number of factors. The past experiences of the animals may be controlled as much as is deemed necessary. Animals are readily available for lengthy and/or complicated training schedules. Animals may be motivated by rather extreme stimulation such as electric shock when a high level of motivation is judged to be absolutely necessary. Animals do not have a capacity for symbolically solving simple learning problems as does the mature human learner. These and many other reasons have led to a large amount of research using animal subjects, especially the readily available white rat.

A common approach to the study of complex learned behaviors is to analyze them into functional parts. Complex learned behaviors might be more easily understood (some theorists believe that they may *only* be understood) by such analysis in terms of the known principles of apparently simpler learned behaviors. An understanding of the principles underlying the learning of a simple movement may guide the study of more complex behaviors. Some of these simple models of learned behavior which have been extensively studied are those that are known by the names *classical conditioning, operant conditioning, instrumental learning,* and *selective (discrimination) learning.*

Pavlovian Classical Conditioning

Classical conditioning was discovered by Ivan Pavlov at about the turn of the century in a Russian laboratory of physiology. In the process of studying the secretion of the salivary gland in the dog, Pavlov noted that on certain occasions the dogs produced salivation in the absence

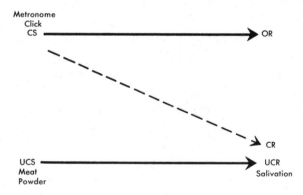

Figure 5-1. The schematic diagram or paradigm of the events in classical conditioning. Presentation of the CS and the UCS together a number of times results in a conditioned connection between the CS and CR like that connection already existing between the UCS and UCR. The CS originally evokes an orienting response (OR) which is not a part of the conditioned response.

of the meat powder and other salivation-producing stimuli placed in the mouth. Becoming interested in this unusual occurrence of salivation, Pavlov investigated the conditions which were sufficient to produce a learned, or conditioned, response.[63]

The basic paradigm or pattern of events of conditioning, as shown in Figure 5-1, involves two stimuli and two responses presented and recorded in a systematic fashion. The *conditioned stimulus, CS,* is presented to the subject slightly earlier in time than the *unconditioned stimulus, UCS.* The unconditioned stimulus always elicits a particular *unconditioned response, UCR.* The conditioned stimulus does not elicit this response before the fact of conditioning but does produce an *orienting reflex.* After the paired presentation of the CS and the UCS on a number of occasions, presentation of the CS alone will evoke a response similar to the UCR if conditioning is established. This new response to the CS is the *conditioned response, CR.* The major interest in conditioning as a study of learning is in the conditions which affect the development or gradual acquisition of the conditioned response to the previously neutral stimuli, CS. (See Figure 5-4.)

In Pavlov's systematic studies, the conditioned response was usually the measured secretions of the salivary gland. The UCS was either meat powder, mild acid solutions, or quinine solutions placed directly into the dog's mouth. The conditioned stimuli that Pavlov used were a variety of visual, auditory, and tactual stimuli. A typical experiment would use a food powder UCS to evoke salivation in conjunction with the beat of a metronome as a CS. Measured saliva flow indicated the strength of the conditioned response on those test trials in which the UCS was not presented. See Figure 5-2 for the essentials of a typical Pavlovian situation.

Figure 5-2. The physical arrangement in a Pavlovian conditioning experiment. The dog must first be adapted to the restraining harness and undergo the surgical insertion of the saliva-collection device before the conditioning may proceed.

TEMPORAL RELATIONSHIPS

Pavlov found that the CS must precede the UCS for conditioning to be established. The interval of time between the beginning of the CS and the UCS in Pavlov's studies varied from nearly simultaneous presentation to a lapse of several minutes. If the CS-UCS interval was sufficiently long, either a brief CS was given with nothing filling the time period before the presentation of the UCS, or a continuous CS was administered, the offset of the CS being delayed until the UCS was presented. The first of these situations was named *trace conditioning;* the second, *delay conditioning* (See Figure 5-3). With either of these

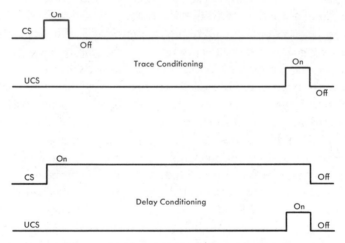

Figure 5-3. The sequence and timing of events in trace and delay variations of classical conditioning. The primary difference is the presence of the CS during the long interval between CS onset and UCS onset.

conditions Pavlov found that conditioning was difficult to produce under conditions of long CS-UCS intervals unless the length of this delay was gradually increased during an extended training period.

EXTINCTION AND RECOVERY

After a conditioned response is established to a CS, the CS may be presented without the UCS. This procedure is called *extinction.* The CR gradually declines in strength during extinction trials. Pavlov found that the speed of extinction of conditioned responses was directly related to the number of conditioning trials used to establish the CR. The greater the extent of the training, the longer the extinction session required to remove the CR.

Pavlov also found that if a period of time intervenes between extinction and a new session of reconditioning, the response previously extinguished to minimal strength spontaneously recovered its full pre-extinction extent (See Figure 5-4). Thus the extinction might be

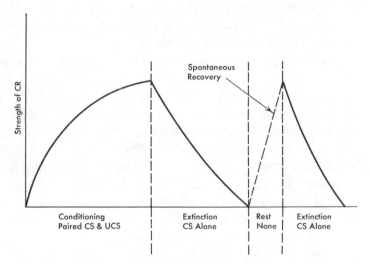

Figure 5.4 An ideal picture of classical conditioning, extinction, and spontaneous recovery of the strength of a response.

likened to a suppression process rather than an erasure of the response. This *spontaneous recovery* was found to be hastened or enhanced by presentation of the UCS now and then during the delay period after extinction. Pavlov found that he could reduce the spontaneous recovery exhibited after extinction by continuing the extinction operation after reaching the point at which the animal ceased to respond. That is, overextinction reduces spontaneous recovery. Full recovery of the CR has not been found in other learning situations, however (See Classical Eyelid Conditioning below).

STIMULUS VARIATIONS

The effect of a novel or unusual stimulus during either conditioning or extinction trials served to reverse the process underway, at least temporarily. A strange stimulus presented during learning of the conditioned response produced a lesser response strength momentarily. This effect is termed *external inhibition*. An unusual stimulus presented during extinction served to increase response strength for a time. This kind of stimulus is called a *disinhibiting stimulus*.

Pavlov also found that if a response was conditioned to a particular stimulus, stimuli similar to that CS would also evoke the conditioned response, but to a lesser degree. This phenomenon is termed *stimulus generalization*. The strength of the generalized response depends upon the similarity between that new, test stimulus and the original CS. Stimulus generalization is found also during extinction. Extinction effects spread to stimuli similar to that used in extinction.

Other experiments by Pavlov established the phenomena called *conditioned discrimination*, in which one CS (CS+) is followed by the UCS and another stimulus (CS−) is not followed by the UCS. The resulting conditioned behavior is a stronger conditioned response to CS+ (which is followed by the UCS) than to CS−.

A peculiar phenomena was reported by Pavlov in these studies of conditioned discrimination. When Pavlov progressively reduced the difference between the CS+ and CS−, the conditioned discrimination behavior was maintained until a small difference between the stimuli was reached. In these very difficult discrimination situations, the animal often ceased responding to all stimuli in the situation and exhibited inappropriate behaviors including falling asleep or fighting the restraining harness. Pavlov termed this reaction to a difficult conditioned discrimination *experimental neurosis*.

MOTIVATION AND CONDITIONING

The extent to which salivary response conditioning was found to be rapid or slow depended to a large extent upon the hunger state of the animal. Pavlov found it nearly impossible to establish a conditioned salivary response using a food UCS when the dog was not hungry. Hungry animals, however, condition readily.

HIGHER-ORDER CONDITIONING

Pavlov also demonstrated *higher-order conditioning*, in which a previously conditioned stimulus now serves, with its conditioned response, as the UCS and UCR for an additional, second conditioning situation. Figure 5-5 presents the schematic representation of such higher-order conditioning. For example, a tone CS has been conditioned to salivation by use of a food powder UCS. This tone is now used as a UCS in an

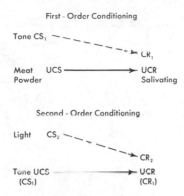

First - Order Conditioning

Tone CS₁

CR₁

Meat UCS ⟶ UCR
Powder Salivating

Second - Order Conditioning

Light CS₂

CR₂

Tone UCS ⟶ UCR
(CS₁) (CR₁)

Figure 5-5. A diagram of the events of higher order conditioning. After the first-order conditioning of salivation to a tone (CS₁), that tone CS is used as a UCS in second-order conditioning of salivation to a light CS₂. Further conditioning using the CS₂-CR₂ as the UCS-UCR relation could theoretically be accomplished, but see the text.

attempt to condition a light CS to salivation. By pairing the light and the tone in the proper conditioning relationship, the light will come to evoke salivation as a CR.

Note that the higher order conditioning situation is also an extinction operation for the acquired UCR. Thus, the second-order conditioning must take place before substantial extinction of the first-order CR (the learned UCR of second-order conditioning) has been effected. Pavlov was unable to obtain higher than this second-order conditioning when the original UCS was food. However, when electric shock was used as the first UCS, Pavlov obtained as high as third-order conditioning.

Classical Eyelid Conditioning

The research situation of conditioning which has received the most attention in recent years is that of the human eyelid reaction to a mild noxious stimulus. The human eyelid closes (UCR) in response to a puff of air to the side of the cornea (UCS). Sensitive apparatus may record the movements of the eyelid and provide evidence that responses of the eyelid do come to be conditioned to neutral stimuli after considerable pairing of some neutral stimulus with the UCS. See Figure 5-6 for a typical eyelid conditioning experimental arrangement.

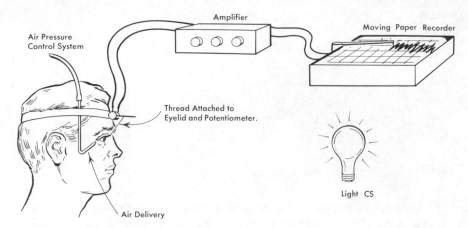

Figure 5-6. The physical arrangement of subject and apparatus in an eyelid conditioning experiment. The movements of the eyelid are transmitted to an electronic amplifier through a headpiece device which presents very little resistance to normal eyelid movements. The subject is free to move his head in a limited fashion. The usual CS are tones and lights. The UCS is an air puff of measured intensity and duration delivered to the cornea. Up and down movements of the eyelid are recorded on moving paper for later analysis.

RESPONSE DEFINITION

A good deal of attention has been paid to methodological problems of eyelid CR techniques, especially the identification of at least four types of eyelid responses in the conditioning situation. These responses are the *conditioned response (CR)*, the *voluntary response*, the *alpha response* to light, and the *beta response*, which is a function of dark adaptation of the subject.

These latter two, the alpha and beta responses, have been shown to be a direct function of the use of a visual CS, and their subsequent identification has neither presented a serious problem nor been a source of argument by workers in the field. The *alpha response* is a very rapid reflex to an increase in light. When the CS is a light, such alpha responses occur very rapidly, before the usual conditioned eyelid response. The *beta response* is also a response to a light as a CS, but of a slightly longer latency and dependent upon the subject being dark-adapted. Some early studies did have artifacts such that the obtained results were different when the effects of these additional alpha and beta reflexes were eliminated from the data.

The difference between a conditioned response and a voluntary response, however, remains a problem. A *voluntary response* is one which is presumed to be given by the subject in a voluntary, volitional manner, apparently so that the subject avoids the unpleasant puff of air to the cornea. One group of investigators has compared the picture (form and speed) of the eyelid response to a stimulus when the subject has been instructed to make voluntary responses, with the picture of the responses of subjects who have admitted after conditioning that their responses were voluntarily produced. The commonality of these responses was noted and summarized in a set of rules for the future identification of voluntary responses.[78] These rules note a difference in the latency, speed, and extent of closure of voluntary versus conditioned eyelid responses. A voluntary response is one with a quick and fast closure yet remaining closed until after the occurrence of the UCS air puff. These empirically derived voluntary-response criteria may be used to eliminate the data of subjects who give a high percentage of such responses. The presumption is made that the responses given by these "voluntary" subjects are a function of different principles than are conditioned responses. Thus the inclusion of these voluntary data might in some way confound and contaminate the study of conditioning. Other investigators have argued against the use of this voluntary response criterion. They have maintained that the responses so identified are simply those of an individual who learns or conditions rapidly, and that the removal of the data of these subjects will distort the picture of conditioning which may otherwise be obtained.[20] This controversy has not been resolved to the satisfaction of all concerned.

MOTIVATION IN EYELID CONDITIONING

Considerable research attention has been directed toward the identification of the source and role of motivation in eyelid conditioning. One such source of motivation has been assumed to be some function of the strength of the puff of air to the eye. It has been found that as the strength of the puff increases, the speed and extent of conditioned responding increases. The relationship seems to be similar to that found between level of motivation and learning performance in other behavior situations. Increases in performance taper off with increases in high levels of strength of puff (See Figure 5-7). The subject may also bring other more personal motivations to the situation. One form of personal motivation is the generalized fear and reactivity called "manifest anxiety." Techniques for objectively measuring manifest anxiety have been de-

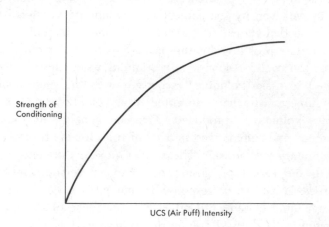

Figure 5-7. A simplified picture of the conditioned strength of eyelid closures after extended training as a function of the intensity of the air puff used during conditioning.

veloped, and high and low anxious subjects may then be compared in conditioning. The evidence has not been unequivocal with regard to either level of conditioning or differences in conditioning as a function of differences in level of measured anxiety, but the majority of studies have indicated that highly anxious subjects condition more rapidly and exhibit a stronger conditioned response than subjects of low anxiety.[79]

STIMULUS FACTORS

The nature of the apparatus controlling and measuring the events of eyelid conditioning allows very close control over the time relations of the reception of the various events. It is not surprising, therefore, that a number of studies have been made of the precise time relationships between the CS and th UCS with a view toward finding that time interval which produces the most rapid and strongest conditioning. Systematic studies have found that approximately one-half of a second (500 milliseconds) is the CS-UCS interval which yields an optimal amount of conditioning (See Figure 5-8). In the eyelid conditioning situation, interstimulus intervals of greater than about two and one half seconds allow little or no conditioning. These facts may be contrasted with Pavlovian salivary conditioning, in which it was reported that conditioning took place at interstimulus intervals of as long as three minutes.

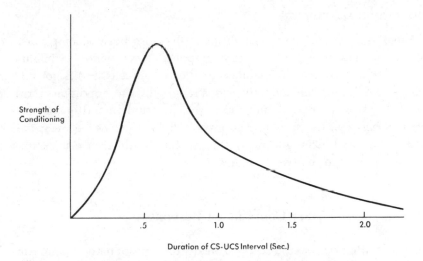

Strength of
Conditioning

Duration of CS-UCS Interval (Sec.)

Figure 5-8. A simplified picture of the strength of conditioned eyelid responding resulting from different CS-UCS time intervals. Very little conditioning occurs unless the UCS follows the CS by about ½ second.

EXTINCTION

It has been found in human eyelid conditioning that the operation of the removal of the UCS in extinction leads to very rapid decrements in CR strength. Conditioned responses that may have taken 50 to 60 trials to be established are seen to decrease to zero strength after but 3 or 4 extinction trials. An explanation for this rapid reduction in response strength has been that the removal of the UCS also removes the motivation to perform the response. That is, once the puff is no longer presented, the motivation of the subject drops to a low level. To avoid this reduction in motivation with extinction, the UCS has been presented at an unconditionable interval after the CS, about two and one half seconds (See Figure 5-8). This extinction technique, which continues presentations of the UCS to the subject, results in a response which loses strength in a much slower fashion, in a fashion similar to that observed in the Pavlovian conditioning situation and to that seen in other learning situations.

Spontaneous recovery has also been demonstrated in human eyelid conditioning, but it has been found to be considerably less in extent than the almost 100 per cent recovery of the conditioned response reported by Pavlov.

Differential or discrimination conditioning has also been accomplished using the human eyelid conditioned response. One neutral stimulus (CS+) is followed by the UCS while the other stimulus (CS−) is not followed by the UCS. The difference in strength of the conditioned response to the two stimuli is a function of the quantitative and qualitative differences between the stimuli. The greater the difference between the conditioned stimuli, CS+ and CS−, the greater the difference in conditioned responding to the two stimuli.

Other Conditioned Responses

Extensive attempts have also been made to condition the change in size of the pupillary opening of the eye based upon the light reflex, the galvanic skin response to electrical shock, the change in rate of heart beat, and other responses for which there are known unconditioned stimuli. These responses differ to a large extent in complexity from that of the eyelid. For example, the galvanic skin response is produced by shock stimulation, but it also occurs to a wide variety of other emotion-producing stimuli. In fact, changes in the galvanic skin response have been shown to be a function of simple skeletal movements. The question, then, must be asked as to which factor in the situation *is* producing the observed galvanic skin response? Was the GSR conditioned directly, or was some other response, say some skeletal movement, conditioned to the CS in such a way that the measured GSR reflected that conditioned skeletal response? Similar questions and arguments can be presented concerning the apparent conditioning of heart rate, of pupillary changes, and others. This is not meant to deny the fact of *some* conditioned response. The fact of the change in the measured response to the presented CS cannot be refuted in most cases. But if these situations are considered as a tool for the study of learning in its simplest form, there remains a question of how many variables and mechanisms *are* affecting these responses, if in fact they are not directly conditioned.

Instrumental Learning and Operant Conditioning

Some simple learning situations require that the animal perform a response to attain a reward. They have been called *instrumental learning* (or instrumental conditioning) situations. The individual's response is instrumental in the attainment of the rewarding state of affairs. Operant conditioning is a similar and overlapping term based upon techniques of changing the strength of existing (operant) responses.

REWARD AND THE PRINCIPLE OF REINFORCEMENT

Under certain conditions some states of affairs appear to be sought after and serve to increase, or *reinforce,* the learning of responses. The *principle of reinforcement* or, as it was described by E. L. Thorndike, the *law of effect,* states that responses which are followed by certain states of affairs are more likely to occur again. That is, they are learned. It is apparent that the definition of a reinforcing state of affairs or *reward* must be accomplished in a separate step from its actual use in the learning situation to avoid a circularity of explanation. As more information is collected about reinforcing situations, a greater certainty emerges about the extent to which certain states of affairs are rewarding.

A rewarding state of affairs is most often the attainment of a goal object or event toward which the subject is motivated. For example, the experience of deprivation of food produces a motive called hunger. Food can then serve as a reward for hungry subjects because it satisfies (reduces) the hunger motivation. A monkey which has been denied normal observation of activities in the laboratory outside of his cage will learn a response for the reward of a peek outside. The suitability of a reward may be determined in each situation by knowledge of the present motivational states of the individual, by knowledge of the principles and laws of motivation, or in some cases, by specific before-the-fact knowledge of which events or situations constitute a reward for the individual in question.

THREE LEARNING SITUATIONS

Three learning tasks which are descriptive of most instrumental learning by laboratory animals are the *runway,* the *operant conditioning box,* and the *shuttlebox.*

The straight *runway* provides observations of the strengthening of a simple response, that of running, in rats. The runway (See Figure 5-9) is typically divided into three functional sections: a starting chamber, a runway section, and a goal section. The animal is released by the removal of a door separating the starting chamber from the runway section. Reward is given in the goal box at the other end of the runway after completion of the run. After each run, the animal is removed from the goal box and either replaced in the starting box for another run or

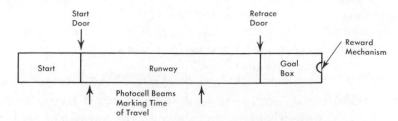

Figure 5-9. **The floor plan of a straight runway for observing the learned running response in rats. The rat is placed in the start section, released according to standard procedures, and removed from the goal box after the run has been completed. The time taken to move through an arbitrary part of the runway is taken as an indication of the present strength of the running response.**

set aside to wait a specified period of time before another run. The time taken by the rat to complete an arbitrary part of the run provides a measure of the response strength. The reciprocal of this time gives a speed-of-response measure of performance.

Operant conditioning, as it is usually employed in the laboratory, uses a small enclosure for an animal, a mechanism for dispensing a reward,

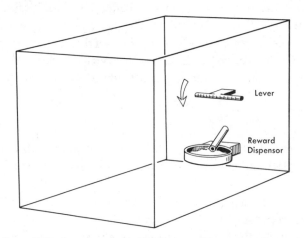

Figure 5-10. **An operant conditioning or Skinner Box for study of the increase in strength of a lever-pressing response. Depression of the lever may produce a food pellet or other predetermined reward. The cumulative total number of lever presses during the conditioning session is usually recorded on moving paper.**

and a simple lever projecting from the wall of the enclosure just above the reward delivery mechanism (Figure 5-10). The animal is placed in the enclosure (called a *Skinner Box* after its originator, B. F. Skinner) for the entire conditioning session; that is, the subject is not removed and replaced between measured responses. Reward delivery and response recording are usually accomplished automatically. After the subject is placed in the Skinner Box, sooner or later explorations are directed toward the lever. Movement of the lever releases a pellet of food. After eating the food the animal is likely to stay near the reward mechanism and lever, and subsequent responses are more probable.

The term "operant" comes from a distinction made by B. F. Skinner,[74] who differentiated *operant* behavior from *respondent* behaviors. *Respondent* behaviors result from known and specifiable stimuli such as the eyelid closure to an air puff or the startle response to a loud noise. *Operant* behaviors are those which simply occur in a situation in which there are no particular instigating stimuli. Animal behaviors of running, stretching, scratching, sleeping and so on may be so described as operant behaviors. The observed frequency of occurrence of the behavior in a situation is called the *operant level*. Operant conditioning results from the application of suitable rewards following each occurrence of the behavior so as to increase the frequency of that behavior. Any operant behavior may be so increased in frequency providing that a suitably rewarding state of affairs is applied properly.

A procedure that is often used to increase the speed of operant conditioning is that of *shaping*. Shaping is the selective rewarding of behavior that is progressively more similar to that desired. At first, any similar operant response is rewarded. Then, the subject is required to approach the lever before reward is given. After an approach response to the lever has been learned, the reward is given only following a touch of the lever, and finally, only complete level presses are rewarded. After a number of such rewards the frequency of operant lever presses increases until the subject presses the lever and consumes the food reward at a high rate. This shaping is also called the technique of *successive approximations*. The selective use of reward can be effectively used to modify almost any response as long as there is an effective reward which can be administered at the proper time.

The *shuttlebox* is a chamber divided into two compartments by a wall with a door or low-wall hurdle (See Figure 5-11). The animal is motivated by an aversive electric shock and is required to leave one side of the two-compartment box and enter the other side. In *avoidance con-*

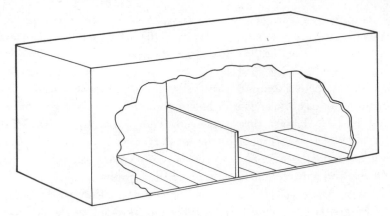

Figure 5-11. A shuttlebox for study of escape and avoidance learning in rats. Electric shock may be applied to the floor in either compartment, motivating the rat to jump to the safe, unshocked side. In simple avoidance learning the onset of the shock is preceded by a warning light or buzzer.

ditioning the cue stimulus is presented some period of time before the grid floor of the box is charged with electricity. The subject has this period of time to reach the uncharged side of the two compartment box. Failure to go there within the time period causes the animal to be shocked. The shock is given until such time as the animal does reach the "safe," uncharged compartment of the box.

In simple *escape learning* the animal is not given a chance to avoid the shock. No cue lights need be presented. The subject is simply shocked by the grids of the floor and the decrease in time taken to escape to the safe compartment with experience in the situation is the measure used to infer learning.

VARIATIONS OF REWARD

Under conditions of consistent reinforcement, the greater the *quantity of reward,* the higher the level of learned performance of the subject. Hungry rats run faster or push a lever more often for a larger than for a smaller piece of food. Figure 5-12 illustrates the typical learning curves obtained for groups given different amounts of reward for the performance of the response. A point is reached, however, where performance does not change appreciably with further increases in the size of the reward. A very large piece of food does not appear to be much more effective as a reward than one which is only slightly smaller.

This relationship between reward and performance must be tempered

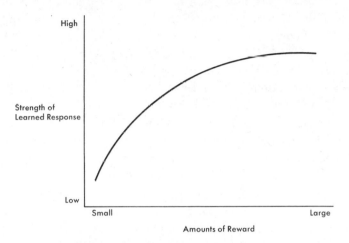

Figure 5-12. A typical relationship between the strength of a learned response after equal amounts of training with different amounts of reward. Performance increases with amount of reward, but less so with increases in larger amounts of reward.

by a qualification. Level of motivation must be held constant. A hungry rat that is fed a large food reward for performing a response will not be hungry very long unless learning trials are widely spaced, allowing further deprivation to re-establish the same level of hunger.

The time that a subject is required to wait for a reward after performing the required behavior is called the *delay of reward.* Long delays of reward produce poor rates of response in most studies. The relationship between delay of reward and performance, however, is not always a simple one. For example, with rats as subjects in a very short runway situation, reward delays of 0, 5, and just less than 10 seconds administered to separate groups produced very little if any differences in performance (average running speed). However, with a delay of 10 seconds or greater, little or no learning of the required response is observed. That is, little or no increase is observed in average running speed with learning trials. These studies indicate that there may be a discontinuous relationship between delay of reward and performance.

NONCONTINUOUS REINFORCEMENT

Reward need not be given after each performance of the required response. What will happen to the strength of the learned response if it is rewarded randomly on half of the learning trials? This is a condition of reward called *partial reinforcement,* in which reward is omitted on some of the learning trials. The subject performs the response, and, on some trials, no reward is given. The performance of partially reinforced subjects is usually compared to that of a control group of subjects which has received continuous (100%) reinforcement.

In most learning situations partial reinforcement leads to a weaker response strength than conditions of continuous reinforcement. In one situation, however (rats as subjects in a straight runway), after substantial training under a partial reinforcement condition, performance has been found to be better (that is, the rats run faster) than under consistent reward.[77] But perhaps the greatest single effect of the partial reinforcement operation is the relative persistence of the partially reinforced response after reward has been discontinued. This will be discussed later as a variable affecting the extinction of responses.

In the operant learning situation, schedule of reward takes on a somewhat more complicated meaning than in simple straight runway tasks. Four basic plans or schedules of nonconsistent reward in the operant conditioning situation can be identified for illustration: *fixed interval, fixed ratio, variable interval,* and *variable ratio.*

The *fixed interval* (FI) schedule fixes a delay period of time between rewarded responses. Under a one-minute fixed interval schedule, after a reward has been given for a correct response, one minute must pass before a response will produce another reward. Responses during the delay period are not rewarded, and subsequent rewards are not given after the completion of that delay period until and unless the response is made again. The rate of response measure under an FI Schedule shows a characteristic set of humps and depressions called *scallops.* Scallops reflect increasing rates of response just before the end of the time period and relatively quiet periods of no responding during the delay period immediately following each reinforcement (See Figure 5-13).

The *fixed ratio* (FR) schedule of reward in operant conditioning is designed so that several responses must be made before the reward is given. Instead of a time period as in the FI schedule, the FR schedule involves the production of a number of responses. An FR schedule of 4 to 1 requires that the animal make four responses; after the fourth response, a reward is given. If the fixed ratio is 10 to 1, the subject is rewarded after performing the tenth response. Relatively high rates of consistent responding can be produced using the fixed ratio schedule and the subject tends to make the required number of responses very rapidly. With high ratios there is typically a post-reinforcement pause in respond-

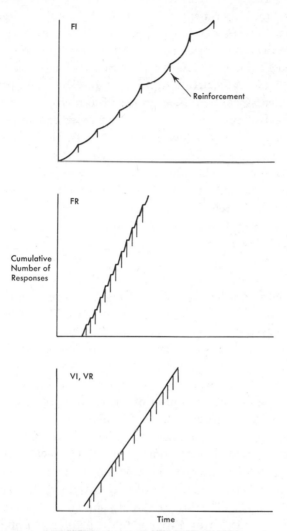

Figure 5-13. Characteristic patterns of responding in operant conditioning under different schedules of intermittent reward. The measure of responding is the cumulative number of responses made since the beginning of the record. A horizontal line reflects no responding, a diagonal indicates a constant rate of response.

ing. A typical pattern of FR responding is given in Figure 5-13. If small increases in the ratio are administered to a rat over a long period of time, performance can be maintained with fixed ratios as high as 200 to 1.

The other two basic kinds of schedules of intermittent reinforcement in operant conditioning are called *variable interval (VI)* and *variable ratio (VR)*. From the experimenter's point of view, one can either vary the interval between responses yielding reward or one can vary the number of responses that the subject must make before each reward. From the trained subject's point of view the application of either of these two schedules is the same. A relatively rapid and consistent rate of response must be maintained since there is no precise information available as to how long a period of time or how many responses intervene between rewards. There may be only a few seconds or a single response before the next response produces a reward, or it may be several minutes or several hundred responses. The rate of response under the varied interval or ratio schedule is consistently stable and relatively high (See Figure 5-13). These VI and VR schedules also produce a very strong resistance to extinction. The VI or VR rewarded response is very persistent in the face of absence of reward.

EXTINCTION

Extinction is accomplished by withholding the reward for a learned response. This is the direct analog of omitting the UCS in classical conditioning. The major performance result of extinction is a decrement in the performance of that response. When the response strength during extinction reaches a level equal to that exhibited before original learning, the response is said to be extinguished. Extinction, thus, is used to describe both the experimental operation of withholding of reward and the observed decrease in the strength of the learned response.

The schedule of reward, as emphasized above, is one of the conditions of reward affecting rate of extinction. A partially rewarded response leads to a much greater resistance to extinction than a response that has been continuously rewarded. This difference is termed the *partial reinforcement effect* or *PRE*. The PRE is highly similar to the resistance to extinction observed after VI or VR schedules of intermittent reward in operant conditioning.

STIMULUS GENERALIZATION

The performance of a learned response in a different situation which is similar to that of learning is termed *stimulus generalization*. The greater the similarity between the stimuli in the original learning situation and the new, test situation, the stronger will be the generalized response. Figure 5-14 describes generalization of a response to similar stimuli varying in intensity. For example, a rat trained to run in a

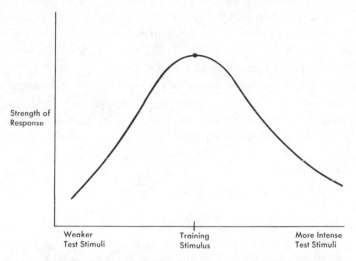

Weaker
Test Stimuli

Training
Stimulus

More Intense
Test Stimuli

Figure 5-14. **Generalized response strength to stimuli differing in intensity from the stimulus used in training. The shape of the function is probably not accurate. The important fact is the monotonically decreasing strength of the response as the test stimulus is made increasingly different from the training stimulus.**

straight black runway will also run in a grey runway, and, at a lesser speed, in a white runway. In this case one dimension, that of brightness of alley color, was varied. Brightness constitutes only a small part of the total stimulus situation, and therefore the consequent effect upon response strength is slight. If a greater part of the stimulus situation were changed between training and test, the generalized response strength would be less. If the color, texture, width, height, and length of the alley were changed, the generalized response would be even weaker; the rat would run much slower.

LEARNED REWARDS

If a neutral stimulus is present at the time that a reward is given for a response, this stimulus may, after repeated such pairings, acquire the power to reward other responses. For example, primate subjects can be taught to perform the specific response of placing a coin-like token in a machine, which then delivers a food reward. After this response has been learned, the subject is presented with a different learning situation in which the reward is the receipt of tokens like those in the first learning task. That is, the animals "work for" a stimulus or object which has been associated with reward. These learned rewards, or secondary reinforcers, may be present in every learning situation. Any cue or stimulus which is consistently present at the time of reinforcement can theoretically acquire rewarding power. The notion of secondary reinforcement is a powerful conceptual tool, potentially explaining the wide variety of situations and stimuli which appear to be rewarding for humans and animals. Common examples often given are the apparent secondary rewarding powers of money, tickets, facial expressions, and other symbols which have conceivably come to signify a rewarding situation. We can describe the effects that these originally neutral stimuli have upon behavior by noting that they are part of and have been associated in the past with other rewarding situations.

NEGATIVE REINFORCEMENT AND MOTIVATION

Learning situations in which aversive stimuli serve as the primary motivator for the learned behavior do not fit readily into the discussion of instrumental learning variables above. The reward for the escape response from electric shock is just that, escape from the shock. Thus the quantity of reward in aversively motivated situations is invariably linked with a significant change in motivation as well. The reduction of the shock which serves as the reward also immediately reduces the amount of motivation. Performance changes are thus a result of two confounded variables. For this reason, aversive or negative reinforcement is here treated as a separate topic.

Systematic studies of the use of electric shock reduction as a reward have indicated that the greater the reduction, the greater the reinforcing power of that reduction. In addition, the stronger the shock, up to a reasonable intensity of such stimulation, the greater the strength of performance of that response. Both of these generalizations ignore the confounding mentioned above.

Analogous to the learned or secondary rewards discussed above, there is a type of learned reward in the aversive motivation learning situation. However, because of the interaction between the operations producing reward and motivation, the stimuli which serve as learned rewards in this kind of situation also function as learned motivators. A hypothetical aversive state produced by these secondary rewards and motivators is called *conditioned fear*. Conditioned fear, in turn, by its reduction, can reward subsequent behaviors. Its motivating properties can also energize behavior.

Perhaps the classic experiment demonstrating these motivating and rewarding properties of a learned fear response was that performed by N. Miller.[57] A rat was placed on one side of a two compartment box and electric shock was applied to the grid floor. The rat was allowed to escape the shock by running through a door into the other compartment which was painted a different color and had a solid rather than grid floor. The escape response was learned readily. In a second part of the experiment, shock was no longer applied and the door was closed. The door would open, however, if the rat rotated a small wheel above the door. With no motivation except escape from the learned fear-producing stimuli, over half of Miller's animals learned to turn the wheel and escape to the non-feared side of the box. Furthermore, the speed with which the rats performed the wheel-turning and escape responses increased markedly with further trials, suggesting that the new response was being reinforced. This new wheel-turning response was performed without the application of the primary motivator, electric shock. The source of the motivation and the reward for this second learned response are theorized to be fear and the reduction of fear, respectively. A number of other plausible interpretations of the results of this experiment have been eliminated by the results of additional experimentation.

The fear mechanism also serves as a theoretical device in the explanation of the persistence of a response acquired in an avoidance learning situation. In avoidance learning the successful subject has learned to respond to a previously meaningless cue to avoid an aversive motivation such as electric shock. After the subject has learned to avoid the shock, there is no obvious source of motivation. Yet such avoidance responses are continuously performed in a vigorous fashion with no signs of the decrease in response strength that one might predict from the observation that there is no further external motivation. The motivation and reward for these avoidance responses are theorized to be fear conditioned to the cue and escape from fear-producing stimuli, respectively. These factors account nicely for avoidance response persistence when shock is omitted.

Selective (Discrimination) Learning

Selective learning in its simplest form consists of rewarding one stimulus-response sequence and not rewarding another. After some training has been given on a simple discrimination task, the performance of the rewarded response may be similar to that of most instrumentally rewarded responses. Performance of the nonrewarded stimulus-response sequence decreases in a fashion similar to that of an extinguished instrumentally learned response. The increasing difference between the strength of the rewarded and nonrewarded response may be noted directly when separate measures of each response are available or it may be indirectly reflected by the subjects' choices between the two responses. As the rewarded response becomes stronger, that stimulus-response sequence will come to be chosen.

A comparison of the phenomenon of generalization with that of discrimination shows that the two appear to function in opposition to one another. Rewarded learning of a response to a particular stimulus increases response strength to similar stimuli. This process is called generalization. Discrimination training defeats this generalization by not rewarding the subject when he responds to other stimuli which are similar to the rewarded stimulus. Thus, discrimination training breaks up the effects of generalization, and it is the effect of generalization which the negative phase of discrimination training serves to eliminate.

Three classes of selective learning problems may be usefully distinguished. First are those problems for which the selection of the appropriate stimulus and the response to that stimulus requires a great deal of trial and error behavior for the subject. A second kind of selective learning experiment rewards responses to one of several slightly different stimuli or a particular pattern of responses to a sequence of stimulus cues. The third kind of selective learning problem rewards one of two very likely stimulus-response sequences. These problems may be named, respectively, *trial-and-error, multiple discrimination,* and *simple discrimination.*

TRIAL-AND-ERROR SELECTIVE LEARNING

The most famous trial-and-error selective learning task is the puzzle-box, originally used by Thorndike.[84] Typically, a hungry cat was placed in the box and allowed to discover the pattern of responses which would effect an escape from the box and attainment of the food reward placed in easy sight outside of the box. The correct mechanism for opening the door in the box was often something like pulling a string hanging from the center of the box. Early attempts by the cat to escape and reach the food reward were usually directed at forcing the door and attacking the cage. Later behaviors were directed at the other facets of the cage, and eventually, the cat would happen upon the string and make the required pull. On a second learning trial, the same cat will again take a substantial period of time doing other things before pulling the string. But gradually the escape is effected in smaller and smaller periods of time. After several training trials, the cat performs the required response to escape almost immediately upon being placed in the puzzle box.

Some important features of this sort of trial-and-error task which distinguish it from other selective learning problems are (1) a low initial strength or likelihood of the solution response, (2) a relative freedom of the animal from being "pushed" by the situation into making any particular response, and (3) a nearly nonexistent connection between the rewarded stimulus-response sequence and the acts required to approach and consume the reward.

MULTIPLE DISCRIMINATION LEARNING

The multiple discrimination learning situation may consist of either a sequence of simpler discrimination tasks or require selection among a collection of equally likely stimulus-response alternatives.

The sequence problem is best illustrated by the complex serial maze shown in Figure 5-15. The subject must make the correct turning response at each of a series of choice points. Reward is given in the goal box. The time to reach the goal box and the number of errors made en route have been shown to decrease regularly with training trials. An analysis of the pattern of errors shows that as training progresses those errors at choice points nearest the goal end are eliminated first.

Another sequence problem which has been used to compare the relative learning abilities of several animal species is the *temporal maze*. Shown in Figure 5-15, this task requires the subject to make a pattern of choices at the same point in the maze. Each choice leads the animal back to the starting point (S) until the proper number and sequence of turning responses at the choice point (CP) have been accomplished. A pattern of single alternation (turns of Left-Right-Left-Right) has been found to be readily learned by most of the species tested. A double alternation problem (Left-Left-Right-Right) was solved only by phylogenetically more highly-developed species, such as the primates. An analysis of the cues available to the subject at the choice point may give some ideas as to the nature of the difference between these two patterns. The single alternation pattern requires only that the subject detect which turn was made on the previous trial. For species such as the rat, this information might become available by smell sensitivity. This will not work for the double alternation pattern, however, since at the time of the second and third choices, the same stimulus information is present, that

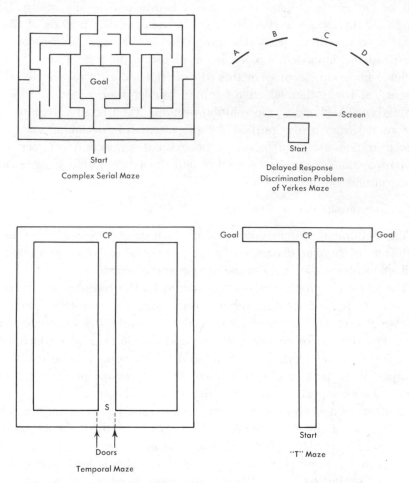

Figure 5-15. Several discrimination tasks for animals. The complex serial maze may take a variety of forms in which a series of choice points face the subject in traveling from "Start" to "Goal." In the delayed response discrimination problem, the subject is placed in the start section, the location of the reward is in one of the four positions A, B, C, or D as indicated, a screen is lowered to prevent visual inspection of the alternatives for a specific length of time, the screen is raised, and the animal is released to get the reward. The temporal maze is a T-maze in which alleyways and doors shunt the animal back to the choice point for several choices in each run. The rewarded pattern of these choices is specified (See text). The T-maze has but one choice point.

the previous turn was to the left. There appears to be no available difference in stimuli at the choice point upon which to base a differential response. One may hypothesize a memory for numbers of previous events or a counting facility in successful double alternation problem solvers.

The multiple response selection form of the multiple discrimination task is illustrated by the Yerkes maze, shown in Figure 5-15. The subject is released to make one response to select the location of the reward. The subject may then be either removed, it an incorrect choice is made, or permitted to find the correct rewarded response choice.

One problem which has been investigated on a variant of the Yerkes maze has been called the "delayed response" discrimination problem. In this task the subject is first taught to select that one of the alternatives which is designated by a cue at the start of the trial. A period of delay is then initiated during which the animal is not permitted to view the discriminanda. After the delay period the subject is released to make a choice. Like the temporal maze problem, this task has been used to compare certain species of animals in intellectual facility. Lower animals, including rats, dogs, and cats, have a great deal of difficulty performing this response correctly when the delays are of any appreciable length greater than about 5 seconds. Some phylogenetically higher species maintain correct choice performance through delays of several minutes between cue and response. Again, an analysis of the available cueing stimuli indicates that this task, like that of double alternation in the temporal maze, requires a sort of memory for events for which there are no present cues. There are no apparent distinctive stimuli to guide the correct response.

SIMPLE DISCRIMINATION LEARNING

The simple discrimination learning selective tasks compare the relative strength of two stimulus-response sequences. One of these sequences is rewarded. The other sequence is not rewarded but is similar on many dimensions of comparison so that it receives a considerable strength by generalization. With training the difference in strengths of these two responses increases such that the subject comes to make the rewarded response with a greater frequency or strength.

The single T-maze illustrated in Figure 5-15 is perhaps the most used simple discrimination task. The discriminanda may be different forms, different colors, or other visual cues, or they may simply be the different responses of turning right or turning left. The subject may be allowed to correct his errors, or he can be removed from the apparatus after making incorrect choices. The Lashley jumping-stand variant of the two-alternative discrimination problem has been judged to be especially effective in guaranteeing that the subject attends to the stimuli which are the cues. In a simple T-maze the subject could make a choice response without attending to the cues, but the jumping stand requires that the subject orient and aim his jump at the chosen one of the cue stimuli which are placed on the front of the landing platforms.

Certain complications of preferences and habits interfere with the study of the discrimination learning in these simple selective learning situations. For example, many rats show a preference for a particular one of the two responses. This has been called a turning preference. Most subjects respond in an alternation pattern on a series of training trials. For these subjects, if a right turn was made on one trial, the probability that a left turn will occur on the next trial is very high. Certain levels of illumination are preferred by rat subjects. If the discrimination is between alleys or large cue stimuli which are painted dark vs. light colors, and depending upon the level of light striking the walls, the rat will strongly prefer one or the other. These complications should serve to illustrate that even this "simple" learning situation is not without numerous technical problems which are not always readily resolved.

A simple discrimination learning task different from the single T-maze and the jumping stand is that presented by the Wisconsin General Test Apparatus.[25] This device, shown in Figure 5-16, was designed to present a series of discrimination problems to primate subjects. A typical problem presents three stimuli which differ on the dimensions of shape, size,

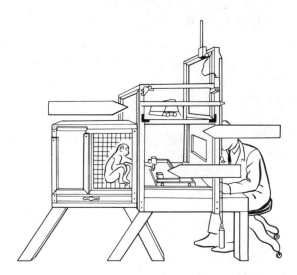

Figure 5-16. The Wisconsin General Test Apparatus permits a variety of similar discrimination problems to be presented to animal subjects.

and color. The subject's task is to select the stimulus which is different from the other two on one dimension such as color. A food reward is placed beneath the blue and not under either of the yellow stimuli. When this discrimination has been learned, a different collection of three stimuli may be presented for which, again, the odd one of the three hides the reward. A series of "oddity" problems may be learned in this fashion. It has been found that with primate subjects each successive problem is learned more quickly. This has been called the development of a *learning set* by H. F. Harlow.[25] The animal has acquired a set to learn; that is, the animal has learned how to learn. After many such problems have been mastered, the subject samples the new collection of cues only once to determine the relevant dimension and maintains correct performance from the first trial.

Considerable research effort has been directed towards some problems of interpretation of simple discrimination learning. The basic question is whether the subject has learned to locomote to a particular *place* where the reward may be found or whether the subject has learned some particular stimulus-response connections. Does a correct turn in a T-maze to the rewarded cue signify that a particular turning movement or approach to a specific cue has been learned or that the animal has learned the overall picture of where the reward is located and has used a kind of "cognitive map" along with any cues which fit into that map to reach the reward? This sort of analysis of the learned discrimination response has not been fruitful for deciding between the opposing theories of learning which generated the views, but it did focus a great deal of attention upon some controls required in the discrimination learning situation. Such research has indicated that the animal will use any cues available as long as they are consistently related to the reward.

Summary

Learning is a concept describing changes in behavior, which result from (reinforced) practice. It is demonstrated by changes in performance after conditions of controlled practice. Learning cannot be observed directly, but must be inferred from performance changes.

Pavlovian classical conditioning is the association of a response (salivation) to a neutral stimulus (a bell) by pairing that stimulus with another stimulus which previously evokes that response (meat powder). Pavlov manipulated aspects of the basic procedure in administering trace and delay conditioning, extinction, external inhibition, disinhibition, higher-order conditioning, and conditioned discrimination. Under other conditions Pavlov noted spontaneous recovery, stimulus generalization, and experimental neurosis.

Classical eyelid conditioning is a modern learning situation much like Pavlovian classical conditioning. The conditioned response is a closure of the eyelid to a tone or light stimulus which has been paired with a puff of air to the side of the eyeball. Though this situation has problems of response definition, it has provided a more accurate assessment of the optimal time relations and the effect of motivational variations upon classically conditioned responses. Several other responses have also been conditioned using similar procedures.

Learning to attain a reward crudely describes instrumental learning and operant conditioning. The effect of reward, according to the principle of reinforcement, is to increase the likelihood of occurrence of responses which it follows. Goal objects which are appropriate to reducing present motivations serve as rewards in many demonstrations of learning.

Typical reinforced learning situations include the straight runway in which the speed of a motivated subject in finding a reward at the opposite end of the apparatus is measured. The Skinner box requires the depression of a lever to produce a reward. Finally, the shuttlebox measures the movement of the subject to the other side of a two-compartment chamber to escape an electric shock.

Some obvious variables affecting reinforced learning include the size of the reward, the delay of the reward, and the schedule at which the reward is delivered (per response). Extinction is the operation of and results from the withholding of reward after the response has been made. Extinction performance is strongly affected by the schedule of prior reinforcement.

Neutral stimuli may acquire the capacity to reward after having been associated with another reward, and are called secondary rewards. Aversively motivated learned responses are importantly affected by secondary rewarding and motivating cues, which produce a state called conditioned fear. Fear-producing cues subsequently motivate and reward behavior in the absence of the original aversive motivation.

Selective or discrimination learning tasks take several forms. Trial-and-error learning permits a relative freedom in response for a subject learning the rewarded behavior. Multiple discrimination learning requires learning either a pattern of limited-choice responses or the selection of one of a large number of similar responses. Simple discrimination learning tasks involve but two stimulus-response sequences, one of which leads to reward.

SUGGESTED READINGS

Deese, J., and Hulse, S. H. *The psychology of learning.* New York: McGraw-Hill, 1967.
A *textbook of learning. From conditioning to complex human learning, the presentation includes the important and accepted situations and generalizations.*

Goldstein, H., Krantz, D. L., and Rains, J. D. (Eds.) *Controversial issues in learning.* New York: Meredith, 1965.
An annotated collection of readings describing theoretical positions on issues of conditioning, rewarded learning, discrimination learning, and others.

Hall, J. F. *The psychology of learning.* New York: Lippincott, 1966.
An empirically oriented presentation of the evidence about learning. Both simple and complex, animal and human research situations are included.

Kimble, G. A. *Hilgard and Marquis' conditioning and learning.* New York: Appleton-Century-Crofts, 1961.
A detailed presentation and summary of conditioning and rewarded learning studies. Some applications to more complex behaviors are also presented.

Prokasy, W. F. (Ed.) *Classical conditioning: A symposium.* New York: Appleton-Century-Crofts, 1965.
A collection of recent research problems in conditioning, presented for the advanced student.

Underwood, B. J. *Experimental psychology* (2nd edition) New York: Meredith, 1966.
Excellent discussions of methodology and experimental design of learning studies.

Woodworth, R. S., and Schlosberg, H. *Experimental psychology.* New York: Holt, Rhinehart and Winston, 1954.
Sections on learning emphasizing the historical development of research problems. Sections on maze learning and certain types of discrimination learning are especially unique.

Chapter 6

HUMAN LEARNING
AND RETENTION

What are the important factors of learning by man of, for example, a new athletic skill? What is the nature of learning new associations and meanings for words? What determines how much is remembered and forgotten? What role does concept learning and language play in how we think?

The study of learning phenomena has been greatly enhanced by the analyses and discoveries made using the simple learning and conditioning situations described in the previous chapter. Study of these simpler learning situations has provided a rich theoretical background for the investigation of learning. These studies of simpler learning have also provided a wealth of concepts and phenomena to be considered for their relevance to other situations. The simpler situations have developed the concepts of motivation, reinforcement, generalization, and incentive, which have been adapted to deal with more complex learning situations.

Different concepts and lines of research on problems of learning have come from study of man's learning of motor skills, verbal habits, concepts, and problem-solving techniques. These approaches have not conceived of the learning situation as an example of the essence of learning, nor have they viewed them as isolating the basic factors determining all of learning. They have concentrated instead upon study of the factors which affect that learning. What factors speed up or slow down the learning of the responses? What factors lead to greater retention of the learning? How may problem solving be controlled and made more efficient? The study of complex human learning has also emphasized the analysis of the overall performance into sub-processes and mechanisms which contribute to and are normally a part of that performance. What sorts of associations comprise a learned motor skill? What affects the association of verbal units?

Four basic human learning research situations will be described along with some of the principles, concepts, and theories which have emerged from study of these situations. These task situations are those of *motor skills, verbal learning, concept formation,* and *problem solving.*

Motor Skills Learning

Sensorimotor skills are learned behaviors which require an interaction between sensory and motor functions. Motor skills studies have demonstrated the importance of particular factors. Careful study of the perfection of patterns of motor activity has emphasized the role of informative feedback necessary for learning, the transfer of training from one task to another, and the effects of relative lengths of work and rest periods.

MOTOR SKILLS TASKS

A variety of simple and complex tasks have been used to study motor skills learning. Some of the most common situations to study very simple motor skills include copying letters backwards and writing or tracing while observing the performance through a mirror. A more complicated task is the *pursuit rotor* which has been very useful for studying the time factors of work and rest periods. The pursuit rotor requires keeping a jointed stylus in contact with a target which moves in a constant-speed circular pattern somewhat like following a dime near the edge of a phonograph record. Variations of the pursuit rotor task may involve altering the pattern of movement of the target or requiring observation of performance through a mirror. A somewhat more difficult task is posed by the *two-hand coordinator,* in which each hand controls one direction of movement of a pointer by means of a crank. A moving target below the pointer follows an irregular but foreseeable pattern at a constant speed. Many variations of tracking tasks are now possible with the use of electronic apparatus and the cathode-ray tube. Spots of light may be used as targets for subject-controlled pursuit lights and these presentations may be manipulated in unlimited patterns and schedules. Finally, the USAF *complex coordinator* (Mashburn apparatus) is a three-control simultaneous tracking task for which the controls and target displays have a rough resemblance to the control dimensions of an airplane. The essential components of some of these tasks are presented in Figure 6-1.

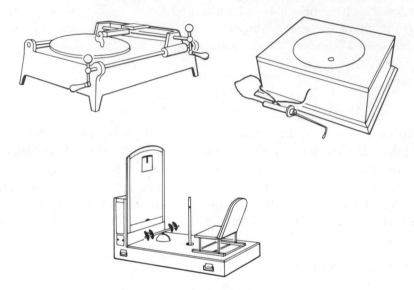

Figure 6-1. Motor skills learning apparatus: the pursuit rotor, the two-hand coordinator, and the complex coordinator. (After Fleishman, E. A., Dimensional analysis of movement reactions. *Journal of Experimental Psychology*, 1958, *55*, 438–453.)

DISTRIBUTION OF PRACTICE

The relative distribution of practice periods during a learning session has been a factor of interest for many years. It has been observed in many different situations that the shorter the work periods, the better the performance upon the task. The length of the rest periods, though, can also be varied independently of the length of the work periods. Rest period length is directly related to goodness of performance. The longer the rest (within limits), the better has been the performance. Performance under *massed practice* for which there is no rest period (and thus the work period is of maximum length) differs from that of *distributed practice* which has moderate lengths of rest and work periods. This difference may reflect both the rest period effect and the work period factor.

The most recent systematic investigations of distribution of practice have concluded that this factor affects only the performance of a skill and does not appreciably determine the amount *learned*.[7] With a substantial rest period intervening between practice and test, there is little difference between groups trained under massed and distributed practice, as shown in Figure 6-2. The increase in performance following rest

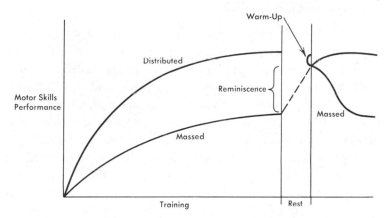

Figure 6-2. Motor skills performance under distributed and massed practice conditions, before and after a substantial rest period. These ideal curves illustrate the increase in performance (reminiscence) observed after a rest period following massed practice. The slight retardation in performance of both groups on the first trials after the rest period, but not thereafter, reflects the lack of and subsequent attainment of "warm-up."

after massed practice is called *reminiscence*. Theoretically this performance difference can be accounted for by the assumption that an inhibitory factor builds up during practice and dissipates during rest periods. The dissipation of the inhibitory factor during the long rest after massed practice conditions accounts for the increase in performance observed after such a rest.

TRANSFER OF TRAINING

The phenomenon whereby learning one skill helps or hinders the learning of a second skill is called *transfer of training*. If training on a first task makes learning a second task easier than it is for a control group which has not learned that first task, there is positive transfer. If learning the first task makes learning the second more difficult, there is negative transfer.

In learning motor skills, negative transfer has not been reliably demonstrated. A pair of tasks has not been found for which learning one significantly retards the learning of the second. Positive transfer among motor skills, however, is both logical and readily demonstrated. Almost any aspect of learning one motor task seems to have some contribution toward making the learning of a different task easier.

FEEDBACK OR KNOWLEDGE OF RESULTS

The factor called *feedback* or *knowledge of results* (KR) has been an especially important variable in the analysis of motor skills learning. KR is somewhat analogous to the reward factor of the simple learning situations. KR, like rewards, may motivate, reinforce, and give information about preceding responses. Rewards in simple learning situations are usually held to be most important for the first of these two properties, motivation and reinforcement, while KR in motor skills learning seems to be most important for the information that it imparts about the responses and their effectiveness. Thus there are likely to be some important qualifications upon the analogy and transfer between rewards for simple learning and KR in the motor skills situation. An analysis of the task and the kinds of responses to be learned is especially valuable in this connection.

Motor skills tasks may be ordered on a dimension of "intrinsic KR." That is, the nature of some tasks allows some amount of knowledge to be conveyed to the subject about the effectiveness of his responses and the overall efficiency of his performance. The pursuit rotor task allows a fairly high degree of intrinsic KR, while many of the electronic cathode ray tube display tracking tasks may be programmed to restrict KR to a high degree. Therefore, adding some amount of KR over that already present in a task would not be expected to greatly improve performance on tasks for which intrinsic KR was initially high, as in the pursuit rotor. However, the addition of KR to tasks where there is little intrinsic KR may greatly improve performance.

Subjects performing tasks with a high degree of intrinsic KR usually have a strong dependence upon that KR for proper execution of the responses. Variations in the amount and time relations of the normal KR may greatly affect performance. If feedback delays are introduced, the responses are distorted as if they too were being delayed to match the information coming later. Distortions of speech may be demonstrated by presenting a subject's speech to his ears after a small time delay. Great difficulty in writing may also be demonstrated when visual observation of the hand movements is delayed through a television system.

Variations in knowledge of results applied after the completion of the task have different effects than would be expected from the analogous effects of reward manipulations in simple instrumental learning situations. The length of the delay of *extra* KR after the performance of the task has little if any affect upon the task. (Lengthy delays of reward, however, make simple learning very slow.) Apparently the KR effects of this kind, when applied between trials on the task, are equally effective whenever they are applied during that period.

Feedback or KR may improve performance on some tasks in which intrinsic feedback is not quick enough or present in sufficient amounts. Addition of KR, called *augmented feedback,* has been shown to improve performance dramatically on some tasks. The responses of many jet aircraft lag appreciably behind the pilot's control responses. This intrinsic KR delay leads to "overcontrolling" and very slow learning of properly sequenced control responses. The application of speeded up KR through the action of a computer which predicts the later performance of the airplane from the present state and control actions makes the task markedly easier to learn. The application of more sensitive and quicker-acting instruments or additional informative display devices improves the ease of operation of many kinds of machinery which otherwise take many hours of learning to grasp the "feel" of the machine. Improving the timing and quality of feedback improves motor skills performance dramatically.

Verbal Learning

The most obvious difference between the behavior of human beings and other species of subjects in learning experiments is the use of language or verbal symbolic processes. The human, with a meaningful word such as "larger," can describe the essence of a discrimination experiment to himself and communicate it to others. With a few words a man, after noting a difference in stimulation, can set up a rule for his subsequent behavior in a conditioning situation: "the air puff probably won't be given any more, so it may be safe to relax and not blink when the light comes on again." From the age of about two years, human beings develop a complicated set of utterances and symbols which allows communication between men and permits the abstraction of experiences and memories into a few simple symbols which are easily remembered.

What is usually called "verbal learning" is the study of the processes which connect these symbols to one another for use in memory, thinking, and communicating. How is it that "car" and "pad" are more easily learned and associated than "hfx" and "tuh"? What kind of word is most easily associated with "xocer"? Who can learn a different language most quickly and how should this learning be undertaken? Present research in verbal learning can give some fairly precise answers to this kind of question.

The study of verbal learning was first systematically investigated by Ebbinghaus in Germany about 1880.[14] Many techniques introduced by Ebbinghaus for the study of memory are still widely used some 80 years later. For example, the nonsense syllable unit, the serial anticipation learning procedure, and certain other procedures and measures of retention were first used extensively by Ebbinghaus. The emphasis upon discovering empirical relations rather than developing global theories of verbal learning, which is characteristic of present research in verbal learning, can also be seen in the early example of Ebbinghaus' work.

GENERAL PROCEDURES

The most often used methods of presentation of materials in verbal learning research are called *serial learning* and *paired-associates learning*.

The *serial learning* task requires the subject to memorize a list of materials in order, as in learning the alphabet, a ten-digit telephone number, or an old English poem. Each item in the list is usually presented alone for a specified period of time. The items are presented for study in the same order. The subject's task is simply to connect all of the items in a chain in memory such that they may be evoked in order upon demand.

In *paired-associates learning* a list of pairs of items is presented and the subject is to recall one item of a pair when presented the other, as in learning the English equivalent of French words or the batting averages of baseball players. No systematic relations are present among the pairs in the list. In contrast to the constant order of the items in a serial list, the pairs are in a random or different order each time they are presented. The response member of each pair is associated in memory with the stimulus member.

There are several variations in these basic methods. One variation is called the "anticipation" procedure, in which each stimulus item of a paired-associates list may be presented alone in a test period prior to the exposure of both members of the pair to the subject for study. From the subject's point of view, the stimulus item of the pair is shown first and the correct response must be recalled in the few seconds before it also appears. The subject must "anticipate" the response. In another variation of paired-associates learning, the "study-test" method, the pairs are presented separately in one phase for study, and in a second period a test is made of the learning by presenting only the stimulus members of each pair.

In these simple learning tasks the items to be learned are presented in certain relationships with the primary attention of the researcher centered upon the ways and mechanisms by which the subjects produce the required responses. When the subject responds correctly, he has, by definition, learned the task. But the way in which the subject performed his job in each part of the task may have varied. Subjects bring to the learning situation a well-established system of verbal habits. Some of these habits are highly personal and unique. For example, the paired-associates items "GED-HAK" may be the initials and part of the automobile registration designation for one of the subjects in the experiment. These items are very easy for that person to learn but may be the most difficult to associate for a number of other subjects. Other associations may be made by using simple rules, bizarre similarities of the items to things which are more easily associated, and a wide variety of other ways limited only by the ingenuity of the subject. Some of the items may even be associated by simple repetition (raw learning) with no apparent or recallable helps.

Considering the number of ways in which the association tasks can be and are performed, it should not come as a surprise that (1) performance of a group of subjects on these tasks is quite variable, and (2) factors which are assumed to affect the learning process will likely have various effects depending upon the kind of techniques that the presented task allows the subjects to use. A major point is that the verbal learning tasks are not especially suitable for the study of "raw learning" defined as the formation of associations between unrelated stimuli and responses. The learning of verbal materials in these experiments is complicated and variable because prior associations do exist to some degree and the performance upon different items reflects, in part, that strength of association.

The rate of presentation of items in laboratory verbal learning is usually well controlled. In those studies where rate is not a manipulated variable, the usual time given to study a particular pair of items or to produce a response is about two seconds. The number of items in a serial or paired-associates list is generally greater than that number which may be recalled immediately after presentation (see "short term retention"), but not too much longer. Lists of 10 to 15 items to be associated are common.

VERBAL LEARNING MATERIALS

Language habits complicate the study of verbal learning in the laboratory. To control these habits, it has been popular to use memory materials which are not familiar to the subject. Ebbinghaus devised the nonsense syllable for this purpose. Nonsense syllables are three-letter, consonant-vowel-consonant, nonwords such as LEH, TOZ, and FAZ. Other artificial materials which have been used include consonant syllables, (CXZ, LPF, JGK, LPL), paralogs (LOFIP, CARUM), in addition to common words, numbers, and meaningful and nonmeaningful spatial forms.

Unfamiliar, artificial verbal learning materials have internal similarities and differences which importantly affect learning ease. These properties include the factors of *meaningfulness* and *similarity*.

The *meaningfulness* of an item is usually measured by some variation of asking subjects to report associations which occur when that item is presented. Specific definitions have used the number of associations produced in a limited period of time (averaged over a large number of subjects). The speed or latency of the first association response to a stimulus may also define its meaningfulness. Other attempts at assessing meaningfulness have included asking judges to rate how meaningful or familiar an item appears using a scale of numbers or to rate how quickly one might learn that item in the context of a given association experiment. All of these techniques produce scales which are related fairly well to one another. Measured meaningfulness also correlates well with judgments of another factor, "pronounciability."[90]

The greater the meaningfulness of the items to be learned, the faster the learning. This plausible, direct relationship between meaningfulness and speed of learning seems to be exhibited in all presentation situations of verbal learning. The specific definition of meaningfulness used is not important; meaningfulness facilitates learning.

A good deal of attention has been paid to analyzing the factors underlying the facilitation of learning by meaningfulness of learning materials.

Some investigators have tried to show that meaningfulness is the direct result of frequency of experience of the material.[90] This very plausible notion has been only partially successful in explaining the available data, however. Some of the differences in scaled meaningfulness which produce differences in learning have not been shown to be reducible to differences in frequency of probable past exposure.

The *similarity* of materials concerns the amount of redundancy or confusion which exists among the items of a list. This redundancy can be defined and measured by the repetition of letters or some other factor in the learning materials. Such repetition defines *formal similarity. Meaningful similarity* is defined by some measure of synonymity of meaning of the items. Meaningful similarity takes into account the similarity of meaning among words such as ICE, FRIGID, COLD, and SNOW.

The effect of similarity among verbal materials is not quite so simple and straightforward as is that of meaningfulness. The two types of similarity and their effects in different presentation situations must be considered. Serial learning is impaired by the presence of either formal or meaningful similarity among the items. The greater the similarity, the poorer the performance. Formal similarity among the stimulus items of paired-associates lists impedes learning, as in the serial presentation situation. Formal similarity among the response items of paired-associates lists, however, seems to have no effect upon learning of the list of pairs.

The effects of these similarity variations are perhaps more easily understood if the presence of similarity is thought of as reflecting interference or confusion among the items. The greater the confusion, the longer the period of time that is required by the subject to sort out the proper places and relationships among the stimuli. The absence of a retarding effect of similarity among the response members of a paired-associates list may be accounted for by the additional property of similar items that, being alike to some degree, they are more easily remembered as a group. The subject may find it easier to learn such a group of similar items than a comparable group of dissimilar items. This may facilitate the learning of the responses, in that memorizing one group is easier than learning a collection of unrelated items. This response learning facilitation may thus offset the hypothesized interference produced by that same similarity.

PRESENTATION FACTORS

The length of the list will affect the speed of learning in most verbal learning situations. This appears to be a quite obvious function; the longer the list, the longer it takes to learn it. But we find that it is disproportionately true with very long lists, and this simple relationship also breaks down with very short lists. In very long lists, greater and greater amounts of additional time are required to learn successive items as they are added to a list. The average time to learn each item (total learning time divided by the number of items in the list) is greater in very long lists than in moderately long lists. This may be a function of greater total interference among the larger number of items in the longer list. In very short lists learning is more rapid than would be predicted by the average speed of learning items in moderately long lists. When the presented items are so few that they may be immediately recalled, "learning" appears to be very rapid and probably follows a different set of lawful relations. (See the section on "short-term memory" later in the chapter.)

The general rule of time factors in verbal learning is that the faster the rate of presentation, the poorer the performance. There are a number of specific time relations which are important in verbal learning studies. These time factors include the *interitem interval* (and the related duration of exposure of a particular item), and the *intertrial interval* (also called distribution of practice.)

The *interitem interval* is defined as the time between the beginning of the presentation of one item and the beginning of the presentation of a second item. This interval affects learning in combination with the length-of-list factor such that as the interitem interval is shortened, the length-of-list effect is enhanced. Conversely, the greater the amount of time each item is exposed, the less difference the length of the list will make. Evidence from studies which manipulated the interitem interval usually shows a constancy of total learning time. Other things held constant, if the interitem interval is doubled, the trials to learn the list will be halved, while the total study time to learn the list remains the same. This constancy holds over an intermediate range of interitem intervals of about 1 to 6 seconds.

The *intertrial interval* is the length of the rest period between each presentation of the list. Intertrial intervals are usually considered to be either short periods of time less than 8 seconds (massed practice), or longer periods of time greater than 15 seconds (distributed practice). Most of the systematic investigations of intertrial interval have been concerned with the difference between these two kinds of rest periods. A methodological problem is the control of the activities of the subjects during this rest period. The purpose of this control is to prevent the subject from covertly rehearsing the materials of the learning task. Such unobserved learning has been made improbable by a variety of devices. Some of the more commonly used activities are simple color-naming games and perceptual-motor steadiness tasks.

The principal result of the many intertrial interval studies seems to be that there is a relatively small effect of distribution of practice in verbal learning. The effect that has been observed is that distributed practice usually facilitates learning. But there is an interaction with what has been called the conditions of interference among the response items in paired-associates learning.[88] The interference may be caused by formal similarity, meaningful similarity, or simply list length. The interaction between intertrial interval and interference among the response items is such that there is a balance between these two factors. There is an optimal amount of interference which produces a maximum distributed practice superiority. The greater the amount of response interference, the shorter must be the intertrial interval for such facilitation to occur.

SOME INTERPRETATIONS IN VERBAL LEARNING

A common theoretical background of interpretations of verbal learning includes the assumption that one can break the verbal learning task into operationally specifiable stimuli and responses. This is a logical analysis, using stimulus and response concepts in conjunction with rationally conceived mechanisms like interference. In most cases this assumption has been fruitful. Occasionally, however, these basic, conceptual notions may be in question. For example, it has been found that that which is presented as the stimulus is not always identical with that which is actually being used by the subjects to perform the task. That is, the "nominal" or presented stimulus was not the "functional" or actual stimulus.

One principal put forward to summarize this problem of effective functional stimuli is that the subject will use the minimal or least stimulus required to perform the task. The subject will not use any more information than is necessary. This leads to the notion of *encoding* stimuli and responses. A common conception is that the presented materials are encoded by the subjects into units which are easier to use in the task. The parts of stimuli and responses which are excluded in the coding process are reinstated when required in the production of responses. For example, association of the paralogs DIMOG-CATUS may be encoded and associated DOG-CAT. The last of the response word is reinserted when necessary for emission. Factors which facilitate encoding speed up the learning process. Practice at encoding is one of the ways in which skill and speed of learning may be improved. Successful encoding may be the key to fast learning of complex verbal materials.

One logical analysis of paired-associates has been especially useful to understand differences in the speed of learning caused by similarity variations and other factors. The *two-phase* conception of verbal learning,[89] now widely accepted, states that there are two aspects to learning each item pair. First, the subject must "integrate" the responses. That is, he must learn the responses themselves such that they may be emitted in the task. Second, the subject "hooks up" or associates the stimulus and response items so that given the stimulus, the response may be produced.

The first phase, that of response integration, accounts for the increase in time to learn tasks which have poor response meaningfulness. Meaningful responses already have a high degree of integration, while nonmeaningful items consume time for that learning. The lesser effect of meaningfulness when it is applied to the stimuli than when it is applied to the responses in paired-associates tasks follows directly from such notions. The stimuli need not be integrated to the same degree as the responses because the stimuli are always available to the subject and need not be emitted by him. Differences in response meaningfulness, however, affect the overall learning performance. Considering the lesser amount of integration required of stimulus items than of response items, it follows that differences affecting the learning of the stimuli and of the responses will produce corresponding differences in the performance of the task.

TRANSFER OF LEARNING

Transfer of learning is the effect which learning one task has on the learning of another. The simplest experimental arrangement to demonstrate this kind of effect is that provided in Figure 6-3. An experimental group learns both tasks, and a control group learns only the second. This simplest demonstration is subject to certain errors, however. In actual comparisons, other factors must be controlled in order to conclude that there have been specific transfer effects of the first task upon the second. Factors which have been demonstrated to be present include the nonspecific transfer factors called *warm-up* and *learning-to-learn*.

Warm-up is a common and descriptive term for the fact that perform-

	Task A	Task B
Experimental	X	X
Control	No	X

Figure 6-3. A simple experiment designed to demonstrate transfer of learning. An experimental group learns Task A before Task B, while a control group learns only Task B. A comparison of learning on Task B will reveal whether Task A facilitated (positive transfer) or inhibited (negative transfer) the learning of Task B.

ance is generally better after some practice by a "cold" subject. In learning a first list the subject becomes "warmed-up" to the nature of the task and the situation and this positively transfers to (that is, improves performance on) the second task. Warm-up is an effect which is noticeable only in the first few minutes of performance after a rest period. Figure 6-4 shows the warm-up improvements in performance during the first practice periods of each day.

Learning-to-learn describes the improvement in successive, similar tasks undertaken by a subject. This improvement is noted over and above the transfer between the specific contents of each task. This effect is shown in Figure 6-4. Simply practice at performing in that learning situation leads to more rapid learning of each successive task. Mecha nisms which may underlie the phenomenon of learning-to-learn are changes in technique or general performance style that are warranted, paying more attention to relevant as opposed to distracting aspects of the tasks, and the gradual development of a store of useful memory tricks and devices.

The specific transfer between tasks may be positive, negative, or neutral. That is, the second task may be learned more rapidly, more slowly, or at the same rate when preceded by the first task. Some specific theoretical suggestions about the direction of transfer have come from a logical analysis of the similarity among the elements of the tasks. The extent to which the stimuli of the two tasks are similar or different and the extent to which the responses are similar or different make up two dimensions. Four transfer situations using extreme values on these two dimensions are presented in Figure 6-5. The condition of

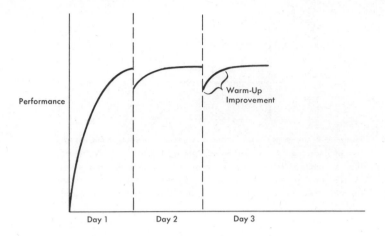

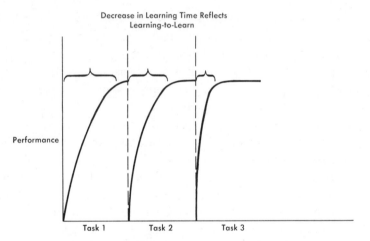

Figure 6-4. **Warm-up and learning-to-learn effects upon the performance of tasks.**

learning the same or similar responses to the same or similar stimuli leads to a high degree of positive transfer. Learning different responses to the same stimuli induces negative transfer. Learning different responses to different stimuli is judged to have no transfer effect, and learning the same responses to different stimuli may yield some positive transfer if response learning or integration is an appreciable part of the tasks. These basic predictions have been verified to a certain degree, although the specification of a dimension of similarity is troublesome. What degree of difference in responses is necessary before negative as

Stimulus
Similarity

	Similar	Different
Similar	Substantial Positive Transfer	Little or No Positive Transfer
Different	Negative Transfer	No Transfer

Response
Similarity

Figure 6-5. **Specific transfer from one task to another as a function of the presence of response similarity and stimulus similarity between the successive tasks.**

opposed to positive transfer will result from learning these responses to the same stimuli? At what point of that hypothetical continuum will there be no transfer observed? Specifications of this kind have not been shown with the materials typically used in learning tasks. The analysis, though, has been useful as a conceptual model of task comparison where some good guesses as to relative similarity are possible.

The degree of original or first list learning and the time delay between the two tasks have effects upon transfer. Positive transfer, when present, has been found to increase with increases in training on the first task. Negative transfer may be maximized, however, when the first task learning is rather weak. Too much first task training removes the negative transfer effect if it is otherwise present. Transfer effects do not seem to be affected by the time interval between the two tasks as long as there are no relatively detailed memories required. Great delays between tasks in which recall of detail is necessary leads to a reduction in the observed transfer.

Retention

Retention is persistence of learning after practice has ceased. *Forgetting* refers to the material which was once learned and is now not available. The many observations about forgetting which man has formulated into folklore are often right but are also contradictory. We have noted that those who learn slowly remember well, but we also have observed that the bright, quick-to-learn individual remembers what he has learned. Though the evidence about memory processes is far from complete, what has been found is somewhat surprising. But first we will need some consideration of the techniques of retention measurement.

MEASUREMENT OF RETENTION

Two direct measures of retention are called *recall* and *recognition*. Situations for the two methods differ in the availability of the responses to the subject. This availability of responses leads to greater amounts of measured retention when recognition is used in place of recall.

Recall tests of retention require that the response be brought from memory in response to general instructions or specific cues. The essay examination is basically a recall measure of retention. Effective recall requires a great degree of response learning or response integration.

Recognition measures of retention of learning require that the "correct" response be recognized or identified from among alternatives. The multiple-choice examination is superficially a recognition test of retention. Response learning is minimal since the responses are presented to the learner.

Relearning is an indirect measure of retention. Relearning requires that careful measurement of the original learning be made. The relearning technique is a comparison of some measure of learning vs. relearning in the same units. The difference in learning and relearning scores directly reflects the extent of retention. The *savings score* of relearning is derived from the difference between original learning and relearning. The relearning technique is judged to be especially sensitive to memories which cannot be recalled or recognized. Any slight improvement in performance during relearning reflects such weak memories.

TWO FACTORS OF RETENTION

The two experimental factors which most importantly affect the amount of material retained are the time interval before retention is measured and the strength of the original learning.

The *length of the forgetting interval* is related to retention in a highly predictable fashion, as shown in Figure 6-6. The longer the retention interval, the less retention. The losses are greater soon after learning, though, than they are after a substantial period of time has passed. The curve of retention after a long forgetting period is so flat that it would appear that there is no further memory loss. Memory losses are slow

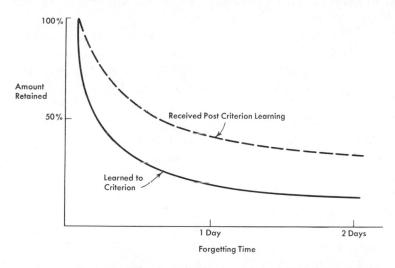

Figure 6-6. **Amount retained over a forgetting interval in which there is no further learning. Large amounts of forgetting occur shortly after practice ceases, but the memory losses become less and less until an almost stable amount of material is retained over further periods of time. The effects of additional pre-test in learning beyond the established criterion are marked. See text.**

after the initial forgetting, but there are still some decreases in retention with further passage of time.

The *degree of original learning* is obviously related to retention. The stronger the original learning, the greater the retention, forgetting time held constant. The importance of the strength of original learning cannot be overemphasized. Careful examination of the effects of a number of plausible manipulations has shown that with degree of original learning held constant these manipulations do not affect retention. For example, retention is the same despite differences in the learning ability of the subject, differences in the relative ease of learning of the materials, or differences in the conditions of interference of the learning materials. Slow learners and fast learners forget at the same rate. Easily learned material is probably not retained any longer than is difficult-to-learn material. These facts are a bit hard to assimilate with what we commonly observe about learning. We note that some things are easily remembered, and it appears that this is so because they are highly meaningful or familiar. These common observations have not been controlled for strength of learning, though. The meaningful materials encountered in uncontrolled commonplace situations are usually learned to a much greater extent.

Added retention resulting from learning after the task is once learned to a particular criterion is often quite marked. Such *overlearning,* as shown in Figure 6-6, leads to slower forgetting and a lesser loss with time.

THEORIES OF RETENTION

Three notions describing the mechanism of forgetting have been advanced. These different theories are not contradictory, and actually complement one another in certain areas. The theories differ primarily in the phenomena observed and in the approaches which the investigator applies to the study of forgetting. The three forgetting notions will be referred to by the names *interference, decay,* and *motivation* theories of forgetting.

The *interference* theory is really a collection of notions which describe the forgetting arising from interfering memories. The basic mechanism is that we forget one item because another item interferes by taking its place. Two interference principles will be described. These are the mechanisms called *retroactive inhibition* and *proactive inhibition.*

Retroactive inhibition and *proactive inhibition* can be formally defined as the differences in performance observed in the simple experiments outlined in Figure 6-7. Retroactive inhibition is the interference with the memory for one task caused by the learning of a second task between

	Experimental Tasks		Delay	Retention Test
Proactive Interference	B	A		A
Control	——	A		A

Retroactive Interference	A	B		A
Control	A	——		A

Figure 6-7. Experimental designs defining proactive and retroactive interference. Differences in the retention of Task A by the two groups indicate the amount of such interference.

the original learning and the retention test. Proactive inhibition is the interference caused by the learning of other tasks before the reference task is first learned. Both proactive and retroactive inhibition are similar to transfer in that they are comparisons of the effects of learning similar tasks in a fairly close time period.

Both kinds of inhibition or interference are increased as the similarity of the reference and interference tasks is increased (to a point—consider the extreme of identical tasks), and both effects are increased by an increase in training upon the interfering task. The effects of delays, however, are different. The greater the retention test delay in the proactive inhibition experiment, the greater is the inhibition, while increases in the retroactive inhibition test period lead to no change or to slight decreases in the interference produced.

Retroactive inhibition is very close to a common sense notion of interference. Later learning covers up and hides the earlier memories. Proactive inhibition, though, is not so plausible and comes in conflict with other common observations about learning and retention. For example, laboratory research has shown that the greater the *number* of similar materials that are learned before the reference task, the poorer will be the retention of that latter task. But this seems to say that as we learn more and more about something, the poorer will be our retention for the most recent learning. A gross prediction could be made on this basis that as we grow older, retention for recently learned materials become poorer, and that the brighter person, as he learns more than his duller friends, will be less able than they to remember what was last learned. But these predictions are not verified by controlled or uncontrolled observation. One can more easily recall recent materials, bright individuals remember better, and age does not produce a decrease in retention in this way.

The solution for this apparent dilemma must come from some other observations of learning and retention. One important factor, of course, is the degree of learning of the materials, which, as noted above, so often makes a critical but unnoticed difference in common observations of learning. As we acquire more knowledge about certain topics, each additional bit becomes more firmly learned than earlier bits because of the meaningful framework which pervades that topic. As one learns more about the principles of human learning, each succeeding fact and observation fits better with the group and is thus likely to be retained better than the earlier facts. The structure of knowledge which is nearly always present in our common experiences of memory is not present in the artificial materials of the proactive inhibition experiments.

A second factor of importance in reducing proactive inhibition in many situations is the operation of a *selector mechanism*.[90] The selector mechanism allows the learner to recognize easily the materials which constitute the present task and thereby to exclude extraneous materials, even though in another sense they are similar and relevant. The task as a whole can be thought of as acquiring some meaning of its own to the extent that its membership is quickly learned. This selector mechanism makes these materials different from other potentially interfering items and experiences of memory. The tasks of the laboratory have also been shown to reflect the operation of a selector mechanism, but after a few similar tasks, it breaks down. As each similar task is presented it becomes more difficult for the subject to distinguish reliably the items of this task from those of the last.

These speculations, in one sense, beg the question of proactive interference with non-laboratory forgetting. Mechanisms are sought and advanced to account for the apparent discrepancies between laboratory based prediction and the commonplace observations of memory. The mechanisms advanced suggest the additional factors which may affect memory outside of the arbitrary controls of the laboratory. The principles which are sound and adequate to describe the narrower range of laboratory learning and forgetting are admittedly insufficient to account for the uncontrolled observations of daily life. As the theory is developed, however, a wider range of phenomena will be included.

The *decay theory* of forgetting can be stated simply that as a function of the ravages of time memories fade away. Less poetically, the decay notion does not speculate on mechanisms of forgetting, but implies that the normal maintenance processes of parts of the body, especially neural regeneration, lead to forgetting. Memory is lost through time and the consequent changes of the body. This notion is quite plausible because our daily experiences with forgetting are that memories seem to slowly recede with time. This notion is also quite difficult to examine scientifically. In an adequate test the effects of interference must be eliminated or controlled during a forgetting period. The decrease in the strength of that memory as a function of time alone must be assessed. The control problems are difficult, if not impossible. Even the state of sleep is not one of minimal interference. The interference mechanisms which are known to produce forgetting will probably never be entirely eliminated. The question of whether there is forgetting through time alone, in addition to the very potent interference factors, remains to be demonstrated. The decay theory is a plausible notion but one that is not very useful to describe the facts of forgetting.

Motivated-forgetting theories are not generally applied except to situations of complex and relatively severe existing motivations. The fundamental notion is one that derives from Freudian personality theory and concerns the mechanism called repression. Memories are repressed when their recall would evoke great unpleasantness for the individual. Retention of happenings involving anxiety, conflict, and frustration is poorer than that for less motivationally involved circumstances. A severe case of repression may be described as one of amnesia, in which the personally relevant memories of a person may be absent for a time. Controlled experimentation is difficult on these topics, and the motivation theories of forgetting are primarily useful notions for dynamic personality description and not for working theories of forgetting.

SHORT-TERM MEMORY

A different set of procedures for studying the retention process are those of short-term memory. *Short-term memory* is the extent to which presented material remains available for short (roughly less than 30 seconds) periods of time. Three varieties of short-term retention can be described: the *immediate memory span*, the *running memory span*, and the newer, *single-unit presentation* method.

The *immediate memory span* is the number of similar bits of information which can be correctly repeated after one exposure. A series of numbers, for example, is presented, and immediate recall is tested. If recall is correct, a new series of numbers one digit longer is presented. The memory span may be defined arbitrarily as the greatest number of digits which the subject has repeated perfectly. This immediate memory span has been found to vary from about 5 to 9 items for most of the normal population tested, and has led some investigators to believe that this limit reflects an inherent limitation of the capacity of man to process information.

The *running memory span* is much the same, except that the subject cannot actively prepare to repeat back the series, as is often done during the presentation of the digits to measure immediate memory span. The running memory span is the number of items which can be correctly recalled backwards in the series just presented at a point indicated by the experimenter. A continuing series of some length is presented to the subject. At some point the subject is asked to start at the last given item and list backwards the previous items presented.

The *single-unit presentation* method of measuring short-term retention is a relatively new technique in which one bit of information is presented and the subject immediately engages in some activity which prevents him from actively attempting to rehearse or memorize that item. The item to be recalled has often been a nonsense syllable and the intervening activity has consisted of counting backwards rapidly from a three digit number. After the desired interval has passed, the subject is interrupted and asked to recall the nonsense syllable. Measuring the short-term retention of a large number of subjects at each of several retention intervals results in a curve of the forgetting of that item like that shown in Figure 6-8.

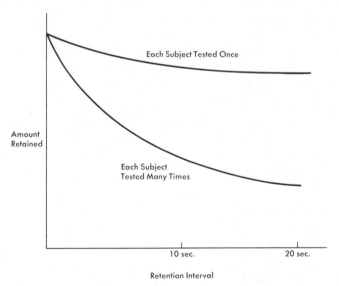

Figure 6-8. Short-term retention for nonsense verbal units over periods of time which are filled by unrelated activities.

Proactive and retroactive inhibition has been found to be an important factor in these studies of retention also. If more than one measurement is made with each subject using the single-unit presentation technique, it has been found that the average memory losses over time are much greater. Apparently, the proactive inhibition of the earlier short-term retention tests produces more rapid forgetting of later bits of information. Single-unit presentation studies have also shown greater retroactive inhibition effects as the intervening (anti-rehearsal) activity is more similar to the units to be recalled.

Concepts and Thinking

The complex activity which we call thinking has been described as the development and manipulation of symbolic representations of the world. Problems may be solved and new works created by the internal processing and reorganization of symbols. The symbols may be words which describe concepts, or the symbols may be less specifiable ways of organizing the experiences of that individual in the world. The discussion of this sort of higher activity of learning will be limited to a consideration of the formation of concepts, the relationship between language and thinking, the solution of specifiable problems, and some comments on the process of creative thought.

CONCEPT LEARNING

The concept reflects an inference about an individual's capacity to classify objects. A *concept* is a relationship or rule for classifying, rather than something possessed by the objects or the subjects. An individual has formed a concept when his behavior in classifying is in accord with the system or rules defining that concept. Knowledge of the concept "redness" is expressed by the subject in classifying or identifying objects which are red as opposed to non-red.

One distinction which can be usefully made between ways of acquiring concepts involves the degree to which the items are already perceived as different. Using the notions of verbal learning, one may express this difference by the degree of response learning which the subject must complete in identifying instances of the concept. The identification of "redness" among items which are either one value of red or of a greatly divergent hue requires little response learning and has been called *concept attainment* by some investigators. This concept attainment may be contrasted with *concept formation,* in which the subject must learn to distinguish the relevant difference in characteristics before the classification may be demonstrated. The concept of wind-packed vs. loosely-fallen snow may require considerable perceptual learning before the subject is able reliably to distinguish these varieties, especially if the subject has lived only in tropical climates where snow seldom or never occurs. Concept formation involves both the discrimination and the classification.

A second distinction which is useful between concept learning examples is the extent to which correct concept identification requires mere observation as opposed to formulation of a principle or rule for guiding choices. Another way of making this distinction is to note that the first of these learning tasks requires only that the experimenter present positive and negative instances of the class, for example, red vs. non-red, wind-packed vs. non-wind-packed snow. This has been called *attribute learning*. The second or rule-guided concept learning involves a more complex relationship defining the concept such as "the larger square in the presence of a circle *or* the triangle in all other displays of stimuli" or, in baseball, the conceptual rules defining a "strike" include "a pitched ball reaching the "strike zone" in front of the batter which is not hit *or* a hit ball which is "foul." This rule-guided concept learning may be called *principle learning* to distinguish it from the attribute concept learning.

Systematic study of the factors influencing concept learning has been undertaken on a large scale only very recently. Consequently, only some tentative and somewhat non-specific generalizations can be made. Concept learning has been found to suffer under conditions of greater stimulus complexity and more informative stimuli. Further, the less perceptible the stimulus differences, the poorer is the concept learning. Time delays during presentation and confirmation of stimuli and responses during controlled concept learning have been found to have some effect. Delays up to eight seconds before knowledge of correctness of the classification have not been shown to have an effect upon concept learning. Delays after that KR but before the next instance of stimuli is presented to the subject have been found to improve concept learning. A delay of about ten seconds, for example, after the KR of one trial and before the next stimulus display is presented has been shown to lead to better concept learning than does a condition of no such delay. In some theoretical approaches this factor has been reasoned to allow time for the subject to process the KR information and perhaps develop a new strategy for classification.

Individual differences of motivation, intelligence, and past experiences with similar concepts would be expected to have an influence upon concept learning, but have not yet been extensively investigated.

The symbols which we call language are obviously a vehicle by which we convey information about the results of thinking to others. But to what extent does language structure thinking activity? Language facilitates performance on many kinds of concept learning tasks, but it is not logically necessary in all such situations of conceptual learning. Clearly, the application of verbal responses to stimulus classes provides a measureable response dimension from which to infer thought. Words are what we observe. Without language, the study of thought processes becomes much more difficult. For example, recall the complexity and involvement of the temporal and delayed discrimination situations described in the previous chapter as tests of the thought capacities of nonverbal animals.

The primary question is whether language processes, which are available and used in the communication of the results of thought, are also influential in the determination of that thought. One writer suggested an affirmative answer which has since been named after him, the Whorfian hypothesis.[95] This notion states in part that language differences between peoples caused differences in the ways that those people view the world. Some evidence for this notion can be readily gathered. Eskimos, who have a greater number of words describing types of snow, find it easier to think about problems relating to snow than do natives of tropical regions. It can be shown that there are differences in thought between individuals who have different language structures relating to that particular subject. Note that such evidence is not analytical, but merely presented an observed relationship between presence of language and presence of thought measures. The causal relation has not been established. This very plausible and provocative notion of the influence of language on thought has been a source of considerable argument and has remained only a hypothesis.

PROBLEM SOLVING

Problem solving is directed thought—thought processes aimed at specifiable goals. A particular set of circumstances which we call a problem requires a set of solution responses. Problem solving has been studied for a longer period of time than have other types of thought. A few important factors affecting problem solving have been isolated.

One collection of factors which impede problem solving may be described as those which elicit inappropriate responses. *Mental set, func-*

tional fixedness, and the *implicit assumptions* which the subject has made about the problem are examples of factors leading to incorrect solutions.

The factor of *mental set* may be illustrated by the water jar problems of Luchins.[44] This set of problems requires the subject to attain a given quantity of water from an unlimited supply by use of three measuring devices, jars of specified capacities. The quantities involved in the consecutive tasks are described in Figure 6-9. It may be seen that the first

Problem Number	Jars to be Used			Required Amount
	A	B	C	
1	29	3	—	20
2	21	127	3	100
3	14	163	25	99
4	18	43	10	5
5	9	42	6	21
6	20	59	4	31
7	23	49	3	20
8	15	39	3	18
9	28	76	3	25
10	18	48	4	22
11	14	36	8	6

Figure 6-9. Luchins Water Jar problems. Assuming an unlimited water supply use the measuring jars A, B, and C to obtain the required amount. See text.

few of these tasks (2–6) are solvable only by a particular order of pouring operations (B–A–2C). Several test tasks are solvable by that same order but also by a much simpler rule (7, 8, 9, 10, 11). A further test task (9) is *not* solvable by the well-established procedure of the first tasks, but only by a different order. The extent to which these latter test examples are attacked by the old rule or require a longer time period for solution than that required by other subjects who have not experienced the earlier order measures the effect of the mental set that those procedures have developed. Thus, by structuring the past problem-solving experiences of subjects, a set to respond in a less–than–optimal fashion may be formed.

The factor which has been labelled *functional fixedness* is the impedance to problem solving which is introduced by the well-known function of certain of the presented stimuli. Functional fixedness may be illustrated by the task which requires that the subject tie together two strings which are hanging from the ceiling in a room. The strings are sufficiently separated that the subject cannot reach one while hanging onto the other. The only tool supplied is something like a pair of pliers or a mousetrap. Either of these tools has a definite and specific function. The solution to the problem requires that these tools be used in an unconventional manner, as a simple weight at the end of one string. This weighted string is then set to swinging toward the other and may be reached as it swings close by. The kind of tool supplied in this situation affects the likely solution time. The more fixed and invariant is the use for the tool, the less likely will an early solution of the two string problem be made with that tool.

The effect of *implicit assumptions* upon task solution may be illustrated by the 9-dot problem shown in Figure 6-10. These nine dots, arranged in a square pattern, are to be connected with four straight lines which are drawn without removing the writing instrument from the paper. Try to solve the problem before reading on. This problem is usually difficult to solve because of the assumptions which the subject makes about the task which in this case are a function of the perception of the stimuli. The primary hindering assumption is that the four drawn lines must stay within the confines of the square. The problem may be solved by lines which leave the area described by the square pattern of dots.

Figure 6-10. The nine-dot problem. Connect the nine dots with four straight lines without lifting your pencil from the page.

These examples do not exhaust what is known of problem solving, but do serve to describe the importance of impeding factors. Certain strategies in solving problems have received experimental attention in practical applications. For example, what are the optimum strategies for finding the malfunction in a piece of electronic gear? One such strategy involves applying a set of tests which isolate the trouble. Questions are asked which have a yes-no answer and which limit the problem to more and more restrictive areas of the apparatus.

Problem-solving analysis has also been made using computer simulation procedures. A computer program is devised to mimic the problem-solving behaviors (successes *and* errors) of actual subjects. The various logic steps and correction procedures used by the subject are thus emphasized.

Creative Thought

Two kinds of creative thinking may be distinguished by the terms *free-association* and *problem-oriented*. *Free-association* is the sort of running thought which is always present when no particular purpose to thought can be identified. Such thoughts are free in the sense of not being purposefully directed to some end. Day dreams and night dreams are well-delineated examples of this kind of free-associative activity of the thought processes. Free-associative thoughts have provided a tool and a source of information for the study and understanding of personality, and will be considered again briefly in a later chapter. *Problem-oriented* creative thought can be more readily manipulated for controlled observations. Some notions of the conditions which lead to or suppress directed creative thought may be ascertained. Aspects of personality which are correlated with creative responses have also been identified.

The thought conditions which lead to a creative performance include having available a relevant set of facts, a problem requiring a creative or new solution, and a pattern of thoughts having the characteristics of producing remote connections between the aspects of the situations. This latter condition appears to be the crucial difference between many creative persons and those who appear equal in other respects but are not creative. The frequent production of ideas which seem unrelated to previous ideas will logically lead at some time to an idea which solves a problem and in a creative way. It is, of course, necessary also that the creative thinker recognize the connection as being useful for the problem solution. But this may only be another way of saying that the creative thinker makes a different connection between the elements of the situation.

Some of the characteristics of creative persons have been assessed by comparing creative scientists and artists with the "normal" population. These characteristics identified include a preference for the intrinsic beauty of solutions and a tendency to prefer theoretical formulations. The creative are above average in intelligence test scores, but are not necessarily outstanding. They have a rather good memory for detail and also seem to produce those memories at what seem to be unusual times. These are not characteristics which will allow precise identification of the creative person from a given collection of people, but they do seem to point toward the dimensions underlying creative thought.

One kind of creative endeavor deserves special mention. The technique called "brainstorming," which involves grouping people to solve a problem in a free environment, has been widely used and alleged to be useful. To the extent that the individuals are actually free in producing ideas for evaluation, the technique allows a rapid and efficient development of a solution. But the brainstorming technique has not been shown to produce any greater numbers or more effective solutions than would be obtained by setting the same individuals to working alone on the problem. That is, it does not function to change the qualitative aspects of creative thinking, but it does perhaps make the information transmission more rapid.

Summary

Motor skills tasks are performed better when practiced during distributed sessions. Positive, but not negative, transfer is readily demonstrated with motor skills. An important factor for learning and performing motor skills is the kind and amount of informative feedback of the performance of the skill.

The learning of verbal materials in the laboratory usually follows the serial or paired-associates procedures. Important factors of verbal learning include meaningfulness, similarity, and time factors of presentation of the materials. The association task as actually undertaken by the learner often involves mediation through other associations and processes of encoding and simplifying the presented stimuli.

Retention of learned materials may be assessed by the basic methods of recall, recognition, and relearning. Retention is primarily determined by the strength of the original learning and the length of the retention interval.

Mechanisms presumed to produce forgetting are retroactive and proactive inhibition. These inhibition mechanisms, together with a collection of other assumptions, make up what is called the interference theory of forgetting. Forgetting occurs because of interfering past and future associations which are similar. Other notions of forgetting include the decay theory and motivated forgetting.

Short-term memory describes the availability of presented materials for short periods of time. Three assessment techniques are the immediate memory span, the running memory span, and single-unit presentations.

Concept learning involves the classification of objects. Some concept learning requires only the discovery of the classification rule, while other problems present stimuli for which the relevant dimensions for classifying must first be perceptually identified and its quantities distinguished.

Language is used in the expressions of thoughts by man, but is it the vehicle for thinking? The Whorfian hypothesis answers that problem solving is better upon topics for which more language concepts are available, and that different languages are correlated to thoughts by those using that language.

Problem solving is directed thought. Problem difficulty may be effected by mental set, functional fixedness, or the limitations imposed by the subject's expectation about the problem solution.

Creative thought is assumed to be a function of conditions which allow the unusual association of ideas.

SUGGESTED READINGS

Bilodeau, E. A. *Acquisition of skill,* New York: Academic Press, 1966.
  Papers presented at a conference concerning the acquisition of motor-skills, in which the emphasis is upon learning rather than the skills.
Cofer, C. N. *Verbal learning and verbal behavior,* New York: McGraw-Hill, 1961.
Cofer, C. N., and Musgrave, B. S. *Verbal behavior and learning.* New York: McGraw-Hill, 1963.
  Both books present papers and discussion on topics of verbal learning which were presented at a conference of leading researchers.
Deese, J., and Hulse, S. H. *The psychology of learning.* New York: McGraw-Hill, 1967.
  A basic text in learning. Several chapters discuss human learning and retention of verbal habits and motor skills.
Ellis, H. C. *The transfer of learning.* New York: Macmillan, 1965.
  An original paperback describing the methods and findings of studies of transfer. Several selected original papers concerning transfer are enclosed.
Hall, J. F. *The psychology of learning.* New York: Lippincott, 1966.
  A basic text in learning. Several chapters concern human learning and retention.
Klausmeier, H. J., and Harris, C. W. *Analyses of concept learning.* New York: Academic Press, 1966.
  Presented papers at a conference concerning classifying and learning concepts. Topics range from the philosophy of concepts to the teaching of concepts in the classroom.

Melton, A. W. *Categories of human learning.* New York: Academic Press, 1964.
Papers by seven researchers ostensibly concerned with definitional problems and interrelationships among the several separate areas of human learning.
Underwood, B. J. *Experimental psychology.* New York: Meredith, 1966.
A good presentation of methods of studying human learning is presented in the last few chapters.
Underwood, B. J., and Schulz, R. W. *Meaningfulness and verbal learning.* New York: Lippincott, 1960.
A readable chronology of experimentation concerning the effects of meaningfulness in verbal learning tasks.

Chapter 7

SOCIAL PSYCHOLOGY

What is the nature of a personal attitude? How may a personal attitude be changed? How does communication between individuals affect personal behaviors? Is one very strongly affected by group consensus and pressure? Is leadership a constant quality of an individual?

A very general definition of *social psychology* is that it is the study of those aspects of behavior which result from interaction among individuals. This definition serves to separate social psychology from most of developmental psychology, physiological psychology, and other broad areas of study in psychology, but it in no way presents sharp boundaries delineating social psychology.

Social psychology may also be defined as a study division including many special topics. Topics such as the study of attitudes, values, cultures, leadership, group membership, communications effectiveness, and group functions are some of those that are frequently mentioned. To some extent such a listing of topics differentiates social psychology from other parts of psychology, but this too is a fuzzy way to define the area.

Social psychology is marked by a very broad range of conceptual approaches. Some social psychologists approach the study of social interactions from a biological background, others from language study, cultural factors, learning theory, certain perception viewpoints, and from psychoanalysis. Each of these backgrounds may present a different organization and a different range of topics for social psychology. This variety of conceptual approaches provides a liberalness and range of approaches to these complex topics which has been fruitful. The different approaches also illustrate the fact that social psychology is an integral part of psychology, and its topics blend with and are generalized from the backgrounds of many other parts of psychology.

Two major areas of social psychology are discussed in this chapter. One collection of concepts and evidence concerns the individual as a function of the forces of society. The other part of this chapter considers the individual only as a part of that behaving society, as part of the operating whole in which the individual's behaviors are not important except as they contribute to that whole.

Inter-individual Factors

Some of the ways in which society shapes the behavior of an individual concerns the topics of attitudes and attitude change, the effectiveness of communications and propaganda, and the effects of society and cultures as they affect the individual. These topics by no means exhaust society's influence upon the individual, but they illustrate the most often considered factors in this part of social psychology.

ATTITUDES

The behavior of an individual is organized and stable. To a certain extent the behavior of an individual is consistent and hence predictable. One of the factors which summarize parts of this consistency is an *attitude*. An attitude comprises an organization of behaviors which have an affective component, that is, feelings, along with cognitions and tendencies toward certain behavior patterns. From another point of view, an attitude describes a predisposition to become motivated.

The object of an attitude may be anything that has the property of existing for the individual. There is both a direction and a degree of feeling associated with the object of the attitude. Attitudes may be pleasant or unpleasant in many degrees.

Attitudes do not exist in isolation. Clusters or systems of attitudes are present in a sort of balance. A change in one attitude is usually balanced by a change in the system. The attitudes interact and support one another, and this organization of attitudes reflects the personality of the individual. Figure 7-1 illustrates a set of attitude objects which are

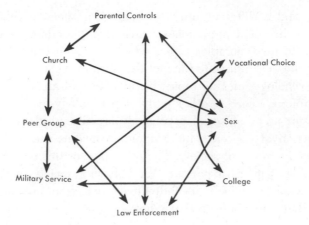

Figure 7-1. A hypothetical set of attitude objects which define
the system of attitudes of a particular young adult. Connecting
lines reflect some of the attitudes which are likely to change,
given a marked change in one such attitude.

likely to be interrelated as a system of attitudes for a particular young
adult.

Attitudes are general motivational states reflecting an organization of
motivated behaviors for an individual. Attitudes serve the goals of the
motivational needs of the individual. Incoming information having to do
with an attitude is selected and shaped according to those more basic
motivational needs. Thus it has been found that new information which is
congruent with a need satisfaction supports and strengthens a weak
attitude. Information coming from varying sources is accepted according to the authority of the source in line with the strength of the
personal needs. Since the motivational needs are satisfied by the attitude
and resulting behaviors, new information supporting such attitudes is
accepted and it in turn supports the attitude. For example, the attitudes
of groups to which the individual belongs also may affect the personal
attitudes, but there has been found to be some picking and choosing
among the beliefs of the group, selecting those which are consistent with
the present attitudes and the personal motivations of the individual.

Attitudes are usually measured by *attitude scales.* Such scales are
collections of statements to which the individual is to indicate approval
or disapproval Some of the sample attitude scale statements in Figure
7-2 give an idea of the makeup of such tests. The statements are selected
for inclusion in the attitude scale by considering facts about and past

Obedience and respect for authority are the most important virtues children
  should learn.
What this country needs most, more than laws and political programs, is a few
  courageous, tireless, devoted leaders in whom the people can put their faith.
There is hardly anything lower than a person who does not feel a great love,
  gratitude, and respect for his parents.
If people would talk less and work more everybody would be better off.
People can be divided into two distinct classes: the weak and the strong.
Human nature being what it is, there will always be war and conflict.

Figure 7-2. Examples of statements from an attitude scale of "authoritarianism" developed at the University of California several years ago. Agreement with a certain number of these conventional statements indicates an authoritarian personality.

responses by individuals known to hold certain attitudes. Attitude scales may also be constructed in line with the construct validity technique. Construct validity (See Chapter 9) gives indirect support for the value of a measurement by considering the extent to which groups measured by the device differ in consistent and expected ways. Do those measured by the scale as having strong pro-religion attitudes behave in ways consistent with that measurement, and do they differ significantly from individuals measured as indifferent to religion?

Another technique of attitude measurement is that of interviewing. Direct questions about attitudes are of two types: *open-ended,* for which the interviewed person must supply answers in his own words, and *fixed-alternative,* allowing only a choice of several given answers. The fixed-alternatives have the disadvantage of supplying words which might bias the individual's response, but this method has been found to be more reliable for attitude measurement. Obviously, the usefulness of the interview technique will depend upon the neutral wording of the questions, the interaction with the interviewer, including his apparent interest and relationship to the interviewed person's answers, and the kind of questions being asked. Personal questions about sex attitudes asked by an attractive member of the opposite sex who appears to be hanging on your every word and using questions being phrased in "you do agree, don't you" manner, will not reflect the same measurements of attitudes as those made under the opposites of each of these conditions. The interview must avoid being an important *object* of attitude evocation unless that is the purpose of the study.

Attitudes may also be measured indirectly by carefully planned circumstances in which actual behaviors in response to certain objects are measured. Comparisons may then be made between actual behaviors, expressed attitudes to direct questioning, and the attitude measurements which result from the attitude scales.

In summary, attitudes arise to objects and consist of beliefs or cognitions, feelings or affects, and behavior patterns such as social actions. Attitudes may be measured by attitude scales, indirect contrived situations, and by direct interviewing. The pattern of attitudes is unique to each individual and is a complex, interacting system such that individual attitudes do not exist in isolation.

ATTITUDE CHANGE

Two kinds of changes occur in attitudes. The change may be one of valence, for example, from "for" to "against." The change may also be a shift in the strength of the attitude. See Figure 7-3. A strengthening or weakening of an existing attitude is judged to be easier to accomplish than a change in valence of the attitude, but it is difficult to assess such changes unless a good measurement device of units of strength of attitudes is available.

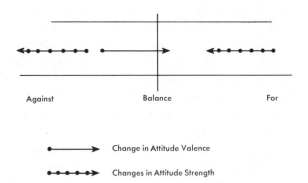

Figure 7-3. Attitude changes of strength and of valence. The difference is primarily that a change in attitude valence requires a crossing of the neural balance point.

One change in attitudes was the recognition noted above that attitudes gain in strength with increases in information relevant and consonant with that motive and attitude. This describes a change in attitudes relative to their formation.

The change in valence of an attitude may be accomplished in several ways. A valence change is easier the weaker the original attitude, but this generalization may be obvious since such attitudes, being closer to the dividing line, have less to change. Nevertheless, several of the factors of attitude change are related to and depend upon the attitude being relatively weak.[81] Strong attitudes which are central to the personality of the individual are probably not changeable anyway, short of drastic treatments akin to the "brain-washing" procedures in which there is total control over the life and situations of the individual.

The first factor or method of change in attitude valence is the production of a change in the *information* or perception of the properties of the attitude object. The change may come about through an actual change in the properties of the object. With improvements in the equipment and procedures of air travel, the resistant attitudes of individuals may be changed. But the attitude may also be changed by bringing new information about the object of the attitude. Advertising may call attention to different aspects of air travel such as the per-mile-travelled safety record which is superior to the well-accepted automobile travel. Attitudes may be changed about air travel by simply pointing out that parachutes are not carried, or that the glamour and comfort of air travel is much greater than with other forms of transportation. The changes may arise from new information about the attitude object which arises from actual changes in the object or simply from new perceived dimensions of information about the object. This method is most applicable when the original information about the object is relatively sparse. At the difficult-to-change extreme of attitudes, the very well-known object yields attitudes for which change is difficult simply because there is no new information which may be presented. The more that is known, the less is the likelihood that new information will be found. The concept of *central attitudes*,[60] attitudes which are basic and highly interrelated in the personality of the individual, also suggest an attitude which is difficult to change. This is partly because of the great deal of information that is known about a central object, but also because there is a higher motivational involvement with maintaining that attitude. The greater the service of the attitude to the motivational needs of the individual, the stronger and more resistant to change is that attitude.

A second sort of approach to attitudinal change is that of *persuasion*. Persuasion is a socially mediated information transmission. An attempt is made to provide new information, called a *message*, through another person. The success of persuasion revolves around the concept of *source credibility*.[60] Source credibility depends upon the perception of the persuador as being expert and free from bias. The greater the expertness of the source (and corresponding lack of expertness and lower self-perceived intellectual ability of the receiver) and the greater the perceived freedom of the source from bias, the greater will be the acceptance of the information. The success of the attitude change, then, depends upon the quality of the information as it relates to the attitude.

The message itself may take a variety of "appeal" forms, including the use of humor, fear, strong emotional states, pride, and so forth. The message may be presented in a direct, positive way, it may be phrased in a negative vein, or it may be presented in an unbiased "both sides of the question" manner. These technicalities of the delivery have not been shown to be very important except as they relate to the credibility of the source and the nature of the information. It is important, though, to hide the discrepancy, called *attitudinal distance*, between the attitudes of the persuader and the receiver, especially if that discrepancy is very large or generalized,[33] or if the motivational relevance of the attitude is very great.

A third manner of changing attitudes, labeled *information direction,* is not a different technique but describes a particular aimed direction for the information. It has been found that effective changes in attitudes follow from messages comprised of new information which meet the motivational bases of an attitude. Consider two individuals who have negative attitudes toward air travel. Neither has or wants to enter an airplane. The first holds this attitude because of a distrust of the skills of the pilots, based perhaps upon the daredevil exhibitions of the barnstorming days and the present distorted newspaper coverage of aircraft accidents. The second person holds this attitude because the expansion of an airport once caused his dislocation with some hardship. A factual message pitched towards the high standards of safety and pilot training from a credible source might well change somewhat the attitudes of the first individual but leave that of the second untouched. The relevance of the message to the motivational bases of the individual's attitude must be strong.

A fourth factor or technique which produces attitude change may be called *commitment and participation.* Though different, these factors seem to involve the same sorts of principles. When an individual takes an active role concerning the objects of an attitude, a change is more likely. The participation may be in discussion of information about the object or it may be an actual "role-playing," behaving in a manner different from that of the attitude originally held. Oftentimes there is a delayed effect of such active participation, in that immediate changes in the attitude do not appear, but are significant later.[18] Commitment refers to an active verbalization or other set of circumstances in which an individual expresses behaviors in line with the new attitudes. The pressure of social circumstances and majority opinions may lead one to profess a different attitude than that actually held. This commitment has been found to lead to an actual change in attitude, perhaps through the additional thought and learning experience the person has in the new role.

COMMUNICATION AND PROPAGANDA

Communication is the interchange of meanings among individuals. Communication most frequently takes place through the vehicle of language, though a variety of movements, expressions, and behaviors also convey meaningful information to others. For such communication to be successful, there must be some commonality of past experiences which have led to similar cognitions, wants, and attitudes in response to symbols. Communication depends upon words and other symbols for objects evoking common cognitions, motivational states and attitudes. Communication may be said to be accomplished when there is knowledge of the cognitions, etc. held by the communicating individual. The conventional symbols of society are required. Knowledge of such communication is assessed by indications of feedback from the receiver in the form of similar verbal or other signs.

Communication serves a very necessary part of our relations with others. In addition to the conveyance of information, however, our dependence upon communication with others for the receipt of knowledge and information about experiences which we could not have sampled has come to be a goal in its own right. The process of communication itself becomes the total purpose and object of the behavior. Deprivation from communication leads to a strongly motivated behavior toward some such interchange, exemplified by the frequent wifely complaint to her husband, "Why don't you *talk* to me?," even though there is nothing really to be said, as shown by the typical answer "What about, dear?"

The purpose of communication among social beings is somewhat obvious. Language effects the transmission of the concepts and norms of that society. There are built up explicit or denotative meanings for each symbol as well as broader suggested or connotative meanings. Both kinds of meaning come to be used in the process of communication, denotative meanings for the base for business and scientific language, and the connotative meanings form the richness or variety of expressions of an idea or concept. As discussed in relation to thinking, language is thought by some to form the structure and stuff of the thought process.[95] The form and complexity of the thought process is held to be determined by the adequacy of the language available for the task. Though doubtful in its entirety, this notion does have some support in studies of thinking which have shown that problems are more easily solved when relevant symbols of methods of solution are available. Language supplies the cues and materials which are the stuff of thought.

The notion of propaganda is really a simple one. In the terms which we have been using, *propaganda* is an attempt to change specific attitudes in a particular direction. Propaganda is usually like persuasion in that the social relations between the individuals are important. Propaganda is also generally verbal in nature. But neither of these is necessarily true. Propaganda may be a collection of information presented in a seemingly *inanimate* way. The parading of a captured enemy spy plane stands as mute evidence requiring no words or direct verbal contact for its persuasive effects upon others. But the same considerations of attitude change as discussed earlier apply to the effectiveness of propaganda. Also relevant are the principles of advertising discussed in Chapter 13, Applied Psychology.

One technique of propaganda which deserves special note could also be discussed equally well under attitude change or advertising. This method is called by some "the big lie." The basic notion is that the constant repetition of some fact or idea under as many conditions as possible will lead to the eventual acceptance of that fact or idea as being true. Though the notion to be assimilated would be seriously doubted when first presented, after continuous repetition the notion becomes well learned and indistinguishable from other notions which are not doubted. This method operates in an unfortunate way in much of our lives even when there is no intention of deceit. A weakly supported fact or principle is repeated by some vehicle, such as a textbook. The "fact" is carried along by another writer and numerous readers. After a period of time the "fact" is unquestionably accepted and presented. Later contrary evidence, though often much more firm and sure than that establishing the first notion, is discounted since the old notion is held so firmly. This brief glimpse of one of the mechanisms affecting the psychology of the scholar or scientist illustrates why facts should never be unquestioningly maintained. Scientific observers are also men in society. Though the original observations may have been reasonably accurate, the interpretation and dissemination of the resulting information is affected by the principles of communication and propaganda like any other utterance of man. Absolute freedom from such influences is a myth.

SOCIETY AND CULTURE

Society is a collection of organized and interacting individuals with common goals and common beliefs, attitudes, and behavior patterns. *Culture* refers to the accumulation of ways of living which have been built up over time in that society. The dividing lines between different societies is an arbitrary one. Whatever distinction is useful can be made. One may compare western vs. eastern societies of the world, or Canadian vs. USA, or even Ames, Iowa vs. Columbia, South Carolina. Comparisons between such defined societies may consider differences in goals, beliefs, attitudes and behavior patterns. The effects of those differences in society upon the individuals may be expressed in terms of the position, role, and social class membership of that individual.

The *positions* of an individual in a society are his memberships in categories such as sex, position in birth order of the family, and other unchangeable facts of existence of importance to the society. Along with such positions are certain specified rights and obligations which are recognized by the society.

The *roles* assumed by the individual are under some control by the individual. Depending upon his experience, a young man may choose an occupation, marital status, and educational level. Each role assumed will determine some behavior patterns. The members of each role are expected to behave in certain ways in standard situations. The uniformity of such response in part determines the role.

Finally the *social class* of the individual will dictate the sort of environment and cultural training which he will experience. Within each society there are classes of individuals having certain rights and privileges which separate these individuals from other social classes. On the basis of a number of criteria, we have distinguished lower, working, middle, and upper classes in our society. Certain patterns of child rearing, social interactions, and even beverage consumption have been found to differ in these groupings. These social class influences shape the social behavior of the individual along with all of the other factors of society.

Structure and Dynamics of Groups

For some time social psychology was focused upon the individual and his reactions to social factors, with little consideration for the situation in which the individual may be found. More recent effort and interest has been directed towards the study of social behavior in specified and controlled group frameworks. There has emerged an approach to understanding the properties of the behavior in the group as well as some clues to the effects of that specific group structure upon the individual.

PURPOSES AND PROPERTIES OF GROUPS

A *group* may be simply a collection of interacting individuals. This breadth of definition includes nearly every case of structures which have been studied by social psychology. It includes groups having a formal basis like a fraternal order and those which are purely informal such as a hastily gathered golf foursome. The group may be composed of individuals with specific characteristics (physicians), the group may have a particular purpose (wildlife protection), or it may be simply a chance collection of individuals caught in a stuck elevator. There may be a great deal of communality among the members or just one common factor. Regardless of the kind of group or its history and origin, there are some principles which guide the development of the group as long as it exists and there are some specific effects which the group may have upon each of the members.

Groups of some particular basis other than chance interaction usually are drawn together because of the motives of the members. An organization has some purpose related to the motives of the members. After the grouping a certain influence is felt upon the attitudes and the action of the members. A modification of the motives and attitudes of the members is accomplished toward the consensus of the group.

Groups have a number of properties. Factors such as size of the group are usually independent of the properties of each of the members. Other group properties, including the attitudes and structural organization of the group, are derived directly from properties of the members constituting that group. The consensus of group attitudes follows directly from some function of the attitudes of each of the members. Further properties like cohesiveness of the group follow from properties of the members but also require some important interaction experiences before they appear.

INDIVIDUAL BEHAVIOR IN A GROUP

Two examples of the influence of the group upon the members' behavior are those manipulations leading to conforming behavior as a result of social pressure, and the complex topic of leadership.

A collection of experiments concerning the effects of social pressure to conform has been performed by Asch.[4] Eight individuals were present in an experimental group ostensibly involving a study of simple perception. Three lines of somewhat different length were presented with the instructions to choose that one of the same length as that line presented on another card. Seven of the individuals in the group were confidants of the experimenter and selected an incorrect line. The test of conformity was whether the lone subject would follow his senses and report what he saw or follow the group so as not to be different. About 25 per cent of the subjects tested disagreed with the group and reported the line equal in length to the standard. The other 75 per cent, however, made some number of errors, that is, conformed to the group opinion on some of the 12 test trials. Two further manipulations in subsequent experiments concerned the size and agreement of the group exerting pressure. It was found that a ratio of 3 to 1 was necessary to demonstrate the conformity but that further increases in the majority were not particularly effective in improving the effect. The presence of dissenters was a potent factor. Apparently just one additional dissenter in the group is all that is necessary for many subjects to disagree with the group and make no "errors."

Conformity to the majority opinion in this fashion affects the attitudes of its members as well as specific behaviors. The more subtle the difference between the "true" state of affairs and that of the group, the greater the likelihood of conformity. In the terms of the line experiments of Asch, the more difficult the actual discrimination the more likely the subject will conform to group selections. A weaker attitude which diverges from that expressed by the group will be easily changed to conform.

Relative leadership and its complement of following-the-leader is nearly always present in groups. Leaders may be simply defined as those who have influence upon others. This is not a quality which is present or not, but rather a quantitative characteristic which everyone expresses to some extent. Leadership is a form of social interaction of influencing others in some way. The leadership may be directed toward accomplishing a bit of group labor, selecting music for a group, or determining the stylish patterns of dress for the group. Each of these things may be done by different "leaders." A leader in one group behavior may be a follower in terms of another.

The leader has been found to fit the expectations of the group as well as satisfy their motives. The leader must be conceived as being one of the group as well as the best of the group in that particular factor.

Some research attention has been paid to the kind of leadership structure in a group and the relative success and cohesiveness of that group.[43] Typical comparisons have been made between authoritarian, democratic, and laissez-faire structures. Groups with democratic leadership have been found to be more cohesive. Authoritarian leadership led to more aggression among the members and less stability within the group as measured by constructiveness of work when the leader was absent.

The related factor of *status* of the members with respect to one another is somewhat more permanent and less flexible. Status may be accomplished by an acknowledged superiority of some members over others in factors like wealth, intelligence, or given political power. Military groups have established rankings in which the status is fixed and likely to affect the performance of individuals in a small group. For example, it has been found that the status of the members in a military group makes group efforts at solving problems less efficient.[85] The group performance is impeded because of the tendency for those of lower rank to defer to those of higher rank. Instead of "natural" leaders taking over for each separate activity, the status factor results in suppression of others in favor of one overall leader.

Group Behavior

Some examples of behaviors of groups include mob or riot behavior at one extreme of social acceptability and team sports activities at the other. In these cases the behavior of the individual is primarily a function of the factors affecting the group and does not differ from other individuals in that group. Regarding any one individual, the behavior pattern is much different from what would be expected of that person if he were alone.

MOB BEHAVIOR

The factors which are believed to be most important in directing the behavior of all the individuals in a mob are the anonymity, suggestibility, ease of emotional arousal, and the freedom from the usual inhibitions to certain behaviors. The direction of the mob behavior, however, is formed by each individual's perception of the situation and his expectations of what will happen.

Each individual seems to be lost in the mob and does not react as would a solitary individual. There are strong feelings of being protected and shielded by the crowd such that individual behavior will not be noticed or remembered. This anonymity leads to a loss in inhibitions and other moderating influences as, for example, fears of reprisal for present behavior. Because the usual controls over personal behavior are missing there can be free expression of motives in the direction suggested by the crowd or by personal perceptions of the situation. Whatever feelings and motives are present in the group may be easily brought into action by simple suggestion. The harangue of the riot inciter is most effective because there are few braking devices on the behaviors of each of the individuals. The effect is further enhanced by the ease with which emotions may be raised. Because of the feelings of anonymity, inhibitions to expression of motives are weak and the mob may be brought to an emotional tension and action by the suggestions of a spokesman or the sudden appearance of a provoking situation like a fire or an undefended scapegoat.

Mobs may be described by the sort of behaviors which the individuals undertake. In the face of great personal danger the members of the mob panic and escape as in a theater fire. Aggressive acts of harm to individuals or general damage to anything in the way mark the behaviors of other individuals in a mob. Finally, the behavior of those in a mob may be directed to personal acquisition and satisfaction, as in "runs on the bank," food hoarding, nondirected "be-ins," and religious revivals.

Summary

Social psychology studies factors of behavior resulting from interactions with others. The contributions of the individual in the group and the effects of the group upon the individual must both be considered.

Attitudes are beliefs, feelings, and behavior patterns in response to objects. They may be measured by attitude scales, direct interviewing techniques, and by contrived situations evoking samples of behavior. Individuals have unique and complex patterns of attitude systems.

Attitudes may be changed in strength or in valence. Factors affecting attitude change include the information held about the properties of the attitude object, properties of the individual attempting persuasion, the relationship of the attitude and information about the object to the motivational needs of the individual, and the degree of publicly displayed commitment and participation which the individual has undertaken concerning the attitude.

Basic to social interaction is communication, the interchange of meanings. Propaganda is a communication designed to effect a change in attitudes.

A collection of expected social behavior patterns arise from an individual's positions, roles, and social classes in a specific society.

A group is simply a collection of interacting individuals, usually having a particular motivation in common. The size, attitudes, and organizations of the group all affect the behaviors of the individuals which together describe group behavior. The group exerts some pressure upon the members toward conformity to a common set of attitudes and behaviors. The leadership of the group can importantly effect the group productivity.

Mob behavior is usually directed toward expression of the personal motives of the individual in the absence of the usual social inhibitors and group motivators.

SUGGESTED READINGS

Backman, C. W., and Secord, P. F. (Eds.) *Problems in social psychology.* New York: McGraw-Hill, 1966.
A collection of experimental reports and papers describing the breadth and detail of research in social psychology.

Hollander, E. P., and Hunt, R. G. (Eds.) *Current perspectives in social psychology* (2nd edition) New York: Oxford University Press, 1967.
A collection of papers describing present empirical problems, prominent viewpoints, and the diversity of social psychology.

Krech, D., Crutchfield, R. S., and Ballachey, E. L. *Individual in society: A textbook in social psychology.* New York: McGraw-Hill, 1962.
A comprehensive and popular introduction to social psychology.

Newcomb, T. M., Turner, R. H., and Converse, P. R. *Social psychology: The study of human interaction.* New York: Holt, Rinehart and Winston, 1965.
A beginning textbook in social psychology.

Prohansky, H., and Seidenberg, B. (Eds.) *Basic studies in social psychology.* New York: Holt, Rinehart and Winston, 1965.
Foundation research studies of note upon which much of present social psychology experimentation is based.

Secord, P. F., and Backman, C. W. *Social psychology.* New York: McGraw-Hill, 1964.
A textbook recognizing a change in emphasis of social psychology toward new kinds of research.

Steiner, I. D., and Fishbein, M. (Eds.) *Current studies in social psychology.* New York: Holt, Rinehart and Winston, 1965.
A collection of papers describing more recent research in social psychology complementing the Prohansky and Seidenberg volume above.

Chapter *8*

DEVELOPMENTAL PSYCHOLOGY

Are behaviors inherited? What simple genetic mechanisms describe the passing of characters from parents to offspring? What are the patterns of behavior development? How does growth relate to processes of learning? What are some examples of developing behavior patterns?

Patterns of behavior may be thought of as being shaped through the action of three kinds of factors: *heredity, maturation,* and *learning.* These factors correspond roughly to the structural equipment of the organism, its growth or development, and the effect of the experiences which it has. There is continuous interaction between these factors. It is probably unwise to seek "pure" examples of inherited patterns of behavior, or those which are formed entirely through growth processes. Learning is always playing some role, direct or indirect, in the formation of a sequence of new responses. Structure always limits development and the range of possible behavior changes. And especially at certain periods of life, the development of a capacity will make possible certain kinds of different behaviors. Some important examples of combinations of these factors determining particular behaviors will be given later.

Heredity

The science of heredity is called *genetics.* Genetics deals with the similarities and differences between related organisms resulting from inherited structure as it relates to environment. The transmission of genetic characters from parents to offspring depends upon the splitting and recombinations of patterns of *genes*, which are believed to be complex, self-perpetuating protein molecules which convey information affecting the formation of cell structures of the body. Genetics deals with the principles of such patterning which lead to similar offspring, as well as the various roles which environment factors may have in effecting differences between individuals. *Behavior genetics* concerns the transmission of automatic behaviors and predispositions to certain behaviors by heredity. Behavior genetics is the study of behaviors which are caused primarily by differences in structure.

SOME GENETIC PRINCIPLES

In a normal cell nucleus, elongated bodies may be observed called *chromosomes.* Chromosomes appear in pairs and are usually constant in number in the cells of any one kind of plant or animal. In man there are 23 pairs of chromosomes, the female having 22 chromosome pairs called autosomes and one pair of X-chromosomes and the male having 22 autosomes and one X-Y pair of chromosomes.

In the normal process of cell division (*mitosis*) and consequent multiplication of cells within an individual, each of the 46 chromosomes is duplicated and the cell divides to form two identical cells. In the production of germ cells prior to the formation of an offspring, a variation called *meiosis* occurs in which there is but one duplication of the 46 chromosomes, but there are two divisions of the cell. Thus, there are

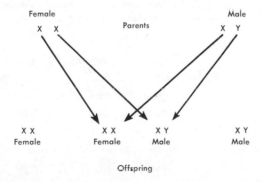

Figure 8-1. Pairings of the sex determining, mismatched chromosome in germ cells. Random selections of either X-chromosome from the female are matched with a random choice between the X or Y chromosome of the male to produce an offspring. It can be readily determined that the male, and not the female, contribution to the new pair determines the sex of that offspring.

only 23 chromosomes in the germ cell of the male (sperm) and 23 chromosomes in the female germ cell (ova) which unite to form a new cell. The sex of the new cell will be determined by the chromosome of the mismatched pair from the male (X or Y) which was a part of that new cell. In Figure 8-1 it can be seen that the sex of the child is thus a function of the genetic contribution of the father.

The term *gene* has been used to represent a hypothetical unit factor of heredity. Each chromosome is assumed to contain a very large number of these gene units of information. *Genotype* refers to the totality of genetic information which is present in the cells. *Phenotype* describes the expressed characteristics of the individual, roughly, the collection of genetic information which is used. The notion of *dominance* of some genes over other recessive genes describes, in part, the genotype-phenotype difference. Genes which are dominant will be expressed in the characteristics of the individual when they are present. Consider, as in Figure 8-2, a pair of genes for hair color. Dark-hair genes are dominant

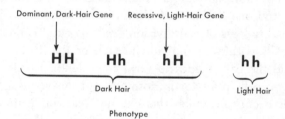

Figure 8-2. The possible pairings of dominant and recessive genes for hair color. The dominant gene, if present, will produce a phenotype having the dominant characteristic.

over light-hair genes. An individual having but one of these dark genes will have dark hair. Only if two light-hair genes are present will the phenotype be of light hair. Some other characteristics which are known to be dominant in man are curly hair, brown eye color, normal color vision and hearing, and immunity to poison ivy.[23]

Genes which happen to be carried in the mismatched chromosome pair differentiating sex have some additional properties. Any genetic information which may be carried in the male Y-chromosome is recessive and plays no part in the phenotype display. Thus, the phenotype of the male will be identical to the genotype of the information of the X-chromosome. Figure 8-3 shows the genotype and phenotype of indi-

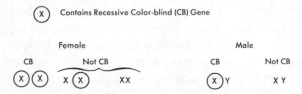

Figure 8-3. **Possible pairings of recessive color-blind and non-color-blind genes and the resulting display of color-blindness. One can logically derive the necessary and likely parents for each kind of offspring and derive facts like those suggested in the text.**

viduals with regard to a recessive gene for color-blindness. Several facts can be expressed about this *sex-linked trait*. Color-blind daughters have color-blind fathers. Color-blind sons have color-blind or "carrier" mothers (gene present but not expressed). Color-blind women have all color-blind sons, and so on.

This survey of some simple genetic concepts and principles is probably a gross oversimplification of the actual process, but it does provide a feel for the notion of inherited properties. Undoubtedly no behavior patterns or predispositions to behavior are determined by these simple rules of combining single pairs of genes. Assuming two pairs of genes in certain combinations determine particular behaviors obviously complicates the conception of the mechanism. Greater and greater numbers of gene pairs entering into the determination lead quickly to the use of probability analyses and statistics of considerable complexity to model the process. Thus, empirical approaches to questions of inherited behavior have been the concern of behavior genetics.

BEHAVIOR GENETICS

Variations in the genetic information of a restricted population may come about in several ways. Individual pairs may be *selected* and mated on the basis of phenotype. By rejection of divergent individuals, the genetic variability of the genotype is likely to be reduced. Mating in a small, closed population of individuals would also tend to limit the pool of genetic information after a time. Other changes in the genetic information pool may come about through *mutation* or change in the genes caused by outside forces. These mutations are commonly thought to be responsible for the gradual evolution of organismic forms.

Experimental study of the genetic basis for behaviors may produce many of these kinds of changes in the populations of genes. After phenotype selection, breeding in a closed population, and similar systematic manipulations of genetic background, the relative occurrence of a phenotypic behavior may be studied. Selection for mating of only those individuals which display a given behavior with others which display that same behavior should result in offspring with a higher frequency of that behavior. Similarly mating among selected individuals which do not display that behavior should, if the behavior is in part heritable, result in offspring which are less likely to display that behavior. After a number of generations of using this selection process, using only those who "have" in one strain and those who "have not" in the other, a point will usually be reached for which further selection does not result in an improvement in the frequency of occurrence of the trait. In this way rats have been selected which are "emotional" vs. "nonemotional" or which learn quickly in a maze vs. perform poorly in that maze.[86] Similarly, dogs have been selected which are aggressive and fearless, yet learn quickly and are docile to a particular handler.

Demonstrations like these must be interpreted with caution. It is not likely that particular behavior patterns have been inherited as such. It is probably not the case that a particular response to specific stimuli may be differentially inherited in groups. But some basic structural difference *is* heritable and is probably the factor determining differences in behavior patterns in test situations. Evidence suggests, for example, that "emotional" animals have enlarged adrenal glands. The factors behind the production of a larger adrenal gland may be at least part of the heritable difference. Selection of emotional and non-emotional animals may have been, in fact, a selection of individuals developing large vs. small adrenal glands. In similar speculation one may link the variance of personality which is attributable to heredity with endocrine gland functions of different sorts. Such linking of heritable behavior to structural differences is one rational account of the differences produced.

In the study of the inheritance of intellectual processes and abilities there is a decided lack in knowledge of such underlying structural differences. That some parts of intellectual behavior differences are inherited has been shown in a number of ways, including studies using IQ measurements of identical and fraternal twins. Identical twins, who are identical genetically, are more alike in IQ than are fraternal twins, who are no more alike genetically than are normal siblings.[32] Environment differences are presumably constant in such comparisons. Selection experiments with such species as rats have demonstrated that within a very few generations a wide separation in maze learning "brightness" and "dullness" can be achieved,[31] though the intellectual basis of the heritable difference has been doubted.

Comparisons of these kinds, which start with phenotypes and seek to change the occurrence of that phenotypic behavior, have been most popular. These studies answer the question of whether there is some genetic basis for a given pattern of behavior which has been observed. The functional question of the methods in which different behaviors are developed from differences in genotype, however, is more difficult to answer. What genotype leads to a particular behavior pattern? What is the relationship of environment or life history to the formation of that behavior pattern? These sorts of questions may be partially answered by experimentally manipulating genotype with environmental differences held constant or accounted for during the development of the behavior character. This sort of manipulation is obviously difficult to accomplish. Some speculation has been made that such studies will find a complex interaction between patterns of genes and particular environmental factors in the production of heritable behavior.

Maturation

The term *maturation* refers to the process of change (usually growth) of an individual which occurs primarily as a function of aging or time. Maturation is assumed to be not influenced by experiences and environmental conditions except as they are necessary for the normal physiological functioning of the individual. Maturation excludes the effects of practice and experience. A pattern of behavior, however, cannot be formed entirely by the action of maturation. A behavior which is made possible by maturational changes is also partly based upon learned responses and will be affected by the peculiar structure of that individual and by the particular situation in which the behavior is observed. Maturation is a hypothetical determinant of behavior changes. Like the concepts of motivation and learning, maturation is not a "thing" which exists and is made hard to measure by its entanglement with other things, but is instead one of many conceptual, hypothetical factors which accounts for certain antecedents and aspects of behavior, thus helping to account for such behavior in a consistent and orderly fashion.

PATTERNS OF DEVELOPMENT

Certain generalizations can be made about development. Development is an orderly process. Its rate is not constant, but is variable in and between individuals. Different parts and systems of the body develop in largely independent patterns and sequences. Development leads to behavior processes oriented toward better discrimination and generalization of stimulation and responses. The end product of the earlier years of development is called a *mature* individual, one who functions in a consistent and useful pattern.

Development as an orderly process proceeds in some consistent directions. The maturation of structure leads to changes in behavior from the head toward the lower parts of the body, from the center toward the extremities of the body, and from a general mass-action of large systems of the body to specific systems of smaller parts of the body.

The patterns of development of control over self-orientation and similar movements in young children follows these sorts of principles. During the first month after birth, a baby will develop some motion control over his neck and head. By four to six months of age the child can hold his head upright while lying on the stomach. The development and strengthening of neck muscles is such that the head need no longer be firmly held when the baby is picked up. Rolling is often observed at about 6 to 7 months, and standing alone without support is usually possible by the 18th month after birth. Behaviors such as crawling and walking appear through a wide span of time of 10 months to 18 months after birth. This pattern of development of self-locomotion illustrates increasingly specific rather than general, massed-action patterns of behavior, as well as reflecting the head-to-tail, inward-outward development patterns.

The *rate* of behavior development in an individual is not constant, nor is it comparable to that of other individuals in any meaningful way. The rate of maturation of physical processes proceeds by "fits and starts" rather than in a continuous, smooth fashion. In overall patterns of growth, the rate of maturation of the early years is not matched by similar growth in later childhood. A particular child should not be expected to conform to the norms or average rates of development like those outlined above concerning body movements and positioning. Each child's development proceeds at a unique rate. A child which has achieved a sitting position without support at an early age of 6 months, may not walk alone until close to two years of age. Though parents

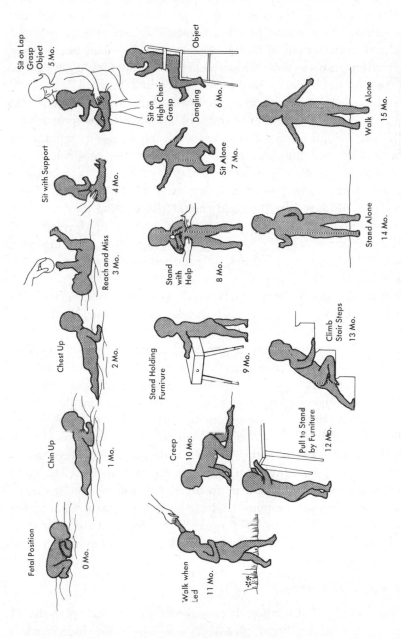

Figure 8-4. Stages of motor behavior development as measured in a careful study of 25 children. (After Shirley, M. M., The first two years: A study of twenty-five. Vol. II. Intellectual development. Minneapolis: University of Minnesota Press, 1933.)

Fetal Position
0 Mo.

Chin Up
1 Mo.

Chest Up
2 Mo.

Reach and Miss
3 Mo.

Sit with Support
4 Mo.

Sit on Lap
Grasp Object
5 Mo.

Sit on High Chair
Grasp Dangling Object
6 Mo.

Sit Alone
7 Mo.

Stand with Help
8 Mo.

Stand Holding Furniture
9 Mo.

Creep
10 Mo.

Walk when Led
11 Mo.

Pull to Stand by Furniture
12 Mo.

Climb Stair Steps
13 Mo.

Stand Alone
14 Mo.

Walk Alone
15 Mo.

commonly become concerned over less than average rate of physical development and are pleased when their child achieves some milestone ahead of the averages, there is little of predictive value for such accomplishments. These marks of relative progress have not been found to be related to the extent of the child's later development, nor do they predict anything about the child's intellectual capacities. Slow motor development in a physically healthy child is quite "normal."

Different aspects and systems of behavior develop at different and probably independent rates. The rate of physical development, for example, may be quite unrelated to rates of acquiring communication skills or problem solving capacities. The appearance of evidence of sexual maturation is often unrelated to the development of social and emotional maturity. The fact of different rates of development of behavior systems displayed by the child should also caution parents about concern over poor physical progress in early months of development. Physical development which is slower than average in no way indicates that the child is generally "behind" or retarded in other respects such as intellectual growth.

Related to the notion of progress in development from general to specific behaviors is the pattern of development toward both more specific and well-defined aspects of stimulus situations. Finer and finer discriminations are made between presented stimuli with development. But the child also develops a capacity for inductive generalization of specific behaviors into principles and larger unified wholes of behavior. The child learns first the larger class of animals before specific species are named and reacted to in a systematic fashion. Further differentiations of "your dog" and "my dog" develop following experiences with individual animals. In the other direction development moves from smaller to larger systematically organized units of behavior. The child comes eventually to put together in an organized fashion the "steering," "pedaling," and "sitting" responses which have been acquired in other situations into tricycle riding. The organization is more than the sum of the individual skills, since there is additional timing and spatial coordination necessary.

MATURATION AND "READINESS"

One concept of the relation between maturation and patterns of behavior is that of *readiness*. Behaviors for which the individual is maturationally "ready" appear efficiently, given the proper stimulating circumstances. If the readiness is lacking, that is, the individual has not developed or matured sufficiently, the behavior pattern will be both difficult to evoke and very slow to develop. For example, reading is a fairly complicated behavior pattern which depends upon a number of fine perceptual discriminations, motor movements of the eyes, and intellectual processes of discrimination and concept formation. These abilities depend upon both maturation and learning. The child who is not ready in one of these processes such as the perceptual capacity to perceive and respond differentially to the letters "p" and "q" will require considerably greater amounts of training than will children for whom such a perceptual discrimination has been already developed.

Training an unready child to read is far from impossible, but it is also far from being efficient, or from another standpoint of childhood experience, wise. Forcing the production of behavior for which the child does not appear to be ready requires a greater amount of effort, and the disappointment for the child may seriously impede his motivation toward that behavior. Such unfortunate consequences may persist even after readiness is assuredly reached. Another practical difficulty with such forcing is that it does no lasting good. Its benefits are only temporary. Careful studies have shown that a child who is given early training to perform skills before he is ready will not be superior at those skills *after* he has achieved sufficient maturation.[31] After some time has passed for the "normal" learning of those skills, the child will be no better than if early training had not been given.

Readiness is an assumed state of maturation which probably cannot be distinctly measured. The states of being "not ready" and "ready" do not necessarily imply that there is a sharp time line between them. The moral of the readiness concept is clear, however. Most efficient development of behavior patterns occurs after readiness has been reached.

MATURATION AND EXPERIENCE

The development of behavior depends upon experience in both an indirect and a direct manner. Directly, experience shapes patterns of behavior depending upon the situation and capacities of the individual. Indirectly, experience has been shown to affect the progress of maturation by withholding or supplying certain environmental conditions which are involved with that change in structure.

One study of the vision of monkeys which were reared in darkness for the first seven months of their lives failed to show certain reflexes of vision such as blinking to an approaching stimulus. After a period of experience with light, however, the monkeys developed a normal pattern of such reflexes. The development was arrested until certain experiences were provided.[67]

Another class of research has shown more permanent effects of early experiences. In one experiment [41] white rats were subjected from birth to one of three conditions: mild daily electric shocks which lasted a short period of time, handling like that received by the shocked rats (but no shocks), and no disturbance at all beyond necessary laboratory cage care. It was expected that the emotional stress of electric shocks at an early age would have some permanent deleterious effects upon the rats. The result was unexpected. The shocked and the handled groups of rats were quite indistinguishable from "normal" laboratory rats. The control animals which had not been disturbed, however, displayed a pattern of emotional behavior indicating "shyness" and fear along with a poorer physical development indicated by slower than normal gains in weight.

These studies along with a growing literature on "early experiences" of various kinds suggest that the early days of life are far more than just a period of automatic development during which only certain physical needs of the body need be looked after. It is apparent that extremes of experience or deprivation are quite likely to have important effects upon the pattern of development and may possibly have permanent effects upon both structure and behavior. Note also the descriptions of the experiments in Chapter 3 concerning rearing monkeys from birth by artificial "mothers" and the adverse effects such deprivation had upon later social and behavior development.

Some Developmental Topics

The following sections describe some representative patterns of development of behavior in children. Some facts and theories of the formation of perceptual patterns, language behavior, cognitive and intellectual capacities, and certain social behaviors are included.

PERCEPTUAL DEVELOPMENT

The responses of the neonate indicate that the perceptual processes of the newborn infant are diffuse and disorganized. A mass-action response occurs to any stimulus which is strong enough to produce some response. A few specific responses do exist at the time of birth. The newborn child is able to locate the nipple and grasp objects which are placed against his hands.

The early development in perception is an acquisition of more detailed perceptual responses. Specific perceptions follow from an "active" exploration of the stimulus environment. When motor processes are sufficiently mature to allow some exploration, a marked increase in the organization of the variety of sense impressions occurs.

An example of the perceptions of younger children being less oriented and responsive to the details and specifics of situations is given by Figure 8-5. The subparts of the figures are not usually reported by

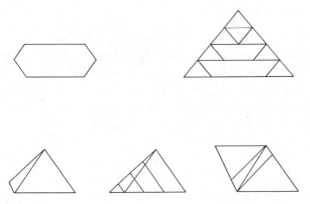

Figure 8-5. The simple figures at the left are hidden in the more complex figures on the right.

children and often cannot even be located upon request. This perceptual skill has been shown to be highly related to rate of development and has thus been used as part of tests of intelligence which measure "mental age." See Chapter 9. The more embedded figures, that is, those whose identification and location is well hidden by a symmetry and regularity of the embedding pattern, may even be a problem to experienced adults.

The development of other perceptual processes describes the importance of the learning processes in shaping perceptual responses which appear to adults to be "natural" and are thus often taken for granted. Some stimulus constancies illustrate this perceptual learning. The child of less than 6 months of age has no perceptual constancy of size. The young child, for example, will not consistently reach for that one of two toys which is smaller and close rather than the other which is larger but further away. The toys are proportionately identical. The child apparently responds to the retinal image of the toy alone. By about 6 months of age, however, the perceptual skill of size constancy requiring depth perception cues appear to be learned. The constancies of brightness and color of objects are also undeveloped before the age of 2 years and continue to develop, equalling the performance of the adult observer at the age of 10 years. Young children respond to the sense impression information of brightness disregarding the surrounds. Similarly, colors are called as they appear rather than as they are later learned to be identified in consideration of the surrounds and illumination.

LANGUAGE DEVELOPMENT

Except for the early improvement in motor abilities, the development of language is perhaps the most obvious change marking the stages of development of a child. There are many aspects of the conditions under which language is learned, but they may be organized in one fashion by considering the purposes of that language, at least for the young child. Language makes the child's needs known to those in attendance. Language expresses the feelings and emotions of the child. Language is an "input" channel of information for the child. And finally language provides a means for social interaction for the child. These different purposes of language actually allow for different kinds of learning situations for words and utterances. Words used to make needs known are not likely to be reinforced or learned in the same way as are those words which express the child's feelings. This analysis need not be carried further to convey the notion of the different directions which language development may take.

Some consideration of the expected stages of language behavior in children is also instructive. The first attempts at language are imitative of the language of parents. Single sounds and short "almost words" appear from about the beginning of the period when the child appears to be aware that he can voluntarily make sounds. The next stage is the use of single words of some clarity, primarily nouns describing familiar objects and interjections signifying feelings. By about two years of age the typical child puts together a group of words which are not usually grammatically correct but are meaningful. "Teddy bear nappy" and "Mamma owwa" are examples which a child may use to "tell" her father of the important events of the day, namely that her teddy bear took a nap with her and that her mother bumped her head on the lamp.

From this period on, the length of the strings of words become longer and the grammar more closely approximates the accepted form.

The relative degree of articulation with which the child makes his utterances also improves over this period and is usually free from obvious defect by six years of age. The standards and examples which the parent set will affect that articulation. Some consideration should be given to the view, however, that a good learning model for very young children is speech that fairly closely mimics what the child emits rather than a perfectly correct pronounciation. The parent may mimic the child's speech occasionally. Much like looking in a mirror, the child may more easily observe his own actions. Such knowledge of results may point out errors and allow more efficient language learning. This view gives some justification for parents to use some "baby talk." "Baby talk" gives the child some "feedback" experiences which may be readily compared to normal conversation of the parents which is overheard by the child. At the very least, however, the parent should probably avoid punishing or appearing to disapprove the utterance made by the child. Positive encouragement is more likely to be effective and disapproval may impede interest in all talking rather than just modify the particular responses punished.

CONCEPT AND COGNITIVE DEVELOPMENT

The formation of the concepts which become a part of the child's materials for intellectual activity is closely related to the development of perceptual and language skills. Evidence of the existence of particular concepts usually comes from language behavior in response to particular stimuli. One sort of simple concept is nothing more than a specific perceptual response to one part of a stimulus. Responding to the color or the relative sizes of a collection of dissimilar items illustrates a concept. More complex conceptual behavior involves the use of a bit of language as a go-between or mediator. "These things are green," and "These blocks are larger and square."

Concepts which involve mediators or for which mediators simplify the task are characteristic of a later stage of conceptual development. This difference in development may be distinguished by presenting to differently aged children a problem of selecting the object of a pair which is larger. If the child is allowed to discover in a first pair that the larger of the stimuli is correct or that that choice leads to a pleasant reward of some kind, his responses on a second pair of stimuli may tell what sort of concept he has learned. The second pair includes the

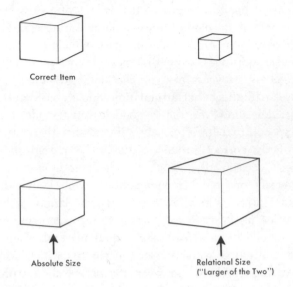

Correct Item

Absolute Size

Relational Size
("Larger of the Two")

Figure 8-6. Items which may be used to test the sort of concept that children have formed. The top pair is presented with the larger item designated as "correct." The lower items are presented as a test for the concept of "larger." See text.

same item as the larger of the first two, but in addition, a second even larger companion stimulus is presented for test. See Figure 8-6. Younger children will respond to the absolute size of the correct item, that is, they will choose the same item as was correct earlier. Older children, however, will make a relational judgment and pick the larger item in the second pair as well. The older child has the capacity to use a verbal mediator "larger" to guide choices in such comparisons. Similarly, language mediators make it easier to learn several tasks. After a particular discrimination has been learned among the members of a group of stimuli, the "correct" dimension is now reversed from what it was; young children, like white rats, often take longer to learn the new task than they did the old. Older children with some language capacity and concepts for mediation, however, learn reversed responding almost immediately.[38]

The concept of quantity can also be followed in its development in the early years of childhood. By the age of 2 to 3 years, children can usually perform the greater-than, less-than operation on objects. They can distinguish between one and more than one. They can often "count" two items but are likely to call any amount greater than 2 as "2" also. By five years of age, most children can count objects in a meaningful way over and above the simple serial learning of the cardinal number labels of "one," "two," "three," and so on. But even at this stage some peculiarities of quality may be revealed in the children's concepts if a test situation is structured appropriately. Jean Piaget performed a simple demonstration using an equal number of flowers and vases.[66] The children established the equality of the flowers and vases by placing one flower in each vase. The flowers were now placed together, the vases placed together. The child still described them as equal in quantity. Piaget then removed the vases from that position and scattered them in a broad area about the child. The child younger than four years of age then typically reported that there was a greater number of vases than flowers. Piaget claims that the child has not learned the idea of conservation of things and is responding, instead, on the basis of how many there appear to be. Things which cover a greater area look like they are greater in number. But this demonstration also indicates that the child is not counting or applying a quantity concept in the fashion of an older child or adult.

Piaget has outlined some theoretical stages of cognitive development in children. These stages in his theory indicate increasingly adaptive behavior from the diffuse and somewhat non-specific responses of the newborn child to the organized and logical behavior patterns of adults. Piaget's notion of development is that it is a *reorganization* of the information which is gradually accumulated. The three major blocks of development include the *sensorimotor activities* following birth, the era of *concrete* operations, and the succeeding era of *formal operations* which leads into adult cognitive structure.

Sensorimotor activities fill the interval of time from birth to about two years of age. (Ages given are only averages from which the individual child may deviate without being abnormal.) Beginning with some reflexes which are innate, the child develops coordination among responses. He learns to anticipate stimuli and make responses in the anticipation of changes of stimuli. The child begins experimentation and exploration of new or different aspects of the world. He begins to acquire different means to achieve goals. The first stages of thinking are present near the end of this sensorimotor stage in the child's attempts to deal with "things not present."

The era of *concrete operations* fills the period from two years until adolescence. The primary stuff which the child manipulates and considers are observable concrete aspects of the world. Thinking does not proceed much beyond the particulars of examples. An early stage of the concrete operations era is the *preconceptual stage* of about 2 to 4 years. During this period the child begins to respond to and use symbols of various kinds. The use of such symbols may be noted in play behavior and in the language of the child. The playful activities deal with imaginary situations of people and objects in the child's life. The boy may pretend that the stuffed dog is asleep. The little girl may "iron clothes" like her mother did earlier in the day. The existence of such symbolic behavior describes a further step in the cognitive development of the child. The stage of *intuitive thought* fills the approximate age range of 4 to 7 years. In this stage the child classifies objects, has a developed concept system, and responds to groups of objects rather than just the selected examples of experience, as was typical in a younger age. The specificity of the concepts allows a finer distinction and yet a more realistic generalization among objects in his experience. At about seven years of age the concepts or principles of "reversibility" and "conservation" as described above appear to shape cognitive responses. The child learns that objects are not altered with every change in the way they appear. Processes are found to reverse in direction and not damage or change the objects involved. The capacities of logic and reasoning are well developed in the later stages of the concrete operations era, but only with respect to things and classes which are concrete and specifiable. Ten year olds, for example, have no problem in distinguishing the order of height of several sticks placed before them, yet they have great difficulty with hypothetical word problems such as "John is smaller than Billy; Peter is taller than Billy; which of the three is tallest?"

The final of Piaget's three levels of cognitive development is that called *formal operations*. At about adolescence the development of logic processes and reasoning using only abstract symbols becomes possible. The child may perform various intellectual operations solely with symbols. Problems may be solved with words, rather than objects of his past experience. The adequate development of these formal operations marks the cognitive maturation of the individual.

DEVELOPMENT OF INTELLIGENCE

The capacity which we call intelligence is not really different from considerations of language and concept development. Tests of general intelligence or IQ are based upon the relative development of the capacity to use words, concepts, and operations with symbols.

Test of intellectual development before the age of 18 months have not been found to be useful in predicting the intellectual ability of the person after that age. Tests at this age are useful only for detecting gross differences in mental deficiency, like that caused by organic damage or sensory defect. The development of various sensorimotor activities which make up the behavior of children at this age proceeds, by and large, at a rate which is not related to the rate and extent of development of other processes at a later age. An estimate of the relative development of motor skills then will not reliably reflect the stage of development of mental capacity now or in the future.

One aspect of the development of intelligence is the question of the relative contribution of genetic, inborn determinants as opposed to the effects of environmental experiences. Are the differences in intelligence a function of heredity or are they a result of the experiences which the developing child has undergone? To anticipate the answer, both factors seem to account for some of the differences in IQ, and it does not seem to be useful to say which factor is most important.

Two kinds of comparisons have been made which have led to this conclusion. One comparison is that between the IQ's of children who have had a significant change in environment after placement in foster homes. Foster home placement usually results in some change in IQ toward that of the new foster parents, but correlations show that there is a stronger relationship between the children's IQ and that of their natural parents than with the foster parents.[76] Intelligence changes with environment but is still related to heredity. The other comparisons leading to similar conclusions are those between two kinds of twins and normal brothers and sisters. Identical twins are developed from the same cell and are genetically identical, while fraternal twins have developed from different cells and are no more alike genetically than any random pair of siblings. Twins, though, are more alike in environment than are siblings of different ages by the nature of being in many of the same places at the same times and the efforts of parents to treat the twins alike. The identical twins differ from fraternal twins in heredity but are the same in environment, while fraternal twins are the same as random siblings genetically but differ in environment. Identical twins have been found to be more alike in IQ than fraternal twins, indicating that genetic differences contribute to the measured intelligence. But fraternal twins are also more alike in IQ than are random siblings of different ages, indicating that the environmental similarity also shaped the measured intelligence.[30] Neither factor can be said to be more important than the other in these studies, because there is no scale to compare units of difference in genetic background with units of difference in environment.

DEVELOPMENT OF SOCIAL BEHAVIOR

A chronological patterning of the development of social behaviors with peers may give some insight into this rather complex topic. Many topics of social behavior are closely related to personality formation of the individual and are also a direct function of the influences of the larger society of the child including the parents.

Social interactions between infants before the age of 8 months are nonexistent. When any response at all is made to another infant, it is as if the other child was another object or toy placed for the first child's convenience. Between roughly 9 and 13 months the infants pay some attention to one another but primarily in the form of squabbles over toys. In the ensuing months there is a greater attention to similar children and less squabbling. By the beginning of the 19th month there is developed some cooperation and mutual social contact. At preschool age children tend to spend less and less time in nonsocial (parallel and noninteracting) activities. Conflicts gradually decrease and the formation of some close friendships with individuals begin. Close friendships of these earlier years develop into a concern with gang and specific ingroup activities in the 7 to 12 year age range. These gangs become more structured in the social groupings of 10 to 14 year olds by such activities as the Boy Scouts and the Campfire Girls. The socialization from these adolescent group activities leads to a common core of interests and activities of the children.

The function of social development may be viewed as benefiting both the social groups in which the child operates and also the individual himself. Society imposes certain restrictions upon behavior while providing the objects, people, and situations with which the individual lives. The standards of each social grouping shape the behavior of the new members, thus perpetuating the overall behavior of that group. Analytical knowledge of social development is the empirical base upon which changes in the social structure may be designed. That is, true control over the changes in the societies of the future depends upon knowledge of and control exerted upon the developing social behaviors of children.

Summary

The factors of heredity and maturation were described in this chapter. Behavior is shaped by the structure of the individual and the nature of his growth process.

The science of heredity—genetics—considers the transmission of features from parents to offspring. Behavior genetics considers such transmission of behavior patterns. Simple genetic concepts of dominance and recessiveness of genetic units are adequate to describe certain features. Behavior patterns, however, assume a far more complex pattern of genetic information, which is studied empirically by noting the presence or absence of characteristics in a specific population of offspring. By breeding in a closed population and selective mating the relative frequency of a behavior in offspring may be noted and used to infer genetic structure underlying that behavior.

Maturation is the process of growth of an individual which is different from learning factors, and the like. Development in children follows an orderly pattern, but at a variable rate. Development proceeds toward peripheral specific acts of the child from central mass-actions. Readiness describes the state of development sufficient for the appearance of a behavior pattern. Normal development depends upon the availability of certain early experiences.

Perceptual development follows time patterns and depends upon experience. It proceeds in the direction of more detailed consideration of the total stimulus which is present. Language is learned as it furthers the needs, feelings, and social behaviors of the child. Concepts, including language, change in quality and extent of use with further experience. Piaget describes three stages of mental development involving successively sensorimotor activities, concrete operations, and formal operations. These stages describe a reorganization of accumulating information as the child matures. Intelligence as measured by IQ tests has been found to be determined by both heredity and environment. Finally, the social behaviors of the developing child reflect the society of the child and the nature of the personality and values that he will hold in later social interaction.

SUGGESTED READINGS

Breckenridge, M. E., and Murphy, M. N. *Growth and development of the young child* (7th edition). Philadelphia: Saunders, 1963.
A textbook of child development during the first five years of age, including topics of both psychological and physical development.
Fuller, J. L., and Thompson, W. R. *Behavior genetics.* New York: Wiley, 1960.
An introduction to the viewpoints and techniques of behavior genetics, combined with a survey of the experimental literature. Some genetics study background is assumed.

Gardner, D. B. *Development in early childhood: The preschool years.* New York: Harper and Row, 1964.
An introduction to child development, with an emphasis upon the achievement of "self-hood."
Jersild, A. T. *The psychology of adolescence* (2nd edition). New York: Macmillan, 1963.
Adolescent behavior considered from the youngster's knowledge of himself and his knowledge of other forces.

Chapter 9

INDIVIDUAL DIFFERENCES
AND TESTING

How may a score on a test be interpreted? What can "statistics" contribute to the use of tests and test scores? What makes up a "good" test? What principle lies behind aptitude tests? What is the nature of intelligence and IQ scores? What is wrong with trying to measure the differences in intelligence between groups?

The assessment of differences and similarities among individuals may be called simply *testing*. The word "testing" is meant in the broad sense of measuring both performances and capacities for performance. The basic applications of testing have been the assessment of individual differences in *capacities* (for example, intelligence), the measurement of *achievements* after training, and the measurement of behavior patterns of *personality*.

The actual tests used to measure individual differences may be arbitrary in origin, rationally conceived, or based upon a background of empirical knowledge. They may be good or they may be bad. But what does it mean to have a test that is "bad"? What makes a test "good"? Measures of the "goodness" of a test depend to a great extent upon the methods of construction and purposes of the test. To understand these kinds of measures of tests as well as the language of test scores, a background of some simple statistical notions is helpful. With these statistics the worth of the test and of individual scores may be assessed. Certain approaches to test construction and improvement will also be discussed, followed by a more detailed examination of the development and uses of one of the psychologist's most well-known tests, the IQ test.

Statistical Tools

Two basic applications of statistics may be distinguished by the kinds of questions that they are intended to answer. *Descriptive statistics* makes a collection of information more meaningful and more easily grasped by presenting a summary of that information. These techniques only describe the given information and make no predictions or value judgments about it. *Inferential statistics* allow answers to questions about the meaning of the given collections of numbers. Questions answered concern the likelihood that two collections of numbers are different or

Sleepy Experimental Group			Rested Control Group	
15	17		15	13
16	15		17	14
12	14		12	13
20	13		10	16
19	15		16	11
18	17		14	12
14	19		16	15
16	17		13	12
16			13	
16.06		Average	13.65	

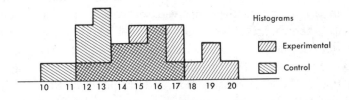

Histograms

Experimental

Control

Minutes to Solve Problems

Figure 9-1. A hypothetical sample of scores to illustrate descriptive and inferential statistics techniques. See text.

whether a set of numbers obtained as measures of behaviors would be expected to occur simply by chance factors alone.

These two kinds of statistics may be distinguished by this example. Suppose that a collection of 15 problems were presented to each of a group of 34 subjects. A measure of problem solving is the total time taken to solve the problems. Seventeen of the subjects were not permitted to sleep for two nights preceding the test. A collection of scores for each group are obtained and shown at the top of Figure 9-1. To make this collection of scores more informative, one descriptive statistic, the average score, is presented below each collection. For further description the scores may also be pictured as shown in the lower half of Figure 9-1. The average scores and the pictures from the two groups appear to be different, but what is the likely source of this difference? What is the probability that this difference is only one of chance? Or can the "chance" interpretation be rejected with some confidence? This question can be answered by inferential statistics. Inferential statistics asks whether this difference is greater than that to be expected, considering the variability in the scores. The answer expresses the probability that the difference was one of chance.

DESCRIPTIVE STATISTICS

The statistical techniques used to describe a collection of numbers include those of picturing the numbers or constructing "curves," describing the central tendency of the collection of numbers, measuring the variability of the numbers, comparing individual scores to groups of scores, and expressing the degree of relationship between two sets of numbers which represent two measures from the same individual.

One method of describing numbers by pictures is the histogram, as shown in Figure 9-1. The frequency of each score along the horizontal baseline (the "abscissa") is expressed by the height of the bar. More commonly, the center point of each bar is connected by a straight line, resulting in a frequency polygon or *frequency distribution*. The frequency distribution is often used to describe a collection of test scores. The most frequently occurring shapes of frequency distributions are the *normal curve*, which is symmetrical and bell-shaped, the *skewed curve*, which looks as if the normal curve was pushed to one side, and the *bimodal* or two-humped *curve*. These oft-occurring frequency distributions appear in Figure 9-2.

How might the central tendency of a frequency distribution be described when the distribution cannot be visually inspected? Three

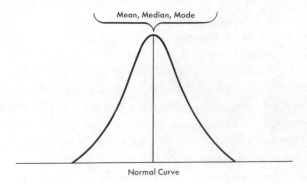

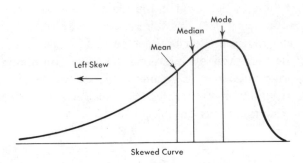

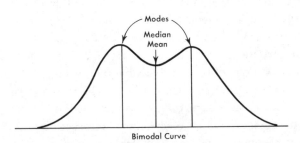

Figure 9-2. **Common frequency distribution shapes and the position of measures of central tendency.**

measures of central tendency are commonly used: the *mean*, the *median*, and the *mode*. The *mean* is the simple arithmetic average of the scores—the total sum of the scores divided by the number of scores. The mean is the same as the "average," as the word is commonly used in describing baseball player performance, and the like. The *median* is the centermost of the ordered scores. That value at which half of the scores are greater and half are smaller is the median. This 50% point is not affected by the size of scores at the extremity of a distribution but only by the effects of their being greater than or less than the median. Thus, the change in size of a score at one end of a distribution *will* change the size of the mean, but it *will not* affect the value of the median. The *mode* is the most frequently appearing score in the distribution. It is the highest peak on the frequency distribution.

Symmetrical curves such as the normal distribution have a mean, median, and mode which are approximately equal. But if the curve is skewed, such as that in Figure 9-2, the mean is positioned further from the mode than is the median. The mean, being sensitive to the size of variant scores, is pushed in the direction of those fewer but more important scores. The median, sensitive only to the number of scores on either side, is not displaced as far from the mode. These facts lead to the notion that an accurate description of the central tendency of non-symmetrical score distributions must include both the median and the mean. Similarly, one can "lie" in reporting the central tendency by selecting but one of these measures. Suppose that the first examination in a course such as Introduction to Psychology yielded a very highly skewed curve like that in Figure 9-2. There were a few very low scores and a bunching of scores near the high end of the distribution. Two things served to change the situation before the next test. First, a large percentage of the individual's making low, failing scores dropped the course. Second, the instructor noted the large number of high scores and made the next test somewhat more difficult. The first change, removing the extremely low scorers, served to raise the mean of the second test a great deal. The increase in the mean was accompanied by a lesser increase in the median, due to the loss of scores at that low end. The tougher second test, however, resulted in a lower score for nearly everyone, shifting the median (and the mean) down slightly. The mean, though, was raised more than it was lowered. If the instructor wished to berate the class, he may report that the median went down 2 points (thus, Get to work!) while praise could also have been applied by reporting that the mean had risen 4 points.

The problem of reporting the variability of the scores is pictured by the distributions in Figure 9-3. Both have the same number of scores and the same mean, median, and mode, and are of the same general shape, yet they obviously differ in "fatness" or *variability* of the scores. Again there are three measures which may describe this property: the

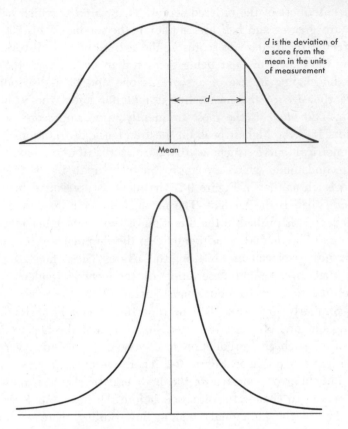

d is the deviation of
a score from the
mean in the units
of measurement

Mean

Figure 9-3. Two normal distributions of equal numbers of scores
and central tendency, but which differ in variability of score
values.

range, the *mean deviation,* and the *standard deviation.* The range expresses the difference between two selected scores in the population. It
may express the difference between the largest and smallest scores, or
it may express the difference between the scores falling at the 25 per
cent and 75 per cent points. This latter "interquartile range" is the distance between the values at which one fourth of the scores are less and
one fourth of the scores are greater, respectively. The interquartile range
is easy to compute and is not subject to the obvious distortions which
the simple range might include in estimating the variability of distributions which had very long, unusual "tails." The *mean deviation* is simply
the average of the differences between each score and the mean of the
distribution. Generally, this average distance is not used in descriptive

statistics because of the additional use and value presented by the standard deviation in other statistical calculations. The *standard deviation,* like the mean deviation, calculates the distance in score units of each score from the mean, but squares each value before averaging. The square root of this average is then taken. Thus, the standard deviation is the square root of the average, squared deviation of the scores from the mean. This statistic has some usefulness in describing properties of the normal curve as described below.

The technique of comparing one score to a collection of scores include the percentile ranking of ordered scores and the relationships of the scores in a normal distribution using the concept of the standard deviation. The *percentile* ranking of a score is simply that percentage

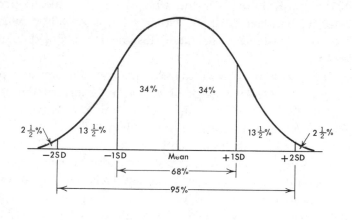

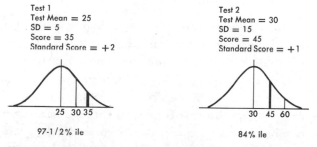

Figure 9-4. The relationship between percentile scores and standard scores in a normal distribution. An example shows the comparison between relative performances on two different tests by using standard scores and percentiles, derived from knowledge of the test mean and standard deviation.

of the total scores which are lower in value. Thus a percentile of 64 expresses the fact that that score was equal to or better than 64 per cent of the scores in the reference distribution. The 50th percentile is the same as the median in most cases.

Scores which are normally distributed may be described by some properties of the normal curve. In the normal curve of Figure 9-4, the standard deviation units are indicated as +1 SD, −1 SD, etc. away from the mean. The properties of the normal curve are such that knowing the distance from the mean in standard deviation units allows calculation of the percentage of the total scores in that area. Thus, the distance between the mean and 1 SD contains roughly 34 per cent of the scores, and between the mean and two standard deviations lie about 47 1/2 per cent of the scores. Looking at both sides of the curve, 68 per cent of the scores lie between the +1 and −1 SD's and 95 per cent of the scores lie between ±2 SD's. Other percentage values which correspond to certain standard deviation distances are tabled in statistical handbooks.

These relationships allow an easy comparison of scores and percentile ranks requiring only knowledge of the mean, standard deviation, and the score itself, along with the appropriate table. Relative performance on tests which differ as to mean and standard deviation may then be compared by looking at the percentile ranks on each of these tests. But this comparison between different tests may also be made without computing percentile scores. Knowledge of the deviation units of each score allows the same comparison. If the raw scores are translated into standard deviation units they become *standard scores*. Again, only the mean and the standard deviation of each distribution need be known to compare relative performance. The examples in Figure 9-4 describe this simple relationship.

The *correlation coefficient* describes the degree of relationship between two sets of scores obtained from the same individuals or objects. Thus, if one is interested in the extent to which persons who get high grades in math are also likely to have high grades in chemistry, the correlation describes this relationship in a single number. The simple correlation, or "r," ranges in size from 1.00 through zero to −1.00. The size of the number, usually expressed in two decimals, such as .45 or .19, determines the strength of the relationship. If there was a strong relationship between chem and math grades, the value might be something like .89, while if the relationship was almost nonexistent, the r may be .17. The sign (+) or (−), describes the direction of the relationship. Positive correlations are direct relationships, while negative correlations are inverse relations. A negative correlation such as $-.78$ would mean that the grades in math and chem are inversely related or that persons with high math scores have low chem scores, and that persons with low math scores have high chem scores.

Care must be taken in the interpretation of a correlation. A high correlation between scores is not evidence that one factor "caused" the differences in the other. That smoking causes cancers cannot be demonstrated by the correlation of the measurements of these two factors in a group of people. An inference of causation requires a controlled demonstration of the presence of one factor evoking another. Correlation applies no control over other factors, and hence makes no inference about the origin of a factor. Correlation does allow prediction, however. A high correlation between smoking and incidence of cancer allows an accurate prediction that smoking individuals will indeed be more likely to also have cancer. The correlation does not show that smoking causes cancer, but simply that smoking and cancer in the same person is a frequent observation.

INFERENTIAL STATISTICS

The problem of making decisions about the differences between groups of numbers is the general task facing inferential statistics. Three parts of this problem will be discussed: the notions of sampling from populations and consequent errors of sampling and measurement, a very simple comparison *statistical test,* and the end-product notion of inferential statistics, *significance statements.*

A *population* is the group of all possible cases about which some question is asked. If practicable, the entire population may be tested, and in this case there would be little need for inferential statistics. The usual case, though, is that of a population which is impossible to measure in its entirety. One such population which could not be entirely measured is that of all the students who *are* now taking this course in psychology, all who *have* taken it, and all who *will* take it in the future under the present rules. This is a common population about which questions are asked in psychological research. Research questions are tested using samples from this very large population.

Suppose that we consider again the problem-solving experiment from earlier in the chapter. Do the conditions of deprivation from sleep and no such deprivation from sleep produce a difference in the time to solve the problems? Two groups of 17 subjects each were randomly

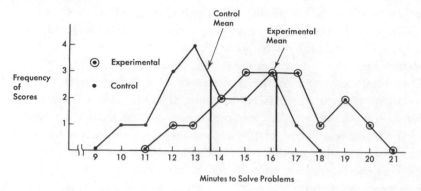

Figure 9-5. Frequency distribution of the hypothetical data presented in Figure 9-1.

selected from the population of psychology students and administered
the treatments. Two kinds of differences may be noted among scores of
these subjects. As shown in Figure 9-5, the scores within each group
differ and conform roughly to a normal distribution. Secondly, there
is an apparent difference between the two groups of scores. The
frequency distributions indicate that there is a substantial separation
between the two curves.

What factors have produced these differences? Two kinds of general
errors in experimental measurement contribute to the differences in
scores. The two kinds of errors are *errors of measurement* and *errors
of sampling. Errors of measurement* include a miscellany of differences
in performance caused by uncontrolled conditions affecting the dependent variable. Distracting factors of light and noise may interrupt the
behavior being measured. Different interactions between the personality
of the experimenter and that of the subjects being measured may affect
performance, and similarly other random effects of the conditions of
measurement influence the scores. Other contributions to the errors of
measurement come from the measuring techniques themselves. The variability may be introduced by the crudeness of the measuring devices,
or the nature of the response measured. The errors of measurement are
responsible for much of the variability of scores within each of the
groups of the experiment. *Errors of sampling* are more closely related to
the reasoning leading to the statistical inference test. These errors result
from the operation of drawing a sample from a population of variable
individuals. The errors of sampling describe the fact that a sample is

never exactly representative of the population from which it was drawn. The differences between different such samples drawn under the same conditions provide an estimate of the errors of sampling.

The difference between the two samples of the problem-solving experiment may have been caused by errors of sampling but also by the effect of the experimental treatment. Statistical inference will give us an estimate of the probability that the difference was caused by the errors of sampling alone. A test is made of the hypothesis that there was *no* effect of the experimental treatment, the *null hypothesis*. This test is based upon a comparison of the difference between the obtained samples and the difference that would be expected by chance between any two random samples.

Suppose that a large number of pairs of groups of twenty subjects were sampled and tested in the manner of one of the groups in the experiment. For each of these pairs of samples, the difference between the mean performance on the dependent variable was computed and plotted as one point on a frequency distribution. After a large number of these pairs of samples have been sampled, the characteristics of the distribution of these differences-between-means may be noted. The standard deviation of this distribution allows us to compute the percentage, or expected frequency of occurrence, of obtained differences of each magnitude. With this distribution it can be estimated that a difference between means as great as that of two standard deviations would occur only in 5 per cent of such pairs of samples. A simple test of the relative likelihood of obtaining means of a specific difference may be made by comparing that difference to the standard deviation of the distribution of such sample pairs. Thus, the test may be simply a ratio between the obtained difference in means to the standard deviation of a distribution of population of such differences. The ratio, called a *critical ratio*, results in a number in standard deviation units which may be translated into percentage and hence probability terms.

The actual calculation procedures for such tests do not require that these multiple samples of pairs be made and measured. The appropriate factors may be estimated from certain properties of the experimental samples. The expected variability between obtained samples may be estimated by the observed variability among scores within those samples, according to statistical theory.

The results of statistical tests of inference are statements of the probability that the obtained differences arose from chance sampling factors alone, or conversely, that the differences may have resulted from other factors, including the independent variable (task differences) of the experiment. The probability statements are called *significance statements*. It is said that an obtained difference is *statistically significant* when the probability that it was caused by chance is so small that the experimenter is *not* willing to accept that chance was the only causative factor. Thus, if a critical ratio of 3.0 was obtained in our experiment, the probability of a difference this large occurring by sampling factors alone is less than 1/4 of 1 per cent or a chance of about 1 in 400. It is thus reasonable to believe that other factors, presumably the independent variable, were at work to produce the differences. As a working decision level, the experimenter is usually willing to accept a significance at the 5 per cent level, or odds of about 1 in 20, as the point of separation between the two conclusions of sampling error alone caused the difference or that some other factor in addition to sampling produced the obtained difference.

It should be clear from this introduction to the logic of tests of inference that the tests do not prove a difference in an absolute sense. The significance probability may be so small that chance factors are almost certainly not the only source of the difference, but it is still a case of *almost* certainty. The rare occasion of a large difference by chance can and does occur in the frequency described by the probability statement. Once in 20 occasions with differences of that size the researcher must expect that the conclusion of rejecting the no-difference or null hypothesis is in error. There is, on this rare occasion, no difference between the groups other than that produced by chance.

Ability Testing

A broad definition of *ability testing* is that it is the use of devices to ascertain some information about an individual, his past or predictable future behavior. Measuring past learning and probably future behavior by assessing present behavior is an important part of ability testing. How much psychology has the student learned after completing the course? What is the likely grade point average of this freshman at the end of his junior year? Who are the most gifted individuals upon which to confer scholarship gifts? Which of a given group are most likely to be exceptional candidates for astronaut training? Which of those around you is likely to suffer some sort of personality disturbance in the near future? Answers to these kinds of practical questions may be attempted most easily by the construction of tests.

P. G. HENKE

A description of the purposes of different tests will first be considered, followed by some of the terms used in testing, along with a consideration of the factors by which the goodness of a test may be measured. Finally, some of the ways of actually constructing tests will be considered, supplemented by some criticisms which have been leveled at psychological tests.

ACHIEVEMENT AND APTITUDE TESTS

Two basic purposes of tests are to measure *achievements* and to estimate *aptitudes*. These are assessments of the effects of the past and predictions of the future, respectively. This difference in purpose, however, is not matched by an important physical difference in the actual achievement and aptitude tests. The content of the tests used for each of these purposes does not necessarily differ. In both cases, measurements of present behavior are made. The kind of test and its purpose is determined by the use to which those measures of behavior are put. Thus, achievement tests require some assumptions about the extent to which the test is really measuring the achievements which it is intended to measure. The reasoning behind the use of an aptitude test is somewhat more complex. An aptitude test assumes that the past exposure of the individuals being tested has been the same and that the present measured performances will then reflect the individual differences in ability to profit from that exposure. Thus, a "mathematical aptitude" test assumes that all persons taking the test have been exposed equally to similar mathematical problems and that the differences in performance on the test problems reflect the ability of the individuals to work with and learn to use such mathematics. This assumption of equal past exposure will be discussed again in connection with the uses of intelligence tests.

Different ability tests reflect different purposes. The examination given at the end of this course is intended to measure the student's relative achievement in mastering the presented content of psychology. If the same test had been given before the course with the intention of using it to predict learning of psychology, it would have been called an aptitude test. The test and its content would be the same, but the purposes would differ.

TEST TERMINOLOGY

The terms used to describe testing procedures and results are based upon descriptive statistics. Test scores are often reported as *percentiles*. An individual's score at the "64th percentile" means that that score was equal to or better than 64 per cent of some group of scores. The particular scores against which a given score is compared are referred to as the *norms* of that test. The scores on the tests which you may have taken as a freshman beginning college may be compared to the norms which were derived from the scores of the entire freshman class or they may be compared to the norms from the larger sample of several freshman classes of the past. By comparison with these norms and by using percentile scores, the student may easily see his relative position in the class. As aptitude test norms, these tests may then be used to estimate relative scholarship, the likely amount of effort that the student will have to put into his studies to "get by," and other similar future academic performances.

TEST NAMES	FIGHTER PILOT	NAVIGATOR
Arithmetic Reasoning		Yes
Biographical Data	Yes	Yes
Dial and Table Reading		Yes
General Information	Yes	
Instrument Comprehension	Yes	
Mechanical Principles	Yes	
Numerical Operations		Yes
Reading Comprehension		Yes
Spatial Orientation	Yes	Yes
Speed of Identification	Yes	
Complex Coordination	Yes	
Discrimination Reaction Time	Yes	Yes
Rudder Control	Yes	
Two-Hand Pursuit	Yes	Yes

Figure 9-6. Tests which were administered to potential fighter pilots and navigators. A composite score on these tests was compared against a cutoff score to determine acceptance for training.

When a collection of different tests are given for roughly the same purpose, the collection of tests is referred to as a *test battery*. If the tests are to be used as a selection device, a *cutoff score* may be determined by some combination of the scores on the different tests such that those whose composite score falls on one side of the cutoff score are separated from those whose scores fall on the other side. An example of a test battery which led to the use of a cutoff score is given in Figure 9-6. The selection of air-crews for WWII aircraft used these tests.

A collection of scores from a test battery may also be displayed as a *test profile*, as shown in Figure 9-7. The personality test of this example

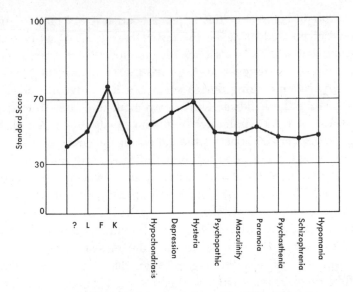

Figure 9-7. A profile of scores from the MMPI diagnostic test of personality patterns. (See Chapter 10.) At a glance, the pattern of scores and any unusual scores may be noted.

describes the extent to which the tested individual answers the questions in the same manner as individuals who have been separately diagnosed as displaying particular behavior disorders. At a glance one may note which scores fall into the ranges of abnormally high and abnormally low scores. The graphic presentation of a test profile in this manner is considerably more efficient than comparing one at a time, each score with the established norms on each scale.

The two concepts which are used to describe the "goodness" of a test are *reliability* and *validity*. *Reliability* describes the extent to which the test measures the same way and yields the same score each time it is given under the same conditions. *Validity* is the extent to which the test measures what it is intended to measure. A test may be reliable but not valid, but a test is never valid if it is not reliable.

An example of these "goodness" concepts may help their understanding. A test of "honesty" is to be developed. How might the relative honesty of a group of students be measured? One approach would be to test each student by flipping a coin. As each student passes in front of the tester, the coin is flipped: Heads-honesty, Tail-dishonesty. The heads are then allowed to participate in an honor system for examinations and the Tails are watched suspiciously for the remainder of the course.

"But," you might complain, "this is not a good test of honesty." Indeed, each time a given student passes the tester there is an equal chance that the measurement will be "honest" or "dishonest." A better test is needed. A second approach, designed to improve the test reliability, would be to use a physical measuring device such as a hand dynamometer. Each student squeezes the handles of this instrument and the strength of his grip is measured by a pointer reading. The greater the strength of the squeeze, the greater the honesty; the values on the scale are called units of honesty. Now the objection of unreliability is partly answered. There will be a fairly high correlation between successive measurements for each student. The test-retest correlation would be high, a good reliability index. But if these measurements are closely examined, two humps on the frequency distribution may be noted, corresponding fairly closely to the sex of the student, females are measured as being generally less honest (less strength of grip) than the males. The girls of the class will be quick to point out that this too is not a good test of honesty. It measures the same way each time, but it does not seem to measure what is generally meant by honesty. An even more reliable test could be devised. Honesty may be measured by the number of hairs on the right arm divided by distance between the pupils of the eyes in millimeters. Here is a measurement that would be highly reliable. The numbers would not change from one measurement to the next within the limits of the formation and disappearance of hair. But this test may be criticized also because it does not appear to be related to honesty. It should be clear that a test may be very reliable but not valid.

How might a test be developed which is both reliable *and* valid? It will not be valuable to gather items for the test without some consideration of what is to be measured, without considering the validity of those items. Honesty was purposefully chosen for the example because it is one of those characteristics of behavior for which there is no general definitional agreement. Abilities which are explicitly defined are usually easily measured by tests, the test incorporating the parts of the definition. Honesty has no accepted definition and the source of the test is thus more obscure.

Four kinds of validity may be usefully distinguished to further explain this problem of test construction. Face or *content validity* refers to the extent to which a test appears to test what it is intended to test. Tests of the motor skills of potential airplane pilots have a good deal of face validity. However, a valid test of pilot proficiency may also be composed of things which have no content validity at all. A test may predict or have *predictive validity,* without apearing to be measuring what it does predict. Pilot selection tests may include questions of American history or of rural sociology. These items may do a good job of selecting pilots for reasons unknown. The existence of such test items illustrates that a test may have low content validity but high predictive validity. A third sort of validity is *concurrent validity,* a measure of the extent to which different parts of a test battery measure the same. A final examination which is composed of objective (say, multiple-choice) questions and essay questions about the same material may illllustrate concurrent validity. The objective questions are said to be valid if they correlate well with the essay questions which, in turn, are often assumed to be valid. Finally, *construct validity* is the technique of validating tests of concepts like that of our example above. Certain ways of behaving, such as those described by the terms honesty, anxiety, and intelligence are validated in an indirect fashion. The extent to which individuals who score high and low on the test, for example, behave as expected by theory or other less formal expectations, gives validity to the test which has separated those individuals. Thus, if a test separated a group of honest and dishonest students, and later tests showed that the honest-measured subjects performed consistently as expected, and the dishonest-measured students also performed in behavior situational tests as we would expect of dishonest individuals, the test is judged to have construct validity. The degree to which the construct as measured by the test "fits in" with other information is construct validity.

Now, how can a test of honesty be devised? Probably it can be devised from test items which are in part rationally developed. At this point a good deal of experience and skill enter the construction picture. Items may be improved or removed by checking the contribution each has made to measuring a construct which in turn did a "good job." This approach to test construction fits well with the next topic, that of developing tests to do a specific job.

CRITERION TEST CONSTRUCTION METHODS

The predictive validity of a test is directly measured by comparison of the extent to which the test correlates with some other measure of that performance. This other measure of performance is called the *criterion* for the test. The test constructor attempts to develop a test which correlates as high as possible with the criterion scores of that same behavior which are available under certain circumstances. Suppose that a test is needed for selecting those who would perform well in assembling television tubes. A practical criterion could presumably be developed by some measure of later skill at the job. A test must be devised which discriminates between those who will eventually do well at the job and those who won't. Again, the source of questions is primarily a rational procedure which is easy or difficult depending upon the test constructor's experience, familiarity with similar tests and relevant aspects of the job performance, and the subtleties of test item writing itself. Ideally, a fairly large collection of test items are administered to a group of job candidates, all of whom are later given training on the job. At the time that training has been completed and the workers seem to be doing the job to the best of their abilities, ratings of performance, the criterion, are determined. The test constructor can then use this criterion performance to select and refine items in the test. That is, those items which correlate well with performance of tube assembly are retained, and those which are not so related are eliminated. Presumably, the resulting test would have a good predictive validity. Further checks could then be made by readministering the test to a new group and repeating the whole process.

Obviously this method of test construction, though excellent in principle, is quite inefficient for its purpose if it must be carried to this extreme for each job in a given industry. Corners can and are cut in practice with a consequent loss of predictive efficiency. A test constructor could simply apply the invented test items to a group of established workers at the job to find the items that separate these individuals from some control sample of workers on different jobs. Those items which discriminate these groups are likely to predict performance of that skill.

Construct validity test construction methods do not differ a great deal from this technique used to develop predictive tests. The primary difference is in the specifiability of the criterion which is available. Tube assembly is much easier to specify and agree upon than are honesty, intelligence, and creativity.

One common mistake of those who would criticize the use of psychological tests is to confuse content validity and predictive validity. By dissecting and evaluating certain sample items which are presented as representative of the tests as, for example, those for national scholarship competition, the critic can show how, in his opinion, a bright student might be led to make a different answer than that scored as "correct." Ignoring the problem of the source of the rational evaluations of items, this criticism overlooks the most important criteria for inclusion of the item, which is "does it work?" The scoring of the test is not capriciously devised, nor do the constructors have ulterior motives, as is often implied. The items are selected for their effectiveness in producing a total score which correlates well with a criterion. In this sense, individual items should not be criticized after the development of the test except by the comparison of the performance on that item and the total score. The only "bad" items are those which, when removed, will produce total scores which correlate higher with the criterion.

Other kinds of just criticism may be made of the "goodness" of present tests. It is quite apparent that even the most highly valued tests in our society are not perfect. They are far from it. Such tests are neither perfectly reliable nor perfectly valid. Because they are not the best that could be devised, criticism can and should be directed toward improving the techniques of construction. One of the difficulties of obtaining better tests for certain jobs is a basic lack of information about behavior in general. Test constructors cannot logically derive items from a consideration of an organization of knowledge about that behavior because that organized knowledge simply does not exist. Instead, a considerable guessing skill and luck enter into the choice of one item rather than another. Further, careful judgment must be exercised in the rules of administration of tests, considering the factors of test-takers attitudes, immediate past experiences, fatigue, and so on, which might unduly influence scores. Basically, test construction is still an art based upon empirical knowledge. It is not the automatic application of the science of behavior that its more enthusiastic supporters and salesmen would have one believe.

Measurement of Intelligence

One of the oldest and most useful of the tests of behavior is that which is intended to measure and predict the intellectual capacity of man. The test of intelligence had a very practical origin in selecting grade school children who would profit from different training. Intelligence tests have since been devised which are useful for assessing differences among adults. The intelligence test has been analyzed for its contributions to the understanding of various performance differences among men. And finally, the intelligence test has been widely misused as a device to prove the superiority of one group of men over another.

TEST DEVELOPMENT

The first successful test of intelligence was that produced by the French physician, Alfred Binet, about 1904. This test was designed to select the dull students in Paris schools so that they might be trained by different methods. Binet developed a test on the basis of his notions of intelligence. He noted, as he observed his own children, that intellectual capacity increases with age. He reasoned that the intelligent person would be less susceptible to distraction, more likely to adapt the situation to achieve a goal, and likely to criticize his own work. These notions were worked into the first Binet tests. In 1916 L. M. Terman revised the Binet tests into what then became the yardstick for comparison of the future intelligence tests, the Stanford-Binet.[82]

The practical needs of the U.S. Army in World War I led to the officer selection and classification test, known as the *Army Alpha*. This test was aimed at assessing ability to follow directions, reason, do arithmetic, and recall information. Recent developments in testing have improved the efficiency of these tests, increased the reliability and improved the norms, but they are not noticeably different in content. The validity of present intelligence tests has come from a rather informal application of construct validity. Tests that reliably selected individuals as desired were considered to be "good" tests.

Binet's testing of school children classified individuals into levels of mental development which he called *mental age* (M.A.). A child's mental age is the age in years of an average child of that mental development. Thus, Binet's test items were graduated into steps measuring

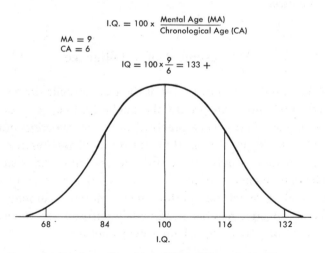

$$I.Q. = 100 \times \frac{\text{Mental Age (MA)}}{\text{Chronological Age (CA)}}$$

$MA = 9$
$CA = 6$

$$IQ = 100 \times \frac{9}{6} = 133 +$$

Figure 9-8. **IQ is easily computed from MA and CA. IQ scores of a large sample are normally distributed with a mean at 100 and a standard deviation at about 16.**

intellectual development. In taking the test the child solved the problems to as high a level as he could. The step at which the child began to make mistakes was defined as the measured mental age of the child. By comparing this mental age with the individual's actual or *chronological age* (C.A.), relative intelligence measurements can be compared regardless of actual age. This comparison is called the intelligence quotient, or *IQ*. The IQ is obtained by dividing the child's mental age by his chronological age (and multiplying by 100 to avoid decimals). An average intelligence score is 100, since that score results when the CA and MA are the same. Figure 9-8 gives examples of these computations and a typical distribution of IQ scores from a large population. The normal distribution of intelligence from Binet's techniques had a mean of 100 and a standard deviation of about 16. These facts, of course, allow predictions of the numbers of individuals to be expected at each IQ level in the average population. These same IQ scores are the end product of nearly all tests of intelligence. Actual scores on the tests may be converted to IQ scores by the simple processes described above using descriptive statistics.

CHARACTERISTICS OF IQ TESTS

The revised Stanford-Binet and other modern tests of intelligence have been examined for systematic variations in the qualities which they appear to measure. Applied to younger children, the tests appear to emphasize judgment and attention, while older children are tested for their verbal abilities and reasoning capacities.[48] The Wechsler IQ tests are divided into two parts: a verbal scale much like the Binet tests and a performance scale which requires responses to items which are nonverbal in nature.[93] The performance scale has been shown to correlate fairly high with the verbal scale for persons of normal verbal facility, and it is reasoned that this scale might more accurately assess the abilities of individuals with a verbal handicap. But in spite of such attempts at minimizing the effects of verbal abilities in assessing intelligence, verbal facility still makes a sizeable contribution to the IQ test score. For example, the test instructions and other test-administration procedures are strongly affected by relative verbal facility.

The use of tests such as the Stanford-Binet and the Wechsler is a person-to-person matter. The tests are not designed to be taken by simply following printed instructions. Each question is presented by a trained test-administrator in accordance with fairly complicated orders of procedure. Thus, the closeness of relationship between the test-taker and the test-administrator, called *rapport*, will affect the scores which result. The training of the test-administrator includes a standardized procedure of presentation of the items and a carefully cultivated avoidance of emotional biases and personality clashes with the test-taker. This problem of rapport will be considered again later.

What effect has age in the adult years upon IQ scores? If the IQ scores of later years are compared to those of roughly 30 years of age, it is found that verbal ability declines from about 30 to 65 years of age, rapid rate.[94] Be careful not to interpret this decline in IQ score as a reduced competency to perform in an intelligent manner. This set of test observations more nearly reflects the reduced ease or facility of the older person to gain new knowledge. The same older person has a background of already learned information which may allow him to guide his life in a more intelligent manner than a younger person with a higher IQ test score but less experience. IQ tests are aimed at assessing adaptability and attention to solving problems, and these sorts of items are more sensitive to the sharpness and quickness of youth than the factor of experience.

The IQ tests have provided a tool for the assessment of exceptional intelligence. Either very high or very low IQ scores suggest an exceptional intellect and that exceptional care might be needed to realize fully the potentials of that individual. Very low scores distinguish the mentally subnormal classes of *mentally retarded* and *mentally defective*, while high IQ scores indicate individuals who are said to be *mentally gifted*.

Subnormal intelligence which has been produced by known factors such as damage to structures of the brain is classified as *mental defective*. Subnormal intelligence which has arisen from the normal processes of mental growth in an individual known to be normal in other physical development is called *mental retardation*. A practical difference between these two groups is often indicated by the kind of handicap suffered by the defective. The intellectual capacities of the defective individuals are often not uniformly below normal, but are affected selectively. For example, severe perceptual interpretation losses may characterize some mentally defective children, while these children may be near normal in other behaviors.

The mentally retarded label is not an easy one to apply in a practical sense, because the degree to which the individual may be able to manage his affairs and live normally depends to a high degree upon the demands made by society. A particular mentally retarded person may be helpless in an industrial environment, for example, but may carry out a normal life in a situation demanding less adaptability. A great deal of attention has been directed to the educability of the mentally retarded, referring to attempts to train each individual to the limits of his ability. By realizing the full capacity of the mentally retarded, acceptable performance in many semi-skilled occupations can be achieved. Early diagnosis of mental retardation has been deemed especially important, so that more effective teaching and less of the frustration of not keeping up will be experienced.

The intellectually gifted have similar problems of requiring special treatment for the maximum realization of the available intellectual capacity. Less is known about the correct manner of training the superior student. Procedures for training individuals of subnormal intelligence may be selected by comparing the results against the criterion of the performance of those with an average IQ score. But what is the criterion for selection of education procedures for the gifted? It is generally believed that more personal attention to a program of intellectual challenges tailored to that individual is superior to keeping the gifted student at the pace of the normal classroom.

Study of the life patterns of gifted individuals from early school years to middle adulthood has indicated that the mentally gifted are superior or above average in most other factors as well.[83] Contrary to popular folklore, which holds that intellectual prowess is compensated for by disabilities of physical constitution, study of the intellectually gifted has shown them to be above average physical specimens; being larger, in better health, and exhibiting better social relationships and leadership than their colleagues of moderate intelligence.

GROUP COMPARISONS OF INTELLIGENCE

One illustration of the misuse of the intelligence tests comes from certain attempts to answer questions about intellectual capacities of established groups. Do those who differ in nationality or location of their homes differ also in intelligence? The basic misunderstanding concerns the question which *is* answered and the question which investigators would *like* to answer by such comparisons. The question which *is* answered is "Do these tested groups of individuals differ in IQ score?," while the question for which an answer is sought is "Do these two kinds of people differ in intelligence?" Several factors about intelligence tests make an answer to the first question an unsatisfactory indication of an answer to the second. These factors are those of the adequacy of *sampling* and the reference population, the validity of the test in situations different from that in which it was *standardized,* and the *techniques of administration* of the test to the different groups.

The first of these problems relates to the difference inherent in a sample from a larger population. Since the entire population cannot efficiently be tested to answer the question, samples must be tested instead. It is easy to see that these samples must be representative of the population. But before this can be assured, the population itself must be adequately specified. If a comparison is to be made between Northern and Southern Europeans by some division of the countries, how might the sampling be made? Would a comparison of first generation descendants of immigrants to the U.S. from those European locations constitute a reasonable group from which to sample? Assuredly not. What are the reasons for the immigration from those countries? In what other ways do those samples differ? Socio-economic status? Occupation? Does not this comparison of children of certain immigrants restrict the population to which one may safely generalize to just that: children of immigrants from the various localities? Note that this is not the same sampling problem which was considered in discussing inferential statistics. In that case there were two random selections of subjects from a common population which experienced but one difference, while in this case the samples are drawn from different populations and one of many differences between those populations has been measured. There is no effective answer to this problem of inference except to note that this method of comparison does not answer questions about larger populations from which the samples were derived, unless it can be shown that all other relevant factors have been held constant, to preclude an accident or bias of selection.

The question of the validity of the IQ test applied to different situations is simply one of whether the same intellectual capacities are measured in groups which are known to differ on other relevant dimensions. IQ tests as they have been considered are quite specific to the groups on which the test was standardized and validated. One of the basic assumptions of an ability test is that it reflects capacities only when the assumption of equal past experience with the materials of the test can be upheld. Especially the factor of verbal facility, which was seen as playing a dominant role in most IQ tests, must be carefully examined for its relevance to comparisons of different groups. Obviously, most Americans would do poorly on an IQ test administered in French, and the French would not do well on tests in English or Tagalog. But the more subtle differences in language variations, such as urban north vs. rural south, or adult vs. teenager, are often overlooked. Generally Nebraskans and Western Iowans, for example, refer to "scooping" snow, while those from Illinois and Eastern Iowa refer to "shoveling" snow. Such minor and apparently trivial differences in word usage may be very important for children and others whose experience with the language form used in the test is limited. Simply the frequency of experience with certain words is much greater in some social classes than in others. Unfamiliarity with the use of a word may lead to a different solution to a problem than would be expected from more verbally experienced test-takers. Which of the following is different from the other: "pot," "point," or "fix"? A narcotics addict might answer "point." An experienced navigator might say "pot," while others may be impressed by the similarity of the beginnings of the other words, and thus select "fix" as the odd one. The example points out some of the difficulty which test constructors have in devising items of equal past experience to the members of different groups. Attempts at developing performance tests which would be culturally unbiased have not been successful. The cultural influences upon behavior may be minimized by some kinds of questions, but they cannot be removed. Consider again the Whorfian hypothesis which holds that the manner in which one thinks is a function of his language structure. This indirect influence upon IQ scores by verbal factors would be difficult to control completely.

Some final problems in the comparison of groups upon test-measured factors such as intelligence concern the way in which that test is administered. The Binet-type IQ tests require a personal interaction between the test giver and the person taking the test. This relationship, called rapport, will be affected by the sorts of feelings and differences which are common between the members of different groups. The test administrator belonging to one group would find it very difficult to hide effectively personal feelings while testing members of another group. One approach which has been partially successful in meeting this problem is to train members of each group to administer the tests to the members of their own group. But the group comparisons are now confounded by a difference in test administrators.

Overall, comparisons between groups which are different enough to be of interest are also different enough on other characteristics and ways of behaving that make those comparisons worthless. Even if a test could be developed which is fair to both groups and could be impartially administered to samples from those groups, there remains the problem of ascertaining the representativeness of that sample to larger populations. This is by no means a trivial problem. One reasonable answer is that the wrong question is being asked when an attempt is made to assess the difference in the layman's concept of intelligence by use of an empirically derived, highly specific IQ-measuring device.

There is another approach to IQ assessment which appears to be very simple and thus has a good deal of appeal. Why not develop some physical measure of intelligence like brain size in certain areas or the speed of brain reaction to stimuli of special kinds? Analysis has shown, though, that the same problems of interpretation still exist for this sort of IQ measure, plus some new ones. The physiological bases of learning and performance are not known to anywhere near the degree that would be required to isolate rationally a measure of IQ. Why not then sample various physiological measures and correlate them with traditional IQ measurement devices in the hope of chancing upon some reliable observation? Now the same problems of validity are again present. Suppose a measurement was devised which correlated very highly with IQ scores? Is this now a valid measure for other groups of individuals than that upon which the criterion test was standardized? Just because it is a physical measurement does not necessarily mean that this measurement is not also a function of experience, cultural factors, use of verbal facility, etc. The physiological changes which underlie learning may be behind the physical change which is being correlated with IQ scores. Can these changes and structural features be assuredly independent of the quality of past experiences of the learner?

The problem is again one of a difference in performance, which one would like to interpret as caused by a difference in a hypothesized causative factor. Attempts at measuring this mythical factor independent of its effects upon performance are not likely to be successful. Intelligence is a product of our imagination, to put it bluntly, and it has become so common in our ways of thinking that care must be taken that it does not become sought as a thing which is independent of its effects.

Summary

Testing is the process of measuring differences and similarities among individuals.

Descriptive statistics are values and pictures which summarize the important features of a collection of numbers. Frequency distributions, measures of central tendency, and measures of variability are the most useful descriptive statistics. The position of one score in a collection may be reported by percentile rank or by standard score. The correlation coefficient describes the relationship between scores from the same individuals.

Inferential statistics apply statistical tests to collections of scores, and, if certain assumptions have been met, the likely cause of the difference between the scores may be expressed in significance statements.

Ability tests answer questions of past and future behaviors by measurements of present behavior. Ability tests measure achievements and infer aptitudes, the difference being one of use for the scores rather than one of test content.

The goodness of a test is described by its reliability and its validity. Reliability measures the consistency of the test, and validity reflects whether the test actually measures what it is intended to measure. Tests may be reliable yet not valid. A valid test is always reliable. Four kinds of validity are content, predictive, concurrent, and construct validity, reflecting different procedures and problems in test construction.

Intelligence tests date from the early attempts of Binet to select school children of differing ability levels. Binet measured mental age (MA) which, in a ratio with chronological age, determined the IQ score.

IQ tests are strongly influenced by verbal ability. Administering individual tests on a person-to-person basis requires a standard relationship between those individuals called rapport. Age has an influence upon IQ score, but may not affect competency of performance.

High IQ scores mark the mentally gifted. Low IQ scores define mental retardation and those who have known neurological damage (mental defectives). Mentally gifted individuals have been found to be above average or equal to others in physical health, social relationships, and leadership, contrary to folklore. The mentally retarded vary in their response to special training designed to make the most of their limited abilities.

IQ tests as they presently exist cannot answer questions about the relative intelligence in different groups of people. Problems of samples tested, the basis of the test standardization, and the techniques of administration all make test score comparisons between samples a poor basis for conclusions about the intelligence of the population groups sampled.

SUGGESTED READINGS

Anastasi, A. *Differential psychology*. New York: Macmillan, 1958.
A textbook of the nature and measurement of individual and group differences. An excellent starting point for gathering information on these topics.
Anastasi, A. *Psychological testing*. New York: Macmillan, 1961.
An introduction to test construction, evaluation, and use. Detailed information upon many standard tests is presented.
Cronbach, L. J. *Essentials of psychological testing* (2nd edition). New York: Harper, 1960.
A textbook presenting the principles of testing. A comprehensive presentation of ability and performance tests highlights this well-known work.
McNemar, Q. *Psychological statistics* (3rd edition). New York: Wiley, 1962.
Tate, M. W. *Statistics in education and psychology: A first course*. New York: Macmillan, 1965.
Two of the many presentations of basic statistical techniques and their applications.

Chapter *10*

PERSONALITY

How do we usually "size up" another person? What factors lead to personality differences? How can these differences be measured? What are the essentials of personality theories?

Personality is the characteristic pattern of behaving of an individual. Others view this behavior pattern as personality, while the individual considers it the *self*. The behavior patterns of personality result from a complex interaction of bodily structure (including appearance and internal factors) and from past experiences which have been instrumental in shaping motives, emotional predispositions, and other relevant habits. The understanding of personality is much the same as the goal of psychology. Obviously, the wealth of information which would be necessary to build an understanding of personality from simpler laws and generalizations is not yet available. Instead, studies of larger wholes and consistencies of the behavior of individuals are undertaken. By use of objective personality inventories and by use of individual case-history records, the commonalities and unique aspects of behavior patterns may be separated and identified. The understanding and prediction which arises from this kind of study is necessarily gross and nonspecific, but some useful empirical facts and background for understanding individual differences in behavior have emerged.

Personality Formation

The development of personality has been identified closely with conditions of heredity, early experience, and maturation. Theories of personality have been very much involved with the specification of stages and patterns of such development. Freud's notion of psychosexual development through stages, the learning-theory approaches to the formation of aspects of personality, and extreme hereditarian views of individuals as being composed of innate predispositions to behave in certain ways, have each had an important influence upon the general views and approaches to understanding personality formation.

COMMONALITIES AND UNIQUENESSES

The formation of an individual's way of behaving may be viewed as resulting from the action of two kinds of factors: those which are *common* to many individuals and those which are *unique* to the individual.

The common influences resulting from the group memberships of an individual have a great deal to do with personality development. The western middle-class patterns of child rearing, the family social grouping, the availability of certain kinds of medical and dental care, for example, all play important roles in the formation of certain aspects of the individual's behavior. Membership in narrower groups such as school systems, the social and economic role of parents, and the sorts of playmates available also have a lasting influence upon the way that individual behaves. The effect of these commonalities upon the individual's behavior may result from both the learning of new habits and the structural and other physical bounds that these factors may pose.

The behavior of an individual conforms to the expectations of the culture concerning his group membership. The role played by an individual in different social situations conforms to the expectations of society. Standards of behavior while attending a concert differ from those at football games. Responses to new acquaintances in church differ from those expressed at a fraternal lodge. The consistency of behavior in each of these situations allows prediction of future behavior in such situations and also contributes to the general behavior patterns of the individual.

The experiences of each individual are quite unique. Though the general patterns of social behavior may be outlined, the exact ways of behaving of each individual within the limits of these patterns do differ. Limitations to complete conformity are imposed by features of the person's structural make-up given by heredity mechanisms and by the specific, unique experiences of the situations which he has already faced. The effectiveness of the same situation may be quite different for the individual members of a group. The way that the situation is interpreted is a function of both the past experience and the make-up of each individual, and will in turn affect the extent to which that experience will influence future behavior patterns.

As the individual comes to have some knowledge of his pattern of ways of behaving, or self, deviations from that pattern are noted and may be corrected. One may consider the development of a "conscience" as a way of speaking of this cognizance of the self and the attempts of the individual to maintain a consistent mode of behavior.

IDENTITY FORMATION

The process of achieving a consistent, well-integrated personality has been described by Erikson as *identity formation*.[15] This useful, conceptual process considers the successive identifications which a child has with different important people in his life. From identifications with parents, siblings, friends, and others, the child may acquire some part of his own later pattern of behavior. Before this eventual harmony is achieved, however, Erikson describes a state of *role diffusion* in which the child has not integrated the various identifications, but is torn at once between them. In role diffusion, which may be a source of abnormal behavior in adult life, a child may try to act the role of a parent, a brother, a coach, and a minister at the same time. During the transition from identifications to a consistent individual behavior pattern, the individual may "try out" a number of ways of behaving. The transition period between being a child and an adult, called adolescence, follows such a sampling of behavior patterns.

As the identity becomes more firm, characteristics of that behavior also become more fixed. The patterns of interests and attitudes, needs and values become more stable and relatively unchangeable. The adolescent, who at one time experimented with dissent, severe conformity to a group, and seeking only pleasure, will likely achieve an identity which resembles very little these different roles, and may eventually assume values like those of the average semi-skilled worker in a machine shop.

To understand the personality of any individual, it is apparent that the common experiences, unique experiences, and identities which that individual has experienced must be known in some detail. The behavior being presently sampled may be a function of any one of these factors of the past.

Measurement of Personality

There are a number of ways to measure personality, and there are a number of uses to which these measurements may be put. Since personality is essentially the uniqueness and the commonality of the behavior of individuals, measurements of that behavior must be oriented toward separating groups of individuals who are alike or different in some behavior pattern. What sorts of measurements may be made to separate personality differences and communalities? What kind of factors of behavior affects these personal behavior patterns? Guilford has discussed seven "trait modalities" called aptitudes, interests, needs, physiology, morphology, aptitudes, and temperaments.[2] In one sense, these terms describe some dimensions of the factors behind personality differences. Definitions of those terms which are unfamiliar appear in the glossary at the back of the book. Other writers have proposed similar but somewhat different lists of dimensions. Some of the devices for the measurement of personality have been aimed at assessing differences along such dimensions as these. There is no complete "personality test," but instead there are a number of ways of measuring certain aspects of behavior.

This section concerns some of the approaches to assessing personality differences and commonalities. They range from well-validated objective tests to subjective devices to evoke an unspecified kind of behavior. Some are practically oriented and others are concerned with the measurement of concepts having a place in a theory of personality. Personality measurement is quite incomplete in the sense of providing a range of devices for all aspects of personality assessment. The selection below, though not exhaustive of the personality measurement devices, gives a grasp of this incompleteness.

PERSONALITY INVENTORIES

In the category of tests which are likely to be objective and reasonably well-validated are the *personality inventories*. These devices generally require that the subject rate or describe himself on the extent to which he conforms to certain ways of behaving by answering questions such as those in Figure 10-1. Each personality inventory is developed for a specific purpose, though other uses for them are often developed.

> I do not like everyone I know.
> At times I feel like swearing.
> Children should be taught all the main facts of sex.
> Someone has been trying to rob me.
> I believe in a life hereafter.
> I am troubled by attacks of nausea and vomiting.
> I have been told that I walk during sleep.

Figure 10-1. Sample statements from the MMPI. Items are sorted into the response categories of "True," "False," or "Cannot Say."

The Minnesota Multiphasic Personality Inventory (MMPI) is perhaps the most well-known and often-used of the personality inventories. One form of this test is composed of about 495 short statements which are to be judged as "True," "False," and "Cannot say." Several groups of questions comprise different "scales" of the inventory. The original purpose of the MMPI was to detect the presence of certain kinds of abnormal patterns of behavior. Figure 10-2 lists these basic scales and a brief description of the sort of behavior which that term includes. The items were originally selected by the extent to which they were

Hs	Hypochondriasis—abnormal concern for bodily functions.
D	Depression—mood state of pessimism and depression.
Hy	Hysteria—using physical symptoms to cover up conflicts.
Pd	Psychopathic deviacy—amoral and asocial personality disorder.
Mf	Masculinity—presence of masculine interests.
Pa	Paranoid—presence of delusional beliefs.
Pt	Psychasthenia—obsessions, compulsions, and abnormal fears.
Sc	Schizophrenia—withdrawal, delusions, and disorientation.
Ma	Hypomania—overactivity and emotional excitement.
Si	Social introversion—withdrawal from social contacts and responsibility.
?	Cannot say score—frequency of defensive reaction.
L	Lie
F	Validity } Validating scales
K	Correction

Figure 10-2. The scales of the MMPI.

involved with medical and neural symptoms. The items composing the scales were validated against a criterion of the responses of clinically diagnosed psychiatric cases. Since the names and descriptive categories have not themselves proved to be stable and acceptable to all in clinical practice, the corresponding scales have acquired further meaning by construct validation.

The MMPI has, in addition to these basic scales, several "validation" scales. The degree of use of the "cannot say" category, the consistency of response indicative of lying or "role playing," and the extent to which the answers reflect patterns of response indicating a poor test-taking attitude (such as personal defensiveness or the other extreme of an exhibition of personal troubles) describe the most important validation scales of the MMPI.

The Edwards Personal Preference Schedule (EPPS) attempts to measure the 15 basic motives or needs as they were suggested by Murray's theory of human motivation.[59] The EPPS requires that the individual choose between the members of 225 pairs of items of description. The pairs are arranged so that they are equal in such factors as social desirability and conformity to the expectations of society. The relative preference or ascendancy of each motive pattern is the end-product of this test.

The *16 P F Test* was developed by Cattell as a technique to measure 16 personality factors which were factor analyzed from a variety of descriptions of behavior.[12] Factor analysis is a statistical technique for determining the commonality among the items of a test. Though the 16 P F Test suffers from a low reliability, which is probably due to its shortness, this approach to personality test construction does hold promise.

The *Allport-Vernon-Lindsey Study of Values* is designed to measure the values which are named theoretical, economic, esthetic, social, political, and religious.[2] The form of the test requires part true-false and part multiple-choice answers to statements of the individual's activities and beliefs.

The personality inventories, by the nature of their administration, are subject to a variety of deviations from the expected ways of responding. This may range from deliberate falsifying to special patterns of responding like that called *social desirability*. If the measurement device is intended to classify persons in particular categories like those of the MMPI, several kinds of errors in classification may result from these deviant ways of responding. One sort of error is the *false positive* in which the person is falsely classified as being of that group. The *false negative* classifies individuals as *not* having characteristics which they really have. In terms of the original purpose of the MMPI of detecting abnormal behaviors, the problems of these classification errors are obvious. The inappropriate response pattern, that is, one which is not in accordance with the construction of the tests, may not be a *deliberate* falsification or adherence to a pattern of choices, but may be the result of problems of self-deception inherent in the adjustment mechanisms of that person. The seriousness of these kinds of errors depends, in part, upon the capacity of the test to account for them or make valid predictions in the face of them.

The personality inventories are different from the ability tests in that the scoring of each item is not determined by its correctness but by the responses of a criterion population. The scoring of the answer to statements such as "I am ashamed of my teeth" for each scale depends upon the empirical comparison with the answer actually given to that item by criterion groups. Whether the answer is "true" or actually descriptive of the respondent's behavior is not important for empirical validity. The only behavior being used by the test is that which the subject indicates by the answers Yes and No. A "False" answer may be keyed as contributing to the Paranoid scale and a "True" response as part of the Interests scale. Thus, a rational attempt to falsify some of the responses, if not based upon a good knowledge of the actual test scoring, may not turn out as the person might expect.

The problem of response styles of agreeing with an unusual proportion of the statements (or disagreeing) or conforming to the expectations of society by giving a socially desirable answer have required an increased sophistication in the construction and use of personality inventories. Both response styles, of course, by their very presence describe one aspect of the person's personality. But the point for test construction is that, for these individuals, the test may not be useful. The response styles cover up or mask the factors which comprise the purpose of the measurement.

PROJECTIVE TESTS

What have been traditionally called the *projective tests* are perhaps not well-named. The use of the word "test" in its narrower sense is not appropriate because these techniques of personality assessment are not devices which separate individuals into groups on some basis. Rather, the projective techniques are a method of obtaining unstructured information about the individual. They might more accurately be described as personality-evocation devices.

The *Rorschach ink-blot* test is the most famous of the projective techniques of personality measurement. The stimulus figures are complex patterns created by spilling ink upon a paper and folding the paper so as to produce a symmetrical pattern when unfolded. Standard forms of ink-blots have been selected and a considerable backlog of response experience allows some expectations about the likely responses. These responses have been categorized according to certain notions of personality and some success is claimed by users in classifying or identifying some characteristics of personality. Generally, the test has not been shown to be useful in a measurement sense. The classification attempts have not been convincingly validated. But the test does enjoy moderate use in coordination with other information by clinicians who feel that the variable responses to the stimuli may be re-examined in many lights. The Rorschach ink-blot test provides a rich flow of verbal behavior from the individual.

The *Thematic Apperception Test* requires imaginative stories about

Figure 10-3. The administration of the Thematic Apperception Test. (Courtesy of the National Association for Mental Health, Incorporated, New York.)

relatively ambiguous pictures of people in situations. The subject is asked to tell stories about 20 successive pictures, guiding those stories by the questions "what is happening, what led up to the scene, and what will be the outcome?" The subject is instructed that his imagination is being tested. Again the subject is assumed to project himself into the story. The responses will be guided by the experiences, motives, and attitudes of the subject. The interpretation of the story is directed at the themes of the behavior. The recurrent motives and patterns of happenings provide the source material about the personality of the subject.

Several assumptions lie behind the projective techniques of personality assessment. One assumption is that the responses evoked by the presented stimuli have some relevance to the personality structure of the individual. This somewhat logical and reasonable assumption is that the imaginatory responses of a person must be at least partially a product of his personality. The invented stories resulting from the projective stimuli must come from some storehouse of information, and the most reasonable assumption is that the individual puts into the story some parts of his own characteristic ways of responding. This assumption must be questioned with each individual, however, as there is no guarantee or other assurance that this assumption is not in error.

A second assumption, often expressed as the major value of projective tests, is that they measure the hidden aspects of personality. The notion is again a rational one and based upon the preceding assumption. The inventions of the person are not only likely to be a reflection of that person's personality, but are likely to reflect aspects of the personality which would not be admitted directly. Whether the notion is expressed in the more extreme case of the projective devices discovering unconscious personality or in the milder fashion that they reveal parts of behaviors which are simply not apparent in other expressions is perhaps not different. Basically, the assumption is that the deeper, guiding factors of personality may be discovered without the subject's public awareness of the discovery.

The subject is said to "project" his personality into the answers. The responses are relatively unstructured in comparison to the alternative choices of the personality inventories, and the materials presented are more ambiguous. Some writers have claimed that the more ambiguous the stimulus presented, the deeper into the unconscious the technique will probe.

The value of the projective techniques in studying personality lies

not so much in their contribution to the rigorous measurement of behavior, for this they do not do at all. Their value is in their use as a
standard method of evoking responses from a subject, responses which
are assumed to reflect that subject's personality determinants. By providing a starting point for organization of what is often highly individu-
alistic clinical or counseling technique, the communalities of the personalities may be emphasized rather than the uniquenesses. A further value
of these projective techniques in the eyes of many psychologists is that
they allow the study of personality as a complete whole or structure
as opposed to the analysis of personality by the inventory methods.

PERFORMANCE MEASURES OF PERSONALITY

Another approach to the assessment of differences in personality is
to observe the behaviors in "natural" or nonartificial settings. If practical information is required about the likely behavior patterns of a
person in a certain situation, that situation may be presented in a
realistic fashion. These kinds of personality measurements have been
called *assessment techniques* after their frequent use by the Office of
Strategic Services in World War II. If there is a need for a stable pattern
of leadership for construction of certain structures under difficult conditions, the assessment technique aims at mimicking the conditions and
stresses which will be in operation in that task. Those who behave
according to the requirements of the task are separated from those who
are not likely to behave in the correct manner. This assessment technique was often used in conjunction with all other available methods of
personality measurement, including the projective test, group discussion,
stress interviews, rating by peers, and observations during "rest" periods,
meals, and social events. More recent assessment methods are being used
for selecting engineers, executives, and the like, often under the guise
of "training programs."

Generally the assessment method has not had a high predictive validity when it was used to select those who would pass or fail as members
of a particular role. Analysis has shown that the ratings by peers and
those who have occupied that role in the near past judge more accurately the success of applicants than do trained psychologists. The
relevant factor seems to be the amount of information which the assessor
has about the exact nature and requirements of the role. As the performance test is made more nearly like the role to be assumed, the predictive
success of that test becomes greater.

Personality Theories

Personality theories attempt to organize the complexity of individual behavior. The representation may be done by "typing" the individual in which personality is categorized upon the basis of some easily distinguished characteristic of structure or personality. The theory may analytically break behavior into "traits." The trait theories represent the uniqueness of each individual by the combination of strengths of measured traits. Other theories are more elaborate constructions of rational principles and invented hypothetical mechanisms which act in an intricate fashion to describe the development and dynamic functioning of personality. Representative theories of each of these varieties will be discussed below.

TYPE THEORIES

The sorting of individual cases into categories is the most common approach to organizing the world of experience. Classifying kinds of plants and animals, chemical compounds, and groups of stars has been the beginning to the systematic study of these things. Classifying men into personality or behavior types is also a very common avocation of man. The oldest writings display classifications of this kind. But on what basis is man's personality to be typed? Are there some simple, easily recognized behavior patterns which will allow understanding of personality?

Type theories may be constructed on the basis of a primary characteristic of behavior such as honesty (George Washington), fanaticism (Adolf Hitler), or sexiness (Marilyn Monroe). These dominant or cardinal characteristics are presumed to guide the pattern of behavior comprising the personality. Other theories have typed personalities on the basis of group membership or shape of body. The spinster is expected to have a personality of a certain kind. The salesman's behavior also is expected to follow certain patterns. Individuals of certain racial and national groups are expected to behave in different stereotyped fashions.

There is often a germ of truth to these type notions. The commonality of experiences of individuals belonging to the same group is likely to lead to certain similarities in personality. The expectations of society for members of a group to behave in certain ways may also direct the personality of each member slightly in that direction. But as a useful device to separate the personalities of individuals and to understand the existing differences, these kinds of type theories are not likely to be more than *very* rough approximations.

One type theory which has been provocative and hence well investigated is that of body types, most recently espoused by Sheldon. Three basic types of body are presumed to reflect different hypothetical biological processes which in turn determine personality. Measurement of body types then reflects personality. The three types are the endomorph, characterized by fat and softness; the mesomorph, muscular and athletic; and the ectomorph, tall, thin, and fragile. The endomorph likes the pleasures of life and tends to be sociable and jolly. The mesomorph, being athletic, is a direct and energetic person. The ectomorph tends to react with shyness, worrying, and withdrawal from society. Individuals may be measured to determine their body type and, consequently, their personality. Notions like these are found in the "common sense" of the layman. The average man believes that the fat man is jolly, that the skinny is shy, and that the athletic is straightforward. Evaluations of Sheldon's theory have been somewhat confounded by this basic belief. When ratings by friends are the source of personality information to compare with physical measurements of the body, the relationship is always much greater than if impartial personality inventories or other tests are the behavior assessment devices used in the comparison.[87] We tend to judge the fat man as more jolly than he really behaves, the skinny as more worrisome, and so on.

Carl Jung developed a well-known theory of personality type on the basis of certain kinds of basic patterns of behavior, the *introverted* and the *extroverted*.[37] The characteristics of the introvert and the extrovert are perhaps well known to all. The introvert is withdrawn and shy, and the extrovert is the glad-handed, outgoing, and forward person. These two kinds of behavior patterns have been found to be on the ends of a continuum. Tests of this behavior characteristic have resulted in a distribution of scores which is not too different from the symmetrical normal distribution with introverts on one end and extroverts on the other. This indicates that there is not an obvious dichotomy between introverts and extroverts, but that these terms describe only the end regions along a continuum. The majority of persons having middle scores, have been called *ambiverts*. The test defining this introversion-extroversion scale has been found to be composed of a number of behavior characteristics. Depression, the tendency to changing moods, and similar behavior patterns have been found to be related to the scores on the introversion-extroversion dimension.

The type theories generally try to describe too much of behavior with too little information. This is a tendency which is always present when a complex task is faced. Behavior patterns are hopelessly complex at a first exposure. It is so much easier to pay attention to only a small set of details and act as if this small part were descriptive of the entire personality. Of course, this approach is not likely to be successful in the understanding of the complexity of personality, though it may provide a serviceable first-classification system for acquaintances. As one usually finds in social situations, the first impression or sampling of the behavior of a person is strong, but it generally turns out to be hopelessly inadequate, if not entirely inaccurate. The boorish snob at the party may be found to be an intelligent, outgoing person on a second encounter.

TRAIT THEORIES

The trait theory of personality considers the consistency of behavior. Rather than attempt to describe the dynamic changes in behavior which result from the stimuli in each situation, the trait theory tries to note the consistent patterns of behavior. By measuring a number of the consistent patterns, the behavior of an individual may be understood by the extent of usage of the patterns.

The source of the complex of named traits of consistent behavior patterns may be rational derivations, or they may be suggested by the statistical commonality among items in tests of behavior. Raymond Cattell's "factor theory" psychology is a statistical approach to the study of personality.[11] Cattell has distinguished between *surface traits* which are based upon frequently occurring observed behaviors and *source traits* which are presumed to underlie and determine those behavior patterns. These kinds of traits differ in "depth," with the deeper source traits more stable and more general in their effects upon behavior. Some of Cattell's traits are assumed to have environmental origins and others arise from constitutional factors, not necessarily heredity. Source traits of a constitutional origin are called *ergs,* while source traits of environmental basis are called *metaergs.* Some example of the traits of Cattell's theory are given in Figure 10-4.

Personality develops, according to Cattell's theory, by the changes in ergs and metaergs. One metaerg is the self sentiment. It is developed through experience and is composed of both a realistic estimate of

Strength of Character vs. Moral Defect
Realism vs. Neuroticism
Balance, Optimism vs. Agitation, Melancholy
Intelligence, Training vs. Its Lack
Self-assertion Dominance vs. Inhibition, Modesty
Toughness vs. Sensitivity
Sociability vs. Hostility
Emotionality vs. Placidity
Friendliness vs. Suspicion
Expressiveness vs. Reserve
Imaginativeness vs. Smugness
Disorderly vs. Persevering and Pedantic

Figure 10-4. Some representative traits of Cattell's personality theory.

what the individual can do and an idealistic goal of what that person would like to be. Personality changes occur after the outcomes of a series of six stages. These stages are choice-points called "dynamic crossroads" and present different possibilities of response in the face of each experience with an erg or metaerg. The modification or socialization of ergs and metaergs describes not only the development of normal behavior but also the development of symptoms of abnormal behavior patterns.

Cattell's theory of personality is a tight, logically consistent formulation. It is based upon the statistical tool called factor analysis. To the extent that the information analyzed by that tool can be accepted by the reader as representative of all aspects of behavior, then the theory so developed may be a good descriptive analysis of personality.

Gordon Allport's trait theory of personality is based upon study of the normal and well-adjusted individual.[1] Allport has emphasized the conscious determination by present forces as opposed to the unconscious effects of past experiences in other personality theories. This system considers the trait to be the unit of study which will reveal the consistency of behavior patterns of individuals. Allport believes that more detailed study of the individual's personality pattern will reveal significant information of the form of expression of the individual, his "style of life."

Allport uses the descriptive terms of common speech to name the traits to take advantage of the flexibility, subtlety, and backlog of information which they convey. These common traits, though usefully considered only in relation to an individual's personality, may be measured in a population of individuals and are found to vary in a normal distribution. Traits which are unique to the individual cannot be measured at all in this fashion. Some of Allport's traits are motivational or dynamic, while others are directive in nature. The traits are not believed to be independent from one another. For this reason, study is best made of the individual pattern of relationships of the traits of each person. In the pattern of traits, Allport claims that certain traits can be described as *central*. Others are *secondary* for that person. Some individuals are characterized by having a personality dominated by a single trait around which the others are focused.

PSYCHOANALYTIC THEORIES OF PERSONALITY

One of the distinguishing features of Freud's psychoanalytic theory of personality is the hypothesis of two modes of thinking: the *primary process,* a more primitive thinking which obeys the *pleasure principle* and is characteristic of the unconscious, and the *secondary process,* which is the method of thinking at the preconscious and conscious levels obeying the *reality principle.* Some of these terms require further clarification. The *pleasure principle* refers to seeking of pleasure and avoidance of pain. The *reality principle* refers to the control of behavior by the real world, operating according to the expectations of the future as well as the present situations. *Preconscious* refers to those unconscious thoughts and influences which may be accessible to consciousness by directing attention to them. *Unconscious* thoughts are not consciously available, theoretically because they are not "acceptable" to the person.

In addition to the biological motivations of the body, there are two sources of motivation or forces which Freud held to be especially important in shaping behavior. The forces of *sex* and *aggression* become disguised, displaced to other stimuli, or repressed from consciousness if not readily gratified. Freud included under the term sex, all of the bodily pleasures, including the other meanings of "love," tastes, and so on. Aggression usually arises from frustrating situations in Freudian theory. The forces of sex and aggression are the primary sources of conflict in the dynamics of this personality theory.

Three divisions of the personality which act together and in opposition to resolve the conflicting forces of sex and aggression and the demands of socialization trainings are the *id,* the *ego,* and the *superego.* Unconscious thoughts of sex and aggression originate in the id. The id uses only the primary process of thought according to the operation of the pleasure principle. Psychic energy is put into these primary process thoughts by the id and this investment is called *cathexis.* The ego serves to keep the thoughts of the id from affecting behavior. The ego has been called the mediator between the demands of the id and the outer forces of reality. The energy of the ego which opposes that of the id is produced by *countercathexis*. The ego may operate at the unconscious level with the impulses of the id and at the preconscious and conscious level with the reality principle. The superego maintains the standards of the personality. A "bad conscience" acts through guilt and self-prohibitions, while the positive rewarding part of the superego is often called the ego ideal. The *ego ideal* sets aspirations and goals for the individual.

The personality system of id, ego, and superego is said to be a closed energy system in which psychic energy amounts are fixed. Thus, if the ego expends energy in counteracting impulses of the id, there is less available for other pursuits according to the demands and goals of the superego. The unconscious struggles between parts of the personality consume energy and thus there may be apparent fatigue with no observable cause. That struggle implies an interaction of psychic energy reserves with the physical energy available.

The development of the adult personality in Freudian theory proceeds according to stages named *oral, anal, phallic,* and *genital.* A great deal of adult personality is understood in Freudian theory by the successes of the individual in these various stages.

The *oral* stages fill the first years of life. Sucking behavior is the first sexual expression, in that such movements and sensations are pleasurable. One phase of the oral stage results when the infant learns to control the onset of the food by getting it from the adults about him. In addition to the control of pleasure stimulation is the notion that the infant seeks to swallow and thus incorporate part of the adult which has supplied food. Similarly there is a fear in the child of being eaten. An oral sadistic behavior of biting and other aggressive behaviors appear with the development of teeth.

The *anal* stage occurs during the recognition of the stimulation from the excretory organs and from the attention from the parents during the period of toilet training. Control of excretion may lead to retentive and expulsive patterns of behavior in the child corresponding to the oral-sadistic and the passive-receptive phases of the oral stage.

The *phallic* stage includes sexual love in childhood of the opposite-sex parent. This sexual love of one parent, called the *oedipus complex,* is accompanied by dislike and rivalry toward the other parent. Fear of reprisal from the father centers about removal of the sex organs or *castration anxiety*. The growth of awareness of differences in sex lead to *penis envy* in little girls. During the phallic stage the children grow toward giving up the oedipal complex and the formation of a strong identification with the like-sex parent. The youth then introjects the values of that parent into the superego. The superego comes to dominate behavior for a time until about eight years of age, when the personality structure becomes more able to adjust to the demands of reality.

A latency period intervenes prior to adolescence, in which other objects and activities such as studying in school, sports activities, and the like, dominate. Learning in this transition stage is aimed at reality, the way the world is. During adolescence there is a growth in the strength of the urges of the id arising from the bodily changes of puberty. Severe conflicts between the id, ego, and superego occur and center the attention of the individual upon himself. The adolescent is thus primarily selfish.

The *genital* stage is that of "normal" adulthood. If there are no residual difficulties of adjustment from the earlier stages, the individual has normal heterosexual relationships in a manner acceptable to the superego.

Differences in personality of individuals are described in terms of the successful passing of each of the stages. An individual is said to be oral if he depends upon others, equates love with food, has strong habits centering around the mouth, or other similar characteristics. An anal character may be overly stingy or stubborn, compulsively neat and orderly, etc. The phallic character is reckless in behavior, often compelled to defend his sexual prowess in an excessive manner without feelings of love. Phallic women often take on a masculine role.

A number of revised psychoanalytic theories have come from earlier collaborators of Freud, who become dissatisfied with parts of the original theory. Adler stressed the feelings of inferiority of the child as basic to the development of personality in the adult. Jung is most famous for his concepts of the introverted and extroverted personality types, though he made other significant changes in the original Freudian notions. Rank gave a special importance to the separation during birth, a painful separation which creates anxiety and shapes aspects of personality throughout life. But the basic notion of the unconscious mental process and its dynamic role in shaping the personality of the individual remains intact in these revised theories.

SELF THEORIES OF PERSONALITY

A self theory of personality holds that the basic organizing factor of personality is the self. The self, in turn, is defined in many ways, but it may be conceptualized as a "picture" into which behavior fits. It represents past experiences, behaviors, and other influences upon the individual. The self theories are not dynamic in the sense of the opposing forces hypothesized by the psychoanalytic theories, nor are they entirely static descriptions as the trait and type theories tend to be. The picture of the individual which constitutes the self is a changeable mold which both determines and is determined by behavior. Its functions are to monitor and organize ongoing behavior, though the mechanism of this action is not clear.

The self theory of Carl Rogers is also called phenomenological personality theory.[70] Rogers' theory was developed, like Freud's theory, from observations made in clinical practice. Rogers advocates a "non-directive therapy" in which the individual comes to change his self-picture by his own effort. The self-picture or self-awareness comes from experiences which result from actions of the individual. Rogers believes that the direction of change of the self is toward improvement, growth, and independence. This tendency for changes to occur in these directions is called the *actualizing tendency*. This actualizing principle is assumed to be fundamental to all life as an active process directed toward improvement and reproduction. Rogers' theory emphasizes the conscious processes of the personality and believes that the unconscious serves only a very small role.

S-R LEARNING THEORIES OF PERSONALITY

S-R theories of personality begin with assumptions of the relevance of the approaches and knowledge from the laboratory study of learning, motivation, and perception to the understanding of personality. S-R theory is a personality theory presumably based directly upon the evidence from S-R studies of the traditional laboratory topics of psychology.

The S-R theory formulated by John Dollard and Neal Miller is the most complete attempt to wed the knowledge of the laboratory with the complex problem of describing personality.[13] They took as their basic framework of personality the psychoanalytic formulations of Freud and tried to account for many of the parts of that system in terms of the stimuli, habit, response, and similar concepts of behavior theories in the Hullian vein. Dollard and Miller's theory of personality revolves around the circumstances of four factors: a drive, a cue, a response, and a reward. The habits between cues and responses, which are motivated by the energy from the drives and are rewarded by reduction of that drive, comprise the permanent structure of personality. Both Hullian and Freudian theory use the pleasure principle or law of effect concerning seeking pleasure and avoiding pain. Typical analyses by Dollard and Miller are those of the origins and resolution of conflicts and the factors of fear and guilt which lead to neurosis. The basic technique is the explanation of the content of psychoanalytic theory by the principles and methods of S-R theory.

Summary

Personality is the behavior pattern of an individual. It is formed by factors common to the individual and factors unique to the individual. One view of personality development is called identity formation, in which parts of the personalities of others are assimilated by means of identification.

Personality inventories are objective tests which permit a self-rating about specific behaviors. The agreement of the subject with certain of the statements about behaviors in the test gives an estimate of the strength of particular behavior patterns in that person. The kind of personality factors measured vary widely according to the purposes of the test.

Projective tests of personality are not tests in the same sense as the personality inventories. Projective tests present a standard stimulus to evoke a sample of behavior. Under the guises of telling a story or reporting what is seen in ambiguous forms, the subject is led to emit verbal behavior which presumably is informative of his own personality and is a largely hidden aspect of his personality. The subject is said to project his personality into the verbal responses.

Personality may also be measured by assessments of behavior in realistic settings. The closer the presented situation is to the real situation, the better are the predictions of likely behavior in that real situation.

Type theories attempt to describe personality by sorting individuals into categories. Body shape and extroversion are two well-known varieties of type theory.

Trait theory measures consistent patterns of behavior and describes the behavior of an individual by his scores on the collection of traits.

Psychoanalytic theories are hypothetical collections of mechanisms and constructs which describe the formation and causes of behavior patterns. The constructs of id, ego, and superego in Freud's theory are the embodiment of past experiences and present forces as they attempt to shape the behavior in a dynamic fashion.

Self theories view personality as organized by the picture which each individual holds of his past experiences, present behaviors, and capabilities.

S-R learning theories have been an attempt to put the constructs and dynamic mechanism of psychoanalytic theory into testable experimental situations.

SUGGESTED READINGS

Cameron, N. *Personality development and psychopathology: A dynamic approach.* Boston: Houghton Mifflin, 1963.
A unified textbook of personality, adjustment, and psychopathology. The text coordinates these topics from a biosocial position.

Gordon, J. E. *Personality and behavior.* New York: Macmillan, 1963.
A textbook of personality presented in the language and framework of the experimental psychology of learning.

Hall, C. S., and Lindzey, G. *Theories of personality.* New York: Wiley, 1957.
A textbook of personality theory.

Millon, T. *Theories of psychopathology.* Philadelphia: Saunders, 1967.
A collection of essays and critiques concerning psychopathology and normal personality theories.

Sahakian, W. S. (Ed.) *Psychology of personality: Readings in theory.* Chicago: Rand McNally, 1965.
A collection of readings of personality theory.

Chapter *11*

ADJUSTMENT

How can we describe the problems that we face in daily life? What is the nature of frustration and to what does it lead? What principles affect conflicts? How does one defend himself from the anxieties and guilt arising from conflicts and other situations?

Individuals are said to have "problems" which lead them to seek a better "adjustment" in life. The freshman must "adjust" to the different social life of the college. Loss of a child requires the parent to "adjust" to that loss. Attainment of puberty forces the adolescent to "adjust" to the newly acquired capacity to engage in sexual behaviors.

Adjustment may be defined as a process of interaction between behavior and the conditions of the environment, including those originating within the individual. A meaningful interaction of behavior with a physiological need like hunger is one such adjustment. Included also are the adjustments of behavior patterns to the social and self motives of the individual in relation to the environmental circumstances of the time. The term adjustment also is used to describe an end state of the process, the achieving of a satisfactory "adjustment" to the situation. The end state of adjustment should not necessarily be equated with a lack of wants, needs, or other sources of strong stimulation, but rather as a balance between those needs and a reasonable absence of "abnormal" states. This description may be recognized as circular, but there is no suitable way to specify the balance of needs and behaviors which are the reasonably "normal" amount. Inactivity with a minimum of need states, however, is not the goal of adjustment processes.

Implicit in this description of an adjustment process is the occurrence of "poor" adjustment. Describing some examples of relatively poor adjustment and mechanisms of overcoming it may make clear what "adjustment" means. The study of adjustment usually centers around the conditions which produce and lead to unfavorable interactions of behavior and those conditions. What sorts of behavior and mechanisms overcome that unfavorable interaction?

The concept of *frustration* is used to describe the most frequent interactive state of maladjustment. The special case of frustration called *conflict* will be developed as one of the major adjustment problems facing an individual. The consequences of frustration and conflict motivate "adjustive" behaviors which minimize those conditions, at least temporarily. This chapter describes some frustrations, conflicts, and "adjustive" behaviors.

Frustration

What is meant when a person is described as frustrated? The definition may take the example form of the "Peanuts" comic strip characters describing "happiness." Frustration is rushing to an 8 o'clock class to find it canceled. Frustration is a 1.999 grade point average when 2.0 is required for graduation. Frustration is a missing page at the end of a mystery book. Frustration is choosing between the sultry brunette and the cute blonde. What do these situations have in common? They all describe a motivated behavior or behavior tendency which is prevented from reaching the goal condition. *Frustration* is defined as a state arising from a motivated ongoing behavior or behavior potentiality which is blocked or thwarted.

SOURCES OF FRUSTRATION

The situations which are described as leading to a state of frustration involve blocking or thwarting agents of several different kinds. Some of the blocks are of a physical nature, others arise from a personal deficiency, and still others may be described as a conflict of motivated behaviors.

Physical blocks may be actual mechanical preventatives as in being stopped by a locked door, or failing to start an automobile engine. Other physical blocks arc from situations which are different from that expected, like the cancelled appointment or the change in the requirements for graduation. Though these sorts of frustration are frequent in occurrence, they usually do not lead to difficulties in adjustment. The physical blocks are often easy to overcome or circumvent. The solution usually requires only a different response rather than a change in the motivation-goal state of affairs.

Other frustration states arise from a goal blocked by a *personal deficiency.* An individual may have low entrance examination scores for medical school or may flunk the physical exam for pilot training. These blocks usually require a change in the goal direction of behavior. The goal state as it was expected is quite unattainable and either the motive for reaching the goal must be changed or a substitute goal must be sought. Re-evaluation of the goal in the light of more realistic information about personal capabilities often leads to a reduction in frustration.

The introduction of frustration by the *conflict* of two or more motive-goal tendencies present at the same time is a frequent source of frustration which is difficult to remove. The variety of complex relationships between goals which are not attainable at the same time or lead to conflicting consequences is the rule in daily life rather than the exception. This complex kind of frustration-producing situation will be considered in greater detail in a later section of the chapter.

RESPONSES TO FRUSTRATION

Frustration has often been described as leading to varied responding. The variety of response during a state of frustration makes prediction in any single case a very difficult task. But certain characteristic patterns of responding have been noted with some frequency. Behavior patterns labelled *aggression, regression, apathy, stereotypy,* and *restlessness* are some of those patterns of responding to frustration.

The *aggressive* response to frustration has a place in theories of personality such as Freud's psychoanalysis. The notion that basic aggressive behavior patterns arise from frustrating states has also been proposed by S-R personality theorists. Aggressive behavior can be readily observed in simple learning experiments with animals. Experimenters who have trained rats to run in a straight runway and then have withheld reward during a period of extinction often have noted that the rat engages in destructive behavior toward pieces of the apparatus which are vulnerable and may also take a nip at the experimenter's hand when about to be removed. The behavior of man is not too different. We kick the door which sticks, pound on the malfunctioning radio, and shake the machine which does not deliver the product for which we have inserted a coin.

Some of these examples of aggression from frustration situations describe hostile behavior at the blocking or thwarting agent. This has been called *direct aggression*. The aggression may also be directed toward some other part of the total situation. This is called *displaced aggression*. Kicking the door which does not open when expected may be called direct aggression but kicking the cat which happens to be walking past at the time would be an example of displaced aggression. In social situations, displaced aggression seems to be a less dangerous aggressive response. Aggression towards the person who has blocked your motivated behavior will usually only lead to greater social difficulties. Aggression toward another, less-important person, however, does not worsen the situation. A man is usually safer in yelling at his wife than at the employer who refused the raise in pay.

Regressive behavior to frustrating circumstances involves responses which are more primitive or are characteristic of an earlier point in the development of an individual. If the individual returns to an earlier form of behavior, that behavior is called *retrogressive*. If the behavior is of a more primitive type, though not necessarily used previously by that individual, it is called *primitivation*.

Regression has been demonstrated in both children and rats in carefully controlled laboratory studies. A famous example was a study by Barker, Dembo, and Lewin[5] in which children were at first rated in terms of the goodness or maturity of play in a small group with some average toys. They were then allowed to enter another area in which more interesting facilities were present (e.g., a model pond and a doll house). After a period of exposure to the more desirable toys, the children were removed from that area and separated from it by a wire screen. The constructiveness of play with the original toys was now rated again. Frustration was evident by the degree to which children engaged in direct aggression to the screen, indirect aggression to the toys and probably the experimenters, and other responses such as reduced responsiveness or apathy. The rated maturity or constructiveness of play with the original toys after the frustration operation was definitely lower when compared to the earlier ratings. A similar demonstration with rats has been made in a learning situation in which a lever was to be pressed after the onset of a cue light to prevent an electric charge to the floor of the cage. After this lever pressing response was learned, the required response was changed to turning a wheel attached to the side of the cage. This second response was also easily learned. After more training on the wheel response, the test state of frustration was produced by making the wheel inoperative in preventing the shock, and a shock on the wheel itself was added for good measure. The most frequent response to this state of frustration was to return to the lever pressing which was previously effective in the situation.

Regression is also quite apparent in daily situations. "Childish" attitudes and responses are frequent when frustration reaches a certain intensity. Pouting and complaining, characteristic of children who do not "get their own way," occur frequently also in adults. The "take my marbles and go home" behavior is also very common. Regression is often combined with aggression, which itself may be viewed from the standpoint of "civilized" society as inherently regressive. The primitive hostilities are not adjustive responses in our society, according to our guiding courts of law.

The *apathetic* response is in one sense directly opposed to aggression or regression. It describes the act of doing nothing rather than acting, however ineffective that action may be. But the apathetic response to frustration is an "active" inactivity. The inactivity is a goal "activity" as opposed to inactivity in non-motivating situations of resting or boredom. The activity may at first be measured, perhaps, by changes in physiological indices of emotion. After a time, though, the apathetic response to certain frustrating states of affairs may be a well-learned habit which actually does a great deal to lessen that frustration. By ignoring frustration, the cues may be removed more effectively than if an active aggression or other activity was set into motion. As an individual, doing nothing when mention is made of the threat of nuclear disaster may be an effective response pattern to reduce that frustration. Though it is obviously not an effective pattern of behavior for nations, the individual who cannot make effective responses in the situation may be most adjustive by being apathetic and allowing the cues to go away sooner. Though campus "organizers" and governing groups of the student body may decry the apathetic student, a certain amount of apathy is justified toward those activities which are likely to make other goals (e.g., obtaining an education and a degree) more difficult to obtain. Limitations of time and resources makes an active intent to participate in all activities, though they may all be worthy, quite frustrating.

Stereotypy refers to a pattern of behavior which appears rigid and fixed in the face of the frustration situation. The fixated response often appears stupid to the view of the observer who is not aware of the background experiences and motivations which led up to that response pattern in the situation. A student may persist in the same studying techniques which have led to failure in the past. With each new unsuccessful experience, persistence in inefficient techniques, like cramming for tests, appears to be greater. In the face of difficult discrimination tasks, rats have been shown to adopt a consistent pattern of responses which are only partially successful in the solution of the problem.[46] The rat which adopts a "position habit" of always turning to the left though the food reward is equally often on the left and right in accordance with a complex set of cues is said to have fixated upon that particular response. Great amounts of training are often insufficient to reduce the strength of that "stupid" position response. The interpretation of such stereotyped responses is equivocal, but the apparent unusual strength of the responses and the emotional reaction which often results when they are interfered with, suggests that frustration has played a strong role.

The response of *restlessness* in the face of frustration is often present along with other patterns of response. An increase in the vigor of responses and the tension of the muscles making the responses are related to this factor. These effects of frustration may be described as similar to an increase in generalized, non-specific motivation or emotional state. Behaviors associated with "having nothing to do" increase during frustration. Smoking increases in frequency and intensity. The "butts" are shorter and ashes more frequently spilled. Gum chewing increases in rhythm, and the tongue stands a greater chance of being damaged. Tightened muscles in the arms are easily noticed, and the strength of grip upon carried objects increases markedly.

Conflict

When two or more motive-goal states are aroused at the same time and they are incompatible, the result is a kind of frustration called *conflict*. Experienced conflicts are quite complex and involve many more than two motive-goal states in varying degrees of strength. Several basic types of conflict, though, may be isolated for analysis. The likely responses and factors in the solution of these conflict situations give some understanding of the more complex experienced conflicts. Finally, some discussion of commonly occurring conflicts in the affairs of individuals will be examined.

SIMPLE MODELS OF CONFLICT

Three basic patterns of simple conflict have been isolated and named the *approach-approach,* the *avoidance-avoidance,* and the *approach-avoidance* conflicts. Each of these conflicts will be presented in a spatial model, as if the behaviors of approach and avoidance refer to actually getting physically closer or further away from the goal. Other situations, however, require that "distance from the goal" be understood as a metaphor implying degrees of attaining that goal.

The *approach-approach* conflict is diagramed in Figure 11-1. The two positive goals are spatially separated and the individual must make a choice between them. Further bounds on behavior in the situation

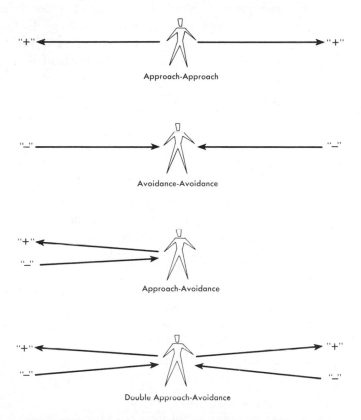

Figure 11-1. Several basic models of conflicts in which the individual is pushed toward and pulled away from any goals of different value.

require that only one response be made, and that after a choice is made it cannot be rescinded. Both in analysis and in conception, this conflict is easy to resolve. The legend of the jackass who starved to death half way between two bales of hay, undecided, has little support in actual observations of behavior.

The *avoidance-avoidance* conflict is diagramed similarly, in Figure 11-1, with the goals separated. The situation is again such that the individual must make only one final choice, but an additional requirement in this conflict situation is that he *must* make one of the choices. If there were no pressure to make a response choice, an effective strategy would be to make neither choice in the situation, or to ignore the situation entirely, called *leaving the field*. This avoidance-avoidance conflict situation is difficult to master and leads to a great deal of indecision.

The *approach-avoidance* conflict situation, again diagramed spatially in Figure 11-1, involves two opposing response tendencies to the same goal. The goal is both desired and unwanted at the same time. Often the consequences of attaining the goal are desirable and repulsive at the same time. A piece of cream pie is inviting but also evokes the knowledge that it would probably lead to putting on weight. The girl is cute but talks too much. The course sounds interesting but the instructor is dull. Approach-avoidance conflicts also lead to a difficult vacillating decision process. However, this is for different reasons and is of a different nature.

Other, more complex combinations arise when these basic models of conflict are combined. For example, the double approach-avoidance, shown also in Figure 11-1, has two goals which must be considered and both have positive and negative aspects about them. One car is fast but expensive, while another is cheap but doggy. The choice must often be made between studying, which is a requirement for attaining an education, but which that night will also lead to missing a particular occurrence of entertainment, and attending the entertainment, which is enjoyable but likely to lead to failing a course exam. Similarly, more complex chains of multiple motive-goal states with positive and negative values may be seen to be the stuff of which the daily experienced conflicts are made.

PRINCIPLES OF CONFLICT RESOLUTION

Experimental analysis of simple conflict situations has yielded four general rules for conflict resolution.[56] (1) There is a gradient of strength of approach which increases the nearer one is to a positive goal. (2) There is a gradient of strength of avoidance which increases the nearer one is to a negative goal. (3) The avoidance gradient is steeper than the approach gradient. That is, for a certain change in distance there is a greater change in the avoidance tendency than there is in the approach tendency. (4) The level of approach or avoidance gradients is a function of the strength of the motive to attain or avoid that goal. These four rules are summarized in Figure 11-2. These rules of conflict

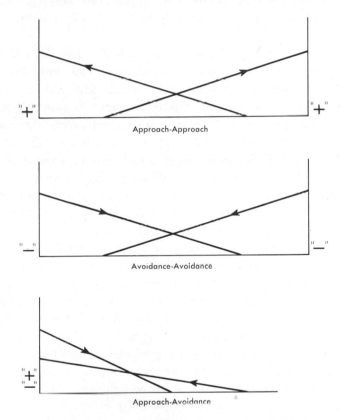

Figure 11-2. Gradients of strength of approach and avoidance permit a rapid graphic portrayal of the forces upon an individual at any point of a conflict. See text.

resolution are directly applied to the simple models of conflict described earlier to yield predictions about the likely solution behaviors in those situations.

The approach-approach conflict involves only rules 1 and 4. There are gradients stretching away from each goal such that the nearer the individual is to a goal, the stronger will be the tendency to approach. If the conflict is presented when the individual is placed in any position but that at which the two goals are equal, the solution will be easy and immediate. The stronger approach draws the individual to that goal. At the point of equality, theoretically, there should be considerable indecision and conflict. But this is somewhat like balancing an egg on its end. The precise balance between motives and responses would not be likely to remain constant for any appreciable length of time, the individual would soon be at one side of the balance and be drawn to that goal.

The avoidance-avoidance conflict is similarly diagrammed, but the direction of forces upon behavior is reversed. The individual at any point different from the balance point would find that the repulsion from the goal with the stronger avoidance tendency pushes him toward the center point of balance. With some amount of inertia, the momentum of the repelled behavior would result in a position on the other side of the balance and the direction of forces would reverse. Repeating this state of affairs would lead to vacillating behavior about the balance point. Unless a time pressure to make a response is introduced (now it is no longer a simple conflict) the individual would remain in oscillation about the point of equal avoidance tendency.

The approach-avoidance conflict also leads to vacillation. With simultaneous approach and avoidance tendencies about a single goal, the situation at relatively distant points from the goal is one of a stronger approach tendency. But because of the steeper avoidance gradient, at points close to the goal, the pressure to avoid the goal is dominant. Thus, at points more distant from the goal than at the balance of tendencies, one is led to approach the goal, but at positions closer than the balance point, the pressure is to avoid. Again an oscillation of behavior about the balance point is likely to result. This oscillation is different, though, in that in one direction it is an attractive force and in the other it is a repulsion. Note that leaving the field is not a solution to this conflict because at points more distant from the goal the dominant tendency is to return toward the goal. The indecision from this conflict is particularly difficult to remove.

Any of these conflict patterns may be changed by the operation of rule 4. If the strength of the motive to attain the goal is changed, the relative level of approach and avoidance is also changed. The approach-approach conflict might be changed to favor one of the goals. The avoidance-avoidance and approach-avoidance conflicts would be changed toward making the oscillation closer to one of the goals.

SOURCES OF CONFLICT

The sources of conflict are as rich as the variety of motive-goal relationships of responses which can be in opposition. From the simple clash between responses to the same stimulus to the pattern of major decisions of the course of one's life, conflicts are likely to be part of daily behavior.

Conflicts may arise from the tendency to make more than one response in a situation. This is similar to the negative transfer design of human learning. When new responses must be learned to a set of cues, a certain amount of interference between the two sets of responses results. When both response tendencies are of about equal strength, neither response may be made, and some increase in tension may arise from the frustration. After a childhood of steering carts and sleds by bending the front end of the vehicle with the feet, a fairly strong habit to push the foot opposite to the direction of desired turn will develop. A vehicle requiring the opposite feet movements, for example, the rudder control of an airplane, will be difficult to steer at first. Somewhere along the course of learning the new habits of foot-steering, the two sets of responses will be almost equal and result in considerable oscillation between the two habits, and consequently a hesitation in properly steering the airplane. After living through this phase, the newer response will become more and more dominant until all traces of conflict in the habits will be gone.

Other habit conflicts may be found in attaching names to things or faces. A new acquaintance who is very similar to an older friend will at first be named incorrectly. But as the new name is learned there will be a period when neither name is emittable due to the conflict of the equal tendencies to make both "name" responses. With further experience the new name will be evoked consistently to the face.

Conflicts are most frequently identified with conflicting motives of the sort used to analyze conflict earlier. Where there are easily identifiable motives and goals operating, the conflict is most easily seen in behavior towards those goals. One laboratory study of such a conflict of motives was the approach-avoidance conflict reported in cats by Jules Masserman.[47] The conflict was developed by first teaching hungry cats to open a small lid over a dish of food in one corner of a restraining box. This habit was easily learned. Now a conflict was introduced by blowing a stream of air at the cat's nose when it opened the box to get food. Since an air puff on the nose is greatly disliked by cats, it was sufficient to lead to avoidance of the dish of food. After several tries at opening the lid and being struck by the air puff, the cats ceased further attempts at reaching the food. Masserman's cats then began to show strange and unusual patterns of behavior. Many of the physiological indicators of an emotional reaction were present. Some cats showed unusual startle reactions to simple common stimuli, and others developed strange patterns of response like pacing in an elliptical pattern. Masserman interpreted these behaviors as indicating an experimentally produced abnormal behavior. Further experimentation has concerned various "cures" for these "neurotic" behavior patterns.

Another common example of motivational conflicts is given by the attempts one occasionally makes to give up the strongly motivated habits of smoking, excessive eating, or chewing fingernails. The approach-avoidance conflict is a very intense one which, if one is successful in his resolutions, leads to a gradual change in the motive state for the behavior. The cognitive resolution to refrain from smoking becomes stronger with knowledge that one has been successful for a time, and this successful avoidance also brings a slight weakening in the power of the smoking cues to break the abstinence. The individual who announces to all and sundry his intentions never to smoke again has used the power of social "face" to enhance the resolution. It becomes more difficult to begin smoking with the knowledge that others will lose respect for you because of it. Gradually, learning which produced the habit will remove it. The cues to engage in that behavior become less and less effective until the approach tendency becomes nearly nonexistent.

Many of the conflicts of life come from the values which we hold and their interaction with other circumstances. The proverbs of our culture often require adherence to patterns of behavior which may be seen to be less than optimal for success and happiness. "Early to bed and early to rise, etc.," suggests a life which would make an active participation in social and cultural activities quite difficult. One can argue that the real source of happiness and wealth resides in the contacts of various sorts that one makes with people in social activities which are largely evening affairs.

The learned patterns of personality which are called values often conflict with necessary behaviors. The values taught by religion contrast sharply with those which must be followed in a developed, competitive business community. The honesty which is learned in the church and the home must be tempered by the expediency of business in selling used cars for "Slippery Sam's No-Money-Down Car Emporium," and the expectations of society are in accord with this difference. Concepts or behavior patterns like honesty vary considerably from place to place. At some educational institutions widespread cheating is the implicitly condoned rule rather than the exception, and various groups of individuals actively collect examination questions in files through "systems." The behavior which would be repudiated as abject dishonesty by those at most schools is regarded at other schools as a sort of game between the students and the faculty with no particular rules. Adherence to some laws of society is considered mandatory while others (e.g., the laws regulating traffic and taxation) are considered to be breakable if the unlawful behavior can be hidden from the executors of the law. Conflicts of values in such situations are quite complex.

On a broader scale still the general form or style of life may often conflict with situations experienced. The demands of studying and of playing while in college must be faced continuously. The larger goals of preparing for life's work and the momentary pressures of other activities are often at odds. Lucky indeed is the person for whom the activities necessary in this preparation, studying, and other intellectual activities, are enjoyable in their own right. The approach-approach conflict of choosing between two desirable activities results in less frustration and pressure than does the approach-avoidance conflict of those who consider learning to be a chore.

A frequent source of broad conflicts in the life of most young people concern the choice of a direction for their life. The choice of a vocation or avocation often leads to conflicts with abilities and past experiences which are difficult to resolve without introducing further conflict. Arthur Miller's play *Death of a Salesman* chronicled the conflicts of a man who was in a life's work for which he really felt he was unsuited. Willie resolved the conflict in the story by ending his own life. Conflicts are often built from the circumstances of having more than one job or duty. The young man serving his country in the armed forces may feel that he is being asked to violate the intentions or purpose of his planned life's work. Those in the "helping" professions of social welfare or medicine often express such a conflict of interests. During the process of growing-up the young person first reaching into the world of the adult often feels bound by the conflicting roles and demands upon a child and an adult simultaneously. Thus, the adolescent is prevailed upon to act like an adult but is simultaneously required to be off the streets by 10 P.M. and face a discriminatory punishment if he should violate a minor traffic law. These sorts of conflict arising from the role assumed by an individual may appear to be easy to resolve from the viewpoint of another person, but the motivations and perceived values of the situation of the one in the conflict are usually in a finer balance.

Defense Mechanisms

What are some of the methods by which one can circumvent frustrations and remove conflicts? As discussed earlier, according to Rule 4 of conflict resolution, the motivational value of a goal may be changed to alter the conflict situation. The motivational value may be changed by denying its existence or by disguising its true nature. A behavior pattern or mechanism which results in such a self-deception has been called a *defense mechanism*.

FUNCTION OF DEFENSE MECHANISMS

Defense mechanisms remove the anxiety and other uncomfortable aspects of frustration and conflict by disguising the motivation for behaviors which are likely to lead to those feelings. The mechanisms are said to enhance the self-esteem of the individual and permit a better adjustment of that individual to the precipitating situation. The denial or disguise of the motivation behind a behavior reduces the anxiety from the frustrating situation to an acceptable amount.

The classification of defense mechanisms is somewhat arbitrary. There is considerable variability in the length and content of lists of the mechanisms described by different writers. Classifications of defense behaviors according to their probable function often requires a considerable amount of inference about the background motivation and self-perception by an individual. This leads to a classification and labeling which is neither precise nor discrete. A behavior pattern may be labeled differently by writers and judged by others to fall half-way between categories.

Care must be taken also that such labeling of behavior mechanisms does not imply an explanation of the behavior. Labeling does not explain except to the extent that it refers the behavior to membership in a class of things about which more is known. Some amount of understanding of the probable function of a behavior does result from labelling as a defense mechanism, but the limitations of the classification system in precision and sharpness of boundaries reduces its usefulness.

COMMON DEFENSE MECHANISMS

Six varieties of defense mechanisms are discussed below to illustrate this sort of adjustment device. Other reactions to frustration and conflict are also listed by some writers as defense mechanisms, but the listing here is that of the majority of writers.

Perhaps the most famous defense mechanism and the most commonly used is that called *rationalization*. Rationalization is the application of different reasons to replace the real reasons for a behavior. Excuses are made up to hide or disguise the true motive for a behavior. A student may "explain" his poor grades by complaining of poor teaching and unfair exams. We often claim to have "needs" which will justify our purchasing a high-horsepower car to "climb hills" or to "pass other cars quickly." Advertisers are careful to supply such imagined needs to justify the purchase of their product. One may compare himself with others to rationalize his conflict and resulting guilt: "Everyone else was drinking at the party."

The rationalization is used to some extent by nearly everyone. It removes minor inconsistencies that might otherwise be apparent to others and to oneself. The search for reasons for behavior sometimes leads to a more consistent and valuable view of oneself. By explicitly pronouncing a reason for a behavior even though it is not correct in entirety, the reduction in anxiety over inconsistency justifies the discrepancy from fact. Needs claimed for certain states of affairs, when they become assimilated into the perception of the self, tend to become needs in fact; learned needs based upon the repeated rationalization. Rationalization also, however, may take the place of logical reasoning and lead to a greater reliance on an unreal conception of the world. For overall adjustment there must be some balance between covering up problems by rationalizing and facing them for other solutions.

Reaction Formation is a mechanism which requires some knowledge of the actual motives and sources of behavior. Reaction formation is the expression of the more socially accepted though weaker of two conflicting motives. The opposite of the true motive is expressed. Those who advocate severe censorship of all materials of a sexually suggestive nature might be using this mechanism if it could be revealed that that individual had strong inclinations toward using the materials which he wished to censor. The mother who did not really want her child might react by displaying a great ostentatious affection for the child. An overly affectionate and complimenting friend might be really covering up to others and to himself a basic dislike for you. But the key to identifying this mechanism is the knowledge of the actual direction of the various motives and alternatives.

Substitution or compensation is like reaction formation to a degree, but the cover behavior is a largely unrelated behavior rather than an opposite one. An acceptable behavior is substituted for one which is less acceptable to that person. A student who is doing poorly in his studies might substitute an active social life at the school. Occasionally some undesirable feature of physique or personality may be disguised or hidden by an emphasis upon excelling in political power or story-telling. Substitution often becomes a useful mechanism by providing a strong impetus toward directing personality in an acceptable channel. The energy which is directed in the new cover behavior provides an unusually great motivation for that behavior. If the resulting behavior is useful to the person, a much greater than expected achievement may be attained in addition to removing the problems from the focus of attention. The person who feels himself to be rather dull may take upon the outward appearances of the bright stereotype; appearing attentive, asking questions, displaying a marked enthusiasm for intellectual pursuits, and so on. As long as the sham is not publicly exposed, the frustration of the personal inadequacy will be disguised to others and to himself. The compensation may take the form or working through the exploits of others. The parents who wish their children to have all the "advantages" that were denied to them are perhaps compensating for the achievements that they did not themselves attain. An individual may substitute the desirable motives and abilities which he can assume in the fantasy of daydreams to disguise their lack in the real world. Each of these varieties of substitution and compensation disguises and covers the frustration and consequent anxiety by focusing attention upon some other behavior. These mechanisms may have a usefulness in the potential value of the resultant behavior, but they also may lead to quite undesirable behavior and further difficulty.

Projection is seeing in others the motives which lead to frustration and problems of conflict in oneself. By assigning our own undesirable motives to others often in an exaggerated amount, we make our own motives by comparison seem less conspicuous. And by calling attention to the behaviors of others, the attention is not focused upon our own motives and behaviors. Projection, again, requires that the true motive states in both the accuser and the accused be known. Because some name-calling behavior is observed does not mean that the caller is projecting his own problems. He may be describing the true state of affairs. But if the charge is obviously unjustified, there is reason to look for the projection mechanism. This mechanism sneaks into our daily behavior in many ways. The basic distrust we have of merchants who seem to be making a good profit lies in part in placing our own motives into their behaviors Simply the statement that "there is a little larceny in all of us" reflects a bit of projection. And the flirt who accuses her boy friend of unfaithfulness may be projecting.

Repression is an escape from the undesirable aspects of a frustrating or conflict situation by a loss of memory. Knowledge of the conflict is simply not available. Repression may be as extreme as a complete denial of the motive state. Some cases of amnesia have been seen to follow this sort of mechanism. There is complete loss of memory about the parts of a person's life which have to do with a rather uncomfortable situation. Other memories of a general nature are present, but the relevant details of the conflict source may be absent. An example of this kind of memory loss was recently given by the inquiry records of an airplane crash in which an apparently improper emergency procedure for the loss of one engine's power was executed. Neither the pilot nor co-pilot had any recollection of the happenings and acts from the time just before the engine power was lost until just after the crash, though this was a considerable period of time and many responses were obviously executed by both men. Simpler examples of repression come from daily memory losses of appointments which we did not wish to keep as opposed to those which we anticipated enjoying. Students often "forget" the instructions for term papers or other unwelcome assignments. Such observations of selective forgetting are quite uncontrolled but this kind of forgetting mechanism is widely held as a means of conflict and frustration adjustment. Repression is a basic part of the dynamics of Freud's theory of personality (See Chapter 10).

Identification as a defense mechanism is related to its role in the normal growing process of children. Identification is trying to be like some other person and living the motivated behaviors of that person. In children it is a normal part of the experiences of trying out different new personalities. In an adult with an established life pattern, identification covers up conflicts and unexpressed motives. By assuming the desirable qualities and behaviors of another for a while, by *being* in fantasy that other person, one may escape the conflicts and frustrations of his own life. Perhaps the appeal of viewing plays, movies, and television and the attraction of reading novels of whatever quality may be explained by the identification experience they give to that observer. By becoming for a time the bold character of 007 or the romantic charmer of Cleopatra, some relief is gained.

Identification is also more than fantasy behavior. If one identifies with a person, there is likely to be some mimicking of the behavior of that person and its effects may be permanent. One may learn new ways of behaving by assuming parts of the observed role of others. By adopting the mannerisms and diversions of a person or group one becomes like that group, perhaps reducing the frustration of not appearing to be like that person or group. If one has very strong feelings of dislike for someone who cannot be ignored or be allowed to discover those feelings, the identification mechanism is an effective guard. By acting and behaving like that disliked person, one comes to see himself as the same as that person. Since there is little difference between these two people, one cannot dislike the other. The conflict is minimized by a change in value and the second person is well on the way to being much like the initially disliked person. This sort of mechanism is difficult to detect in ourselves. Often the source of dislike concerns a sort of jealousy about the apparent motives and behaviors of the other person and the dislike is hidden by assuming those behaviors.

DANGERS IN DEFENSE MECHANISMS

Labeling the behaviors does little in the way of explaining them. Some function of the mechanism may be assumed by its inclusion in a category, but usually not anything that was not apparent in each individual case.

Everyone uses defense mechanisms to some degree. Some persons rely heavily upon rationalization, others upon reaction formation. Still others make up for frustrating circumstances largely by identifying in fantasy. The point is that they are normal behaviors in nonexaggerated amounts and are probably present in all people. This does not mean, however, that they are harmless or of no consequence for that person. Here is a case of a little knowledge being a dangerous thing. The glib exposure of all of the mechanisms that your friends appear to be using may lead to serious personality problems for them and indirectly for you. The serious exposure of carefully designed rationalizations may expose to that person's view conflicts which he cannot handle, and lead him to unfortunate behaviors. Remember that the mechanism is serving an adjustive function which implies that there is a source of frustration or conflict which must be dealt with. The defense mechanism is doing that job by disguising or denying its presence. Careless exposure of such emotional problems may lead to an uncontrollable situation.

Lest this has overly exaggerated the seriousness of the exposure of the mechanisms it should also be said that the motives underlying the behaviors, like all motives, are invented by the student of behavior. Motives are not real things which lurk in the mind ready to pounce out at every opportunity. The motives describe some hypothetical causes for patterns of behavior. The danger of exposure, too, is hypothetical and a result of similar inferences. That the inferences might be and often are correct should caution your uninhibited psychologizing of those whom you do not know very well.

Defense mechanisms hold other dangers for those who use them. It has already been mentioned that rationalization may lead to a reliance upon unreal logical formulations and that the adjustive behaviors of reaction formation, compensation, and substitution may not benefit the person or society, and that fantasy may lead to excessive withdrawal to an unreal world. The behaviors which result from defense mechanisms are not always useful, though they can be.

The major weaknesses of defense mechanisms as adjustment devices for an individual are (1) that their excessive use usually leads to greater social and personality difficulty, and (2) that they do not generally solve the problem which required their use in the first place. Though momentary motivational problems of frustration and conflict may be removed by the mechanisms, little is usually done by the mechanisms to change the basic problems of personality structure which lead to those motivations.

Other Modes of Adjustment

WITHDRAWAL

Opposed to the active society-directed behaviors of the defensive reactions to frustrations and conflicts are the *withdrawal* and escape responses. Like the escape behavior of avoiding physical harm is the avoidance of anticipated psychological harm by withdrawing from contact with the situations. Reliance on withdrawal is, like the defense mechanisms in general, useful for its own purposes, but likely to lead to further difficulties with society and not likely to allow sufficient contact with the sources of the problems for a better solution to be developed. An active form of withdrawal is that of *negativism*. Negativism is a purposeful rebellion against the requests and wishes of others. It is frequently present in children but also in the behavior of adults. The resistance may take the form of following "orders" blindly and to-the-letter when they describe something we did not wish to do. The fantasy of identification and compensation is also a sort of escape reaction. (This overlap illustrates some of the problems of attempting too tight a classification system.) Finally the regressive reactions to frustration are also a withdrawal. Withdrawal to earlier rewarding situations and behaviors which were once appropriate provides an attempt at regaining what existed once to escape the reality of the present.

FEARS AND ANXIETY

Fear is a normal reaction in anticipation of danger. Some degree of fearful anticipation of the hazards of physical and psychological situation is necessary for an individual to survive. But fears, too, may be exaggerated until they are out of proportion to the danger. A moderate fear of having too few friends may develop into a guiding force which drives a person to actually fearing to be alone. A need for social companionship may cultivate a fear of not attaining enough friendships and this may lead to an unfillable need for having people nearby all the time.

Anxiety was discussed earlier as a non-specific, generalized fear. Anxiety was also mentioned in connection with some of the other mechanisms of adjustment as reflecting the undesirable consequences of a frustration or conflict situation. If anxiety is not effectively reduced by a solution to the conflict or frustration, the result is a non-adjustive state of affairs. If the anxiety appears to direct behavior, the individual may be responding to the conflict by anxious behavior alone. Symptoms of such an anxious behavior reaction include unpleasant feelings of emotion, helplessness, and unpleasantness. Some bodily responses of fear states occur alone with the experienced feelings. Unresolved fears and anxiety which do not constructively benefit the structure of personality are very close to neurotic reactions, which may require expert help for resolution of the precipitating conflicts.

Summary

Adjustment is a process of interaction between an individual's behavior and the conditions of the environment. Adjustment is often aimed at minimizing states of frustration and conflict.

Frustration is a state arising when a motivated behavior is blocked. Blocking may come from a physical barrier, a personal deficiency, or a conflict of motivated behaviors. Frustration may lead to responses of aggression, regression, apathy, stereotypy, or restlessness.

A conflict may be simplified into approach-approach, avoidance-avoidance, or approach-avoidance patterns for analysis and study. Conflicts are viewed as being influenced by four principles which have been derived from behavior theory. Conflicts may arise between two or more habits, motivational factors, or general styles of behaviors and roles in life.

Behavior mechanisms which use self-deception to remove frustrations and conflicts are called defense mechanisms. Some often used defense mechanisms are rationalization, reaction formation, substitution, projection, repression, and identification. Defense mechanisms are normal methods of adjustment when used in moderation. Their major weaknesses are that they do not solve the problems which they cover up, and their excessive use usually leads to greater social difficulty, creating further needs for adjustment.

Other mechanisms of adjustment include withdrawal from contact with frustrating situations and the development of a generalized fear response called anxiety.

SUGGESTED READINGS

Jourard, S. M. *Personal adjustment* (2nd edition). New York: Macmillan, 1963.
A textbook of normal patterns of adjustment. The book develops from considerations of individual personality to the social relations of the normal individual.

Shaffer, L. F. and Shoben, E. J. *The psychology of adjustment.* Boston: Houghton Mifflin, 1956.
A textbook of normal and abnormal patterns of adjustment. The viewpoint of the book is predominantly that of experimental and empirical psychology. The strong influences of learning are emphasized.

Chapter *12*

BEHAVIOR
DISORDERS

*What is the nature of deviant behavior? How do neuroses and psy-
choses differ? What are some common behavior disorders? How
might deviant behaviors be changed? What are the techniques
and professions which treat behavior disorders? How might one
avoid deviant behaviors?*

The study, cure, and prevention of deviant behavior is generally known
by the term "mental health." This name is believed to be unfortunate by
some writers because it implies a particular viewpoint for the study of
that behavior. The use of the word health implies a perhaps unjustified
similarity to the study of physiological disorders. It implies the "medical
model," which will be discussed in the chapter.

More acceptable terms to describe most of the content of this chapter
might be *psychopathology* and *psychotherapy*. *Psychopathology* is the
science of deviant behavior and *psychotherapy* is the process of changing deviant behaviors. Along with these two topics, principles of personal
improvement of personality will be presented which are likely to prevent
the formation of many sorts of deviant behavior.

Psychopathology

There are a variety of approaches to the identification of deviant, mal-
adjusted, or abnormal behavior patterns. These kinds of behaviors

usually are marked by feelings of personal unhappiness, discomfort, or distress, along with a certain inappropriateness of that behavior. More serious examples of deviant behavior are marked by a break with reality, experiencing and reacting to perceptions and beliefs which have no basis in fact. These definitions have considerable flexibility and allow a freedom in individual case categorization depending upon the needs and purposes of that classification.

What then *is* mental illness? *Mental illness* is a certain pattern of behavior of an individual which is judged to be seriously inappropriate and uncomfortable and which represents a considerable handicap and unhappiness for that individual. The exact behavior patterns which fit the criteria are somewhat different from one person to the next but some further general classifications of kinds of deviant behaviors have been found to be useful.

The distinction between an individual who displays a deviant behavior pattern and one who appears normal is one of the difficult problems of classification facing the student of psychopathology. A second quite similar problem is the distinction between varieties of deviant behaviors. One classification of deviant behaviors is that of neurotic and psychotic patterns of behavior. What is the nature of the distinction between these behaviors and the implications which each hold for treatment? This section will describe first the nature of the problems of classification of deviant behaviors, and then consider some frequently used neurotic, psychotic, and character disorder behavior labels. Sufficient description of these deviant behavior examples will be given for the reader to develop a "feel" for recognizing them.

DISTINGUISHING MENTAL DISORDERS

Deviant behavior which is very similar to normal adjustive response patterns, but which is exaggerated, somewhat damaging, and partly ineffective for the individual, has been called *neurotic* behavior. Neurotic patterns of response appear to be on a continuum of effectiveness-of-adjustment-mechanisms, in that the usual mechanisms are present, but their value or strength seems to be different. This view of neurotic behavior holds that neurotic behavior is not qualitatively different from that of normal adjustment, but that the effectiveness of the adjustment devices or the use of certain mechanisms in exaggerated amounts results in its classification as a deviant pattern of behavior.

Other, more severe patterns of deviant behavior do not seem to be on this same continuum of normal and neurotic behavior patterns. Psychotic behaviors often appear discontinuous from those of normal individuals. Patients who refuse to wear clothes, who chew on parts of their own body, or who refuse to move from a fixed position for hours on end do not seem to fall on the same dimensions as those with neurotic and normal behaviors. Though this distinction appears very great when extreme cases are considered, it is difficult to specify and measure. There appear to be too few criteria which are effective in distinguishing more than a small percentage of actual collections of neurotic and psychotic behavior patterns. The classifications which have existed for some time, then, are of a disjunctive nature. That is, they define a deviant behavior of a certain label if it conforms to any one of several patterns. The category of psychosis is defined by a collection of criteria.

The most commonly expressed difference between a neurotic and psychotic patient is in terms of *reality contact*. Reality contact is an inferred construct which may be measured explicitly in a number of ways. The presence of *hallucinations* (false sense perceptions) may indicate poor contact with reality. The existence of *delusions* (false beliefs) are also evidence that a patient may be living in his "own little world." The patient may also indicate a poor reality contact by being disoriented in time or place. He may assume another identity—the "Napoleon" whom the entertainers picture as the typical mental patient. Finally, the motor behavior of the patient may indicate poor reality contact. Holding bizarre positions of the limbs for hours at a time, or making gestures which have no apparent meaning are examples of deviant motor behavior.

Other attempts at defining neurotic-psychotic differences have used the relative *efficiency of behavior*. Behavior which is focused toward the motivational goals is characteristic of normal functions, while diffuse behavior is directed toward nonrelevant goals in the presence of the motivation and suggests deviant behavior. Random motor movements in a motor skills task, and irrelevant talking while attempting a simple description would indicate relative inefficiency, and thus deviant behavior, when used to excess.

A different behavior approach of distinguishing neurotic and psychotic behavior has been to examine the degree to which these two kinds of deviant behaviors are *produced or removed by learning processes*. If psychotic behaviors may be shown to be the result of similar but perhaps more extensive experiences of the kinds leading to normal adjustment and neurosis, then the neurotic and psychotic behaviors may be seen as continuous. Similarly, if they are "cured" or removed by the same techniques, they would not appear to be different in kind.

The *social reaction* to the behavior may also be considered in forming the distinction. Psychotic behaviors usually appear less desirable to members of society and this is reflected in part by the hospitalization of psychotics. Neurotics are nearly always treated as out-patients, whereas most psychotics are given institutional care.

Whatever the basis for the present classification, attempts at justifying it and improving it have run into difficulties. Part of this problem involves the question which is being asked. Instead of the question of the nature of the difference between neurotics and psychotics, a functional or practical question might better be asked: What are the determining conditions? How may the behavior be modified, and what may be done to prevent such a deviant behavior from forming? The answers to these questions would form a functional rather than taxonomic question for the science of psychopathology. The answer to the question of the sort of difference, qualitative or quantitative, between neurotic and psychotic behavior patterns would follow from the functional knowledge.

NEUROSES

The observable bits of deviant behavior are called *symptoms*. These bits or patterns of behavior are assumed to result from a past history of events and conditions. The name for the neurotic pattern is usually derived from some characteristic of the origins and pattern of symptoms. Study and removal of the neurotic pattern in a particular patient, however, may not necessarily be determined by this label. The pattern of past conditions leading to the neurotic pattern must be considered to suggest the proper direction for therapy. Four types of neuroses are considered below: the *anxiety reaction,* the *phobic reaction,* the *hysteric reaction,* and the *obsessive-compulsive reaction.* These types appear rather often and give a good flavor of the neurotic reaction.

The *anxiety reaction* may be viewed as a partial failure of the individual's defenses. Those mechanisms which function to prevent the individual from facing the fears and anxieties of past experiences fail partially and allow a sizable vague fear to be forced into consciousness. There is no awareness of the reasons for the fear, but there are feelings that dreadful things are likely to happen to the person soon. Some bodily symptoms may occasionally be present. Feelings of breathing difficulties, "heart trouble," pounding heart, speeded pulse, trembling and so on are often reported along with the nonspecific fear.

The *phobic reaction* has been defined as a specific fear of unusual intensity of some object, act, or situation. It is more than a normal fear reaction, in that there is usually no actual danger. The phobic reaction may be viewed as being a symbol of some other factor which is the "true" source of the fear. A collection of terms were once used to describe these sorts of dreads. Some terms like "claustrophobia" (for a fear of enclosed places) and "hydrophobia" (for fear of water) have persisted into our daily vocabulary, but the ascribing of an X-phobia for each sort of un-natural fear has been largely discontinued.

The progress of phobic reactions has been frequently found to follow a pattern. The phobia often dates from a critical, intense fear-producing situation which occurred during early childhood. It has been subesquently forgotten or repressed, and its memory would bring out feelings of guilt or anxiety. Finally, the effective treatment of such phobias has been found to include a re-evaluation of the guilt feelings arising from the situation once the critical incident has been recalled.

Hysteric reactions are symptoms which express converted impulses and motives. The pattern of behavior into which the problem has been converted may be a dissociative condition having to do with memories of personality, or it may concern a physiological disorder. A dissociative reaction may be a brief *amnesia,* a longer loss of memory, in which the person often changes his identity, called a *fugue,* or a memory loss for an extended period of time during which the individual expresses a new personality, usually quite different from the former one. The second personality may also form over a period of time in an alternating pattern with the original identity in cases of multiple personality. The forgetting in these cases involves the conflicts of the individual and may be viewed as an extreme withdrawal mechanism.

The hysterias which are connected with physical symptoms are commonly called *conversion reactions.* Conversion reactions are physical disorders which have a psychological basis. The disorder symptom is usually an insensitivity or paralysis of some parts of the body. Occasionally the disorder covers a spatial area which has no anatomical basis, as for example, an insensitivity corresponding to the area covered by one sock. Conversion symptoms like blindness or tunnel vision (peripheral vision has disappeared) were noted by earlier workers and in some cases, were removed by use of hypnosis. At other times they disappeared while the patient participated in engrossing physical sports activities. The reaction may be viewed as a conversion of the conflict and anxiety into a particular symptom as a symbol and cover to hide the memory of that particular set of events which are feared. Often a careful process of re-evaluation of the recalled conditions are sufficient to remove or change the hysterical symptoms.

The *obsessive-compulsive reactions* are similar to the symptoms of phobias and hysterias in that their presence defends the individual from some more devastating memory or confrontation with conflict. Obsessions and compulsions are thoughts and actions which occur repetitively and are not consciously controllable. As long as they are present, the patient may be said to be warding off anxiety attacks. When they are interfered with or interrupted, the patient experiences great anxiety. The contents of these symptoms are usually related to themes of aggression and sexual impulses or to self-correcting behaviors like orderliness, cleanliness, and various self-imposed duties and punishments. The obsessive-compulsive reactions are usually easy to diagnose and are very close to being consciously available to the patient. The conflicts and motivations yielding the obsessions and compulsions are richly represented by symbolization and closely corresponding behaviors.

PSYCHOSES

Only those psychoses of a psychogenic origin, having no known physical cause or structural change in the brain, are considered in this section. These psychoses are often called *functional psychoses* to distinguish them from the *organic psychoses* to be considered in the following section. Three classes of functional psychosis are considered with some examples of subclasses which have been observed frequently. Those classes are the *affective, schizophrenic,* and *paranoid reactions.*

The *affective reactions* concern various patterns of mania and depression. In its weakest degrees, *mania* is much like a state of high spirits. There is a general overactivity of actions and thoughts, much like that of mild alcoholic intoxication. In more severe mania there appears to be a strong pressure to action of some kind, a pressure to talk constantly and with frequent changes of subject matter, and a drive to physical action which easily leads to anger if slightly thwarted. In extreme degrees, mania is a violent and disorganized behavior. *Depression* states may be similarly viewed in stages. The weakest depression is not too different from discouragement and underactivity. In greater depression stages there is an acute melancholia in which the patient often feels worthless, full of sin, and frequently contemplates suicide. In severe depression there is a condition of acute immobility and speechlessness often called a *depressive stupor.*

Many patterns of mania and depression are found in the affective psychoses. An individual may have a cycle of behavior from severe mania to severe depression, from mania to mild depression, or just from mania to a normal affective state. Similarly the stages of depression may cycle with different depths of mania. The timing of different stages is also quite variable.

Schizophrenia is the most frequent diagnosis of psychotic behavior. The schizophrenic pattern of behavior is one of withdrawal from participation in society and a consequent life in response to a world within oneself. A common pattern of schizophrenic development is from an early schizoid behavior (nonpsychotic withdrawal), through stages of greater withdrawal, to an eventual psychotic state. Some theorists view it as a gradual destruction of the central integration of personality, a change in the associative connections which organize behavior.

Four varieties of schizophrenia serve to illustrate the many patterns which the withdrawal may take. Each of these types is unique, yet a particular patient may exhibit combinations of these behavior patterns. The four varieties are *simple, paranoid, hebephrenic,* and *catatonic* schizophrenia.

Simple schizophrenia entails a gradual loss of interest in life, accomplishments, and social participation. Showing no ambition and some apathy, these patients appear to be contented and quiet. There is some reaction to pressure from others, but usually in a self-destructive, negative vein. The patient makes no effort to improve his condition or social contacts.

The *paranoid schizophrenic* is marked by a systematic and logical organization of delusions. The *delusions,* which are mistaken beliefs about the world, are often subtle and accompanied by *hallucinations,* which are false sense impressions. The delusions are also accompanied by a systematic use of projection and other formal accusations toward others. The paranoid schizophrenic also displays a loss of interest in the world and a general disorganization of personality. The paranoid (delusional) aspects of the behavior are like those of paranoia psychosis to be described later, but here they are combined with the breakdown of personality organization and self-centered behavior which is the hallmark of schizophrenia.

The *hebephrenic schizophrenic* is characterized by silliness, bizarre thoughts and actions, disorganized speech containing words of the patient's invention, and an unorganized set of delusions and hallucinations. Compared with the paranoid schizophrenic, the hebephrenic is illogical and inconsistent, appearing to change topics rapidly and with a disorganization of feelings and content. Hebephrenics, for example, may laugh at the suggestion of the death of close friends and become upset when telling of their own good health. The onset of hebephrenic schizophrenia is relatively rapid, the disorganization appears marked after a relatively short period of time.

The *catatonic schizophrenic* is markedly inactive. The attention of this deviant behavior pattern is on the movements and movement thoughts called "motility." The patients may display peculiar and unusual positions of the limbs and body for long periods of time. A short intense manic phase often alternates with the deep stupor of some patients. In catatonic mania the patient holds real danger for himself and others, while in the marked motor depression, the patient may not move at all, refusing to eat or perform the simple acts of the body necessary for living organisms. In some cases a behavior that has been described as "waxy flexibility" takes place in the stupor state in which the limbs may be placed in various positions and, like a wax model, they will not move. The extremes of immotility often are rapid in onset and disappearance. The catatonic patient has often come out of the state of stupor instantly and reported everything that went on around him during the state. The acute motor negativism apparently does not necessarily interfere with his perceptions.

The third form of psychosis, the *paranoid reaction,* is like the paranoid schizophrenic except there is an absence of the general personality disorganization characteristic of the schizophrenic. The paranoid has an elaborate delusional system which allows strange interpretations of the events about the patient. Hallucinations are generally absent. The patient perceives correctly but misinterprets what he perceives. Often the complex yet logically tight verbalizations of the patient leads one to wonder why the patient was labeled psychotic. The relationship of reality to the premises of that highly logical argument, however, indicates a break from reality in interpretation of the events and intentions of others. The paranoiac is seen to use the mechanisms of projection extensively, "seeing" plans of others to do him harm, believing that there is an organized attempt to do in the patient, and similar themes.

Paranoia is used to describe a pattern of behavior of normal individuals as well and had been extensively used as a term to refer to feelings that others are plotting against one and that more than chance is affecting the circumstances of his life.

DISORDERS OF ORGANIC ORIGIN

The organic psychoses are those in which some impairment of the function of brain tissue is known or likely to be causing the deviant behavior pattern. Some common forms of organic disruption are the "senile psychoses," produced by age, psychoses resulting from excessive intake of drugs and alcohol, and the results of progressive neural destruction such as that caused by earlier contact with venereal disease. Patterns of behavior resulting from organic destruction are varied, but there are some consistencies which have been noted.

Senile psychoses result from the ravages of age and are characterized by disorientations in space and time. The patient often does not know the present date and his location, but may carry on vivid conversations with individuals and at apparent times long since past. Hallucinations are frequent and varied.

Alcoholic psychosis (delirium tremens) is commonly marked by a violent restlessness with accompanying hallucinations of a terrifying nature. A certain degeneration of motor control is often indicated by the trembling of the patient.

General *paresis*, which is destruction of neural tissue, leads to loss of certain motor control and eventual death. The paretic psychotic often exhibits delusions and hallucinations along with an exaggeration and an absence of various reflexes of the body. This condition has been commonly found to be the result of contact with the venereal disease syphilis at a much earlier time, though the patient thought he was then cured.

CHARACTER DISORDERS

A character disorder is a personality pattern of socially deviant behavior. The individual does not usually experience the degree of anxiety and emotional stress typical of neuroses and psychoses. Instead the person with a character disorder has not learned the customs and morals of his society. He usually responds to his own needs in an impulsive fashion.

Character disorders include the socially deviant behaviors of delinquency, sexually deviant behaviors, drug addiction, alcoholism, and outright felonious acts. One frequent antisocial reaction is called the *psychopathic reaction*. The psychopathic individual has had no moral development in his society. His self-centered, impulsive, and criminal acts are not premeditated. He shows no emotional response (lie detectors are useless on him) and does not seem to be stressed in his life role. Obviously, many of these characteristics are present in mild amounts in everyone, especially during the personality developing teen-age years. The psychopathic, like the neurotic, falls at the extremes of a continuous dimension of behavior patterns from normal to deviant. The psychopathic reaction is often quite resistant to treatment.

Psychotherapy

Psychotherapy is the process or method by which deviant behaviors are changed or "cured." There is no unified plan or organization of those processes. Instead of a common viewpoint there are many viewpoints. There is little agreement on even the simplest criteria to judge or measure the effectiveness of a treatment. This jumble of approaches and procedures has led to one facetious definition of psychotherapy as an undefined technique applied to unspecified problems with an unpredictable outcome. Part of the problem may be traced to the state of development of the science of psychopathology. But other parts of the confusion may be traced to the kinds of influences prevailing upon the psychotherapist, both historical and political. Finally, the various differences between psychotherapists as men must be considered for their effects upon the process, taking into account the needs and behaviors of these men. In the following section a discussion of several "models" for the classification and treatment of deviant behaviors will be sketched. Some of the basic procedures of commonly used psychotherapy will also be discussed, followed by a description of the background and functions of psychotherapeutic workers.

MODELS OF MENTAL DISORDERS

The models of deviant behavior may be seen to correspond somewhat to the theories of personality considered earlier. The medical models correspond roughly to the type and trait theories. The behavior models are very similar to the S-R theories of personality, and the dynamic models are the same as the Freudian and neo-Freudian theories of personality development and function.

The *medical model* is an inheritance from the medical backgrounds of early psychopathologists. Using the conceptions and terminology which have been successful in the treatment of structural disorders, the medical model has dominated the present viewpoints of deviant behavior, especially as they are pictured by society. The very term "mental illness" implies a particular disease which must be diagnosed and treated. The deviant behaviors are assumed to be only symptoms of this usually hidden cause. The classification of deviant behaviors in the previous section is based upon the "diagnostic classifications of mental disorders" outlined by earlier medical views and approaches to the problem.[3]

A. Disorders caused by or associated with impairment of brain tissue function
  1. Acute brain disorders (11 specific disorders)
  2. Chronic brain disorders (23 specific disorders)
B. Mental deficiency
  1. Mental deficiency, familial or hereditary
  2. Mental deficiency, idiopathic
C. Disorders of psychogenic origin, or without clearly defined physical cause or structural change in the brain
  1. Psychotic disorders
        Involutional psychotic reaction
        Affective reactions
          Manic-depressive reaction, manic type
          Manic-depressive reaction, depressive type
          Manic-depressive reaction, other
          Psychotic depressive reaction
        Schizophrenic reactions
          Simple type
          Hebephrenic type
          Catatonic type
          Paranoid type
          Acute and undifferentiated type
          Chronic undifferentiated type
          Schizo-affective type
          Childhood type
          Residual type
        Paranoid reactions
          Paranoia
          Paranoid state
        Other
  2. Psychophysiologic autonomic and visceral disorders
        Psychophysiologic skin reaction
        Psychophysiologic musculoskeletal reaction
        Psychophysiologic respiratory reaction
        Psychophysiologic cardiovascular reaction
        Psychophysiologic hemic and lymphatic reaction
        Psychophysiologic gastrointestinal reaction
        Psychophysiologic endocrine reaction
        Psychophysiologic nervous system reaction
        Psychophysiologic reaction of organs of special sense
  3. Psychoneurotic disorders
        Anxiety reaction
        Dissociative reaction
        Conversion reaction
        Phobic reaction
        Obsessive-compulsion reaction
        Depressive reaction
        Other
  4. Personality disorders
        Personality pattern disturbance
          Inadequate personality
          Schizoid personality

Cyclothymic personality
Paranoid personality
Personality trait disturbance
   Emotionally unstable personality
   Passive-aggressive personality
   Compulsive personality
   Other
Sociopathic personality disturbance
   Antisocial reaction
   Dyssocial reaction
   Sexual deviation
Special symptom reactions
   Addiction
   Learning disturbance
   Speech disturbance
   Enuresis
   Somnambulism
   Other
5. Transient situational personality disorders
   Gross stress reaction
   Adult situational reaction
   Adjustment reaction of infancy
   Adjustment reaction of childhood
   Adjustment reaction of adolescence
   Adjustment reaction of late life

Figure 12-1. A listing of mental disorders defined by the American Psychiatric Association.[3]

But there are some traps and pitfalls in a complete adherence to the medical model. What is a disease when that term is applied to mental function? What constitutes a "diagnosis" of a hebephrenic schizophrenic? A disease is usually defined as a disturbance in the function of some part or organ of the body. A diagnosis is both the process and result of inference of that disturbance. What is the disturbance which is inferred to define the hebephrenic? Is not the mental disorder classified on the basis of patterns of behavior and not an inferred cause? When pursued further, language problems of this sort become even more sticky because of the relative vagueness of the definitions which exist for various deviant behavior categories.

The *behavior models* take the accumulated knowledge of the normal function of learning, motivation, perception, and similar processes as a basis for the understanding and treatment of deviant behavior. There is no single organization of these facts which stands out as a unitary model, but rather there is a literature of experimental research information which is used to understand the deviant behaviors. The behavioral approach considers the deviant behaviors to be understandable in the terms which are used to describe and explain normal behaviors. The behavioral model emphasizes the effects of past experiences, learning, and the current motivation implied by the situation.

The *dynamic models* of deviant behavior and psychotherapy are those of Freud and others who have modified Freud's notions in a minor way. The therapy techniques which follow from this viewpoint are termed *psychoanalysis*. The main assumptions of this dynamic notion is that a closed system of energy exists in the individual which shapes behavior. Disturbances and incompletion of various stages in the development pattern of the individual result in the channeling of energy toward specific behaviors. For example, deficiencies in the anal stage of development are predicted to produce compulsive symptoms in adult behavior. Each deviant behavior is presumably traceable to a particular stage in the dynamic development of personality.

The preceding orientation to some of the background beliefs of those who engage in psychotherapy is intended to organize somewhat the various sorts of procedures which are used in psychotherapy. Some understanding derives from knowing the guiding beliefs of the protagonists in controversies over techniques and prognosis. One such argument concerns the existence of the phenomenon called *symptom substitution*. This phenomenon, which follows directly from the assumptions of the medical model, describes an expected appearance of new symptoms in a patient for which only the previous symptoms were removed and for whom there was no attempt made to remove the "causes" of those symptoms. This concept implies that there is a "disease" which is hidden and is lurking behind the observed symptomatic behaviors. Therapists with the orientation of the behavioral model would view a deviant behavior as simply a learned pattern of behavior which is inappropriate and undesirable. Removal of the "bad" behavior removes the entire problem. The medical model view predicts that new undesirable behaviors would take the place of those which were removed. Empirical evidence on this question has not been overwhelming. Interpretation of existing evidence is difficult because many of the behaviors which may be labeled as new symptoms arising from the unremoved disease may also be predicted to appear by the behavioral viewpoint. Because a certain set of experiences and environmental conditions are assumed to lead to deviant behaviors, removal of one such behavior pattern will probably be followed by another deviant behavior pattern unless the precipitating environmental conditions are also changed. Thus, a test of the notion of symptom substitution would require the demonstration that new symptoms appear when the old ones are removed, even after the environment which led to the first deviant behavior patterns had been changed or improved.

Similarly the patterns of therapy in psychoanalysis follow directly from the implicit assumptions of dynamic theory. Terms and concepts such as "resistance," "repression," "identification," and others describe phenomena in psychoanalysis which are a part of the dynamic theory. Each approach to psychotherapy is quite different, both in its view of the nature of deviant behavior causes and in its view of the probable susceptibility of that deviant behavior to change.

COUNSELING TECHNIQUES OF PSYCHOTHERAPY

Two basic kinds of counseling have been used to treat deviant behaviors. One of these has been called *traditional counseling* and the other is called *client-centered counseling*.

Traditional counseling is much like the relationship between the professional and the layman seeking legal advice, medical help, or a cure for a bad golf swing. The professional is assumed to be more knowledgeable, more experienced and somewhat better able to take an objective look at the problems. The basic form of the relationship is the presentation of the problems and the administration of professional advice about solutions to those problems. In traditional counseling the patient's problems are interpreted and specific behavior analyses and recommendations may be presented. The success in removing those problems is likely to hinge upon the patient's willingness to follow that advice. But one of the recurring problems of many individuals is that they have had too much information presented and may have a genuine inability to carry-out any such new plans. There may be a conscious and active rejection by the patient of the content of the interpretation and the suggested therapeutic steps. For reasons such as this, other counseling techniques have been devised which are more effective in certain counselor-patient relationships.

The *client-centered counseling* approach was devised by Carl Rogers after his dissatisfaction with the traditional techniques of diagnosis and interpretation.[69] Rogers' view of counseling is that it must be led by the client and only subtly directly by the counselor toward certain goals of adjusted behavior. Client-centered therapy directs the patient toward developing his own methods of solution of the problems and should be effective in making the patient able to solve his problems unaided after a number of sessions. The primary tool of the therapist in this method is the restatement of the affective or feeling aspects of the patients remarks rather than their factual content. When the client talks of his grades as reflecting his study habits and not his true level of ability, as in an example given by Rogers, the therapist responds by emphasizing the feelings of the patient, that he is concerned about his low grades and fears that they may be taken as reflecting that he is stupid. This kind of reply by the counselor is often difficult to make and requires at times some evasive answers. For example, if the patient asks outright for advice, the counselor must reply stating that the patient feels that he would like help with his problems. The client soon learns that he must take all of the initiative himself.

Variations of these counseling techniques have been used. Special differences concern the sort of assumptions which the therapist maintains about the course of change in the patient's behavior. A counselor who leans toward a dynamic theory will interpret the behavior of the patient in those terms and recommend changes in behavior based upon those theoretical notions. A counselor with an S-R theory orientation will similarly view the deviant behavior in terms of principles of learning and motivations in a situation. Thus, the model which one counselor uses to organize the deviant behavior may differ greatly from that used by others.

OTHER THERAPY METHODS

A collection of other methods of changing deviant behavior patterns of individuals include the modification of the precipitating environment, giving therapy in groups, and some special techniques which have been useful with deviant behaviors in children.

The *modification of the environment* of the person with a pattern of deviant behavior may be sufficient to change that behavior. The modification may be intentional and directed at producing a certain relationship between the patient's behavior and what it yields, or the change may be an unspecified one which removes the apparent causes for the difficulty, but with no specific notions of why it happened. The latter technique is often used with individuals who have existed in an impoverished or socially degenerate environment. The change from that location to the quite different world of the hospital is often sufficient to effect a permanent change in behavior patterns. Similarly a regression back to deviant behaviors is often noted when the patient returns to those old environmental haunts. Another sort of environmental modification involves a planned set of behavior contingencies according to notions of learning and reinforcement of behavior. These techniques follow from the behavioral model viewpoint and are an attempt to reverse the existing situation so that now the deviant behavior will be nonreinforced and "unprofitable."

Group therapy is often applied in situations where a number of patients might be profitably gathered together for treatment, as in hospitals and other confinement institutions. There are two obvious advantages to group therapy. First, it is a more efficient use of the therapist's time to give treatment to more than one person at a time. But also, and perhaps more importantly, group therapy gives practice and experience in social relationships. The members of such a group are often the most critical contacts which the patient is likely to confront. They are not usually tolerant of other patient's troubles and after they have gained some experience, are likely to be quite outspoken in giving advice. This sort of therapy is often alleged to be most useful for the patient who has first had some treatment on an individual basis. The group therapy sessions also give some feelings of camaraderie and

Figure 12-2. A session of group therapy (Courtesy of the National Association for Mental Health, Incorporated, New York).

Figure 12-3. Play Therapy with a child (Courtesy of the National Association for Mental Health, Incorporated, New York).

"belonging" to that group. Group therapy, too, develops some social relations, "tools" which many patients need to guide their future behaviors in normal society.

Therapy with children who have behavior problems may take the form of *play therapy, release therapy,* or an *interpretative relationship* with the child. In *play therapy* the child acts out his difficulties with toys and dolls designed to represent the principal characters in his troubles. The lack of verbal skills in the child may be compensated for by the expression of feelings and problems in play activities. In *release therapy* the child "releases" emotions by engaging in aggressive behavior toward symbols of troublesome situations. After the emotion has been expressed in an open manner, the child becomes more relaxed and the therapist may describe or interpret those feelings to the child. By acknowledging the existence of strong feelings toward others and conveying to the child that the feelings are quite normal, the child may be trained to guide these emotional feelings in a more effective manner.

Interpretative therapy concerns noting the indications of problems in the play activities of the child, allowing some expression of feelings toward otherwise quite unassailable persons and things in the child's life, and finally the interpretation of these behaviors in ways that the child can understand and use to develop more effective adjustments to the frustrations and conflicts.

SOMATIC THERAPIES

Somatic therapy reduces the occurrence of deviant behaviors in patients by biological changes. Changes may be brought about by the application of *drugs* and other chemical agents to parts of the body. The production of *convulsions* by electrical or chemical stimulation has also been shown to have an effect upon deviant behavior patterns. Finally, deviant behaviors have been treated by destruction of certain tissues of the body by *surgical operation*.

Two major varieties of psychopharmocological agents have been useful in the treatment of persons with deviant behavior patterns. *Tranquilizers* depress the activity of the sympathetic (emotional) nervous system. The ideal tranquilizer would affect only the emotional system and have no side effects upon motor behavior, intellectual clarity, and other functions. The elimination of the feelings of anxiety would presumably allow an evaluation of problems which are hidden by effective defenses and other patterns of behavior. Other tranquilizers which *do* suppress motor activity are useful in the control of manic and other violent behaviors in patients. *Stimulants* facilitate sympathetic nervous system activity. Stimulant drugs may be used to lessen the degree of depressions, but they have also been found to heighten anxiety and increase deviant behavior patterns in psychosis. Another kind of drug which has been used in experimentation in relation to psychopathology is the *hallucinogen*. Mescaline and lysergic acid diethylamide (LSD) have been reported to have a marked effect upon feelings and perceptions as well as upon the thought processes. These agents are thought to produce behaviors which mimic those of psychotic disturbances.

Convulsive therapy techniques involve the administration of either drugs or electric shock in an amount sufficient to produce convulsions (similar to those of a grand mal epileptic convulsion) followed by a coma. Some memory loss for the events immediately preceding the convulsion is experienced after return to a conscious state. Convulsive therapy is usually given in a series of shocks administered every few days. Its effects appear to be to hasten one's recovery to normal states from periods of depressed behaviors. Other abnormal behaviors do not seem to be significantly affected by the treatment.

Psychosurgery as a treatment for mental disorders has not been looked upon with favor in recent years. Psychosurgery usually includes the destruction of neural connections between the frontal lobes of the brain with other brain areas. The change in behavior has been described as a lessening in the emotional reactions of the subject and hence affecting related deviant behaviors. The behavior change seems to come about by a reduction of the inhibition mechanisms of sensory input. That is, the patient reacts more readily to distractions and his activity is determined to a large extent by impinging stimuli. Many of these same effects can now be produced with drugs, which have the additional value of not producing permanent changes and which do not have the substantial risk of side effects upon brain function including death.

PSYCHOANALYSIS

Psychoanalysis is a psychotherapy based upon the dynamic theories of personality and mental disorders. The analysis follows different rules in the counseling setting and is a more integrated "system" than are the other various treatment techniques.

Two principal methods of obtaining information in analysis are the methods of *free association* and *dream analysis. Free association* requires the patient to become relaxed in the therapy situation and relate everything that comes to mind. The patient is instructed to freely associate and report those thoughts to the analyst. At first the patient will resist relating content which would bring out unpleasant feelings of guilt or anxiety. The psychoanalyst interprets and analyzes the content of the associations in terms of the dynamic theory. By an analysis of symbols and themes of the associations, the analyst comes to understand the personality structure of the patient in dynamic theory terms. Dreams are also reported to the therapist and serve as another source of symbols reflecting the dynamic personality. They may also be used to start the free association process. By the process of *interpretation* the therapist describes the origins of the *resistances* of the patient in terms of the theory and thus breaks them down. Content which is especially emotional will be evaluated to the patient in relation to the infantile stages. This relatively objective understanding of feelings lessens their control over verbal behavior.

The goal of psychoanalysis is an understanding by the patient of his personality in the terms of the theory. During the course of psychoanalysis several phenomena are likely to occur. At some stage the therapist may be viewed as that individual who constitutes the focus of the patient's problems. The *transference* may involve reacting to the therapist as though he were the patient's mother, father, etc., depending upon the structure of personality. An intense reliving of an emotional experience is called an *abreaction*. The development of more effective behavior patterns to situations is referred to as *working through*.

The goal state of psychoanalysis is the achievement of *insight* into the structure of one's personality. Insight is an understanding of the person's emotional reactions and behaviors in terms of the infantile development stages of dynamic theory. Therapy of deviant behavior results from this insight and the consequent self-correction by the patient.

PSYCHOTHERAPEUTIC WORKERS

Five names may be distinguished and identified as applying to persons engaged in psychotherapy. These names are *psychiatrist, clinical psychologist, psychoanalyst, psychiatric nurse,* and *psychiatric social worker*.

The *psychiatrist* is a physician who has limited his practice to treatment of deviant personality and behavior. The psychiatrist takes additional training in psychiatry after his internship and attaining of the M.D. degree. This dual training in medical and "mental" backgrounds of behavior allows medical evaluation and treatment of the disorder which is not possible for the non-medical psychotherapists. Psychiatrists are often "pure" therapists in the sense of having interest only in applying therapy rather than the investigation and accumulation of new knowledge of behavior pathology. The psychiatrist is also often limited by the viewpoint of his training to the use of but one theory of behavior therapy, often that of the dynamic theory of psychoanalysis.

The psychologists interested in psychotherapy are primarily *clinical psychologists* though the distinction between the activities of these persons and those of *counseling psychologists* is rather vague. The clinical psychologist has a Ph.D. degree, and has had one year of internship in supervised psychotherapeutic activities in a clinic or hospital. There is a strong orientation in the clinical psychologist training towards the development and evaluation of a classification of deviant behaviors and techniques of therapy. The clinical psychologist is more likely to be interested in theory development and research on problems of psychopathology. Not all psychologists are interested in the study of deviant behavior, though, just as all physicians are not psychiatrists.

The *psychoanalyst* is usually a psychiatrist but may also be a psychologist or a layman. The psychoanalyst is one who uses psychoanalytic techniques in therapy. The name does not imply training requirements or degrees, though nearly all analysts do have either an M.D. or Ph.D. degree.

The *psychiatric social worker* and the *psychiatric nurse* are individuals from the indicated professions who have had additional training and are specializing in dealing with patients with deviant behavior problems. The psychiatric nurse is often responsible for the day to day administration of treatment in the hospital. The psychiatric nurse may also be able to contribute to the information about a patient concerning his hospital ward activities and the effectiveness of the prescribed therapy outside of the observational sphere of the psychiatrist or psychologist in charge. The psychiatric social worker contributes information about the surroundings of a patient before and after his deviant behavior pattern was noted. The legwork involved in ascertaining the "facts" of environment is accomplished by this specialty, along with the out-patient and post-discharge contact necessary for evaluation and maintenance of normal behavior.

Maintaining Mental Health

A discussion of deviant behavior problems would not be complete without some self-help suggestions for prevention of behavior problems. Even though the precise causes and mechanisms of deviant behavior are not known, several important factors of a reasonably general nature have been isolated. Some of these factors have been used in the formulation of the following six rules for maintaining mental health.

Maintain good physical health. Several direct relationships between physical health and behavior have been noted in this book. It should appear obvious that behavior will be affected by the state of health and consequent feelings arising from poor health. Even slight disturbances which last a long time, like a sore elbow or a very mild toothache, affect one's disposition and one's reactions. Oftentimes, mental health is impaired by the anxiety which one feels over the thought of going to a physician. The knowledge that something is probably wrong and requires treatment may evoke conflicts in a person. All too often, the long term poor adjustment that a person appears to maintain is traceable to a session of poor health. Mild debilitating diseases like many instances of infectious mononucleosis may produce no symptoms strong enough to direct the person to medical help, but the continued tired feelings and general rundown outlook on life may easily lead to poor academic or work performance which in turn may have a lasting influence on that person's life.

Know and accept yourself. Know what your dominant wants, needs, and goals are. Evaluate objectively your capacities to fulfill those goals. Face your limitations and your shortcomings. But accepting yourself as you are does not mean that you should remain as you are and make no attempts to improve. Self-improvement should be a part of the self picture which you understand and promote.

Know and accept others. Recognize the wants and goals of others and avoid interpreting those goal-seeking behaviors as hostile to your own goal attainment, even if there is a competition of sorts. Avoid attempts at molding or changing others into different patterns. Accept the adjustment mechanisms of others as they may be. Much damage can be done by an amateur exposure of the adjustment mechanisms of your friends.

Have a confidential relationship with someone. Maintain at least one friendship which allows you to talk of your problems and goals in confidence. Discussion of your feelings with a good listener promotes a better self-adjustment by exposing to consideration parts of problems which may not have been admitted before. The presentation of these things to others will require that one give them a certain amount of consideration which might otherwise be repressed. The advice of the confidant need not be considered or followed, though some such consideration is, of course, necessary to continue the friendship.

Maintain some social participation. Contact with others is a necessary part of knowing what the world is like. A realistic set of goals and values can only be held after exposure to the outside world. Social participation need not be a formal participation in groups or a systematic series of engagements with others. Rather, an informal contact with and interest in others allows a greater contact with people as they are rather than as they would pretend to be.

Engage in satisfying work or other creative experience. A sense of purpose in daily activities and a value for your life can often be found in doing a job which you enjoy and consider worthwhile. If you feel that your work is unimportant it is likely that you will consider yourself unimportant. A satisfactory substitute for this sort of deficit is the undertaking of some other activity which allows satisfaction and creativity. The extra activity may be a constructive hobby in which the creativity potentialities are obvious or it may be a sports activity where the satisfaction is primarily personal. In either case, the development of some activity which attracts and satisfies is excellent insurance against the feeling of despair and worthlessness of poor adjustment.

SEEKING PERSONAL HELP

The steps which one should take when behavior problems are suspected should be fairly clear from the discussion in this chapter. A first step should establish the state of your physical health. In an academic setting, the next step is easy. Make contact with the student counseling or guidance center. Student clinics are usually equipped to evaluate and treat minor problems of adjustment, especially those related to academic choices of vocation, poor study habits, or simple social difficulties.

Where an established counseling facility is not known, ask your physician to recommend a source for further treatment. There are usually mental health centers giving out-patient care within a reasonable distance. Unless your financial resources are without limit, it is usually not wise to seek out a psychiatrist in private practice unless you have been strongly advised to do so. In addition to the financial factor, many psychiatrists are interested only in severe forms of deviant behaviors. Treatment of personal adjustment problems are often outside their interest and capabilities.

There are two dangers for the student who has had some contact with the study of adjustment and psychopathology. The first is the tendency to see in one's own behaviors the symptoms of a deviant behavior pattern. This has been called the "medical student's syndrome" in that the student believes that each disease studied is characteristic of his own troubles. The other danger is the opposite extreme of covering up problems with a little (usually *too* little) knowledge of adjustments. Psychological terminology may be given as an explanation and defense for maintaining deviant behavior. The psychological knowledge may give the student a new source of rationalization for his problems and consequent inferior adjustment.

Summary

Mental health is the study, cure, and prevention of deviant behavior patterns. Psychopathology is the science of deviant behavior and psychotherapy is the process of changing deviant behaviors. Deviant behavior is marked by certain personal feelings and discrepancies between behavior and expected reactions to situations.

Neurotic behaviors are ineffective adjustments. Psychotic behaviors may be extreme forms of neurotic behaviors, or they may be discontinuous and qualitatively different from normal and neurotic adjustment.

Anxiety neuroses are marked by emotional reactions which are exaggerated and dissociated from causes. Phobic reactions are extreme fears which are unjustified. Hysteric reactions convert impulses and motives into other behaviors. Obsessive-compulsive reactions channel anxiety into particular repetitive thoughts and acts.

Functional psychoses include affective, schizophrenic, and paranoid reactions. Other psychotic disorders have an organic origin, including senile and alcoholic psychoses, and paresis.

Psychotherapy is the process by which deviant behaviors are changed. Actual procedures depend upon the theoretical assumptions of the therapist in conjunction with the particular problem. Three views of disorders are the medical model, the behavioral model, and the dynamic model.

Counseling psychotherapy may be traditional counseling or client-centered counseling. Therapy is also effected by modification of the environment, group therapy, play therapy, release therapy, and interpretative therapy. Further control over deviant behaviors has been achieved by biological changes through drugs, convulsive shock, and surgery.

Psychoanalysis is a special process of therapy which uses a dynamic theory of personality as a vehicle for the patient's coming to understand his own problems.

Psychotherapeutic workers include psychiatrists, clinical psychologists, psychoanalysts, psychiatric nurses, and psychiatric social workers.

Some simple rules for maintaining mental health include (1) maintain good physical health, (2) know and accept yourself, (3) know and accept others, (4) have a confidential relationship with someone, (5) maintain some social participation, and (6) engage in satisfying work or other creative experience.

SUGGESTED READINGS

Frazier, S. H., and Carr, A. C. *Introduction to psychopathology.* New York: Macmillan, 1964.
A brief introduction to abnormal behavior, including classification, dynamics, and origins of those behaviors. Emphasis is on the functional rather than organic behavior disorders.

Maher, B. A. *Principles of psychopathology*. New York: McGraw-Hill, 1966.
*A textbook of abnormal behavior patterns as a part of behavioral science.
Psychopathology is viewed as depending upon an understanding of the
principles of normal behavior.*
See also the suggested readings at the end of Chapter 13.

APPLIED PSYCHOLOGY

How may the psychology of learning and motivation be applied to the education process? What are the important aspects of machines which man must control? What are the situation conditions which lead to efficient work at a task? How may workers be selected and evaluated in a job? How may the behavior of consumers be measured and directed?

Some of the information about behavior which has come from psychology as a science has found immediate use. Practical interests have also led to the development of additional information using psychology's methods and principles. Certain areas of applied psychology having a definite range of problems have been given the names industrial psychology, human engineering, consumer psychology, legal psychology, and educational psychology. Much like the engineering counterparts of the physical sciences, applied psychology has been developed, beyond the original information of the parent science, into specialized informational systems in their own right. Some of the applied psychology fields are described in this chapter.

Technology of Education

What conditions lead to the most efficient learning? Will machines or other devices speed the learning process? How may different approaches

to presenting material for learning be best coordinated? These are some
basic questions which a technology of education might be expected to
answer. Parts of these questions are not different from those which
underlie research on "learning" in the laboratory. Some of the same
variables and considerations are met in the application of information
about learning that were important in its investigation in the laboratory.
Other aspects of psychology applied to the needs of education are those
of the measurement of individual differences in capacities and achievements, the consideration of developmental readiness for kinds of learning, and some knowledge of personality formation which is characteristic of the school age child. These latter problems of testing and
devolopment will not be discussed here.

DISTRIBUTION OF LEARNING

One of the more direct applications of laboratory knowledge to the
classroom concerns the scheduling of learning experiences. The interference theories of forgetting have demonstrated that the similarity of
the materials to be learned will affect their retention. The greater the
similarity of those materials, the greater will be the interference with
the remembering of any of the material. One task of educational design,
then, is to ensure low similarity between concurrent learning tasks.
Intervening activities of minimal similarity may be planned, along with
attempts to reduce the existing similarity. Similarity may be reduced
by suitable grouping and coding to make the materials appear different.
Simply spreading the many similar items of information over a period
of time may in some cases make the items appear more dissimilar because of the extra time which the learner has available to consider
those items and learn to distinguish them.

Another aspect of the distribution of learning concerns the problem
of when to break larger wholes into smaller parts for learning. Responses
which must be made in a continuous chain may be learned by practicing
that whole chain or by breaking the whole into several parts for separate mastery. The selection of one of these two techniques depends
upon a number of factors of the tasks and of the learner. Tasks which
are rather long or rather short, are meaningful, and are unified will be
better learned by the whole method. The whole method also seems to
be superior when the subjects are intelligent or the practice is distributed. The part method is disadvantaged by the fact that one must learn
not only the separate parts but also the connections between them for
a smooth continuous performance. This disadvantage may be eliminated,

however, by breaking the material into parts which overlap one another.

Helpful techniques to learn somewhat non-meaningful materials include breaking those materials into suitable "chunks" for memory and the use of memory devices. Long numbers may be grouped into *threes* or other divisions which have some meaning. The principle is to achieve a smaller number of more meaningful memory units. Similarly, one may devise simple rules which code the units to be retained. Such rules are called *mnemonic devices*. An example of a mnemonic device is the poem used to remember the number of days in the month, "Thirty days hath September . . ." The variety and effectiveness of such mnemonic devices depend upon the ingenuity of the instructor and the student. The memory devices make more complex and complicated materials easier to learn by virtue of their relationship to a more easily remembered code device. Care must be taken in the invention of such devices, though, that the translation back to the material to be learned is itself well learned or obvious. Little is gained if one can recall the rule, but has no knowledge of what it means for the learned materials.

PROGRAMMED LEARNING

A variety of choices are open to an educational designer facing the development of an effective learning situation. The traditional lecture may be selected with blackboards, visual presentation devices, or other audio-visual aids. A small group-discussion class may be used with many variations in technique. Daring innovators may suggest that a collection of readings from textbooks and other sources is sufficient for the learning task without frequent instructor-student contact. A new technique which has created a rather large impact upon the technology of education is that of *programmed learning* and the associated *teaching machines*.

The basic notion of *programmed instruction* is a mechanical presentation of the material to be learned according to some principles of learning which insure that each individual following the program has "learned" the material. The heart of programmed learning is a carefully constructed program of steps to be followed, not the mechanisms which present that program. Two basic varieties of program have been used: *linear* and *branching. Linear* programs have a continuous series of small steps in a chain, each dependent to some extent, and building upon the earlier steps. Considerable hinting and prompting is applied to allow the learner to make the correct response to each successive question. A "good" program makes sufficiently small steps in knowledge with each frame that the learner makes very few errors. The *branching* program depends upon the answer to each question to direct the learner to new material to be learned. If the answer is incorrect, the learner may be directed to relearn that material or may be given a different approach to the same kind of material. Errors are explained and the learner masters each part before progressing to the next. The linear program assumes that with small enough steps, there will be no errors, while the branching program assesses and corrects wrong answers as the learning goes along.

Lumsdaine has described three important features of programmed learning.[45] The learner (1) actively responds, (2) has immediate feedback of incorrect responses, and (3) may progress in learning at his own rate. Theorists such as Skinner have emphasized the importance of the active responding and suggests that the answers be written out.[75] Others have suggested that an active, motor response may not be necessary. Other research and discussion has concerned the determination of the size of the step for each frame and whether small steps might be less efficient than larger ones. On the one hand, the smaller step leads to the learning of fewer errors, and on the other hand, the

Figure 13-1. One of the many teaching machines which present to-be-learned materials mechanically, ask questions, and give answers to those questions.

small steps probably lead to boredom and lowered motivation for the learner.

Programmed learning does hold an advantage for efficient learning, but the limits of that superiority have not been clearly identified. The kinds of materials, the type of program, the sort of outside pressures to learn, and the characteristics of each individual learner may each play a role in answering the question of the value of programmed learning. The measured gains from programmed learning must always be tempered against practical considerations before a conclusion about the adoption of the general technique may be reached. Does a comparison of Program A with Lecturer X really say much about the relative value of programmed instruction vs. traditional lectures? Can there not always be devised a better program or a better lecture?

The mechanical problems of programmed learning have been met by a variety of devices and machines. In fact there may be more individuals working upon machines than upon programs. The machines range from simple drum-type devices with openings for exposure of each item of material at a time to books which require the user to cover the answers to each frame. Some more elaborate and flexible techniques of programmed instruction have used a computer to ask questions and correct answers. The versatility of the computer in altering the order of materials depending upon the capacities and responses of the learner rivals the experienced individual tutor. The computer has the additional advantage of being unaffected by fatigue and personality impediments to a successful teaching interaction, as well as a great storehouse of detailed knowledge. But the computer is also very expensive to operate and has a "coldness" about its output which tends to discourage rather than develop the kind of enthusiasm for learning which the expert instructor may develop in the student.

AUDIO-VISUAL MEDIA

Other attempts at improving the presentation of materials to be learned have involved the peculiar capacities of films, television, and tape recordings to supply a realism and richness of detail which a lecturer, blackboard, or a textbook lack. The advantages of a standardized presentation through these devices, though, may be offset by the relative inflexibility to the needs and performances of the students at any given time. The experienced lecturer is allegedly able to sample the feedback from his audience and alter his presentation to fit. Smaller classes permit questions to expedite these functions.

Techniques of Self-Instruction

A more familiar title for this section might be "learning to study." One of the sad facts of our existence is that studying is *not* an inborn behavior pattern which is maximally efficient and is ready to provide the student with all the information for which he has capacity. Effective studying, like walking, playing basketball, or flying an airplane, must be learned through extensive and often unpleasant practice. Many different skills make up effective study habits; these include reading-to-learn, note-taking, listening, committing materials to memory, outlining, and others. Each of these separate skills must be practiced and developed.

Learning any skill is hard work and will not be accomplished quickly. Simply a resolve to improve will not do the job either. A resolution must be backed by effective practice over a period of time. The old habits were acquired through many years of sporadic practice and should not be thought easy to dislodge by even the best of intentions to improve. New habits must be practiced until they are stronger than the old.

STUDY HABITS TO BE LEARNED

Five basic skills usually are lacking in the student with ineffective study habits. These include a positive learning attitude, techniques for beginning studying, reading-to-learn, listening to lectures, and taking examinations. Some comments and suggestions from a study of such behaviors are presented here.

Developing a positive learning attitude. A positive learning attitude is the most serious lack in the typical student. Without a driving force to motivate learning, all of the best techniques are somewhat wasted. A positive attitude for learning is learning for its own sake. Acquisition of knowledge and attention to interesting things are the primary motivating factors. The positive attitude or motivator draws the student to learning rather than pushes him toward it. The accumulation of new insights stimulates further study. A positively motivated learning process is painless and enjoyable.

But this is not the way studying is usually pictured to be. The common connotation of studying is that it is drudgery, and, like all drudgery, it is laborious, and inherently unpleasant. This negative attitude does not follow from the nature of learning, but rather from the habits which the student has assimilated over a period of time. New, positive habits must be acquired to overcome the past learning. Learning to enjoy studying takes a great deal of practice and a few temporarily uncomfortable changes in personal behaviors.

One major recommendation leading to the development of a positive attitude for studying is that a new motivation will be acquired if the student *imagines* that he is actively interested, doing a little "play-acting." One must force an interest and active participation in studying. After a period of time, the play-acting becomes less obvious and a genuine self-sustained interest in the materials will develop. The notion behind this recommendation is that social and personal motives depend upon the experiences of the individual. The more experience that one has with being actively interested in some topic, the greater is the strength of the actual positive motivation for that activity. The positive attitude will also grow as other skills of studying are developed. There is a mutual dependency such that a positive attitude is necessary for acquiring effective study habits and that a positive attitude follows from the use of effective studying. The greater the ease of acquiring information and seeking new knowledge, the greater is the enjoyment which that activity provides. But one first step is to "make believe" that you are interested and actively involved in learning.

Learning to begin studying. With self-generated motivation for learning, the student with poor habits is now faced with *beginning the study* of some materials. How does one begin? This skill, like the others, must be developed by practice. Before the skill is well-developed some tricks might be employed. These tricks require planning ahead, a procedure which many students have not mastered.

The development of a plan has several parts. One should plan what to study, when to study and for how long, and prepare for each study session. A schedule must be developed which is realistic and yet allows for all the activities to be accomplished. One must try to allot time so that coverage of studying, social activities, and just doing nothing are adequately represented. The schedule need not be rigorous and specific, but should have enough detail to allow some foresightful anticipation of exams, and so forth.

Before each planned study session make up your mind whether you actually intend to study during that period. If you know that you don't really intend to get anything done and will probably quit at the first sign of something else to do, don't begin in the first place. This is done to avoid developing a habit of breaking one's resolutions. Plan exactly what you intend to accomplish and set a reasonable time limit.

Several ancillary factors about studying include the selection of a suitable place for studying. Studying should be done in a place with reasonable privacy but neither so quiet nor so noisy as to be distracting. Have the tools at hand and other potential distractors out of the reach of your attention. Studying in *one* place has some value in stimulating an attitude of studying whenever you are there, especially for the student just beginning to learn how to study.

Prepare for subsequent study periods by stopping each session at an appropriate place. To make beginning studying easier next time, stop now where things begin to get easy, not where they are especially difficult or put you to sleep. Plan the next beginning to allow yourself to get warmed up to the subject matter in an enjoyable fashion. A series of easy questions or instructions are often useful to start the next study session.

Reading-to-learn. Perhaps the greatest amount of studying time involves reading. It has often been said that many students do not know how to read. All college students know how to read in a basic manner, but many students have not developed the skill of *reading-to-learn.* There is a tremendous difference in the kind of reading skills one employs while scanning a magazine story or newspaper, and the skill which guarantees an efficient learning of the printed material. How can one develop reading-to-learn skills?

Several effective approaches have been described, and an apparent factor in all techniques of reading-to-learn is some guarantee that an active attention and intent to learn are present. In some way the student must insure that none of the material will be just "covered," but will instead be actively considered and learned. Any trained chimpanzee can scan his eyes across the characters on a printed page. That kind of "coverage" of reading assignments accomplishes nothing for the student. The only reason for reading is to learn the concepts and ideas which are presented. Here, presumably, the student can learn to excel over the chimpanzee, yet many do not.

One of the systematic techniques of effective reading-to-learn has been called the *three-step reading process.* The three steps are those of *previewing, learning,* and *reviewing.* Each step has a specific function. Together they should ensure that the facts, concepts, and ideas have been learned.

The preview step is a quick coverage of the reading to learn what sorts of things will be discussed. One should build a rough outline or network of topics which are included in the reading, by skimming section headings, lead sentences in paragraphs, and any other aspects of the text which strike your attention. Play the picture games and look at the summary statements and questions (if any) to get a thorough "feel" for what is to be presented. Such a preview, for an average chapter such as those in this book, should take no more than five or ten minutes. One should avoid mechanical activities of neatly copying section headings in an outline; especially if these exercises take the place of an active mental questioning of the content of the chapter. The end product of learning is not penmanship but an intellectual change called learning.

The second step is a basic reading. The speed of this reading will depend upon the kind of material, the reading habits which one has developed over a period of time, and the relative difficulty and importance of the learning. The intellectual intent, however, should be to learn. One must maintain an active interest in what is being read. Maintaining this active interest is the basic goal for any activities which one may undertake during this reading.

Note-taking should also be designed to help one learn the material. The notes must be an effective tool for acquiring the information presented. To develop more useful notes, reword the statements. Putting concepts in one's own language insures some thought about them and hence some learning probably takes place. Avoid excessively neat underlining when this distracts one from an active intellectual consideration of the content. Underline *after* a paragraph or section has been thoroughly read and understood. Make the underlining a sort of review of the most important concepts and ideas presented. Finally, one should make notes in the form of questions for review. Restate each point as a question that you might expect to be asked on a quiz or examination.

Above all, one should maintain an actively questioning intellectual position while reading. Continuously question the origin of statements, asking how that information was determined. From what does each generalization and statement follow? Such an active participation provides a framework for learning. Simple facts may be joined by logical relationships and organization which includes those facts. Most readings are presented in meaningful paragraphs or larger units of organization. After each such natural division one should immediately quiz himself upon what was just read, trying to describe in his own words what was presented and its importance. Such immediate checks will show the holes in one's learning and allow him to fill them by a re-reading. Being honest with oneself at this point is one of the hardest things for students and even professors to do. It is easy to slip into the next section assuring oneself that having just been "over" that material, he now knows it. One should guarantee that this is so by describing in detail what was just read.

The third step of reading is a review, preferably at a later time, but not too much later. A few hours or at most a few days after the reading, a careful review of the reading should be undertaken. Again the holes in memory and the troublesome sections for longer-term memory will appear. The review may follow the guides of the notes taken. The value of notes in the form of questions is obvious at this stage. Effective but brief questions covering all of the material are invaluable for guaranteeing that learning has occurred. Obviously, holes in memory should be filled by reading again these details with an additional review as a memory check.

If these steps for reading are followed rigorously, probably no additional studying will be needed for examinations, except for a quick review if the delay period is very long. Cramming and frantic studying for exams will be unnecessary and probably of no real benefit.

Note that little was said about speed of learning and reading. Though poor reading habits of eye-movements and similar skills may be important in determining the relative speed of learning by reading, they do not necessarily relate to the extent of learning. If one's reading speed is excessively slow, he should take some steps to improve. Study time is, of course, limited. But one should not substitute reading-speed exercises for attempts to improve what he can learn from reading. The *rate* of learning will be affected by reading speed; *what* is learned depends upon intellectual activities during that reading.

Listening to lectures. Listening to lectures fills a substantial period of the student's time. One estimate of the number of lectures a student will attend in four years of college is about 1800. What skills must the student acquire to profit most fully from lectures? Much poor advice has been given about the best way to listen to lectures. Some have advocated a complete listening with no note-taking. Others advise a careful and thoughtful examination of each statement that the lecturer makes. Others suggest a blind note-taking which approaches the limit of copying verbatim the entire lecture. There are pitfalls in each of these approaches. Neither listening alone nor note-taking alone will insure an adequate learning of the presented material. Without notes memories may be poor with no means for check. Verbatim notes allow almost no learning during the session and often will lead to overlooking the emphasis and enthusiasm which the lecturer has presented. Too much thoughtful examination will lead to lapses in one's attention to parts of the lecture. A balance must be achieved and note-taking skills learned.

The skill of taking notes and listening at the same time is not inherited nor given by divine blessing to a chosen few. It must be learned much like the basics of writing or the intricacies of bridge playing. The skill of listening and faithfully reproducing what was said may be developed to the degree of skill of the court recorder who misses no detail of the presentation. But this limit need not be attained. Some abbreviations and shorthand skills of your own invention may be profitably applied but are not completely necessary. The basic skill which must be acquired is the lag in writing behind listening. Observations of the highly skilled performance of a court recorder or of a telegrapher reveals that the notations are several steps or thoughts behind the speaker. Similarly, the student must learn to make notes on what has been said while listening to what is being said now. This skill should be practiced at every opportunity. One should take notes perhaps at all lectures whether needed or not until the skill is well-developed.

Re-working of lecture notes is another activity overlooked by the poor student. A careful examination, review, and re-working of notes after the lecture serves several functions at once. The student is given an excellent active learning experience which forces an intellectual concentration upon the material. The re-working of the notes allows the student to fill in holes or errors of note-taking while the material is still fresh in mind. The review permits the student to develop a meaningful source for studying and review at a later time, by providing an additional "text" for reference.

Taking examinations. Taking examinations often appears to be the curse of the student, interfering with the happiness and social activities of college life. Such is the view of the student who has not prepared by effective study. The student who has learned the assigned material and has learned how to study usually has no fear of an exam and often anticipates the challenge to what he knows.

The cramming activities of the poor, though not necessarily dull, student are pathetically inefficient preparation for that examination and are often worse than no help at all toward achieving an education. Cramming requires massed practice of materials which are best learned by distributed practice. The thoughtful problem-solving aspects of an organization of facts are lost in the hustle of acquiring facts. The emotional tone of pressure upon the student defeats memorizing and higher intellectual processes. The anxiety and fear of failure which drives the student to cram becomes associated with education and all of its attributes. The cramming behavior destroys and makes even more difficult the development of effective learning techniques. Cramming is a trap, a rigid behavior pattern typical of that made by most animals when pressured to respond in a frustrating situation. The careful development of behaviors which will prevail under emotional states, and those preparations which will avoid the frustration entirely, are characteristic of the intelligent man.

Two basic forms of examinations are those called "essay exams" and "objective exams." They may be crudely distinguished by the requirement of recall versus recognition memory, respectively. Essay examinations provide some cues from which the student is asked to formulate an effective exposition. The objective examinations having a "true-false" and "multiple-choice" format require only that one identify the correct fact or relation. Neither kind of exam is "easier" than the other because difficulty depends upon the grading standards of the examiner, not the format of the questions. But there are different ways of preparing for these different exams. The basic rule is to practice what is required by the exam. If the examination is known to be of the essay type, one should practice writing and answering essay questions. Practice organizing small sketches of information covering aspects of the material. Some knowledge of the typical pattern of the course examination may direct study toward comparisons, toward brief defining essays, or toward outlines of the usually covered facts. Similarly, with objective examinations, effective preparation includes answering objective questions. Student workbooks often are sources for typical questions. It is quite effective (and teaches the student about the instructor's problems of test construction) to make up an examination in the expected format. Write out good multiple-choice questions. This activity, if time is available, may bring out similarities and confusions between what were widely separated parts of the course. A favorite technique of many instructors is to use "foils," alternative choices which sound like or appear superficially similar to the correct answer. They may be from the course or may be invented words of a likely nature. Answering the examination questions which you have devised and those made by other students gives an excellent and often more rigorous review than that of the actual examination. In any case, the review for the exam should be made to be an effective practice of the responses to be made upon that exam.

TRAINING AND EDUCATION

One important distinction which may be made from the view of the instructor is that between *training* and *education*. *Training* implies the achievement of specific objectives of knowledge; particular facts to be acquired have been delineated. *Education* is more of an attitude which has an underlying core of information. Being educated implies a background of information and a provision for continuing the acquisition of information. Being trained is only the state of having acquired certain information.

The technology of instruction varies considerably, depending upon whether the goal is education or whether the goal is merely training. A variety of implications of a training session center around the concept of the motivation of the student to learn, his need for putting out an active effort versus passive reception of material, and so forth. The instructor aiming at training certain limited facts and materials will alter the presentation in whatever ways are effective to impart the information. Liberal use of tricks in the classroom, attention-getting devices, glamorous audio-visual display mechanisms, and considerable showmanship will often be employed. The author recalls an effective trick employed by the U.S. Navy instructors in an "Instructor Training School." One of the first sessions was marked by the appearance of a sloppily dressed ensign who was preceded into the room by his coffee cup and profuse comments about the character and probable ancestry of the students. A substantial fear was instilled in all those students of lesser rank by belligerent, unanswerable questions, and threats of the things to come in the weeks ahead. It was a most convincing performance. He later interrupted this performance with a review of all of the wrong things to do in front of a class of navy men, as he had demonstrated them. This was an unforgettable demonstration of what not to do. As a trick it was highly effective in conveying the intended information. It illustrates the difference in approach often used for training and the information presentation methods which are typical of education.

But the opportunity for education need not be dull and uninteresting. On the contrary, much attention should be directed towards maintaining

the interest of the students in the material. But the interest and motivation is aimed toward the information and the stimulation of study of
similar materials beyond those presented.

The moral of this for the reader is perhaps already clear. College
training is much less than a college education. Simply learning to recite
the collection of facts presented in various assignments is not all that
comprises an education. Being educated includes also an attitude toward
knowledge and learning, an active attitude of seeking, evaluating, and
enjoying that learning.

Human Engineering

Human engineering is not an attempt by psychologists to design a
more useful human being, though to make such an attempt may be
instructive. Rather, *human engineering* is an application of knowledge
of behavior and the capabilities of men which permit the design of more
effective man-machine systems. Any device, whether a simple lead pencil
or a supersonic transport, has been shown to profit by design which
takes into account the human operator. Many examples could be given
to describe this positive help which applied psychology has given to
product design. But many other examples could be presented to illustrate an unfortunate lack of consideration of the capacities of the man
who is intended to use the machine. The many new devices and weapons
systems which were developed in the early years of World War II
often were difficult or impossible to use in a consistent fashion. The
design engineers simply did not take into account such obvious things
as the length of a man's arm, the number of arms which he has, or
the upper limits of sound intensity which he can stand. For example,
three multi-engine military aircraft were designed with important control
functions in different relative locations. A pilot entering one type of
airplane would find the pitch control of the propellers in the position of the throttles of the previous airplane. In an emergency there is
little time to "look and see," and accidents thus happened.

Human engineering applies what is known about the required behaviors along with new empirical investigations to determine optimal
designs when information is sparse, and an educated judgment where
new research is not feasible. Perception and motor skills research have
an obvious application directly to many problems of equipment design.
New empirical tests of various alternative parts of a man-machine

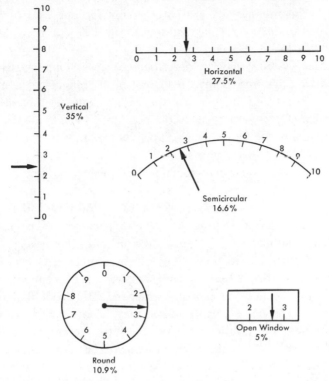

Figure 13-2. Different ways of presenting information by instruments. Studies have shown that the vertical and horizontal dial faces produced the greatest percentage of errors in reading under conditions of a brief exposure to the instrument.

system provide new information of a guaranteed validity. Comparisons between the different display instruments pictured in Figure 13-2 illustrate such an empirical study. In those situations where direct tests of alternative systems are not efficient or where the nature of the task precludes a prior test, as in many phases of the space program, the careful educated judgment of the human factors engineer permits the best approximation to a perfect solution.

MAN-MACHINE SYSTEMS

Machine systems using human operators may be pictured as having the following functions: *input* of information to the machine's system, some *memory* or other functional operation, and *output* of the work of the machine. More elaborate and detailed analyses of machine function have, of course, been made. But these simple views of machine operation may be summarized into two factors for purposes of human control: the *information* display presented to the operator and the *controls* systems to be operated.

Man-machine systems may be described as *closed-loop* versus *open-loop.* *Closed-loop* systems involve feedback of the effects of control of the operator permitting further control adjustments in a continuous, cyclical fashion. Open-loop systems do not have such feedback determining further control movements. Each control movement is largely independent of the previous movements.

The effectiveness of each man-machine system may be judged against a number of specific criteria. Some criteria involve the *output* or effectiveness of the system. The number of bombs on the target, the number of rivets placed per hour, the number of typing errors per page, or the number of automobile accidents per mile all may be criteria of the effectiveness of particular man-machine systems. Another class of criteria concerns aspects of the human link in the system. The effectiveness of *human performance* may be assessed independently from the machine being operated. The human performance may be compared against the known capacities and abilities of man. Thus the goodness of an individual performance in a system may be considered independently from the criteria of operation of the total system. Independent measures of human performance are not always readily developed, but they are becoming more available as more becomes known of the psychological operations and functions of man. Another kind of criterion which is based upon man's performance include measurements of errors, subjective statements of pleasure and displeasure in operation of the machine, and many physiological indices of the *efficiency* of operation of the structure of the human operator. The focus of the human engineer may be upon the expressed fatigue in operation of new and different machines rather than upon the slight differences in output efficiency. In the industrial application of a new machine, the feelings of the workers may constitute a very large part of the overall equation of success with that machine. Still other criteria of man-machine systems concern *reliability,* the number of fallible components operating in the total system.

INFORMATION DISPLAYS

Two aspects of information display must be considered: (1) the abilities and limitations of the operator to receive information, and (2) the characteristics of the information to be transmitted. These aspects are considered together in the design of the optimal information display for the system.

Several dimensions of information processing by the human operator may be identified. One concept is that of *channel capacity*. This is the maximum amount of information that can be usefully received in a given situation. There is a definite limitation upon the amount of information which may be processed in a given period of time, though agreement about the definition of such a limit has not been reached. Informative stimuli differ in *load* and in *speed* when presented in a display. The greater the number of kinds of information, the greater the *load* which is said to be exerted on the system. The number of stimuli presented per unit of time defines the *speed* of the information display. It is desirable that information displays have a minimum load, that is, fewer sources of information. Stimuli are best separated in time by at least one half second. An even better arrangement allows the operator to control the rate of presentation of the stimuli.

Use of more than one sense channel to present the same information increases the likelihood that the information will be received. Similarly, the greater the number of dimensions used in presenting the stimuli (for example, simultaneous variations of color, size, and style of visual information), the greater the amount of information which may be reliably transmitted through the channel. Further, the more realistic the information, that is, the greater the correspondence between the bit of information and the expected natural display of such information, the better performance that display of information will evoke.

The information may be presented by *static* devices such as charts, maps, tables, and so forth, or the information may be of a changing, *dynamic* kind. Dynamic displays may indicate only one of two states (OFF or ON, or open or shut) in a dichotomous fashion, or they may present information in one of several categories differing in quality (red, green, blue, yellow, or violet), or the display may indicate quantitative changes in the state of something (temperature or time). The greatest complication and attention have surrounded the quantitative displays.

The usual criteria for selection among different quantitative, dynamic displays are the speed and accuracy of reading, depending upon the demands of the situation. Comparisons of the instruments shown in Figure 13-2 found them to be differently ranked in effectiveness depending upon such situational factors as the duration of exposure and whether they are moving or indicating a steady state, and depending somewhat upon the criteria of assessment used in the task.[53]

Displays of multiple instruments illustrate some further complexity and problems for human engineering. The placement of similar instruments is best done such that the same pointer reading (such as straight upward) indicates a "nonalarm" state. Any deviation by one of the instruments in the display is then more easily noted. Instruments like those used to present information to an airplane pilot under conditions of no outside visual reference to the ground have been found to be best placed in a pattern allowing scanning movements of related instruments in accordance with the use of the information. An optimal display has been determined empirically by noting the actual time spent looking at each instrument and the frequency of movements between each pair of instruments. A more recent investigation of instrument flying sponsored by the Federal Aviation Agency[16] used some of the most advanced instruments available to determine if the time to learn instrument flying could be reduced. One particular configuration of new instruments was found to cut the normal time to achieve instrument flying proficiency in half. This achievement marked some technical advancement, but more importantly, the gain in performance was a function of the better presentation of required information to the pilot.

MACHINE CONTROLS

Several dimensions of movements of parts of the operator's body contribute to the selection of control devices. Limitations of the structure of the body determine the speed, length, and forces of a movement along with the sort of informative feedback checks which the individual has available to guide that movement. The movement may be an easily distinguished on-off, or the accuracy of positioning of a control may be known only by its effects upon machine output. Feedback of information of machine movements to the operator may be immediate as in steering an automobile, or delayed, as in controlling a jet aircraft. The machine movement feedback may be continuous or present but part of the time. Control movements may require action through preferred or nonpreferred limbs and parts of the body. The control may be always in contact with the body or it may require a blind positioning of a part of the body such as one's foot groping for the headlight beam control in a strange automobile.

A great deal of research has investigated the control arrangement of what have come to be called *tracking* tasks. The function of the operator in a particular tracking task may be to position some control such that errors or differences between the location of the piece of the machine being controlled and where it is supposed to be are minimized. It may be *pursuit tracking,* following a moving target, or *compensatory tracking* in which the operator is given only information about the extent of his present error in positioning. Aiming a gun at a stationary target requires compensatory tracking to line the gun sights with the target. Pursuit tracking may be illustrated in the same vein by attempting to shoot a moving target like a jack rabbit on the run. A variety of relevant dimensions of the tracking system have their counterparts in control systems. The physical shape and kind of movement required in the control, the extent to which the controlling mechanism is coarse or fine, linear or nonlinear, are relevant. The presence of calculated damping or resistances to movement, modifications and attenuations of feedback information, and computer calculation and presentation of information which anticipates control effects (called *quickening*), all have been shown to affect the tracking task importantly in special applications.

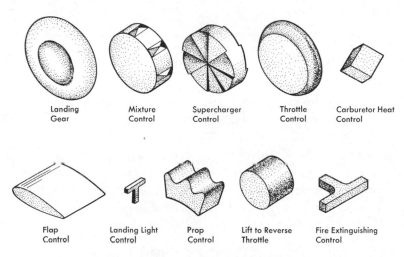

Landing Gear	Mixture Control	Supercharger Control	Throttle Control	Carburetor Heat Control

Flap Control	Landing Light Control	Prop Control	Lift to Reverse Throttle	Fire Extinguishing Control

Figure 13-3. **Control knobs which have been formed to be readily distinguishable and somewhat realistic in shape.**

The main dimensions of a control are the required *force, distinguishability,* and *realism* which it presents to the operator. The control may require too much force, or too little may be required to operate the control most efficiently. The distinguishability of controls which must be rapidly grasped on an irregular schedule will also affect the total

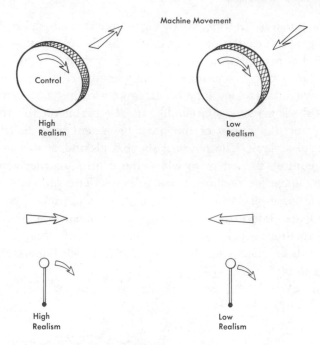

Figure 13-4. Control systems having different amounts of realism. Certain control movements are expected to produce particular results by a majority of treated individuals.

performance in the system. Like the aircraft controls in different positions in similar airplanes some controls demand some sort of added cue so that the operator may reliably select the proper one. The realism of the control is the extent to which it does what one would expect it to do, considering the background of experiences with machines and the learned perceptual habits of the operator. Figure 13-4 illustrates controls which have varying amounts of realism.

Design of Working Environment

A part of the application of psychology which is related to human engineering is the design of an efficient working environment. Like the design of man-machine systems, the working environment may be constructed against output criteria, maximizing short or long-term performance, or criteria of human performance like fatigue feelings may be the primary consideration. In other settings the control over errors may be the most important consideration of the design. Depending upon which criteria are used the situation may have a slightly different arrangement of the working environment.

Three parts of the design of the working environment will be discussed: the considerations based upon sizes and abilities of the human operator called *anthropometry*, the arrangement of the components of the *workspace*, and those outside factors of *physical environment* which surround the human operator.

ANTHROPOMETRY

An effective working environment requires that the parts be presented and arranged in accordance with the features of the operator. Some factors of arrangement depend upon the static sizes of the operators. The height of a working surface, the size and distance of placement of a hand-operated switch, the shape of a chair, and the opening sizes of parts bins all depend upon corresponding dimension of the worker. The number of differently sized individuals who will use the workspace will also affect its dimensions. The design may try to include only a particular range of sizes or it may attempt to include nearly all possible sizes. If adjustments are possible, as in the position of a motor vehicle seat, an even greater range of sizes may be accommodated. A typical range of sizes for which many machines are designed is that which accommodates all individuals between the 5th and 95th percentiles.

Other design considerations include the limits of possible movements of parts of the operator. The normal sweep of the arm and foot will dictate the size of work tables and action of foot pedals. These are considerations of dynamic anthropometry. A considerable number of such facts have been catalogued and are available for equipment designers.

ARRANGEMENT OF WORKSPACE

The coordination of the displays of information, the controls, and the operator into an optimally arranged workspace may take advantage of experience with existing similar job spaces or it may require a careful task analysis. In a task analysis attention is paid to the links between parts of the system which may be connected by movements of limbs, scanning visual movements, and necessary communications. After examination of these links, a new arrangement may be designed considering the sequence and frequency of use of those parts, as well as considerations of accuracy required and realism of control functions relating to the system. The flight instruments and controls of aircraft were analyzed according to these factors and were subsequently standardized in a pattern which was believed to be optimal.

PHYSICAL ENVIRONMENT FACTORS

The illumination of a work space may have an important bearing upon the effectiveness of the operation, depending upon the importance of visual cues. A general rule is that the intensity of light should be rather high, but there is also a danger in having too much light. There is some evidence that too great an intensity of illumination distorts the contrast between different surfaces making the perception of that difference more difficult. Certain work situations are improved when they are illuminated by a local rather than a general light source. The control of glare from light sources or from reflections off of parts of the working environment is an obvious additional consideration in the illumination of the working environment.

The degree of sound which reaches the ears of the operator is often at an adaptable level so that it is effectively ignored. But higher intensities of sound, unusual frequencies, and unusual sounds do not adapt readily and are potential distractors impeding performance. High intensities of noise can lead to temporary or permanent hearing losses. Generally, continuously experienced sounds over 90 decibel units of pressure are sufficient to lead to hearing losses. Sharp, impulsive noises of great intensity are more likely to cause destruction than are continuous moderate intensities of noise. Background noise or music which is in tempo with the rhythm of work will lead to better performances. Lively and pleasant music are believed to stimulate an attentive and ambitious work performance.

The sort of atmospheric comfort which prevails may also affect performance. The temperature and relative humidity may be selected to complement the nature of exertion of the operator. The quality of the air in terms of freedom from contaminants and odors might also be controlled in working circumstances where they are potential distractors leading to subjective discomfort.

Physical factors are in many cases trivially easy to correct as compared to the cost of machine systems changes, though they are often overlooked by those who want to "cut corners" on costs. Often the gain in performance (or loss) which comes about from one important change in the physical stimuli may surpass the advantage gained by major changes in expensive equipment. As long as human operators are a part of the work system, the best human operating conditions must be applied to produce a maximally efficient work output.

Employment Psychology

Part of what is called industrial psychology concerns the application of psychological measurement, job analysis, and a special decision-theory to the selection and evaluation of workers. Personnel decisions may be made most effectively when both the qualifications for the job and the abilities of the applying workers are considered. Not every worker will be most suited for the job available, and conversely, not all jobs will be held by the best possible worker, but the more information about needs and potentialities which are available, the less likely will a truly "square peg" be forced into a "round hole." It should be apparent that a careful selection process may minimize a variety of other problems in the industry. Training programs may be shorter. Morale will undoubtedly increase, and productivity should improve. The "right man in the right job" is an especially desirable goal to shoot for, but, as will be seen, will probably only rarely be attained.

JOB ANALYSES

Both the general characteristics of a worker holding a particular job and the special capacities which are required must be assessed in an effective job analyses. Some notion of general intelligence, requisite (and possible hindering) personality characteristics, and the general background of work experience are included in the general features of the job analysis. The job does not always benefit from the best of these things. High intelligence, for example, does not always lead to an effective performance. A monotonous job requiring simple skills may be performed poorly by an individual of great intellectual endowment because of wandering attention, a need for "stirring up excitement," or simply an interference and threat to the supervisory employees. It has been found that persons with much better than required qualifications do not last long on the job. Either personal advancement, boredom, or other related factors apparently lead to a change in employment.

Personality characteristics of cooperation and empathy with other workers may be required in jobs requiring close teamwork. But, as with intelligence, the best is not always the greatest amount. Supervisors with too much empathy will have a more difficult time making those decisions which are for the good of the job rather than those which help the individual worker. Some amount of "thick skinned" insensitivity is necessary in particular jobs, like that of grading students.

Work background is also a part of the requirements for many jobs.

Not just the specific training and transfer of experience from one job to another, but a more general familiarity with the often unmeasured aspects of that employment. For example, the general "machine sense" which comes from being around mechanical devices is often missing from persons of restricted background experiences and cultures. Some individuals do not recognize the slight changes in the sounds of functioning machines, which would cue others that something is wrong, before the machines actually stop. Simply being in an office tends to impart a general feel for office procedures, good or bad, that are often overlooked in specific office-job descriptions. The small matters of knowledge of protocol, what is and is not expected of office workers, and similar factors which make for a shorter and less difficult breaking-in period are more likely to be present in persons with office-work experience.

The specific capacities of a worker which will best suit him to one job as opposed to another, or from the point of view of the employer, the capacities which will mark the best worker for the job must be carefully gathered and checked in each situation. Sources of relevant information include job manuals, careful logs of the activities of the job, and interviews with those in contact with the job. In each case bits of information which will be useful in selection will be collected. Attention should be paid at this point in the job analysis to the more specific details which make that job different from others. Often the obvious requirement for a job is not an effective distinction at all. That a library clerk enjoys books seems to make sense, but does not really distinguish that job from a variety of others, and in fact may be a negative predictor for some library tasks. It may be best for workers to dislike the possibly interfering activity of reading the books which they must handle.

After the job is well described, the employment psychologist must devise means of selecting those workers who would do the described job in the best way. Such testing devices are called *predictors*. The object of the test is to discriminate between applicants who would and would not perform well on the job, and therefore the best test includes predictors which separate most clearly those who can and cannot do the job. The techniques of test construction are not different in technical considerations from those discussed earlier. The goodness of the predictors depend upon the ingenuity, imagination, and effective groundwork of the test constructor.

The measure of effectiveness of the test for the job is its success in selecting men to do the job well. The next most important step is choosing the criterion by which good job performance is distinguished from poor job performance. What marks a good job performance from one that is not? Here again the employment psychologist must select criteria which mark the most important function of that job. Performance criteria may include amount and speed of production, quality, and waste in production. Other indirect criteria include the amount of time on the job, tardiness, absenteeism, and the number of accidents in which the individual is involved on the job.

Less objective criteria of job performance include ratings by peers and supervisory personnel. The dangers of ratings must be considered, however. In addition to the outright subjective interference by feelings and personal interactions between the rater and the person being rated, there is the possibility of the raters knowing the scores of the workers on the predictor tests and biasing their ratings accordingly. This *halo effect* is the influence upon judgments of job performance characteristics by knowledge of high scores on the predictor devices.

The criteria used should be carefully examined to avoid known distortions. Objective output criteria may be contaminated by factors of differences in tools or working situations. The differences between workers on similar jobs may not be a function of the characteristics of the workers. Assessments should be made under similar conditions or under conditions which have been adjusted for inequalities. Judges often use a combination of criteria to assess an individual's performance on a job. Either a calculated score combining different criteria scores or a simple, informal look at several reasonably independent criteria measures will assure a greater accuracy of the total job analysis.

STRATEGIES OF PERSONNEL DECISIONS

The ideal goal of the employment psychologist is to place all individuals in jobs which suit them and the employer perfectly. This ideal may be approximated, but in practice the personnel psychologist must consider other factors which limit its attainment. There are two extreme positions of personnel actions which may be described: that of *selection* and that of *placement*.

The extreme case of *selection* is the situation of choosing from a group of applicants that one who is most qualified for the job. With job analyses and a sufficiently large pool of applicants, a person with the composite qualifications most closely matching the job specifications will be selected and all others may be rejected. Sufficient candidates are screened to find the one with the right qualifications. This is the selection problem in its purest form.

The other position is that of *placement* of each of a group of individuals into the jobs which most clearly suit them. Assuming unlimited openings, each person is assessed and matched to job analyses. This "pure" selection point of view is like that of the vocational counselor, but is rarely the position of the employment manager.

The actual employment situation may fall along a continuum between these two positions. At times there is but one job to be filled by many applicants, and at others there are many jobs and few applicants, such that each man must be placed most advantageously. A compromise strategy for in-between positions of moderate availability of applicants and jobs requires a wise positioning of persons based upon aspects of both selection and placement. A sort of nonspecific judgmental procedure is most often used in actual practice.

Some of the considerations which may guide a compromise strategy include the numbers of applicants relative to the number of jobs, the cost of wrong placements, the moldability of the men and the jobs, and similar situational and social factors.

When the number of men equals the number of jobs, the greatest likelihood of mismatching is present. Like the personnel assignment problem facing the military services, each man is placed where he is most likely to fit, given the particular jobs available at the time. Apparent mistakes can and do occur, as illustrated by the mismatches which inevitably result from a great need for men to fill jobs for which no one is well suited.

The cost of an error in placement also guides the decision process. Obviously those with a great deal of education and training are more costly and must be matched more closely to the job than assembly line workers, both from the standpoint of production and the relative ease of change of jobs for the men. Filling some jobs, such as those in a research endeavor, for which prediction is difficult and the potential output is very great, may require a selection strategy of hiring any who seem to fit and relying upon later analyses of performance to effect the final selection. Under the guise of on-the-job-training, a large company might underwrite the costs of hiring ten times as many engineers as are actually needed to guard against losing the most productive 10 per cent of the applicants.

Another consideration is the degree of changeability of the job and the man. An especially good applicant who does not precisely fit the job may be hired with the intention of changing the job to fit the man. The applicant may also be trained so that the job fit is somewhat better. Here again the highly educated and trained person may illustrate an extreme case. High degrees of specialization training make a change of the man unlikely, though the potential change of the job to fit the man may be a wise alternative.

Other situational and social factors are also important factors in selecting individuals in job situations. Often the formal job analysis does not include such potentially relevant aspects of the job as the impact of the predecessor, the kinds of co-workers and individuals comprising the social contacts of the job, and the sort of supervisor which the job inherits. Careful placements considering social relations are often overlooked because of the low value of the employee and demands upon the selection officer's time, but errors from these factors are just as important to the overall record of job placement.

Consumer Psychology

At first consumer psychology was primarily concerned with advertising. The concern was in persuasively communicating information from producers to consumers about the product. Later developments in the field of applied psychology worked in another direction. The needs and desires of the consumer were sampled to inform the producers both about products and directions for additional advertising. The various techniques of imparting and gathering information have been the focus of *consumer psychology*. The problems of the discrepancy between what information has been presented, what consumers say that they will do, and what consumers actually do is one that is similar to many of the problems of the study of behavior.

An effective communication from a producer to a consumer must first be noticed by that consumer. Various ways of attracting and holding attention have been studied by advertising psychologists. Given the attention of the consumer, then the communication must convey some bit of information in a way that the consumer accepts its content. The persuasiveness of an advertisement is linked firmly with concepts of motivation and emotion and, more recently, the notion of an "image." Finally the effective communication must produce some desired result. Measurement of the effectiveness of an advertisement in shaping actual consumer behavior has been difficult to implement and is generally difficult to control, but some techniques have yielded satisfactory estimates.

ATTENTION-GETTING METHODS

The likelihood of a printed advertisement being noticed depends upon its size, color, position, and certain factors of its quality. These mechanical factors have been studied in the laboratory by making comparisons between ads while measuring the focus point of the eye, by surveying the readers of periodicals in which ads have been placed, and variations on these themes. There are problems with these measurements. Assessments of the success of an ad are desired which are uncontaminated by sample biases, false verbal agreement by those tested, and the unnatural constraints of the laboratory. But some clear relationships have emerged.

The size of the ad increases the likelihood of its being noticed, but with decreasing gains with further size increases. An ad which is doubled in size will not quite be noticed twice as often. Doubling the size again will yield an even smaller increase in readership, and so on. Size does interact with other factors of the ad, however. Simply doubling the size of an ad may make the printing strikingly out of proportion. Colors and blank areas of the format may appear to be even more outstanding. This

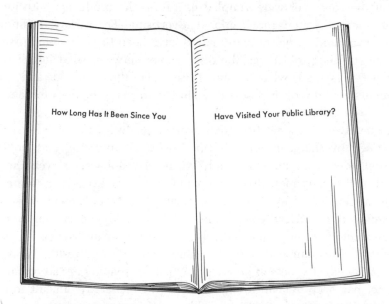

How Long Has It Been Since You   Have Visited Your Public Library?

Figure 13-5. An advertisement may be striking, simply because of the great unfilled space around it.

latter factor is often used effectively. A large blank page in a newspaper with a few lines of information, conspicuous by their small size, will be nearly always attended to by the reader.

Color is effective when many hues have been employed. The simple addition of a third color to the black and white printing already present usually yields no gain in attention. A multicolored display will reap substantial gains in noticeability. But color, too depends upon the surroundings. A colored ad in a surrounding of other colored ads is not necessarily better than a black and white ad in the same colored surroundings. A good black and white ad in between colored ads may be an effective attention-getter. Certain displays are best colored. For example, the color may be used to exaggerate a feature of the product, or indicate a richness which would not be apparent in a black and white illustration.

The position of an advertisement in a periodical or other display of many ads has also been found to determine attention. The ad placed just inside the covers is more often noticed than an ad in any other place in the magazine. It is generally believed that a position which allows an unobstructed view after, say, turning a page, is better than others. The first thing noticed is more likely to be examined closely than are other things on those pages.

Finally, the quality of an ad is a catch-all category referring to outstanding variations of color and space, the shock value of an unusual statement, an attractive picture, or the unusual characteristics of the paper on which it is printed. Quality refers to the factors which are likely to increase its noticeability, not the value judgment of its ultimate worth. The real "grabber" may be quite crude by social standards, but effective in reaching a high percentage of the readership. A scan through any magazine will give many examples of this miscellaneous quality factor which attracts the attention of the reader.

PERSUASION

The most important part of the information of a message is called the *appeal*. This bit of information is that which is expected to influence the beliefs, attitudes, and behavior of the consumer. An assumption guiding the construction and invention of appeals is that the motives and desires of the consumer may be exploited. The major difficulty with the motive approach is the poor state of development of the study of motives in men, but the theories and guesses about motivational constructs which have been available have been used with some apparent success. The notion of manipulating motives with advertisements has been less popular among advertisers recently, and the trend has shifted towards the development of the related image of the product in the mind of the consumer. Rather than focusing attention upon the consumer, the new ads try to set up some beliefs about the product or its manufacturer which will hopefully lead to favorable consumer behavior.

Two sorts of messages may be distinguished—*positive* and *negative* appeals. The positive appeal suggests that the consequences of that product are pleasant and desirable. The negative appeal emphasizes the unpleasant and undesirable consequences of not purchasing and using that product.

Pure positive appeals are somewhat difficult to find. Any ad for one of several similar products necessarily suggests that others are inferior when the one is described as superior. The unanswered question of better than what, faster than what, or more exciting than what are implicitly answered by the knowledge of competing products. Such negative suggestion has usually been avoided whenever possible because of the build up of doubt and negative feelings toward an entire class of products. A reminder of the bad points of a similar product does some damage to the product advertised. Such techniques can also be exploited, as in the rival ads of auto rental firms and in the very effective campaign of a popular imported auto. Examples of appeals which are almost free from negative suggestion are those promoting travel by airplane and the prevention of forest fires.

The negative appeal suggests that any course except that suggested in the ad will lead to some less desirable state of affairs. But again the negative suggestion factor of telling consumers what not to do and pointing out the lack of some quality in competing products is always at least implicitly present. Negative appeals are illustrated by ads for cold remedies, pain supressors, and other quasi-medical products. A more subtle negative appeal is that in the message which suggests that the product advertised will make life more fun or allow new experiences while implicitly, though not always subtly, describing *not* doing these things as undesirable. Soft drink ads allow the individual to insure continuous companionship in beach parties, automobile ads stress the exploration of the country, and smoking ads allow the individual to find privacy away from the crowd.

The distinction between the positive and the negative appeals becomes fuzzy at this point. In product areas having heavy ad competition, there are probably no ads which simply give information. The ads usually promise indirect benefits and manufacture differences between equivalent products to have any effectiveness at all in shaping consumer behavior.

The reliance upon motivational analyses of consumer reaction to advertisement and consumer behavior has borrowed heavily from some speculative theories of motivation and personality theory. The basic notion has been to find the motivational pattern that guides a bit of consumer behavior. By such techniques as depth interviewing and some interesting variation of projective tests of personality, the basic determiners of consumer behavior may be inferred. The implication is that such information will shape the appeal to maximize positive consumer motivation.

The existing needs of individuals may be exploited. A hungry man, for example, does not need much persuasion to eat. A more important task of advertising, though, is to develop needs where they are now weak or nonexistent. Advertising effort is directed toward developing a strong desire into the status of a need. A good "cover" rationalization may convert a desire into an expressed need. The desires which may be expressed in the possession of a powerful automobile have been channeled into a "need" for "power to pass" or to "get out of tight situations" (which usually are not met except by those who use that horsepower unwisely), and so on. Whether such conversions of desires and wishes to needs which direct consumer behavior are good or bad is immaterial, the advertising question is "does it work?"

Other motivational factors include the determinants of *impulse buying*. Along with the motivational analyses suggested above, impulse buying is a topic for empirical research. Many of the present advertising beliefs are based upon educated guesses rather than empirical knowledge. These changes in consumer behavior have strong implications for academic analyses of motivation.

The *image* of a product or producer has been the most prominent focus of modern advertisements. The image is the composite attitudes and feelings which a particular product evokes in the consumer. Some dramatic changes have occurred in consumer behavior and the images which consumers hold of products when ad attention is directed towards modifying the image.

The basic procedure of image change requires an analysis of the present image of the product. This may be done by asking participants to note those of a list of adjectives which describe the product or by asking for ratings of the relative pleasantness, strength, warmth, activity, and the like, which the product suggests. After this assessment, the direction of intended change will be determined by the nature of the product. Automobiles are usually given an image of prestige, fun, or power, while cigarettes must be pleasant and relaxing, and foods have other connotative feelings.

Consumer acceptance depends to some extent upon the nature of the image change. An effective procedure has been to associate the product with outstanding examples of the desired image. Dramatic new images of manliness have been producd for cigarettes by association with outdoors activities and heavy industrial workers. Extra large vegetables were advertised by use of a giant which has since become a household word. The changes in images of automobiles are continuous. Some firms engage advertising agencies simply to keep the image of the company from becoming tarnished. Rather than pushing some particular characteristic, a producer may simply wish to maintain a positive, pleasant image. Large industries which do not deal directly with consumers, including many industrial electronics and aircraft companys, often spend considerable sums upon ads to insure that adverse publicity does not make them appear undesirable in the public's eye.

EFFECTIVENESS OF ADVERTISEMENT

The techniques of determining the effectiveness of advertisements have been imaginative but inconclusive. The difficulty in the way of a controlled study of buying habits may perhaps be appreciated when one introspectively considers the sorts of things which lead us to purchase one brand over another. The location of parking spaces, the lack of a smile on a salesman's face, a dislike for a wrapper may all directly change our actual consumer purchase from what we would have at first bought. The point is that perhaps the ads do not play a very strong role in actual consumer behavior. Personal recollection appears to document such an assertion. This begs the question at hand but also suggests the relative magnitude of advertising effects upon the purchase of many products.

Direct approaches of surveying individuals about their buying habits have been used with some success, though the greatest unknowns in the use of these techniques are the representativeness of the sampled individuals, and the faith which may be put in their given answers. The people available for a survey are often not representative of the buying population. People will say that they purchase only certain brands when in fact they do not. It is not easy for a person to admit to a personable interviewer that one gives little thought to the brand purchased or that he selects the cheapest brand.

Indirect approaches to assessing the effectiveness of advertising include coupon returns and the Nielsen Audiometer. These devices assess the likelihood of exposure to the ad and hence estimate the success of the ad. There are many ways in which the exposure can be estimated, but few offer any firm answers about the actual consumer behavior·

The most obvious approach is the measurement in change in sales. In fact, the level of sales and their changes with different advertising are effective and worthwhile assessors of the overall programs of advertisements, but they are not analytical. There is no efficient way of telling which of the many possible factors about advertisement and its presentation caused the observed change in consumer behavior. It is also quite slow. The cost of mistakes is formidable, leading to the practice of test-marketing in selected areas before a more general advertising coverage.

OTHER ASPECTS OF CONSUMER PSYCHOLOGY

By no means has all of consumer psychology been discussed. Attention has been drawn only to a limited aspect of the problems of advertisement. Consumer psychology is a very broad field covering such other problems as salesman selection and training, testing for noticeable differences in products and their use, the larger economic trends of buying, and analyses of consumer needs, habits, and patterns of life which are related to particular kinds of products. Interested readers may pursue these topics in the suggested readings.

Summary

A variety of different areas of applied psychology have evolved from the study of behavior.

The technology of learning concerns the scheduling and distribution of learning experiences into smaller, more easily learned pieces. Learning may be programmed and presented in a linear or branching fashion by teaching machines.

Self-instruction techniques include developing a positive attitude, learning effectively to begin studying, reading to learn, listening to lectures, and assessing what has been learned. These techniques are fairly direct applications of learning and motivation theory and research. The techniques may differ depending upon whether the goal is one of training or of education.

Human engineering is the design of effective man-machine systems.

The machine to be operated presents both displays of information and controls to be operated. The displays and controls are engineered toward developing the most effective system. The effectiveness of the system may be judged by measures of output, of errors, and of efficient human performance, including subjective reports. Information displays are designed to take into account the abilities and limitations of the operator to receive the required characteristics of the information. Controls must be designed to take maximum advantage of the human operator's past use of controls, physical size, and capacity to distinguish different controls.

An efficient working environment must take into account the physical size of the operator, the arrangement of the components of the workspace, and the physical stimulation environment which reaches the operator.

Effective selection of individuals for employment requires a careful analysis of the requirements of the jobs and the capabilities of the job. Some judgment is still required, because the employment situation usually is such that one man is not uniquely and solely qualified for each job.

Advertisement noticeability depends upon relative magnitude, position, and factors of the quality of the message. Its effectiveness may be estimated by its noticeability, by surveying consumers, and by noting changes in sales. The persuasion of the message is related to attitude change. The message appeal may exploit or develop motivation in the consumer. It may use positive or negative appeals to promote a particular product, or it may consist of a general program to change or maintain a corporate image.

SUGGESTED READINGS

Anastasi, A. *Fields of applied psychology*. New York: McGraw-Hill, 1964. *A textbook of applied psychology, covering personnel and industrial psychology, human engineering, consumer psychology, clinical and counseling psychology, and the contribution of psychology to the topics education, medicine, and law.*

Brown, J. M., Berrien, F. K., Russell, D. L., and Wells, W. D. *Applied psychology*. New York: Macmillan, 1966. *A readable textbook of applied psychology covering, in addition to the subjects of this chapter, the topics of mental health, international relations and negotiations, and aspects of criminal behavior.*

McCormick, E. J. *Human factors engineering.* New York: McGraw-Hill, 1964.
A textbook of human engineering, containing a fair amount of detailed "handbook" information on topics of sizes, shapes, and other dimensions of materials.

Voecks, V. *On becoming an educated person: An orientation to college.* Philadelphia: Saunders, 1957.
An excellent, empirically based philosophy and set of procedures for developing effective skills of studying and learning.

GLOSSARY

This listing contains definitions of terms used in this book which have some-what of a special meaning in psychology not necessarily the same as common usage. Other psychological terms may be found in J. Drever, *A dictionary of psychology*, Baltimore: Penguin, 1952, or H. B. English and A. C. English, *A comprehensive dictionary of psychological and psychoanalytical terms*, New York: Longmans, Green, 1958.

ability test. a device to ascertain some information about an individual, his past or predictable future behaviors.

abreaction. in psychoanalysis, an intense reliving of an emotional experience.

achievement test. a test designed to measure present behaviors and thereby infer the effects of past experiences.

accommodation. the change in focus of the lens of the eye.

acquisition. the course of learning a new response; those procedures.

activation theory. a view of emotion and motivation which describes the continuity of degrees of arousal.

actualizing tendency. the tendency for the self to change in the direction of improvement, growth, and independence.

acuity. the extent of discrimination of small-sized stimulus differences.

adaptation. the process which results in a decreasing responsiveness to a stimulus as a function of constant exposure.

adjustment. a process of interaction between behaviors and the conditions of the environment, including those originating within the individual.

adrenalin. a collection of hormones secreted by the adrenal gland, usually during emotional excitement, and which tend to continue that emotional reaction.

affective reaction. a functional psychosis characterized by states of mania and depression.

afferent neuron. a neuron leading in from a receptor.

alpha response. a rapid eyelid reflex to an increase in a light stimulus.

alpha wave. an EEG tracing characteristic of a resting, yet awake, adult with his eyes closed.

ambiversion. balance between introversion and extraversion.

anthropometry. sizes and functional dimensions of humans.

anxiety reaction. a neurosis in which a vague fear is the primary symptom.

apathy. a purposeful inactivity in the face of frustration.

appeal. the bit of information which is designed to influence the receiver.

aptitude test. a test to predict future behaviors.

assessment techniques. the observation of the behaviors of individuals in "natural" settings for diagnostic and predictive purposes.

association area. cerebral cortex areas of no specific known function.

associationism. a philosophical view that the content of the mind is formed of associations of ideas.

attitude. an organization of behaviors having an affective component, cognition, and a predisposition to certain behavior patterns.

attitude scale. devices to measure attitudes, usually composed of statements presented for agreement.

attitudinal distance. descrepancy between the attitudes of the persuador and the receiver.

attribute learning. concept learning in which the learner must only observe differences in the stimuli.

audition. the sense of hearing.

augmented feedback. additional knowledge of results applied in a motor skills learning situation.

aural harmonics. distortions and changes in a tone produced by the structures which guide the sound to the organ of Corti.

avoidance conditioning. a learning situation in which the subject avoids a noxious stimulus by responding correctly to a cue.

awareness. the active experience of some object or event; often equivalent to consciousness.

behaviorism. a viewpoint of psychology which declares that objective observations of behavior are the only proper contents for psychology.

beta response. an eyelid response to a light from a dark-adapted subject; of longer latency than the alpha response.

behavior genetics. the transmission of automatic behaviors and predispositions to certain behaviors by heredity.

behavior model. a view of psychopathology in which symptoms are assumed to be treatable directly by suitable reinforced learning processes and changes of environment without reference to hidden causes, and so on.

brain. common name for the collection of neural organs located at the head end of the spinal column.

brainstorming. placing a group of persons together to solve a creative problem.

brightness. the psychological dimension corresponding to the amplitude of the light stimulus; the intensity of the light.

catatonic schizophrenic. a schizophrenic psychosis marked by extreme withdrawal and negativism.

catharsis. a release of emotional feelings connected to repressed experiences which are now revealed.

central attitude. an attitude which is basic and highly involved in the personality of an individual.

central trait. the primary way of behaving in an individual's personality structure.

cerebral cortex. the outermost layer of the brain, composed of thin hemispherical layers of folded neuronal tissue.

channel capacity. the maximum amount of information that can be usefully received in a given situation.

character disorder. a personality pattern of socially deviant behavior.

chromosomes. bodies in the cell nucleus which carry genetic information.

clairvoyance. the ESP of happenings at another time and place.

classical conditioning. the evocation of a response to a new stimulus after that stimulus has been repeatedly presented with another stimulus which was adequate to evoke that response.

client-centered counseling. a relationship in which the patient is led to develop his own understanding of his problems and the solutions to those problems.

closure. the tendency to see objects as complete wholes in spite of gaps in the actual physical stimulus.

cochlea. the inner ear structure which houses the vibration sensitive auditory cells called the air cells of the organ of Corti.

color addition. the mixture of colors as in colored lights upon a white surface; the colors are reflected to the observer unchanged.

color subtraction. the mixture of pigments which are illuminated by a white light; the pigments absorb certain colors and reflect others to the observer.

combination tone. an additional tone which is heard along with two presented tones; its frequency is equal to the difference in frequency of the presented tones.

commitment. an active verbalization in which an individual expresses behavior in line with specific attitudes.

compensatory tracking. positioning a variably moving device upon a stationary target.

complementary colors. opposite hues on the color wheel; colors which produce gray when additively mixed.

concept attainment. the process of learning an appropriate classifying behavior using an already available dimension of the stimuli.

concept formation. the process of learning an appropriate classifying behavior which requires learning to distinguish the relevant differences between the stimuli.

concurrent validity. the extent to which different parts of a test battery measure the same.

conditioned response. the learned response in conditioning arrangements.

conditioned stimulus. the stimulus to which a new response is learned.

cones. light-sensitive retinal cells located in the fovea.

conflict. the presence of two or more motive-goal tendencies at the same time.

consonant information. information which does not conflict with information and beliefs already possessed.

construct validity. the extent to which the construct defined by the test scores fits into a theory or more general collection of relevant information.

content validity. the extent to which a test measures what it appears to measure.

context effect. the influence which a range of stimuli presented may have upon the selection by an observer or judge.

control. a goal and characteristic of science, describing the production and regulation of events upon demand; a concept of experimentation which describes the extent to which factors other than those specified have been excluded from the observed phenomena.

convergence. the changing angle between the line of sight of the eyes as the focal object comes nearer.

conversion reaction. a neurotic disorder which has been converted to a physical symptom.

convulsive therapy. a shock to the body which often changes behavior patterns of depression temporarily.

correlation. the degree of relationship between two sets of scores obtained from the same individuals.

criterion. a measure of performance used as a standard against which test scores are compared.

culture. the accumulation of ways of living which have been built up over time in that society.

cut-off score. a score or composite score which marks a selection decision.

decay theory. the notion that materials are forgotten purely as a function of time.

defense mechanism. a behavior pattern which circumvents frustration and hides conflict by self-deception.

delay conditioning. a variation in classical conditioning in which the UCS is delayed for a period of time during which the CS was continually present.

delusion. false belief.

dendrites. the (normally) receptor parts of a neural cell.

dependent variable. the behavior differences of interest in an experimental design.

descriptive statistics. a summary of numerical information.

developmental explanation. the placement of new information into an established, known sequence of behaviors.

direct aggression. hostile behavior at the blocking or thwarting agent.

displaced aggression. aggression directed toward some other part of the total situation than the blocking agent.

distorted room. a room of unusual shape which is made to appear normal from one position.

distributed practice. a moderate rest period intervenes between successive practice or learning periods.

dominance and recessiveness. the action of genetic units for one kind of characteristic over another; the presence of a dominant gene will lead to that character being expressed.

drive. the force or energy of a motivator. A *general drive* view holds that all motivators contribute a bit of energy to a common pool; a *specific drive* notion holds each source to have its own specific energy for relevant responses.

dynamic models. the theoretical views of personality such as those of the psychoanalysts as they are applied to psychopathology.

effectors. the muscles and glands which produce observable behaviors, directly or indirectly.

efferent. a neuron leading out to an effector.

electroencephalograph (EEG). recording of electrical potentials at the surface of the cerebral cortex.

encoding. a process by which items are simplified for memory tasks.

end brushes. the functional ends of a neural cell which join and stimulate dendrites of other neurons.

equilibratory senses. yield neural information about accelerative movements of the head.

error of anticipation. in psychophysical measurement, a tendency to change the response too soon.

error of habituation. in psychophysical measurement, a resistance or inertia against changing a response.

errors of measurement. a miscellany of differences in performance caused by uncontrolled conditions which affect the dependent variable.

errors of sampling. the collection of differences between samples and the population from which they were drawn.

escape learning. a learning situation in which the subject escapes a noxious stimulus by running to a "safe" area.

experimental neurosis. the production of inappropriate behaviors apparently as a function of a difficult conditional discrimination problem.

extinction. the procedure of withholding the UCS or the reward in a learning situation; also, the performance decrement following that operation.

extrasensory perception (ESP). reception of information through other than the known sensory channels.

factor analysis. a statistical technique which determines the communality among the items of a test.

faculty psychology. a philosophical view that the mind of man is composed of a number of inborn faculties.

feedback. the flow of information back from a response.

figure and ground. a phenomena of perception in which one part of a complex stimulus stands out as a figure against the rest of the figure, the background.

fissure of Rolando. a deep vertical fold in each cerebral cortex hemisphere along which lie the body sense and motor control projection areas.

fixed interval reinforcement schedule. an operant conditioning technique in which a fixed period of time is waited before another response is rewarded.

fixed ratio reinforcement schedule. an operant conditioning technique in which a fixed number of responses must be made before a response is rewarded.

fovea. the area at which light strikes the retina from objects centered in front of the eye; the area of greatest acuity.

free association. a technique or process by which a person evokes the chain of things which "come to mind."

frequency distribution. a graphical plot of the frequency of the ordered scores.

frequency methods. a threshold measurement technique in which selected stimulus values are presented separately for a number of times and the frequency of correct judgments against a comparison standard describes a curve from which the threshold is defined.

frustration. a state arising from a motivated ongoing behavior or behavior potentiality which is blocked or thwarted.

functional fixedness. the impediment to solving a problem caused by a necessary component being used in an unorthodox fashion.

functional psychosis. psychoses of a (presumably) psychological origin.

functional stimulus. the actual stimulus responded to in a situation.

functionalism. a historical viewpoint in psychology which used naive intro-spection to study the functional processes of the mind; also, a modern viewpoint which judges its end product by its usefulness rather than theoretical value.

genes. complex, self-perpetuating protein molecules which convey information affecting the formation of cell structures of the body.

genetics. the science of heredity.

genotype. the totality of genetic information which is present in the cells.

gestalt psychology. a modern German viewpoint of psychology which con-siders that phenomenological analyses of the structures or wholes of experi-ence yield the basic subject matter for psychology.

glands. bodies which may pump chemicals directly into the bloodstream (endocrine) or through ducts to other points on the body.

group. a perceived collection of interacting individuals.

group therapy. a session with a number of patients in which free discussion among the patients is urged.

gustation. the sense of taste.

hallucination. false sense perception.

hallucinogen. drugs affecting feelings and perceptions.

halo effect. the influence upon one judgment by knowledge of the individual's performance upon some other task.

handedness. the dominance of one hand over the other for certain responses; most individuals are right-handed.

hebephrenic schizophrenic. a schizophrenic psychosis marked by silliness, bizarre actions, and unorganized sets of delusions.

hedonic theory. a notion of behavior determined by the pleasantness or unpleasantness of its consequences.

hertz (Hz.). a new term for "cycles per second."

higher-order conditioning. the use of a CS-CR reaction as the UCS-UCR of a new conditioning situation.

homeostasis. an hypothesized mechanism which is assumed to regulate the level of some states of affairs in the body such as food stores and temperature.

hue. the psychological dimension corresponding to the wave length of the light stimulus; the "color" of the light.

human engineering. an application of knowledge of behavior and the capabilities of men which permit the design of effective man-machine systems.

hysteric reaction. a neurosis in which a particular pattern of behavior or physiological condition is a symptom which covers another disturbance.

identification. covering up conflicts by living the life of someone else.

identity formation. the process of achieving a consistent, well-integrated personality.

impossible figure. illusory figures composed of parts of drawings having common connecting lines.

independent variable. the manipulation being studied in an experimental design.

inference. a technique used to describe the likely (mental) events lying behind observable behavior.

inferential statistics. techniques which answer questions of the likely differences between collections of numbers.

information theory. a mathematical description of the units of information contained in a particular message form.

inhibition. a process opposing the performance of a response.

insight. in psychoanalysis, an understanding of one's emotional reactions and behaviors in the terms of dynamic theory.

instrumental learning. a simple learning situation in which the performance of a response is instrumental in attaining a reward.

intelligence (IQ score). that factor measured by intelligence tests; a general capacity to behave in an adaptable and acceptable manner.

interactive explanation. the placement of new information into an organization of knowledge of present factors.

interference theory. a mechanism accounting for forgetting; one item is forgotten because another item interferes with the memory of it.

interitem interval. time between presentation of successive items in a learning situation.

interpretative relationship. interpreting the patient's behavior in terms which he can understand and use to develop more effective adjustments.

intertrial interval. the time interval between trials of learning.

intrinsic KR. the knowledge of results which the task naturally gives to the learner.

introspection. a self examination of mental content with an effort toward objectivity and completeness of description.

kinesthesis. the muscle, tendon, and joint sense which gives information about relative movements of parts of the body.

knowledge of results. like feedback, a factor describing the information coming from responses.

law of effect. responses which are followed by certain states of affairs (reinforcers) are more likely to occur again.

leadership. having an influence upon others.

learned reward. a stimulus which has acquired a reward capacity through conditioning.

learning. the relatively permanent change in behavior which results from (reinforced) practice.

learning-to-learn. the improvement in speed of learning successive similar tasks.

leaving-the-field. to leave a conflict situation entirely, to avoid making a choice between undesirable alternatives.

lesion. a specific damage to tissue.

linear perspective. the depth cue of objects becoming smaller (closer together) with increasing distance.

loudness. the psychological dimension of a sound stimulus corresponding to intensity.

mania. an overactivity of thought and actions.

man-machine system. the total design of man-using-a-machine for some purpose.

massed practice. a minimal rest period between successive practice or learning periods.

maturation. the process of change (usually growth) of an individual which occurs primarily as a function of aging or time.

mean. simple arithmetic average.

mean deviation. the average of the differences between each score and the mean of the collection.

meaningfulness. the extent of associations which a stimulus word elicits.

measureability. a characteristic of methods of gathering knowledge describing the degree to which terms and concepts can be precisely specified.

median. the middle value of an ordered collection of scores.

medical model. a view of psychopathology which holds a usually hidden "cause" for the symptomatic behavior observed.

mental age. the age in years of an average child of that mental development.

mental health. a state of having no mental illness.

mental illness. a certain pattern of behavior of an individual which is judged to be seriously inappropriate and uncomfortable and which represents a considerable handicap and unhappiness for that individual.

mentally defective. those individuals with low IQ scores caused by damage to the structure of the body.

mentally gifted. those individuals with high measured IQs.

mentally retarded. those individuals with very low IQ scores.

metabolic rate. the speed of chemical and physico-chemical changes in a living body.

method of limits. a threshold measurement technique in which a series of stimuli are presented in order of magnitude until an instructed observer's response changes.

MMPI (Minnesota Multiphasic Personality Inventory). a personality inventory having scales measuring patterns of behavior like those of individuals having various mental disorders.

mnemonic devices. simple rules which code and decode materials for more effective memorization.

mode. the most frequently occurring score.

moon illusion. the perception of the moon as much larger at the horizon than when viewed overhead.

morphology. the comparative structure and features of an individual.

multiple discrimination. a learning task in which one of several S-R alternatives may be selected, or a sequence of responses is required.

naturalistic observation. a technique of observing behavior in which the investigator only observes and does not interfere with the ongoing behavior.

negative afterimage. a lingering sensation having a reversed dimension from the exposed stimulus.

negativism. a purposeful rebellion against the requests and wishes of others.

nervous system. conductors and organizers of information reaching the receptors and directed to the effectors; central vs. peripheral, and somatic vs. autonomic are two different divisions of the total nervous system. (See Chapter 2.)

neuron. a specialized cell of the body which transmits excitation through a distance; said to be the smallest structural unit of the nervous system.

neurosis. a state of deviant behavior which is very similar to normal adjustive response patterns, but which is exaggerated, somewhat damaging, and partly ineffective for the individual.

new brain action. a conceptual view of brain function describing actions of the phylogenetically newer and more well-developed parts of man's brain; functions like thinking, solving problems with symbols, and other voluntary acts fit into this category.

noncontinuous reinforcement. a learning situation operation of administering reward only after some responses according to a schedule.

nonsense syllables. three letter, vowel-consonant-vowel nonwords used as verbal units in learning studies.

normal curve. a frequency distribution having a symmetrical, bell shape and several useful properties for statistical manipulation of scores.

norms. reference scores of a test.

null hypothesis. the hypothesis that there are no differences except those caused by chance between the observed scores.

object constancy. the perception of an object as stable and unchanging in spite of the changing stimulus properties reaching the observer.

obsessive-compulsive reaction. a neurosis in which a repetitive act or thought is the focal symptom.

old brain action. a conceptual view of brain action describing the automatic, regulatory, and life preserving processes of the body which are also found in phylogenetically "older" and, hence, simple species.

olfaction. the sense of smell.

olfactory rod. the receptors for olfaction.

open-ended questions. questions for which no fixed answers are supplied for the respondent to choose.

operant conditioning. the strengthening of an operant response by the timely application of suitable rewards.

operant level. the observed frequency of occurrence of a behavior.

optic chiasma. the point at which the optic nerves cross.

optic nerve. the bundle of neurons leading from the retina of each eye toward the occipital lobes of the cerebral cortex.

optic tract. the bundles of neural cells leading from the optic chiasma to the lateral geniculate nuclei.

organic psychosis. psychoses having a known physical cause.

orienting reflex. the original response produced by the conditioned stimulus.

overlearning. additional practice after the selected criterion of mastery has been reached.

paired-associates learning. a verbal learning method in which the response is learned to the stimulus in each of several pairs of items.

paradoxical heat. an artificial sensation of "hot" produced by simultaneously stimulating warm and cool receptors.

paranoid. a psychosis marked by an elaborate system of delusion.

paranoid schizophrenic. a schizophrenic psychosis marked by a systematic and logical organization of delusions.

paresis. a destruction of neural tissue leading to psychosis.

partial reinforcement. reinforcement of a fixed percentage of learned responses.

partial reinforcement effect. a high degree of resistance to extinction following partial reward training.

percentile. the percentage of the total scores which are lower in value than a given value.

perceptual defense. the notion that perceptual sensitivity varies to stimuli in such a way as to defend that person from threatening, and similar stimuli.

personality. the characteristic pattern of behavior of an individual.

personality inventory. a personality test in which the individual rates or describes his own behaviors.

persuasion. socially mediated information transmission directed at changing an attitude.

phenomenology. introspective reporting by naive or untrained observers.

phenotype. the expressed genetic characteristics of the individual.

phi phenomenon. a simple stroboscopic movement produced by lights successively lighted in different positions.

phobic reaction. a neurosis in which an unusual specific fear is the focal symptom.

physiological psychology. the study of the structure and physiological mechanisms which underlie behavior.

pitch. the psychological dimension of a sound stimulus corresponding to its frequency.

play therapy. the patient acts out his troubles in a "make-believe" atmosphere.

pleasure principle. seeking of pleasure and avoidance of the unpleasant.

polygraph. a device for recording a number of continuous physiological measurements at the same time.

population. a group of all possible cases about which some question is asked.

power law. an observation in psychophysics which holds that changes in the stimulus which produce equal stimulus ratios result in equal ratios of the reported stimulus.

precognition. the ESP prediction of future events.

preconscious. in Freudian theory, thoughts and influences which may be accessible to consciousness by directing attention to them.

predictive validity. the extent to which a test accurately predicts a criterion.

primary process. in Freudian theory, a primitive mode of thinking which obeys the pleasure principle and is characteristic of the unconscious.

principle learning. concept learning in which the learner must formulate a rule for guiding his classifications.

proactive inhibition. the interference caused by the learning of other tasks before the reference task is first learned.

problem solving. thought processes directed at specifiable goals.

programmed learning. a mechanical presentation of material to be learned according to certain principles of learning theory.

projection. seeing in others the motives which lead to frustration and conflict in oneself.

projection area. cortical surface areas which, by stimulation studies, have been shown to have specific sensory and motor function.

projective test. a personality evocation device; in a test framework an individual is unknowingly led into talking of himself and his problems.

propaganda. a collection of information designed to change specific attitudes.

psychiatrist. a physician who has specialized in the treatment of mental disorders.

psychoanalysis. a theory of personality development and a tool for the treatment of patients with certain mental disorders; originated by Freud.

psychoanalyst. a therapist who uses psychoanalysis; usually a psychiatrist.

psychokinesis. the movement of physical objects by mental powers.

psychological scaling. the "measurement" of a set of stimuli by the instructed responses of human observers.

psychopathic reaction. a behavior pattern indicating a lack of moral development in one's society.

psychopathology. the science of deviant behavior.

psychophysics. the precise measurement and description of responses made to stimuli.

psychophysiology. the study of physiological reactions to psychological stimuli; primary use is made of a medical polygraph for recording changes.

psychosomatic illness. physiological injury which has arisen from an emotional (psychological) state.

psychosurgery. the removal of brain areas to effect a change in deviant behavior.

psychotherapy. the process of changing deviant behaviors.

pursuit tracking. following a moving target.

range. the difference between two selected scores in the population.

rapport. the personal relationship between individuals.

rationalization. the application of different reasons to replace or disguise the true motives for a behavior.

reaction formation. the expression of the more socially accepted though weaker of two conflicting motives.

readiness. the state of having sufficient maturation for the normal appearance of a particular behavior.

reality contact. the meaningful interchange between a person and the observable world.

recall. a retention test in which minimal cues are presented to evoke the responses.

receptors. the mechanisms of receiving energy changes and converting those changes to neural information.

recognition. a retention test in which the responses may be selected from a presented collection of items.

reduction screen. a device to exclude all stimulation except that from the focal stimulus, as a blackened tube held to the eye.

reflex action. a conceptual view of simple nervous system functioning in which neurons connect an effector almost directly to a receptor.

regression. responses to frustration which are more primitive or are characteristic of an earlier point in the development of an individual.

reinforcement. a state of affairs or process which has the effect of changing the probability of occurrence of the responses to which it is applied (or follows).

reinforcement theory. a theory of learning in which the occurrence of learning *depends* upon the application of a reinforcer or reward following the to-be-learned response.

relative movement. the different rates of movement of near vs. far objects which cue the observer as to their distance away.

release therapy. the process of releasing emotions by aggressive behavior toward symbols of the patient's troubles.

reliability. the extent to which a test measures the same and yields the same score on different occasions under the same conditions.

reminiscence. an increase in performance following rest after massed practice.

repeatability. a characteristic of methods of gathering knowledge describing the generality of the observations.

repression. an escape from the undesirable aspects of a frustrating or conflict situation by a loss of memory.

resistance. an occurrence in psychoanalytic therapy of an unwillingness or inability to continue free association; considered to indicate being close to forgotten experiences of importance.

respondent behavior. behaviors in response to known and specifiable stimuli.

response integration. the process of learning and differentiating the responses of a task.

retention. the measured persistence of learning after practice has ceased.

retina. the curved inside surface of the back of the eye which is composed primarily of light sensitive cells.

retinal disparity. the different picture received from a near object by each eye.

retroactive inhibition. the interference with the memory for one task caused by the learning of a second task between this original learning and the retention test.

reversible figure. figures for which the figure and ground changes with continued observation.

rods. the light sensitive retinal cells which are located primarily away from the fovea and relays only black and white information.

role diffusion. a state in personality formation in which the individual is at once torn between several roles.

runway. a simple learning device in which the running speed of the subject is recorded.

saturation. the psychological dimension corresponding to the complexity of the wave form of the light stimulus; the greater the saturation, the less gray or pastel appearing the color.

savings score. a measure of the retention of materials which have been relearned; the difference between original learning and relearning.

schizophrenic. a psychosis marked by withdrawal.

selective learning. a learning situation in which one stimulus-response sequence is rewarded and others are not.

selector mechanism. the ability of subjects to differentiate the materials of a presented learning task from similar materials before the task is learned.

self motive. a motive which contributes to the maintenance of the self concept or ego of the individual.

senile psychosis. a psychosis caused by neural distruction in the aged.

sensation. the aspects of perception which involve the reception of stimulation.

sensorimotor skill. learned performances of behaviors which require an interaction between sensory and motor functions.

sensory isolation. reduction or removal of normal levels of stimulation reaching the individual.

serial learning. a verbal learning task in which the materials are learned in order.

sex-linked trait. a characteristic carried in the XY and XX chromosomes.

shaping. the procedure of selectively rewarding those responses which are progressively more similar to that desired.

short-term memory. the extent to which presented materials remain available for short periods of time during which the memorization activity is curtailed or controlled.

shuttlebox. a two compartment box in which subjects are taught to move from one side to the other upon cue.

significance statement. a conclusion of a statistical test which expresses in probability terms the likelihood of non-chance factors producing an observed difference.

similarity. the extent of redundancy or confusion which exists among verbal items.

skewed curve. a frequency distribution which is distorted and not symmetrical.

skinner box (operant conditioning box). an enclosure in which one operant response is learned to a high degree of performance by the subject as a result of the application of reinforcers.

social motive. a motive which requires the presence or participation of another individual for its expression or instigation.

society. a collection of organized and interacting individuals with common goals and common beliefs, attitudes, and behavior patterns.

somatic therapy. altering deviant behavior by bodily changes.

source credibility. the perception of an information source as being expert and free from bias.

spatial summation. simultaneous stimulation of one neuron by a large number of other neurons.

spontaneous recovery. the recovery of an extinguished response after a period of delay.

standard deviation. the square root of the average squared deviation of the scores about the mean.

standard scores. test scores expressed in standard deviation units.

statistical test. a tool for answering a question about the differences between two or more groups of numbers.

stereotypy. a pattern of behavior in response to frustration which appears rigid and fixed.

stimulus generalization. the spread of a conditioned response to stimuli similar to the CS.

stroboscopic movement. a perceived motion produced by successive presentation of slightly different stimuli.

structuralism. a historical viewpoint of psychology which used introspection to analyze experience into elements called sensations.

subject. an individual in a research project whose behavior is being observed.

subliminal perception. a process by which stimuli are used to affect behavior, but in which the process was not consciously noticed by the observer.

substitution. an acceptable behavior is substituted for one which is less acceptable to that person.

successive approximations. another name for shaping.

superposition. the overlap of close objects on farther ones.

survival motive. a motive based upon a physiological necessity or other condition which may directly affect the survival of that individual.

symptom substitution. the appearance of new symptoms to replace those removed; an assumption of the medical model.

symptoms. observed indicators of some unobservable condition.

synapse. the junction of the end brushes of one neuron and the dendrites of the next.

synaptic transmission. the mechanism by which an impulse passes across the synapse.

taste buds. the receptors for gustation.

teaching machines. a device for presenting programmed instruction.

telepathy. the transmission of thoughts from one mind to another.

temperament. the long term emotional reactivity or predisposition of an individual.

temporal maze. a maze learning pattern in which different responses must be made successively to the same cues.

temporal summation. cumulative effects of repeated impulses reaching a neuron in a short period of time.

test battery. a collection of different tests given for the same purpose.

test profile. the display of a collection of test scores, usually in comparable units.

threshold. the value at which a change in an instructed response is noted.

timbre. the psychological dimension of a sound stimulus corresponding to its complexity.

trace conditioning. a classical conditioning variation in which the UCS was delayed after the offset of the CS.

traditional counseling. an advice-giving, expert-layman relationship.

trait theory. a personality description using the combination of strengths of several measured traits.

transfer of training. the effect of learning one task upon the learning of a second task.

transference. a process in psychoanalytic therapy in which the therapist is viewed with an obvious love or hate previously associated with some other person in the patient's life.

two-phase conception. a verbal learning theoretical notion which considers two aspects to performance: integrating the responses and hooking the responses to the stimuli.

two-point threshold. the smallest distance by which two points of pressure may be separated and still yield a sensation of two separate points rather than one.

tympanic membrane. the eardrum.

type theory. a notion in which personality is typed upon the bases of some easily distinguished characteristics of structure or behavior.

unconditioned response. the original response to the unconditioned stimulus.

unconditioned stimulus. in classical conditioning, the stimulus which originally evokes the response.

unconscious. the state of not having consciousness; in Freudian theory, unavailable, unacceptable thoughts.

validity. the extent to which a test measures what it is intended to measure.

variability. the extent to which numbers differ.

variable interval reinforcement schedule. like fixed interval but with a varying time interval.

variable ratio reinforcement schedule. like fixed ratio but with a varying ratio.

verbal learning. the study of the association of verbal units under specified conditions.

vigilance. the long term attention of an individual towards a selected group of stimuli.

voluntary response. in eyelid conditioning, a voluntary movement of the eyelid.

withdrawal. a form of adjustment to conflicts and frustrations.

warm-up. the initial improvement upon an old task after a long absence.

Weber's law. an early approximation which stated that the size of the difference threshold is a constant proportion of the reference stimulus.

white noise. all frequencies of sound presented simultaneously at an equal loudness.

REFERENCES

1. Allport, G. W. *Patterns and growth in personality.* New York: Holt, Rinehart and Winston, 1961.
2. Allport, G. W., Vernon, P. E., and Lindzey, G. *A study of values: a scale for measuring the dominant interests in personality* (3rd edition). Boston: Houghton Mifflin, 1960.
3. American Psychiatric Association. *Diagnostic and statistical manual: mental disorders.* Washington, D.C.: The Author, 1952.
4. Asch, S. E., "Studies of independence and conformity: A minority of one against a unanimous majority," *Psychological Monographs*, 1956, 70, No. 9.
5. Barker, R. G., Dembo, T., and Lewin, K., "Frustration and regression: an experiment with young children," *University of Iowa Studies in Child Welfare*, 1941, 18, No. 386.
6. Berlyne, D. E., "The influence of complexity and novelty in visual figures on orienting responses," *Journal of Experimental Psychology*, 1958, 55, 289–296.
7. Bilodeau, E. A., and Bilodeau, I. M., "Mortor-skills learning," *Annual Review of Psychology*, 1961, 12, 243–280.
8. Boring, E. G., "The perception of objects," *American Journal of Physics*, 1946, 14, 99–107. Reprinted in Liebowitz, H. *Visual perception.* New York: Macmillan, 1965.
9. Brown, G. W., and Cohen, B. D., "Avoidance and approach learning motivated by stimulation of identical hypothalamic loci," *American Journal of Physiology*, 1959, 197, 153–157.
10. Butler, R. A., "Discrimination learning by rhesus monkeys to visual-exploration motivation," *Journal of Comparative and physiological Psychology*, 1953, 46, 95–98.

11. Cattell, R. B., *"The scientific analysis of personality,"* Baltimore, Penguin Books, 1965.

12. Cattell, R. B. *The Sixteen Personality Factor Questionnaire* (rev. edition). Champaign, Illinois: I.P.A.T., 1957.

13. Dollard, J., and Miller, N. E. *Personality and psychotherapy.* New York: McGraw-Hill, 1950.

14. Ebbinghaus, H. *Memory: A contribution to experimental psychology.* (Translated by Ruger, H. A., and Bussenius, C. E., 1913.) New York: Teachers College, Columbia University, 1885.

15. Erickson, E. H. *Childhood and society.* New York: Norton, 1950.

16. "Federal Aviation Agency Short-cut to an IFR ticket?" *FAA Aviation News,* 1967, 5, No. 8, 4–6.

17. Festinger, L. *A theory of cognitive dissonance.* Evanston: Row, Peterson, 1957.

18. Festinger, L., and Carlsmith, J. M., "Cognitive consequences of forced compliance," *Journal of Abnormal and Social Psychology,* 1959, 58, 203–210.

19. Freeman, G. L., "Postural accompaniments of the voluntary inhibition of micturition," *Journal of Experimental Psychology,* 1938, *23,* 45–61.

20. Gormezano, I., "Addendum on 'voluntary responders.'" In Prokasy, W. F. (Ed.) *Classical conditioning: a symposium.* New York: Meredith, 1965.

21. Grossman, S. P. *A textbook of physiological psychology.* New York: Wiley, 1967.

22. Guilford, J. P. *Personality.* New York: McGraw-Hill, 1959.

23. Hall, C. S., "The inheritance of emotionality," *Sigma Xi Quarterly,* 1938, *26,* 17–27.

24. Hardy, K. R., "An appetitional theory of sexual motivation," *Psychological Review,* 1964, *71,* 1–18.

25. Harlow, H. F., "The formation of learning sets," *Psychological Review,* 1949, *56,* 51–65.

26. Harlow, H. F., and Harlow, M. F., "Social deprivation in monkeys," *Scientific American,* 1962, *207,* 136–146.

27. Harlow, H. F., and Zimmerman, R. R., "Affectional responses in the infant monkey," *Science,* 1959, *130,* 421–432.

28. Hess, E., "Attitude and pupil size," *Scientific American,* 1965, *212,* 46–54.

29. Hilgard, E. R. *Introduction to psychology* (3rd edition). New York: Harcourt, Brace and World, 1962.

30. Hilgard, E. R., and Atkinson, R. C. *Introduction to psychology* (4th edition). New York: Harcourt, Brace and World, 1967. Pp. 453–454.

31. Hilgard, J. R., "The effect of early and delayed practice on memory and motor performances studied by the method of co-twin control," *Genetic Psychology Monographs,* 1933, *14,* No. 6.

32. Holzinger, K. J., "The relative effect of nature and nurture influences on twin differences," *Journal of Educational Psychology,* 1929, *20,* 241–248.

33. Hovland, C. I., Harvey, O. J., and Sheriff, M., "Assimilation and contrast

effects in reaction to communication and attitude change," *Journal of Abnormal and Social Psychology*, 1957, 55, 244–252.

34. Hubel, D. H., and Wiesel, T. N., "Receptive fields, binocular interaction, and functional architecture in the cat's visual cortex," *Journal of Physiology*, 1962, *160*, 106–154.

35. Hull, C. L. *Principles of behavior*. New York: Appleton-Century-Crofts, 1943.

36. Jules, B., "Texture and visual perception," *Scientific American*, 1965, *213*, 38–48.

37. Jung, C. G. *Psychological types*. New York: Harcourt, Brace and World, 1923.

38. Kendler, T. S., and Kendler, H. H., "Reversal and nonreversal shifts in kindergarten children," *Journal of Experimental Psychology*, 1959, 58, 56–60.

39. Kohler, I., "Experiments with goggles," *Scientific American*, 1962, *206*, 63–72.

40. Leeper, R. W., "A study of a neglected portion of the field of learning: the development of sensory organization," *Journal of Genetic Psychology*, 1935, *46*, 41–75.

41. Levine, S., "Noxious stimulation in infant and adult rats and consummatory behavior," *Journal of Comparative and Physiological Psychology*. 1958, *51*, 230–233.

42. Lindsley, D. B., "Emotion." In Stevens, S. S. (Ed.) *Handbook of experimental psychology*. New York: Wiley, 1951.

43. Lippitt, R., and White, R. K., "An experimental study of leadership and group life," In Maccoby, E. R., Newcomb, R. M., and Hartley, E. L. (Eds.) *Readings in social psychology* (3rd edition). New York: Holt, 1958.

44. Luchins, A. S., "Mechanization in problem solving: The effect of einstellung," *Psychological Monographs*, 1942, 54, No. 248.

45. Lumsdaine, A. A., "Teaching machines and self-instructional materials," *Audio-visual Communication Review*, 1959, 7, 163–172.

46. Maier, N. F. *Frustration: The study of behavior without a goal*. New York: McGraw-Hill, 1949.

47. Masserman, J. H., "Experimental neuroses," *Scientific American*, 1950.

48. Maurer, K. M. *Intellectual status at maturity as a criterion for selecting items in preschool tests*. Minneapolis: University of Minnesota Press, 1946.

49. Mayer, J., "Regulation of energy intake and the body weight: The glucostatic theory and the lipostatic hypothesis," *Annals of the New York Academy of Science*, 1955, *63*, Art. 1, 15–43.

50. McClelland, D. C. (Ed.) *Studies in motivation*. New York: Appleton-Century-Crofts, 1955.

51. McClelland, D. C., and Atkinson, J. W., "The projective expression of needs: I. The effect of different intensities of the hunger drive on perception," *Journal of Psychology*, 1948, 25, 205–222.

52. McConnell, J. V., Cutler, R. L., and McNeil, E. B., "Subliminal stimulation: an overview," *American Psychologist*, 1958, *13*, 229–242.

53. McCormick, E. J. *Human factors engineering.* New York: McGraw-Hill, 1964. Pp. 127–132.
54. McGinnis, E., "Emotionality and perceptual defense," *Psychological Review,* 1949, *56,* 244–251.
55. Melzack, R., and Wall, P. D., "Pain mechanisms: A new theory," *Science,* 1965, *150,* 971–979.
56. Miller, N. E., "Liberalization of basic S-R concepts: Extensions to conflict behavior, motivation and social learning," In Koch, S. (Ed.) *Psychology: A study of a science,* Vol. II. New York: McGraw-Hill, 1959.
57. Miller, N. E., "Studies of fear as an acquirable drive: I. Fear as motivation and fear-reduction as reinforcement in the learning of new responses," *Journal of Experimental Psychology,* 1948, *38,* 89–101.
58. Miller, N. E., and Dollard, J. *Social learning and imitation.* New Haven: Yale University Press, 1941.
59. Murray, H. A. *Explorations in personality.* New York: Oxford University Press, 1938.
60. Newcomb, T. M., Turner, R. H., and Converse, P. E. *Social Psychology,* New York: Holt, Rinehart and Winston, 1965.
61. Olds, J., "Physiological mechanisms of reward." In Jones, M. (Ed.) *Nebraska symposium on motivation.* Vol. 3. Lincoln, Nebraska: University of Nebraska Press, 1955.
62. Olds, J., and Sinclair, J., "Self-stimulation in the obstruction box," *American Psychologist,* 1957, *12,* 464 (Abstract).
63. Pavlov, I. P. *Conditioned reflexes.* (Transl. by G. V. Anrep) London: Oxford University Press, 1927.
64. Penrose, L. S., and Penrose, R., "Impossible objects: a special type of illusion," *British Journal of Psychology,* 1958, *49,* 31–33.
65. Pfaffman, C., "Taste, its sensory and motivating properties," *American Scientist,* 1964, *52,* 187–206.
66. Piaget, J. *The child's conception of numbers.* New York: Norton, 1965.
67. Riesen, A. H., "Post-partum development of behavior," *Chicago Medical School Quarterly,* 1951, *13,* 17–24.
68. Rock, I., and Kaufman, L., "The moon illusion," II, *Science,* 1962, *136,* 1023–1031. Reprinted in Leibowitz, H. *Visual perception.* New York: Macmillan, 1965.
69. Rogers, C. R. *Client-centered therapy.* Boston: Houghton Mifflin, 1951.
70. Rogers, C. R. *On becoming a person: a therapist's view of psychotherapy.* Boston: Houghton Mifflin, 1961.
71. Schachter, S. *The psychology of affiliation: Experimental studies of the sources of gregariousness.* Stanford: Stanford University Press, 1959.
72. Schreiner, L., and Kling, A., "Rhinencephalon and behavior," *American Journal of Physiology,* 1956, *184,* 486–490.
73. Schuck, J. R. Personal communication.
74. Skinner, B. P. *Science and human behavior.* New York: Macmillan, 1938.
75. Skinner, B. F., "The science of learning and the art of teaching," *Education Review of Harvard,* 1954, *24,* 86–97.

76. Skodak, M., and Skeels, H. M., "A final follow-up of one hundred adopted children," *Journal of Genetic Psychology*, 1949, 75, 3–19.
77. Spence, K. W. *Behavior theory and learning.* Englewood Cliffs, N.J.: Prentice-Hall, 1960.
78. Spence, K. W., and Ross, L. E., "A methodological study of the form and latency of eyelid responses in conditioning," *Journal of Experimental Psychology*, 1959, 58, 376–385.
79. Spence, K. W., and Spence, J. T., "Sex and anxiety differences in eyelid conditioning," *Psychological Bulletin*, 1966, 65, 137–142.
80. Swets, J. A. *Signal detection and recognition by human observers.* New York: Wiley, 1964.
81. Tannenbaum, P. H., "Initial attitude toward source and concept as factors in attitude change through communication," *Public Opinion Quarterly*, 1956, 20, 413–425.
82. Terman, L. M. *The measurement of intelligence.* Boston: Houghton Mifflin, 1916.
83. Terman, L. M., and Oden, M. H. *The gifted group at mid-life.* Stanford, Stanford University Press, 1959.
84. Thorndike, E. L., "Animal intelligence. An experimental study of the associative processes in animals," *Psychological Monographs*, 1898, 2, No. 8.
85. Torrance, R. P., "Some consequences of power differences on decision making in permanent and temporary three-man groups. In Hare, A. P., Borgatta, E. P., and Bales, R. F. (Eds.) *Small groups: Studies in social interaction.* New York: Alfred A. Knopf, 1955.
86. Tryon, R. C., "Gentic differences in maze-learning ability in rats." In *39th Yearbook Nat. Soc. Stud. Educ.* Bloomington, Illinois: Public School Publishing Co., 1940.
87. Tyler, L. E. *The psychology of human differences* (2nd edition). New York: Appleton-Century-Crofts, 1956, P. 444.
88. Underwood, B. J., "Ten years of massed practice on distributed practice," *Psychological Review*, 1961, 68, 229–247.
89. Underwood, B. J., Runquist, W. N., and Schultz, R. W., "Response learning in paired-associate lists as a function of intralist similarity," *Journal of Experimental Psychology*, 1959, 58, 70–78.
90. Underwood, B. J., and Schulz, R. W. *Meaningfulness and verbal learning.* New York: Lippincott, 1960.
91. Vernon, J. A. *Inside the black room.* New York: Clarkson N. Potter, 1963.
92. Watson, J. B., and Rayner, R., "Conditioned emotional reactions, *Journal of Experimental Psychology*, 1920, 3, 1–14.
93. Wechsler, D. *The measurement and appraisal of adult intelligence* (4th edition). Baltimore: Williams and Wilkens, 1958.
94. Wechsler, D. *The Wechsler Adult Intelligent Scale manual.* New York: Psychological Corp., 1955.
95. Whorf, B. L. *Language, thought, and reality.* Cambridge, Mass.: Technology Press, 1956.

INDEX

INDEX